The Origins of Alliances

A volume in the series

Cornell Studies in Security Affairs

edited by Robert Jervis
Robert J. Art
Stephen M. Walt

A full list of titles in the series appears at the end of the book.

The Origins of Alliances

STEPHEN M. WALT

Cornell University Press

ITHACA AND LONDON

First published 1987 by Cornell University Press
First printing, Cornell Paperbacks, 1990

Printed in the United States of America

Library of Congress Cataloging-in-Publication Data

Walt, Stephen M., 1955–
The origins of alliances.

(Cornell studies in security affairs)
Bibliography: p.
Includes index.
1. Alliances.   2. International relations.   3. Middle East—Foreign relations.   4. Middle East—Politics and government—1945–
I. Title.   II. Series.
JX4005.W335   1987   327.1'16'0956   87-47606
ISBN-13: 978-0-8014-9418-5 (pbk. : alk. paper)

Cornell University Press strives to use environmentally responsible suppliers and materials to the fullest extent possible in the publishing of its books. Such materials include vegetable-based, low-VOC inks and acid-free papers that are recycled, totally chlorine-free, or partly composed of nonwood fibers. For further information, visit our website at www.cornellpress.cornell.edu.

9   10   Paperback printing

Contents

[v]

Preface to the Paperback Edition

When I completed this book in 1986, the dramatic changes now sweeping the Soviet Union and Eastern Europe were largely unforeseen. Although I recognized that shifts in Soviet policy could weaken NATO's cohesion significantly, I did not explore this possibility in any depth. The publication of this paperback edition provides an opportunity to do so now.

States form alliances primarily to balance against threats. Threats, in turn, are a function of power, geographic proximity, offensive capabilities, and perceived intentions. Throughout the Cold War, the Soviet Union posed a greater threat to the major powers of Eurasia than the United States did. As "balance-of-threat" theory predicts, these states balanced by allying with the United States, creating a global coalition that was both remarkably stable and significantly stronger than the Soviet alliance network.

The events of the past three years largely confirm balance-of-threat theory. Domestic reforms in the Soviet Union and the subsequent decision to permit independent regimes in Eastern Europe have sharply reduced the tendency for other states to balance against the Soviet Union. To note a few examples: the NATO countries are beginning major reductions in defense spending; the United States is planning to withdraw a substantial portion of its armed forces from Europe; movement for European unity has slowed; and U.S. reactions to the repression of pro-democracy forces in China suggest that China's value as a counterweight to Soviet power has declined. As a more ominous instance, perceptions of U.S.-Japanese rivalry are growing, now that the Soviet threat no longer provides a powerful motive for cooperation. Significantly, these changes have occurred despite continued evidence of Soviet military might. Instead, the belief that Soviet aims are less dangerous and that Soviet power will be removed from Central Europe

[vi]

lies at the heart of these developments. Threats, not power alone, are crucial.

What does balance-of-threat theory reveal about international politics after the Cold War? By definition, the end of the Cold War implies a diffusion of threats. If current trends continue, we will see a reunified Germany bordering the newly independent states of Eastern Europe, a weakened and internally divided Soviet Union, and a stronger and more assertive Japan (China's future course remains the most difficult to predict). It will be far less clear which states pose the most serious threats; as a result, international alignments will be more ambiguous and less durable. Perceptions of intent will be increasingly important, because the distribution of capabilities will be more equal and geography may not offer clear guidance. Thus the Eastern European states may lean toward the West should Soviet intentions appear more threatening, or tilt back toward Moscow if a reunified Germany poses the greater danger. Similarly, relations among Japan, China, and the Soviet Union are likely to be shaped less by power or geography than by each state's assessment of the others' intentions.

As for NATO itself, the optimistic rhetoric about maintaining the "Atlantic Community" should be viewed with some skepticism. Without a clear and present threat, neither European politicians nor U.S. taxpayers are likely to support a large U.S. military presence in Europe. Although NATO's elaborate institutional structure will slow the pace of devolution, only a resurgence of the Soviet threat is likely to preserve NATO in anything like its present form. And shorn of U.S. protection and the unifying effects of the Soviet threat, the nations of Europe are likely to find cooperation more difficult to sustain, unless economic pressure from the United States and the Pacific Rim overrides familiar security concerns.

What do these trends mean for the United States? On the one hand, the United States' *external* position appears even more favorable now than it did when this book was first published. (Its internal problems may be quite another matter, of course.) The traditional goal of U.S. grand strategy has been to prevent any single power from controlling the combined industrial resources of Eurasia; the decline of Soviet power means that goal will be even easier to achieve. But the end of the Cold War creates new problems as well. Because U.S. protection will be less important to its allies, U.S. influence over these states is virtually certain to decline. At the same time, the United States must avoid a return to isolationism as well as a renewed crusade to "export democracy" to the developing world via military intervention. History suggests that a major war is more likely when the United States withdraws from world affairs. History also suggests that U.S. military intervention in the Third World is more likely to lead to despotism and prolonged civil war than to stable and workable democracy. Paradoxically, therefore, U.S. leaders must show greater imagination, wisdom, and restraint than they did at the height of U.S.-Soviet rivalry, because the problems to be faced will be more ambiguous and the resources available to address them will be fewer.

In short, balance-of-threat theory reveals that the decline in the Soviet threat is creating a world in which the United States will enjoy greater security at less cost and risk. But it is also a world in which policy choices will be more difficult and U.S. influence will be smaller. And it is a world in which perceptions of intent will exert a powerful impact on how other states respond to U.S. actions. Although the United States retains enormous advantages when compared with other nations, it must still strike a balance between encouraging aggression through apparent indifference and provoking opposition through misplaced or unthinking belligerence.

STEPHEN M. WALT

Chicago, Illinois
June 1990

Preface

The ability to attract allies is a valuable asset in any competitive system. By contrast, those who cause others to align against them are at a significant disadvantage. Understanding the forces that shape international alliances should therefore be a vital concern for most statesmen. By elaborating and testing a number of hypotheses about alliance formation, this book attempts to contribute to that understanding.

Like most scholarly endeavors, this project began with several puzzles. While in graduate school, I was struck by the sharp discrepancy between what scholars wrote about alliances and what contemporary policy-makers apparently believed. Indeed, the two groups seemed almost 180 degrees apart. For example, the notion that alliances are formed to oppose strong states was then a truism among scholars. Yet both Soviet and U.S. statesmen repeatedly argued that the reverse was true, that any appearance of weakness would cause their allies to defect. Similarly, although most scholars viewed ideology as a weak cause of alignment, the Soviet fear of "capitalist encirclement," Soviet support for countries in the "socialist commonwealth," and U.S. fears about a "Communist monolith" suggested that the political leaders of both superpowers took ideology quite seriously. Disagreements also emerged over the importance of foreign aid and political penetration as causes of alignment. Because these competing beliefs underlie important policy disputes (including the importance of credibility, the need for overseas intervention, and the political effects of military spending and foreign aid), determining which views were most accurate seemed well worth the effort.

Along the way, as I examined the theory and practice of alliances and considered evidence from the Middle East, additional puzzles emerged. The most important involved balance of power theory. I was convinced that it was the most useful general theory available, but I was disturbed

[ix]

by several anomalies. According to Kenneth Waltz, whose *Theory of International Politics* contains the most elegant and rigorous presentation of this theory, the international system is characterized by a tendency to form balances of power. But if that is so, why did some alliances grow both larger and stronger over time (often dwarfing their opponents), as the Allies did in World War I and World War II? Furthermore, how might we explain the fact that for the past three decades the United States and its allies have controlled a combined gross national product roughly three times that of the Soviet Union and the Warsaw Pact while spending more each year on defense? Although balance of power theory can explain the Soviet response to this situation (i.e., the Soviet Union compensates for its weak allies by devoting a larger percentage of its GNP to military expenditures), it cannot tell us why the Soviet Union is so unpopular in the first place. Furthermore, if balance of power theory is a theory primarily about the behavior of great powers, then how do we explain the alliance preferences of lesser states? Do they balance as well? If so, against whom? Finally, could we incorporate the other factors that statesmen consider when deciding with whom to ally—factors that are not directly related to national power?

The solution presented in this book is a reformulation of balance of power theory which I call balance of threat theory. In anarchy, states form alliances to protect themselves. Their conduct is determined by the threats they perceive, and the power of others is merely one element in their calculations (albeit an important one). The power of other states can be either a liability or an asset, depending on where it is located, what it can do, and how it is used. By incorporating the other factors that create threats to national sovereignty, balance of threat theory provides a better explanation of alliance formation than does balance of power theory.

For reasons developed at length in chapter 1, most (but by no means all) of the evidence examined here is drawn from recent Middle East diplomacy. Unfortunately, there is no comprehensive and reliable diplomatic history of the Middle East. Patrick Seale's excellent *The Struggle for Syria* ends in 1958, and the late Malcolm Kerr's brilliant monograph *The Arab Cold War* is limited to inter-Arab politics from 1958 to 1970. The enormous literature on the Arab-Israeli conflict, by contrast, usually downplays inter-Arab relations. And the best scholarly studies—such as Nadav Safran's *Saudi Arabia: The Ceaseless Quest for Security*, Steven L. Spiegel's *The Other Arab-Israeli Conflict*, and Michael Brecher's remarkable books on Israeli foreign policy (*The Foreign Policy System of Israel*, *Decisions in Israel's Foreign Policy*, etc.)—focus primarily on one country. Having decided to test several hypotheses by examining Middle East alliances, I found that there was no reliable account of the full set of events I sought to explore.

As a result, I was forced to provide that account myself. This requirement was both a burden and an opportunity; chapters 3 and 4 provide the only complete account of postwar alliance diplomacy in the Middle East (including the diplomacy of the two superpowers) of which I am aware. Although this book is by no means the definitive diplomatic history of this region, I hope that both the theoretical and the historical material contained in it will be of use to students of international politics and the Middle East alike.

Writing this book taught me the importance of loyal allies. I was fortunate to have many. Kenneth N. Waltz encouraged me to ask an important question. Even more helpfully, he provided a model for the ways that important answers are reached. George Breslauer was unstinting in his criticism and generous with his praise. The friendship of both these scholars is much appreciated. Walter McDougall sharpened my use of diplomatic history and corrected several errors. I am also indebted to Robert Art, whose comments and encouragement made revising the manuscript much easier.

The following people offered valuable comments on all or part of the manuscript: L. Carl Brown, Lynn Eden, Charles Glaser, Lori Gronich, Fen Hampson, John Mearsheimer, Steven E. Miller, Laurie Mylroie, Kenneth Oye, Glenn Snyder, Jack Snyder, David Spiro, Marc Trachtenberg, John Waterbury, and Lynn Whittaker. I am grateful to all of them. I also thank Jonathan Shimshoni for his friendship and his many suggestions as I began the final draft.

I have profited from interviews with several scholars who helped me find my way through the tangled thicket of Middle East politics. William B. Quandt, Dennis Ross, and Nadav Safran provided advice in the early stages. Seth Tillman and Steven Rosen offered their own insights on the domestic politics of U.S. Middle East policy. In Egypt, discussions with Gehad Auda and Abdul-Monem Sayed of the Center for Strategic Studies at *al-Ahram*, Abdul-Monem al-Mashat of Cairo University, Ann Mosely Lesch of the American Universities Field Staff, and Mohammed Sid Aqmed helped sharpen my grasp of inter-Arab relations. In Israel, Ya'acov Bar-Siman-Tov, Galia Golan, Ya'acov Roi, and Dan Schueftan graciously interrupted their own work in order to discuss mine. I thank all of these scholars for sharing their ideas with me.

The opportunity to give a seminar at the Jaffee Center for Strategic Studies in Tel Aviv helped me refine my ideas further. I thank its director, Aharon Yariv, for the invitation and Shai Feldman for arranging my visit and for offering his own valuable insights.

Support from institutional allies also has been indispensable. The early drafts of this book were written while I was a research fellow at the Center for Science and International Affairs at Harvard University. CSIA was an ideal intellectual home, and I am grateful to its founder, Paul Doty, and the rest of the staff for their help. Some of the research was conducted during my various sojourns at the Center for Naval Analyses, and my associates there—especially Bradford Dismukes, James M. Mc-Connell, Charles C. Peterson, and Robert G. Weinland—contributed greatly to my intellectual growth.

I have received financial support from the Institute for the Study of World Politics, the Center for Science and International Affairs, and the Center for International Studies at Princeton University. A grant from the University Committee on Research at Princeton made it possible for me to travel to the Middle East. In the Woodrow Wilson School, Agnes Pearson handled various administrative details with exceptional competence. Edna Lloyd, Gwen Hatcher, Lynn Caruso, Terry Barczak, and Malilia Clark provided efficient secretarial support.

Portions of chapters 2 and 8 originally appeared in the spring 1985 issue of *International Security* (vol. 9, no. 4, copyright © 1985 by the President and Fellows of Harvard College and the Massachusetts Institute of Technology). I thank the journal and its publishers for permission to use this material here. I also thank Cornell University Press for being tolerant of a young author, and especially Jo-Anne Naples for helping tidy up my prose.

Four others merit my deepest thanks. Stephen Van Evera has contributed ideas and encouragement throughout. He is, quite simply, everything a colleague should be. Helene Blair Madonick knew how much this book meant to me; I hope she knows that she means even more. Finally, I dedicate this book to my parents; the older I get, the more grateful I am.

Stephen M. Walt

Princeton, New Jersey

[1]

Introduction:
Exploring Alliance Formation

This book is about the origins of alliances.[1] I seek answers to questions such as these: What causes states to support one another's foreign policy or territorial integrity? How do statesmen choose among potential threats when seeking external support? How do the great powers choose which states to protect, and how do weaker states decide whose protection to accept? In short, how do states choose their friends?

The importance of this subject is manifest.[2] The forces that bring states together and drive them apart will affect the security of individual states by determining both how large a threat they face and how much help they can expect. At the same time, the factors that determine how states choose alliance partners will shape the evolution of the international system as a whole. The ability to establish durable empires, for

1. I define *alliance* as a formal or informal relationship of security cooperation between two or more sovereign states. This definition assumes some level of commitment and an exchange of benefits for both parties; severing the relationship or failing to honor the agreement would presumably cost something, even if it were compensated in other ways. For a good discussion of the various definitions that scholars and diplomats have employed, see Roger V. Dingman, "Theories of, and Approaches to, Alliance Politics," in *Diplomacy: New Approaches in Theory, History, and Policy,* ed. Paul Gordon Lauren (New York, 1979), pp. 245–50.

2. George Modelski has called alliance "one of the dozen or so key terms of International Relations." See his "The Study of Alliances: A Review," *Journal of Conflict Resolution,* 7, no. 4 (1963): 773. According to Julian R. Friedman, "alliances are the central feature of international political life." See his "Alliance in International Politics," in *Alliance in International Politics,* ed. Julian R. Friedman, Christopher Bladen, and Steven Rosen (Boston, 1970). To Hans J. Morgenthau, alliances "are a necessary function of the balance of power operating in a multiple state system." See his "Alliances in Theory and Practice," in *Alliance Policy in the Cold War,* ed. Arnold Wolfers (Baltimore, Md., 1959), p. 175. According to Ole Holsti, "alliances are apparently a universal component of relations between political units, irrespective of time and place." See Ole Holsti, P. Terrence Hopmann, and John D. Sullivan, *Unity and Disintegration in International Alliances* (New York, 1973), p. 2.

example, will depend in large part on how potential victims respond. Will they work together to thwart these ambitions, or can a potential hegemon keep its opposition isolated and weak? Does aggression become easier with each new conquest, or does resistance increase at a faster rate?

Failure to understand the origins of alliances can be fatal. In the Franco-Prussian War, for example, France entered the war confident that Austria-Hungary would soon join it in battle against Prussia. When the Austrians chose to remain neutral (a decision Bismarck's diplomacy had encouraged), a key element of French strategy collapsed.[3] In the decades before World War I, Germany's leaders ignored the possibility of a Franco-Russian alliance (1892) and an Anglo-Russian entente (1907), only to be surprised when their own actions helped create the very alignments they had believed were impossible.[4] In much the same way, Japan's leaders were convinced that their alliance with Nazi Germany and Fascist Italy would deter the United States from opposing their expansion in the Far East. They could not have been more wrong; the formation of the Axis encouraged the United States to resist Japanese expansion even more vigorously and to move closer to its wartime alliance with Great Britain and the Soviet Union.[5]

In each of these cases, the error lay in a faulty understanding of the causes of alliances. As a result, these states adopted grand strategies that were seriously flawed. In the simplest terms, a state's grand strategy is a theory explaining how it can "cause" security for itself.[6] Strategy is thus a set of hypotheses or predictions: if we do A, B, and C, the desired results X, Y, and Z will follow. Ideally, a statement of grand strategy should explain why these results are likely to obtain and provide appropriate evidence. Because the challenges one may face and the capabilities one can employ will be affected by the behavior of other states (e.g., will they help, remain neutral, or oppose?), the hypotheses that statesmen accept about the origins of alliances should play a major role in determining the strategies they select. The success of these policies will depend on whether the hypotheses they embrace are correct.

3. See Richard Smoke, *War: Controlling Escalation* (Cambridge, Mass., 1977), pp. 127–28, 131–33; and Michael Howard, *The Franco-Prussian War* (New York, 1979), pp. 46–48, 64–65.

4. See Imanuel Geiss, *German Foreign Policy 1871–1914* (London, 1979), pp. 66–68.

5. See Louis Morton, "Japan's Decision for War," in *Command Decisions*, ed. Kent Roberts Greenfield (New York, 1959), pp. 67–68; and Robert J. C. Butow, *Tojo and the Coming of the War* (Princeton, N.J., 1960), pp. 66–67.

6. This conception of grand strategy is based on that of Barry R. Posen. See his *The Sources of Military Doctrine: France, Britain, and Germany between the World Wars* (Ithaca, 1984), chap. 1, especially p. 13.

[2]

The United States offers no exception to these principles. More than anything else, the Cold War between the United States and the Soviet Union has been a competition for allies. As a result, many recurring debates over the conduct of U.S. foreign policy ultimately rest on disagreements about the causes of alliances. The policies that have emerged depend on which hypotheses of alliance formation were endorsed. The question is whether or not these hypotheses are correct. Answering this question is the principal goal of this book.

One central issue is how states respond to threats. Do states seek allies in order to balance a threatening power, or are they more likely to bandwagon with the most threatening state? This basic question lies at the heart of a host of policy issues. For example, should the United States increase its military spending and its commitment to NATO to prevent the growth of Soviet military power from causing the "Finlandization" of Europe? Alternatively, should the United States do less so its allies will do more? Similarly, will the fall of the Shah and the Soviet invasion of Afghanistan drive the Gulf states into a pro-Soviet position, or are they more likely to join forces with the United States and one another? The answer depends on whether states most often ally to oppose a threatening power or try to appease it.

Throughout the Cold War, U.S. statesmen have consistently embraced the latter view. As the "Basic National Security Policy" formulated by the National Security Council in 1953 stated: "If our allies were uncertain about our ability or will to counter Soviet aggression, they would be strongly tempted to adopt a neutralist position."[7] "Pactomania" was the logical result. In the same way, the lengthy involvement of the United States in Vietnam was justified by the widespread fear that U.S. allies would defect if the United States withdrew. As Secretary of State Dean Rusk put it: "America's alliances are at the heart of the maintenance of peace, and if it should be discovered that the pledge of America was worthless, the structure of peace would crumble and we would be well on our way to a terrible catastrophe."[8] Because U.S. statesmen have believed that allies are attracted by displays of

7. "Review of Basic National Security Policy," NSC 162/1, October 30, 1953. Reprinted in *The Pentagon Papers: The Defense Department History of United States Decisionmaking on Vietnam*, Senator Gravel ed. (Boston, 1971), 1: 424. See also Ernest R. May, "The Cold War," in *The Making of America's Soviet Policy*, ed. Joseph S. Nye (New Haven, Conn., 1984), pp. 223–26.
8. Quoted in Franklin B. Weinstein, "The Concept of a Commitment in International Relations," *Journal of Conflict Resolution*, 13, no. 1 (1969): 52.

strength and will, they have sought to preserve an image of credibility and military superiority despite the obvious costs.[9]

A second issue is whether states with similar internal characteristics are more likely to ally than states whose domestic orders are different. The early debates over the implementation of containment, for example, were due in part to disagreements on this point. Where George F. Kennan saw the Communist bloc as prone to ideological rifts and internal divisions (and therefore vulnerable to U.S. blandishments), his opponents in the Truman administration saw the Communist world as a cohesive ideological alliance that had to be confronted militarily because it could not be dissolved through positive inducements. Different beliefs about what held the Soviet alliance system together thus gave rise to very different policy prescriptions.[10] Since then, U.S. opposition to leftist and Marxist movements throughout the world has been based primarily on the belief that ideological solidarity will make these regimes loyal allies of the Soviet Union.[11] Here again, an unstated hypothesis about the causes of alignment has been a key element of contemporary U.S. foreign policy.

Finally, can certain policy instruments cause other states to alter their alliance preferences? In particular, can the provision of economic or military aid create loyal allies? How easily and how reliably? Are foreign agents, advisers, and propaganda effective instruments of influence or control? The belief that these instruments will have a significant effect on alliance choices underlies U.S. concern for Soviet arms shipments to the Third World as well as the widespread conviction that states with a large Soviet or Cuban presence are reliable tools of the Kremlin.[12] Once

9. On the importance attached to credibility in postwar U.S. foreign policy, see Patrick Morgan, "Saving Face for the Sake of Deterrence," in *Psychology and Deterrence*, ed. Robert Jervis, Richard Ned Lebow, and Janice Gross Stein (Baltimore, Md., 1986), especially pp. 137–43; Deborah Welch Larson, "The Bandwagon Metaphor and American Foreign Policy" (paper delivered at the International Studies Association annual meeting, March 1986); and the discussion in chapter 2 of this volume.

10. In retrospect, Kennan's analysis was strikingly prescient, especially with regard to the inevitable tendency for the Soviet Union and China to quarrel. See "U.S. Objectives with Respect to Russia," NSC 20/21, in *Containment: Documents on American Policy and Strategy, 1945–1950*, ed. John Lewis Gaddis and Thomas Etzold (New York, 1978), pp. 186–87. See also John Lewis Gaddis, *Strategies of Containment* (New York, 1982), pp. 43–45.

11. Examples include U.S. opposition to (1) the Greek Communist party during the Greek civil war, (2) the Mossadegh government in Iran in 1953, (3) the Arbenz regime in Guatemala in 1954, (4) the Marxist regimes in Castro's Cuba and Allende's Chile, and (5) the Movimento Popular de Libertaçao de Angola (MPLA) in Angola. The same concern underlies U.S. opposition to the Sandinista government in Nicaragua, the African National Congress, and the Marxist rebels in El Salvador.

12. For classic examples of this type of reasoning, see U.S. Department of State, Bureau of Public Affairs, "Communist Influence in El Salvador" (Washington, D.C., 1981); U.S. Department of State, Inter-American Series 119, "The Sandinista Military Buildup" (Washington, D.C., 1985), pp. 29–39 and passim; and U.S. Departments of State and Defense,

again, an important element of U.S. national security policy rests on an untested assertion about the effectiveness of certain instruments on alignment.

These popular hypotheses paint a dramatic picture of U.S. insecurity. The belief that states are attracted to strength implies that any appearance of weakness or irresolution could damage the international position of the United States irreparably. The belief that ideology is a powerful cause of alignment implies that virtually all Marxist governments and leftist movements are reliable Soviet assets. And if foreign aid or foreign agents can create loyal satellites, then the United States is also threatened when non-Marxist countries receive material support from the Soviet Union. If these hypotheses are correct, in short, the United States faces an extraordinary challenge.

THE ARGUMENT

In the pages that follow, I argue that each of those beliefs is exaggerated. First, I demonstrate that balancing is far more common than bandwagoning. In contrast to traditional balance of power theorists, however, I suggest that states ally to balance against threats rather than against power alone. Although the distribution of power is an extremely important factor, the level of threat is also affected by geographic proximity, offensive capabilities, and perceived intentions. Thus I propose balance of threat theory as a better alternative than balance of power theory.

Second, the evidence shows that ideology is less powerful than balancing as a motive for alignment. Indeed, I argue that many apparently ideological alliances are in fact a form of balancing behavior. The record also shows that certain ideologies are extremely divisive. In other words, states sharing these ideologies are more likely to compete than to form durable alliances.

Third, I conclude that neither foreign aid nor political penetration is by itself a powerful cause of alignment. Even more important, neither is an effective way to gain leverage except under very unusual conditions.

Taken together, these results help explain why the international position of the United States is extremely favorable and likely to remain so. Because states balance against threats, (not against power alone), the United States has been able to create and sustain a global alliance whose

---

"The Soviet-Cuban Connection in Central America and the Caribbean" (Washington, D.C., 1985), pp. 3–10, 27–28, and passim. See also "Excerpts from Reagan's Speech on Aid for Nicaraguan Rebels," *New York Times*, June 25, 1986, p. A12.

capabilities exceed those of the Soviet Union and its own allies by a considerable margin. Ideological rifts (e.g., the Sino-Soviet split) reinforce Soviet isolation. Neither extensive foreign aid nor covert political penetration is likely to alter these tendencies.

Once we understand the origins of alliances, we can correctly judge the burden of preserving U.S. national security. It is relatively light. We can also see how recent U.S. foreign policy has been misguided, and we can identify how present errors can be corrected. Thus an enhanced theoretical understanding of the origins of alliances will yield important practical results as well.

THE ALLIANCE LITERATURE

Although the literature on alliances is enormous, much of it does not address the questions identified here.[13] Most of the existing research on alliances has examined other issues, such as whether there is a relationship between alliance formation and the likelihood of war and whether the rate of alliance formation fits some specified mathematical model.[14] Similarly, although the extensive collective goods literature on

13. One recent survey, based on U.S. sources, identified some 270 articles or books addressing different aspects of alliance dynamics. According to its author, "little of the research on alliances and alliance dynamics has been cumulative." See Michael Don Ward, "Research Gaps in Alliance Dynamics," *Monograph Series in World Affairs*, Graduate School of International Studies, University of Denver, 19, no. 1 (1982): 5. For other surveys of the copious alliance literature, consult Holsti, Hopmann, and Sullivan, *Unity and Disintegration in International Alliances*, chap. 1 and app. C; Bruce Bueno de Mesquita and J. David Singer, "Alliance, Capabilities, and War," *Political Science Annual*, 4 (1973); Philip Burgess and David Moore, "Inter-Nation Alliances: An Inventory and Appraisal of Propositions," *Political Science Annual*, 3 (1972); and Brian L. Job, "Grins without Cats: In Pursuit of Knowledge of Inter-nation Alliances," in "Cumulation in International Relations Research," ed. P. Terrence Hopmann, Dina Zinnes, and J. David Singer, *Monograph Series in World Affairs*, Graduate School of International Studies, University of Denver, vol. 18, bk. 3 (1981).

14. Examples of this genre include Robert Rood and Patrick McGowan, "Alliance Behavior in Balance of Power Systems," *American Political Science Review*, 79, no. 3 (1976); Brian L. Job, "Membership in Inter-nation Alliances: 1815–1865," and Randolph Siverson and George T. Duncan, "Stochastic Models of International Alliance Initiation: 1885–1965," in *Mathematical Models in International Relations*, ed. Dina Zinnes and William Gillespie (New York, 1976), pp. 74–109; George T. Duncan and Randolph Siverson, "Flexibility of Alliance Partner Choice in Multipolar Systems: Models and Tests," *International Studies Quarterly*, 26, no. 4 (1982); R. P. Y. Li and W. R. Thompson, "The Stochastic Process of Alliance Formation Behavior," *American Political Science Review*, 72, no. 4 (1978); W. J. Horvath and G. C. Foster, "Stochastic Models of War Alliances," *Journal of Conflict Resolution*, 7, no. 2 (1963); Jack S. Levy, "Alliance Formation and War Behavior: An Analysis of the Great Powers, 1495–1975," *Journal of Conflict Resolution*, 25, no. 4 (1981); J. David Singer and Melvin Small, "Alliance Aggregation and the Onset of War," in *Alliances: Latent War Communities in the Contemporary World*, ed. Francis A. Beer (New York, 1970); and Charles W. Kegley and Gregory A. Raymond, "Alliance Norms and War: A New Piece in an Old Puzzle," *International Studies Quarterly*, 26, no. 4 (1982).

alliances implicitly assumes that alliances are created to provide security against threats, these models focus on explaining the distribution of burdens within existing alliances rather than on explaining why the alliances were formed in the first place.[15]

Nevertheless, a number of works do examine the origins of alliances. Among the traditional works on international politics are many accounts of individual alliances and several important theoretical treatments. Hans Morgenthau's classic *Politics among Nations*, for example, contains a lengthy discussion of alliances supported by a variety of historical illustrations. Similar analyses are provided by George Liska and Robert L. Rothstein. Like Morgenthau, Liska relies on anecdotal evidence to support his points, whereas Rothstein bases his conclusions on case studies of Belgium and the Little Entente (Czechoslovakia, Rumania, and Yugoslavia) in the 1920s and 1930s.[16]

The traditional literature almost always falls within the broad compass of balance of power theory, although other hypotheses appear as well. Thus Liska writes that "alliances are against, and only derivatively for, someone or something," and Morgenthau refers to alliances as "a necessary function of the balance of power operating in a multiple state system."[17] At the same time, however, Liska suggests that "alignment . . . may [also] express ideological or ethnic affinities," and he states that "opportunistic alignments" may occur when a state believes that the effort to balance power will fail.[18] To complicate matters further, Paul Schroeder has argued that alliances are formed either to (1) oppose a threat, (2) accommodate a threat through a "pact of restraint," or (3) provide the great powers with a "tool of management" over weaker states.[19] In short, although most of the traditional literature relies heavily on balance of power concepts, doubts remain regarding the universal applicability of this hypothesis.

A limitation of the traditional approach is that its proponents rarely offer systematic tests of general hypotheses. Although Liska provides many apt examples, he does not attempt to assess the relative validity of

15. See Mancur Olson and Richard Zeckhauser, "An Economic Theory of Alliances," *Review of Economics and Statistics*, 48, no. 3 (1966).

16. See Hans J. Morgenthau, *Politics among Nations*, 4th ed. (New York, 1967); George Liska, *Nations in Alliance: The Limits of Interdependence* (Baltimore, Md., 1962); and Robert L. Rothstein, *Alliances and Small Powers* (New York, 1968).

17. See Liska, *Nations in Alliance*, p. 12; and Morgenthau, *Politics among Nations*, p. 175.

18. Liska, *Nations in Alliance*, pp. 27, 42–43, 55–56. Rothstein makes a similar point: "Small powers . . . were forced to play a perilous game: moving quickly from the lighter to the heavier side of the balance as soon as an apparent victor . . . could be discerned." See *Alliances and Small Powers*, p. 11.

19. See Paul Schroeder, "Alliances, 1815–1945: Weapons of Power and Tools of Management," in *Historical Dimensions of National Security Problems*, ed. Klaus Knorr (Lawrence, Kansas, 1976).

his many interesting propositions. Case studies on individual alliances can provide more reliable evidence but may not tell us much about how different states would behave in different circumstances. Schroeder fares better on this score, because he supports his arguments with a survey of the major European alliances from 1815 to 1945. But even he does not examine which of the possible motives for alignment is most common or identify the factors that might affect the strength of each.[20] The question of which hypotheses provide the best guide for policy is left unanswered.

The belief that states ally to oppose powerful or threatening states has been challenged by several quantitative studies as well. Using sophisticated indices of national capabilities and a cooperation versus conflict scale created by coding diplomatic events, Brian Healy and Arthur Stein argue that European great power alliances from 1870 to 1881 result from bandwagoning (which they term the ingratiation effect) rather than from a desire to balance power.[21] Because Germany's ascendance after 1870 was associated with increased cooperation from most other states and because an anti-German alliance did not form in this period, they reject the hypothesis that states "act to oppose any state [or coalition] which tends to assume a position of predominance."[22]

Despite the sophistication and originality of this work, there are several problems. First, the methodology is suspect, because it assumes that coders can estimate the true meaning (i.e., the level of conflict or cooperation) of a discrete diplomatic event divorced from its historical context.[23] Second, the results are based on events that were atypical. Germany's favorable position (including the free hand it enjoyed during the Franco-Prussian War) was due primarily to the great effort Bismarck devoted to convincing others that Germany was not an aggressive

20. There may be a conceptual problem here as well. The desire to ally in order to aggregate power and the desire to ally in order to manage weaker states are not incompatible. For example, a great power threatened by another great power may want to ally with weaker states both to increase its capabilities and to influence their behavior.

21. See Brian Healy and Arthur Stein, "The Balance of Power in International History: Theory and Reality," *Journal of Conflict Resolution*, 17, no. 1 (1973). For a related work, see Richard Rosecrance, Alan Alexandroff, Brian Healy, and Arthur Stein, "Power, Balance of Power, and Status in Nineteenth Century International Relations," *Sage Professional Papers in International Studies* (Beverly Hills, Calif., 1974). For an extension that challenges several of Healy and Stein's results, see H. Brooke McDonald and Richard Rosecrance, "Alliance and Structural Balance in the International System: A Reinterpretation," *Journal of Conflict Resolution*, 29, no. 1 (1985).

22. This hypothesis is drawn from Morton A. Kaplan, *System and Process in International Politics* (New York, 1957).

23. For a persuasive critique along these lines, see Paul W. Schroeder, "Quantitative Studies in the Balance of Power: An Historian's Reaction," *Journal of Conflict Resolution*, 21, no. 1 (1977).

[8]

state.[24] Far from refuting the tendency of states to oppose predominant powers, Healy and Stein's work reveals that power can be less important than other factors, such as perceived intentions.[25] In particular, Germany failed to provoke a countervailing coalition because Bismarck's adroit diplomacy made friendship with Germany seem both possible and preferable. The ingratiation effect may thus be largely a testimonial to Bismarck's diplomatic artistry.

Another challenge to balance of power theory has emerged from the ranks of expected utility theorists. Claiming to offer a formal theory of how states choose alliance partners, these authors suggest that states form alliances to increase their utility, measured in terms of security, risk, or welfare.[26] After correlating observed alliance dyads with various measures of utility, Michael Altfeld concludes that "alliances do not appear to be random; . . . potential alliances which fail to increase both partners' security almost never form."[27] In a similar work, David Newman claims to disprove balance of power theory by showing that states whose power is increasing are more likely to form alliances, because they are more attractive partners.[28]

There are serious problems here as well. Expected utility theory does not identify who will ally with whom; it can only predict when states may seek alignment with someone. Furthermore, the fact that states whose capabilities are increasing tend to form alliances does not refute balance of power theory. After all, a state whose security position is threatened will probably attempt to increase its relative power (e.g., by spending more on defense) while simultaneously seeking an alliance with another state. Thus what Newman claims is a causal relationship (increases in power encourage alignment) may well be spurious. Even

24. During the Franco-Prussian War, for example, Bismarck maneuvered France into starting the war and encouraged Russian fears that Austria-Hungary would intervene on the side of France. Russia promptly mobilized its troops, which convinced Austria-Hungary to remain neutral. See Smoke, *War*, pp. 127–28, 131–33. On Bismarck's foreign policy in this period, see Gordon A. Craig, *Germany: 1866–1945* (London, 1978), pp. 101–4.

25. For a related argument by these same authors and their collaborators, see Rosecrance et al., "Power, Balance of Power, and Status," pp. 37–39.

26. Relevant works here are Michael F. Altfeld and Bruce Bueno de Mesquita, "Choosing Sides in Wars," *International Studies Quarterly*, 23, no. 1 (1979); David Newman, "Security and Alliances: A Theoretical Study of Alliance Formation" (diss., University of Rochester, 1984); and Michael F. Altfeld, "The Decision to Ally: A Theory and Test," *Western Political Quarterly*, 37, no. 4 (1984).

27. See Altfeld, "Decision to Ally," p. 538 and passim. This conclusion is based on the fact that 25 percent of all dyads showing positive utility actually form an alliance, whereas only 2 percent of those showing negative utility do so. Of course, these figures tell us nothing about which dyads will be preferred or why 75 percent of the dyads exhibiting positive utility do not ally.

28. Newman, "Security and Alliances," pp. 21, 53–60.

were this not the case, two states whose capabilities are increasing might well form an alliance against a third state that is growing still faster or that appears especially aggressive. This type of response would still be an example of balancing behavior.

Finally, some authors have used game theory to analyze alliance behavior. William Riker's seminal work on political coalitions examines the optimal size of *n*-person alliances, and Glenn Snyder used two-person game theory to illuminate the trade-offs that states face in seeking to maintain allied support while avoiding the risk that their allies will entrap them in unwanted wars.[29] Both authors reach conclusions that are consistent with balance of power theory (i.e., Riker's prediction that the players will seek a "minimum winning coalition" implies that states will join the weaker side).

Unfortunately, because game theory models are based solely on the distribution of power and the structure of possible payoffs, they do not take into account the impact of perceptions, ideology, and geography. Among other things, this limitation helps explain why Riker's attempt to apply his insights to international politics is only partly successful.[30] And as Snyder admits, two-person game theory tells us more about the behavior within coalitions than it does about the players' choice of partners: "game theory does not predict who will align with whom."[31] As with most of the other literature on alliances, in short, game theory has provided interesting answers to a different set of questions.

The existing scholarship on alliances is useful as a source of hypotheses. It does not, however, tell us which hypotheses are valid. As one student of this subject has observed, "We have little if any reliable

29. See William H. Riker, *The Theory of Political Coalitions* (New Haven, Conn., 1962); and Glenn Snyder, "The Security Dilemma in Alliance Politics," *World Politics*, 36, no. 4 (1984).

30. Riker's conclusion, titled "Reflections on Empires," still makes for fascinating reading. Drawing upon his model of *n*-person coalitions, Riker predicts that the Soviet-American rivalry will show (1) the superpowers paying ever-greater prices to attract or keep allies, (2) increased tensions as the outcome of each realignment is seen as increasingly vital, (3) an increased probability of general war, and (4) the eventual decline of the two superpowers as a result of the first three tendencies. Although there is evidence of these tendencies throughout the Cold War, this evidence is probably due as much to misperceptions by both superpowers as to the logic of an *n*-person game. In particular, Riker's deductions rest on his belief that by 1950 "the U.S. was opposed by a minority coalition which could check many American actions and might even reasonably aspire to defeat it" (*Theory of Political Coalitions*, p. 223). If this scenario were true, then Riker's explanations would hold. In fact, however, the United States and its allies were vastly superior to the Soviet alliance network during this period. For example, the West controlled over three times the GNP produced by the Soviet Union and its satellites and spent larger amounts on defense as well. Because many U.S. leaders believed the Soviets to be more powerful than they were, however, and because they accepted several dubious theories of alliance formation, the politics of the early Cold War approximated Riker's prediction, but not for the reasons he describes.

31. Snyder, "Security Dilemma in Alliance Politics," p. 463.

information about the relative potency of the various reasons why nations . . . join alliances."[32] Thus, despite the enormous impact that debates about the origins of alliances exert on the conduct of U.S. foreign policy, the same disputes persist. What is needed is a strategy for resolving them.

RESEARCH METHODS AND PROCEDURES

The method I have employed is straightforward. The principal historical evidence I have used is the diplomatic history of the Middle East between 1955 and 1979.[33] Through a survey of these events, I have identified thirty-six separate bilateral or multilateral alliance commitments, involving eighty-six national decisions. After identifying the motives that led each state to select certain allies at different times, I have compared these results with the predictions of each hypothesis. Two questions are central: (1) Which hypothesis explains the greatest number of alliances? and (2) Are there identifiable conditions that affect which type of behavior is to be expected (i.e., which hypothesis is likely to apply)?

This approach is designed to overcome some of the limitations found in the works described earlier. Although historical case studies provide the most detailed evidence regarding the causes of a particular alliance, attempting to test several general hypotheses through a single case study is obviously problematic. Comparative case studies are more promising, but a large number of cases would be needed to establish valid conclusions. This difficulty is especially troublesome when the hypotheses under consideration are not mutually exclusive (a problem faced throughout this book).

Reliance on historical anecdotes or a large statistical sample is equally troublesome. Anecdotal evidence cannot tell which causes are most powerful or widespread, and statistical manipulations cannot provide direct evidence about the perceptions and motivations that inspired a particular alliance decision. Nor can they readily take into account the novel contextual features of a given case.

In order to overcome these limitations, I have employed a methodology that combines the features of a focused comparison and a statis-

32. Ward, "Research Gaps in Alliance Dynamics," p. 18.
33. I have identified the main alliance commitments of nine Middle East states and the two superpowers. The states are the United States, the Soviet Union, Egypt, Iraq, Israel, Jordan, Lebanon, Saudi Arabia, Syria, North Yemen, and South Yemen. I have also included several others (e.g., Great Britain and France) when excluding them would clearly have been misleading.

[11]

tical-correlative analysis.[34] By examining a large number of alignments (thirty-six), I have enhanced the external validity of my results and increased their robustness. Even if the ambiguity of the evidence leaves my interpretation of a few cases open to debate, my conclusions are likely to be valid as long as most of the analysis is sound. Finally, because my evaluation of each alliance is based on a careful reading of available historical accounts, the results can be informed by evidence on perceptions and motivations as well as the impact of unique contextual factors. Given the objectives of the study, this compromise between generality and specificity seems necessary and appropriate.

Definitions

I use the terms *alliance* and *alignment* interchangeably throughout the book. For my purposes, an alliance is a formal or informal arrangement for security cooperation between two or more sovereign states. Employing this rather broad definition makes sense for several reasons. First, many contemporary states are reluctant to sign formal treaties with their allies. To limit my analysis to formal alliances would omit a large number of important cases. Second, precise distinctions—for example, between formal and informal alliances—would probably distort more than they would reveal. There has never been a formal treaty of alliance between the United States and Israel, but no one would question the level of commitment between these two states. Changes in that commitment, moreover, have been revealed primarily by changes in behavior or by verbal statements, not by the rewriting of a document. Similarly, the Soviet Union and Egypt did not sign a formal treaty until 1971 but were obviously close allies long before then. And the 1971 Soviet-Egyptian Treaty of Friendship and Cooperation was actually a sign of growing tension between the two countries, not a symbol of enhanced commitment. Finally, any effort to take formal statements of inter-Arab solidarity at face value would be fraught with peril, as any student of Middle East politics knows. Thus an attempt to employ a strict typology of alliance commitments could easily be misleading, because the true meaning of either formal or informal arrangements is likely to vary from case to case.[35]

34. On these different approaches, see Alexander L. George, "Case Study and Theory Development: The Method of Structured, Focused Comparison," in Lauren, *Diplomacy: New Approaches*, pp. 61–62 and passim.

35. My decision not to employ a strict typology does not mean that there is no difference between formal and informal commitments or that a typology of alliances is impossible to devise. I have simply decided to rely upon a more subjective assessment of the various alliances examined in this study rather than employ a formal taxonomy that might not accurately reflect the nature of the specific commitment. On the differences between formal and informal commitments, see the perceptive analysis by Robert A. Kann in "Alliances versus Ententes," *World Politics*, 28, no. 4 (1976).

Even more important, establishing a strict typology of commitments is simply not necessary for my purposes. I am interested in identifying the broad forces that lead states to support one another in international affairs, but I do not seek to explain the precise arrangements the parties ultimately choose. The specific commitments that allies accept will reflect a host of idiosyncratic features that are unlikely to be easily generalized. Thus I make no claim to be able to predict exactly how states will choose to implement their mutual commitments, but I do seek to explain why they choose to do so in the first place and to identify which of several potential partners they are likely to prefer. Resolving these questions will be challenge enough.

Why the Middle East?

I have chosen to investigate alliance formation in the Middle East for several reasons. First, the Middle East has been and remains an area of considerable strategic importance. Its importance is revealed by the efforts that both superpowers have devoted to acquiring and supporting allies in the region, efforts that have led to serious superpower confrontations on several occasions.[36] Second, alliance commitments in the Middle East have shifted frequently throughout the postwar period, as these states adjusted to changing internal and external circumstances. As a result, the diplomacy of the Middle East provides a large number of cases for consideration and is likely to reveal more about the factors that determine alliance choices than would examination of a less turbulent region.

Most important of all, the Middle East provides a strong test of many familiar hypotheses. Because most propositions about alliance formation (or international relations theory in general, for that matter) have been derived from the history of the European great power system, it is especially appropriate to examine their utility in predicting the behavior of states that are neither European nor great powers. Moreover, many of these regimes are relatively young and lack the diplomatic experience

---

36. According to Henry Kissinger, "the Middle East lies at the crossroads of three continents. Because of the area's strategic importance, and because it provides the energy on which much of the world depends, outside powers have continued to involve themselves in its conflicts, often competitively." Henry A. Kissinger, *White House Years* (Boston, 1979), p. 285. Richard Nixon termed the region "a powder keg" and stated that "it is like the Balkans before World War II—where the two superpowers . . . could be drawn into a confrontation that neither of them wants." Quoted in William B. Quandt, *Decade of Decisions: American Policy toward the Arab-Israeli Conflict, 1967–1976* (Berkeley, Calif., 1977), pp. 82, 100. By the late 1970s, superpower arms transfers to the Middle East constituted roughly 40 percent of the global total, more than double the amount sent to any other region. See ACDA, *World Military Expenditures and Arms Transfers 1968–1977* (Washington, D.C., n.d.), p. 8.

[13]

and traditions of the European great powers. Thus, if familiar hypotheses apply to this region as well, that is strong testimony to their explanatory power. Furthermore, the Middle East has been swept by intense ideological rivalries, major shifts in relative power, and significant superpower involvement throughout the period in question. As chapter 2 will show, these factors lie at the heart of the most popular hypotheses about alliance formation. Accordingly, the Middle East is an especially appropriate arena within which to assess them.

Methodological Barriers

Despite these strengths, I have faced a number of potential methodological problems in writing this book. Although several can be only partially alleviated, none presents an insurmountable barrier.

As I already noted, the concept of alliance is difficult to define and measure with precision. As will become clear in the next chapter, the same is true for such independent variables as level of threat and ideological solidarity. Moreover, many of the alliances examined in this study are overdetermined: they result from a number of separate causes. In such circumstances, measuring the importance of each different cause precisely (in order to distinguish between different hypotheses) is extremely difficult. To deal with this problem, I consider a large number of separate alignments while remaining alert for crucial cases that support one hypothesis while excluding others. I also include direct evidence (e.g., elite testimony) that identifies which causal factors were the most important in a particular instance.

A second potential difficulty arises from my focus on the Middle East. It might be argued that this region is *sui generis,* that any results derived from examining alliances in the Middle East cannot be applied to other areas or to different time periods. It might also be suggested that adequate understanding of Middle Eastern diplomacy requires specialized training and a knowledge of unique cultural factors that I cannot claim.[37]

Although these considerations are not without merit, they do not present an overwhelming barrier. The argument that the Middle East is *sui generis* applies with equal force to any other region. Yet international relations scholars have long relied on historical cases and quantitative data drawn from European diplomatic history without being accused of

37. For arguments to this effect, see Leonard Binder, "The Middle East as a Subordinate Political System," *World Politics,* 10, no. 3 (1958); Fouad Ajami, "The Middle East: Important for the Wrong Reasons," *Journal of International Affairs,* 29, no. 1 (1979); and L. Carl Brown, *International Politics and the Middle East* (Princeton, N.J., 1984).

a narrow geographic, temporal, or cultural focus. Nonetheless, I have addressed this problem in two ways. First, I have drawn on European history in elaborating the different hypotheses. Second, after testing these propositions on the Middle East, I have applied them to the current array of global alliance commitments. By drawing on evidence from several different contexts, I have significantly reduced the limitations of relying primarily on evidence from the Middle East.

Of course, it may be true that alliances in the Middle East exhibit unique patterns of behavior. If so, that situation is not so much a barrier to theoretical work as a challenge to the theorist. The task is to explain how unique regional characteristics produce the observed behavior. Indeed, that is precisely what I attempt in later chapters, when I examine the impact of pan-Arabism on alliances in the Arab world.

Finally, because I am relying primarily on secondary sources in investigating these alliances, my assessment of contemporary Middle East diplomacy rests on the scholarship that area specialists have provided. Unfortunately, the historiography on recent Middle East politics is uneven—because of the difficulty of archival research and the obvious biases with which many accounts are written. Even primary sources and elite testimony must be treated with caution, given the instrumental motives that most participants in Middle East diplomacy have in offering their accounts. To compensate for these problems, I have tried to document events and arguments as extensively as possible, relying on multiple sources and the most widely accepted historical accounts.

I will proceed as follows. In chapter 2, I will develop the concepts and hypotheses that will guide the remainder of the study. In Chapters 3 and 4, I will describe the evolution of alliance commitments in the Middle East, beginning with the Baghdad Pact in 1955 and ending with the Arab responses to the Egyptian-Israeli peace treaty in 1979. In these chapters, I describe the various alliance relationships formed during this period, identify their origins, and place them within a broader historical context.

These tasks accomplished, I begin the task of comparing hypothesis and evidence. In chapter 5, I explore the competing propositions that states ally to balance against threats or to bandwagon with them. In chapter 6, I consider the importance of ideology as a cause of alliances. In chapter 7, I examine the role of foreign aid and transnational penetration as instruments of alliance formation. Finally, in chapter 8, I provide a comparative assessment of the different hypotheses, extend the analysis to alliances outside the Middle East, and reveal what these results imply for U.S. foreign policy.

A final word. This book is primarily an exercise in international relations theory, not Middle East studies. I have not tried to provide a definitive diplomatic history of the Middle East since 1955. Instead, I have analyzed Middle East alliances in order to resolve several important disputes within the fields of international relations theory and national security policy. I will now consider these disputes in more detail.

[2]

Explaining Alliance Formation

In this chapter I propose five general explanations for international alliances. I explore the logic of the various hypotheses, present illustrative examples, and outline the conditions under which the behavior predicted by each should be expected.

Alliances as a Response to Threat: Balancing and Bandwagoning

When confronted by a significant external threat, states may either balance or bandwagon. *Balancing* is defined as allying with others against the prevailing threat; *bandwagoning* refers to alignment with the source of danger. Thus two distinct hypotheses about how states will select their alliance partners can be identified on the basis of whether the states ally against or with the principal external threat.[1]

These two hypotheses depict very different worlds. If balancing is more common than bandwagoning, then states are more secure, because aggressors will face combined opposition. But if bandwagoning is the dominant tendency, then security is scarce, because successful aggressors will attract additional allies, enhancing their power while reducing that of their opponents.

Both scholars and statesmen have repeatedly embraced one or the other of these hypotheses, but they have generally failed either to frame their beliefs carefully or to evaluate their accuracy. Accordingly, I pre-

1. My use of the terms *balancing* and *bandwagoning* follows that of Kenneth Waltz (who credits it to Stephen Van Evera) in his *Theory of International Politics* (Reading, Mass., 1979). Arnold Wolfers uses a similar terminology in his essay "The Balance of Power in Theory and Practice," in *Discord and Collaboration: Essays on International Politics* (Baltimore, Md., 1962), pp. 122–24.

sent each hypothesis in its simplest form and then consider several variations. I then consider which type of behavior—balancing or band-wagoning—is more common and suggest when each response is likely to occur.

Balancing Behavior

The belief that states form alliances in order to prevent stronger powers from dominating them lies at the heart of traditional balance of power theory.[2] According to this view, states join alliances to protect themselves from states or coalitions whose superior resources could pose a threat. States choose to balance for two main reasons.

First, they place their survival at risk if they fail to curb a potential hegemon before it becomes too strong. To ally with the dominant power means placing one's trust in its continued benevolence. The safer strategy is to join with those who cannot readily dominate their allies, in order to avoid being dominated by those who can.[3] As Winston Churchill explained Britain's traditional alliance policy: "For four hundred years the foreign policy of England has been to oppose the strongest, most aggressive, most dominating power on the Continent. . . . [I]t would have been easy . . . and tempting to join with the stronger and share the fruits of his conquest. However, we always took the harder course, joined with the less strong powers, . . . and thus defeated the Continental military tyrant whoever he was."[4] More recently, Henry Kissinger advocated a rapprochement with China, because he believed that in a triangular relationship it was better to align with the weaker side.[5]

Second, joining the weaker side increases the new member's influ-

---

2. For analyses of the classical writings on the balance of power, see Edward V. Gulick, *Europe's Classical Balance of Power* (New York, 1955), pt. 1; F. H. Hinsley, *Power and the Pursuit of Peace: Theory and Practice in the History of Relations between States* (Cambridge, England, 1963), pt. 1; Inis L. Claude, *Power and International Relations* (New York, 1962), chaps. 2 and 3; Robert E. Osgood and Robert W. Tucker, *Force, Order, and Justice* (Baltimore, Md., 1967), pp. 96–104 and passim; and Martin Wight, "The Balance of Power," in *Diplomatic Investigations*, ed. Martin Wight and Herbert Butterfield (London, 1966). Modern versions of the theory can be found in Waltz, *Theory of International Politics*, chap. 6; Kaplan, *System and Process in International Politics*; and Morgenthau, *Politics among Nations*, pt. 4.

3. As Vattel wrote several centuries ago: "The surest means of preserving this balance of power would be to bring it about that no State should be much superior to the others. . . . [But] this idea could not be realized without injustice and violence. . . . It is simpler, . . . and more just to have recourse to the method . . . of forming alliances in order to make a stand against a very powerful sovereign and prevent him from dominating." Quoted in Gulick, *Europe's Classical Balance of Power*, p. 60.

4. Winston S. Churchill, *The Second World War*, vol. 1: *The Gathering Storm* (Boston, 1948), pp. 207–8.

5. Kissinger, *White House Years*, p. 178.

ence within the alliance, because the weaker side has greater need for assistance. Allying with the stronger side, by contrast, gives the new member little influence (because it adds relatively less to the coalition) and leaves it vulnerable to the whims of its partners. Joining the weaker side should be the preferred choice.[6]

Bandwagoning Behavior

The belief that states will balance is unsurprising, given the many familiar examples of states joining together to resist a threatening state or coalition.[7] Yet, despite the powerful evidence that history provides in support of the balancing hypothesis, the belief that the opposite response is more likely is widespread. According to one scholar: "In international politics, nothing succeeds like success. Momentum accrues to the gainer and accelerates his movement. The appearance of irreversibility in his gains enfeebles one side and stimulates the other all the more. The bandwagon collects those on the sidelines."[8]

The bandwagoning hypothesis is especially popular with statesmen seeking to justify overseas involvements or increased military budgets. For example, German admiral Alfred von Tirpitz's famous risk theory rested on this type of logic. By building a great battle fleet, Tirpitz argued, Germany could force England into neutrality or alliance with her by posing a threat to England's vital maritime supremacy.[9]

Bandwagoning beliefs have also been a recurring theme throughout the Cold War. Soviet efforts to intimidate both Norway and Turkey into not joining NATO reveal the Soviet conviction that states will accommodate readily to threats, although these moves merely encouraged Nor-

---

6. In the words of Kenneth Waltz: "Secondary states, if they are free to choose, flock to the weaker side; for it is the stronger side that threatens them. On the weaker side they are both more appreciated and safer, provided, of course, that the coalition they form achieves enough defensive or deterrent strength to dissuade adversaries from attacking." See *Theory of International Politics*, pp. 126–27.

7. This theme is developed in Ludwig Dehio, *The Precarious Balance* (New York, 1965); Hinsley, *Power and the Pursuit of Peace*; and Gulick, *Europe's Classical Balance of Power*.

8. W. Scott Thompson, "The Communist International System," *Orbis*, 20, no. 4 (1977).

9. See William L. Langer, *The Diplomacy of Imperialism* (New York, 1953), pp. 434–35; and Craig, *Germany 1866–1945*, pp. 303–14. This view was not confined to military circles in Germany. In February 1914, Secretary of State Jagow predicted that Britain would remain neutral in the event of a continental war, expressing the widespread view that drove German policy prior to World War I. As he told the German ambassador in London: "We have not built our fleet in vain, and . . . people in England will seriously ask themselves whether it will be just that simple and without danger to play the role of France's guardian angel against us." Quoted in Imanuel Geiss, *July 1914* (New York, 1967), pp. 24–25.

way and Turkey to align more closely with the West.[10] Soviet officials made a similar error in believing that the growth of Soviet military power in the 1960s and 1970s would lead to a permanent shift in the correlation of forces against the West. Instead, it contributed to a Sino-American rapprochement in the 1970s and the largest peacetime increase in U.S. military power in the 1980s.[11]

American officials have been equally fond of bandwagoning notions. According to NSC-68, the classified study that helped justify a major U.S. military buildup in the 1950s: "In the absence of an affirmative decision [to increase U.S. military capabilities] . . . our friends will become more than a liability to us, they will become a positive increment to Soviet power."[12] President John F. Kennedy once claimed that "if the United States were to falter, the whole world . . . would inevitably begin to move toward the Communist bloc."[13] And though Henry Kissinger often argued that the United States should form balancing alliances to contain the Soviet Union, he apparently believed that U.S. allies were likely to bandwagon. As he put it, "If leaders around the world . . . assume that the U.S. lacked either the forces or the will . . . they will accommodate themselves to what they will regard as the dominant trend."[14] Ronald Reagan's claim, "If we cannot defend ourselves [in Central America] . . . then we cannot expect to prevail elsewhere. . . . [O]ur credibility will collapse and our alliances will crumble," reveals the same logic in a familiar role—that of justifying overseas intervention.[15]

These assertions contain a common theme: states are attracted to strength. The more powerful the state and the more clearly this power is demonstrated, the more likely others are to ally with it. By contrast, a decline in a state's relative position will lead its allies to opt for neutrality

10. For the effects of the Soviet pressure on Turkey, see George Lenczowski, *The Middle East in World Affairs*, 4th ed. (Ithaca, 1980), pp. 134–38; and Bruce R. Kuniholm, *The Origins of the Cold War in the Near East* (Princeton, N.J., 1980), pp. 355–78. For the Norwegian response to Soviet pressure, see Herbert Feis, *From Trust to Terror: The Onset of the Cold War, 1945–50* (New York, 1970), p. 381; and Geir Lundestad, *America, Scandinavia, and the Cold War: 1945–1949* (New York, 1980), pp. 308–9.

11. See Dimitri K. Simes, "Soviet Policy toward the United States," in Nye, *The Making of America's Soviet Policy*, pp. 307–8.

12. NSC–68 ("United States Objectives and Programs for National Security"), reprinted in Gaddis and Etzold, *Containment*, p. 404. Similar passages can be found on pp. 389, 414, and 434.

13. Quoted in Seyom Brown, *The Faces of Power: Constancy and Change in United States Foreign Policy from Truman to Johnson* (New York, 1968), p. 217.

14. Quoted in U.S. House Committee on Foreign Affairs, *The Soviet Union and the Third World: Watershed in Great Power Policy?* 97th Cong., 1st sess., 1977, pp. 157–58.

15. *New York Times*, April 28, 1983, p. A12. In the same speech, Reagan also said: "If Central America were to fall, what would the consequences be for our position in Asia and Europe and for alliances such as NATO? . . . Which ally, which friend would trust us then?"

at best or to defect to the other side at worst. The belief that states are prone to bandwagoning implies that most alliances are extremely fragile.

What is the logic behind this hypothesis? Two distinct motives can be identified. First, bandwagoning may be a form of appeasement. By aligning with an ascendant state or coalition, the bandwagoner may hope to avoid an attack by diverting it elsewhere.

Second, a state may align with the dominant side in wartime in order to share the spoils of victory. Mussolini's declaration of war on France in 1940 and Russia's entry into the war against Japan in 1945 illustrate this type of bandwagoning, as do Italian and Rumanian alliance choices in World War I.[16] By joining the side that they believed would triumph, each hoped to make territorial gains at the end of the fighting.

Stalin's decision to align with Hitler in 1939 illustrates both motives nicely. The Nazi-Soviet Non-Aggression Treaty led to the dismemberment of Poland and may have deflected Hitler's ambitions westward temporarily. Stalin was thus able to gain both time and territory by bandwagoning with Germany.[17] In general, however, these two motives for bandwagoning are quite different. In the first, bandwagoning is chosen for defensive reasons, as a means of preserving one's independence in the face of a potential threat. In the second, a bandwagoning state chooses the leading side for offensive reasons, in order to share the fruits of victory. In either case, however, such behavior stands in sharp contrast to the predictions of the balancing hypothesis.

Different Sources of Threat

Balancing and bandwagoning are usually framed solely in terms of capabilities. Balancing is alignment with the weaker side, bandwagoning with the stronger.[18] This conception should be revised, however, to account for the other factors that statesmen consider when deciding with whom to ally. Although power is an important part of the equation, it is not the only one. It is more accurate to say that states tend to ally with or against the foreign power that poses the greatest threat. For example, states may balance by allying with other strong states if a

16. See Denis Mack Smith, *Mussolini* (New York, 1982), pp. 234–35, 246–50; Adam Ulam, *Expansion and Coexistence: Soviet Foreign Policy, 1917–1973* (New York, 1974), pp. 394–98; and A. J. P. Taylor, *The First World War* (New York, 1980), pp. 88–90, 153.

17. See Ulam, *Expansion and Coexistence*, pp. 276–77; Isaac Deutscher, *Stalin: A Political Biography* (London, 1966), pp. 437–43; and Joachim Fest, *Hitler* (New York, 1974), pp. 583–84, 592–93.

18. The preeminent example of balance of power theory based exclusively on the distribution of capabilities is Waltz, *Theory of International Politics*, chap. 6. For examples of theorists who argue that other factors can be important, see Gulick, *Europe's Classical Balance of Power*, pp. 25, 45–47, 60–62.

weaker power is more dangerous for other reasons. Thus the coalitions that defeated Germany in World War I and World War II were vastly superior in total resources, but they came together when it became clear that the aggressive aims of the Wilhelmines and Nazis posed the greater danger.[19] Because balancing and bandwagoning are more accurately viewed as a response to threats, it is important to consider other factors that will affect the level of threat that states may pose: aggregate power, geographic proximity, offensive power, and aggressive intentions.

Aggregate Power

All else being equal, the greater a state's total resources (e.g., population, industrial and military capability, and technological prowess), the greater a potential threat it can pose to others. Recognizing this fact, Walter Lippmann and George Kennan defined the aim of U.S. grand strategy as that of preventing any single state from controlling more industrial resources than the United States did. In practical terms, it means allying against any state that appears powerful enough to dominate the combined resources of industrial Eurasia.[20] Similarly, Sir Edward Grey, British foreign secretary in 1914, justified British intervention against the Dual Alliance by saying: "To stand aside would mean the domination of Germany; the subordination of France and Russia; the isolation of Britain . . . and ultimately Germany would wield the whole power of the continent."[21] In the same way, Castlereagh's efforts to create a "just distribution of the forces in Europe" revealed his own concern for the distribution of aggregate power.[22] The total power that

---

19. In World War I, the alliance of Great Britain, France, and Russia controlled 27.9 percent of world industrial production, while Germany and Austria together controlled only 19.2 percent. With Russia out of the war but with the United States joining Britain and France, the percentage opposing the Dual Alliance reached 51.7 percent, an advantage of more than 2 to 1. In World War II, the defense expenditures of the United States, Great Britain, and Russia exceeded those of Germany by roughly 4.5 to 1. Even allowing for Germany's control of Europe and the burdens of the war against Japan, the Grand Alliance possessed an enormous advantage in overall capabilities. Thus the formation of the two most important alliances in the twentieth century cannot be explained by focusing on power alone. For these and other statistics on the relative power in the two wars, see Paul M. Kennedy, "The First World War and the International Power System," *International Security*, 9, no. 1 (1984); and *The Rise and Fall of British Naval Mastery* (London, 1983), pp. 309–15.

20. For a summary of these ideas, see Gaddis, *Strategies of Containment*, pp. 25–88. Kennan's ideas are found in *Realities of American Foreign Policy* (Princeton, N.J., 1954), pp. 63–65. Lippmann's still compelling analysis is found in Walter Lippmann, *The Cold War: A Study of U.S. Foreign Policy* (New York, 1947).

21. Quoted in Bernadotte C. Schmitt, *The Coming of the War in 1914* (New York, 1968), 2: 115.

22. Castlereagh's policy is described in Harold Nicolson, *The Congress of Vienna* (New York, 1946), pp. 205–6.

states can wield is thus an important component of the threat that they pose to others.

Although power can pose a threat, it can also be prized. States with great power have the capacity to either punish enemies or reward friends. By itself, therefore, a state's aggregate power may provide a motive for balancing or bandwagoning.

Geographic Proximity

Because the ability to project power declines with distance, states that are nearby pose a greater threat than those that are far away.[23] Other things being equal, therefore, states are more likely to make their alliance choices in response to nearby powers than in response to those that are distant. For example, the British Foreign Office responded to German complaints about the attention paid to Germany's naval expansion by saying: "If the British press pays more attention to the increase of Germany's naval power than to a similar movement in Brazil . . . this is no doubt due to the proximity of the German coasts and the remoteness of Brazil."[24] More recently, President Reagan justified U.S. intervention in Central America in much the same way: "Central America is much closer to the United States than many of the world's trouble spots that concern us. . . . El Salvador is nearer to Texas than Texas is to Massachusetts. Nicaragua is just as close to Miami, San Antonio, and Tucson as those cities are to Washington."[25]

As with aggregate power, proximate threats can lead to balancing or bandwagoning. When proximate threats trigger a balancing response, alliance networks that resemble checkerboards are the likely result. Students of diplomatic history have long been taught that neighbors of neighbors are friends, and the tendency for encircling states to align against a central power was first described in Kautilya's writings in the fourth century.[26] Examples include France and Russia against Wil-

23. See Harvey Starr and Benjamin A. Most, "The Substance and Study of Borders in International Relations Research," *International Studies Quarterly*, 20, no. 4 (1976). For a discussion of the relationship between power and distance, see Kenneth A. Boulding, *Conflict and Defense: A General Theory* (New York, 1962), pp. 229–30, 245–47. For an interesting practical critique, see Albert Wohlstetter, "Illusions of Distance," *Foreign Affairs*, 46, no. 2 (1968).

24. Quoted in Paul M. Kennedy, *The Rise of the Anglo-German Antagonism, 1860–1914* (London, 1980), p. 421.

25. *New York Times*, April 28, 1983, p. A12.

26. Kautilya's analysis ran as follows: "The king who is situated anywhere immediately on the circumference of the conqueror's territory is termed the enemy. The king who is likewise situated close to the enemy, but separated from the conqueror only by the enemy, is termed the friend (of the conqueror). . . . In front of the conqueror and close to the enemy, there happen to be situated kings such as the conqueror's friend, next to him the enemy's friend, and next to the last, the conqueror's friend, and next, the enemy's friend's friend." See Kautilya, "Arthasastra," in *Balance of Power*, ed. Paul A. Seabury (San Francisco, 1965), p. 8.

helmine Germany, France, and the Little Entente in the 1930s; the Soviet Union and Vietnam against China and Cambodia in the 1970s; and the tacit alignment between Iran and Syria against Iraq and its various Arab supporters.

Alternatively, when a threat from a proximate power leads to band-wagoning, the familiar phenomenon of a sphere of influence is created. Small states bordering a great power may be so vulnerable that they choose to bandwagon rather than balance, especially if a powerful neighbor has demonstrated its ability to compel obedience. Thus Finland, whose name has undeservedly become synonymous with bandwagoning, chose to do so only after being defeated by the Soviet Union twice within a five-year period.

Offensive Power

All else being equal, states with large offensive capabilities are more likely to provoke an alliance than are those that are incapable of attacking because of geography, military posture, or something else.[27] Although offensive capability and geographic proximity are clearly related—states that are close to one another can threaten one another more readily—they are not identical.[28]

Offensive power is also closely related but not identical to aggregate power. Specifically, offensive power is the ability to threaten the sovereignty or territorial integrity of another state at an acceptable cost. The ease with which aggregate power can be converted into offensive power (i.e., by amassing large, mobile military capabilities) is affected by the various factors that determine the relative advantage to the offense or defense at any particular period.

Once again, the effects of offensive power may vary. The immediate threat that offensive capabilities pose may create a strong incentive for others to balance.[29] Tirpitz's risk strategy backfired for precisely this

27. The best discussions of the implications of offense and defense are in Robert Jervis, "Cooperation under the Security Dilemma," *World Politics*, 30, no. 3 (1978); Stephen W. Van Evera, "Causes of War" (diss., University of California, Berkeley, 1984); and George Quester, *Offense and Defense in the International System* (New York, 1977). For an analysis and critique of these theories, see Jack S. Levy, "The Offensive/Defensive Balance of Military Technology: A Theoretical and Historical Analysis," *International Studies Quarterly*, 28, no. 2 (1984).

28. The distinction lies in the fact that there are a variety of factors unrelated to geographic proximity that alter the offense/defense balance. Proximity also tends to produce greater conflicts of interest, such as border disputes, between the states involved. These conflicts of interest are the result of proximity but can be distinct from the issue of offensive or defensive advantages.

29. See William L. Langer, *European Alliances and Alignments* (New York, 1950), pp. 3–5; Raymond J. Sontag, *European Diplomatic History, 1871–1932* (New York, 1933), pp. 4–5; Jervis, "Cooperation under the Security Dilemma," p. 189; and Quester, *Offense and Defense in the International System*, pp. 105–6.

reason. England viewed the German battle fleet as a potent offensive threat and redoubled its own naval efforts while reinforcing ties with France and Russia.[30] However, when offensive power permits rapid conquest, vulnerable states may see little hope in resisting. Balancing may seem unwise because one's allies may not be able to provide assistance quickly enough. This tendency may be one reason that spheres of influence emerge: states that close to a country with large offensive capabilities (and that are far from potential allies) may be forced to bandwagon because balancing alliances are simply not viable.[31]

Aggressive Intentions

Finally, states that are viewed as aggressive are likely to provoke others to balance against them. As noted earlier, Nazi Germany faced an overwhelming countervailing coalition because it combined substantial power with extremely dangerous ambitions. Indeed, even states with rather modest capabilities may prompt others to balance if they are perceived as especially aggressive. Thus Libyan conduct has prompted Egypt, Israel, France, the United States, Chad, and the Sudan to coordinate political and military responses against Colonel Qadhafi's activities.[32]

Perceptions of intent are likely to play an especially crucial role in alliance choices. For example, changing perceptions of German aims helped create the Triple Entente. Whereas Bismarck had carefully defended the status quo after 1870, the expansionist ambitions of his successors alarmed the other European powers.[33] Although the growth of German power played a major role, the importance of German intentions should not be overlooked. The impact of perceptions is nicely revealed in Eyre Crowe's famous 1907 memorandum defining British policy toward Germany. Crowe's analysis is all the more striking because he had few objections to the growth of German power per se:

---

30. As Imanuel Geiss notes: "Finding an agreement with Britain along German lines without a substantial naval agreement thus amounted to squaring the circle." See his *German Foreign Policy*, p. 131. See also Kennedy, *Rise of Anglo-German Antagonism*, pp. 416–23.

31. Thus alliance formation becomes more frenetic when the offense is believed to have the advantage: great powers will balance more vigorously, and weak states will bandwagon more frequently. A world of tight alliances and few neutral states is the likely result.

32. For a discussion of Libya's international position, see Claudia Wright, "Libya and the West: Headlong into Confrontation?" *International Affairs*, 58, no. 1 (1981–1982). More recently, both the United Stated and France have taken direct military action against Libya and a number of other countries have imposed economic sanctions against Qadhafi's regime.

33. See Craig, *Germany 1866–1945*, pp. 101, 242–47, and chap. 10; Geiss, *German Foreign Policy*, pp. 66–68; and Kennedy, *Rise of Anglo-German Antagonism*, chaps. 14 and 20.

Non-zero sum worldview

The mere existence and healthy activity of a powerful Germany is an un-doubted blessing to this world. . . . So long, then, as Germany competes for an intellectual and moral leadership of the world in reliance on its own natural advantages and energies England cannot but admire. . . . [S]o long as Germany's action does not overstep the line of legitimate protection of existing rights it can always count upon the sympathy and good will, and even the moral support of England. . . . It would be of real advantage if the determination not to bar Germany's legitimate and peaceful expansion were . . . pronounced as authoritatively as possible, provided that care was taken . . . to make it quite clear that this benevolent attitude will give way to determined opposition at the first sign of British or allied interests being adversely affected.[34]

In short, Britain will oppose Germany only if Germany is aggressive and seeks to expand through conquest. Intention, not power, is crucial.

When a state is believed to be unalterably aggressive, other states are unlikely to bandwagon. After all, if an aggressor's intentions cannot be changed by an alliance with it, a vulnerable state, even if allied, is likely to become a victim. Balancing with others may be the only way to avoid this fate. Thus Prime Minister de Broqueville of Belgium rejected the German ultimatum of August 2, 1914, saying: "If die we must, better death with honor. We have no other choice. Our submission would serve no end. . . . Let us make no mistake about it, if Germany is victorious, Belgium, whatever her attitude, will be annexed to the Reich."[35] Thus the more aggressive or expansionist a state appears to be, the more likely it is to trigger an opposing coalition.

By defining the basic hypotheses in terms of threats rather than power alone, we gain a more complete picture of the factors that statesmen will consider when making alliance choices. One cannot determine a priori, however, which sources of threat will be most important in any given case; one can say only that all of them are likely to play a role. And the greater the threat, the greater the probability that the vulnerable state will seek an alliance.

34. "Memorandum by Sir Eyre Crowe on the Present State of British Relations with France and Germany, January 1, 1907," in *British Documents on the Origins of the War, 1898–1914*, ed. G. P. Gooch and Harold Temperley (London, 1928), 3: 397–420. See also G. W. Monger, *The End of Isolation: British Foreign Policy, 1900–1907* (London, 1963), pp. 313–15. Sir Edward Grey drew a similar conclusion about Britain's alliance policy: "Great Britain has not in theory been opposed to the predominance of a strong group in Europe when it seemed to make for stability and peace. . . . [I]t is only when the dominant power be-comes aggressive that she, by an instinct of self-defence, if not by deliberate policy, gravitates to anything that can be fairly described as a Balance of Power." See Edward Grey, Viscount of Fallodon, K.G., *Twenty-Five Years, 1892–1916* (New York, 1925), 1: 8 and passim. See also Kennedy, *Rise of Anglo-German Antagonism*, p. 431.

35. Quoted in Luigi Albertini, *The Origins of the War of 1914* (London, 1952), 3: 458.

The Implications of Balancing and Bandwagoning

The two general hypotheses of balancing and bandwagoning paint starkly contrasting pictures of international politics. Resolving the question of which hypothesis is more accurate is especially important, because each implies very different policy prescriptions. What sort of world does each depict, and what policies are implied?

If balancing is the dominant tendency, then threatening states will provoke others to align against them. Because those who seek to dominate others will attract widespread opposition, status quo states can take a relatively sanguine view of threats. Credibility is less important in a balancing world, because one's allies will resist threatening states out of their own self-interest, not because they expect others to do it for them. Thus the fear of allies defecting will decline. Moreover, if balancing is the norm and if statesmen understand this tendency, aggression will be discouraged because those who contemplate it will anticipate resistance.

In a balancing world, policies that convey restraint and benevolence are best. Strong states may be valued as allies because they have much to offer their partners, but they must take particular care to avoid appearing aggressive. Foreign and defense policies that minimize the threat one poses to others make the most sense in such a world.

A bandwagoning world, by contrast, is much more competitive. If states tend to ally with those who seem most dangerous, then great powers will be rewarded if they appear both strong and potentially aggressive. International rivalries will be more intense, because a single defeat may signal the decline of one side and the ascendancy of the other. This situation is especially alarming in a bandwagoning world, because additional defections and a further decline in position are to be expected. Moreover, if statesmen believe that bandwagoning is widespread, they will be more inclined to use force. This tendency is true for both aggressors and status quo powers. The former will use force because they will assume that others will be unlikely to balance against them and because they can attract more allies through belligerence or brinkmanship. The latter will follow suit because they will fear the gains their opponents will make by appearing powerful and resolute.[36]

36. It is worth noting that Napoleon and Hitler underestimated the costs of aggression by assuming that their potential enemies would bandwagon. After Munich, for example, Hitler dismissed the possibility of opposition by claiming that British and French statesmen were "little worms." Napoleon apparently believed that England could not "reasonably make war on us unaided" and assumed that the Peace of Amiens guaranteed that England had abandoned its opposition to France. On these points, see Fest, *Hitler*, pp. 594–95; Liska, *Nations in Alliance*, p. 45; and Geoffrey Bruun, *Europe and the French Imperium: 1799–1814* (New York, 1938), p. 118. Because Hitler and Napoleon believed in a bandwagoning world, they were excessively eager to go to war.

[27]

Finally, misperceiving the relative propensity to balance or band-wagon is dangerous, because the policies that are appropriate for one situation will backfire in the other. If statesmen follow the balancing prescription in a bandwagoning world, their moderate responses and relaxed view of threats will encourage their allies to defect, leaving them isolated against an overwhelming coalition. Conversely, following the bandwagoning prescription in a world of balancers (employing power and threats frequently) will lead others to oppose you more and more vigorously.[37]

These concerns are not merely theoretical. In the 1930s, France failed to recognize that her allies in the Little Entente were prone to band-wagon, a tendency that French military and diplomatic policies reinforced.[38] As noted earlier, Soviet attempts to intimidate Turkey and Norway after World War II reveal the opposite error; they merely provoked a greater U.S. commitment to these regions and cemented their entry into NATO. Likewise, the self-encircling bellicosity of Wilhelmine Germany and Imperial Japan reflected the assumption, prevalent in both states, that bandwagoning was the dominant tendency in international affairs.

When Do States Balance? When Do They Bandwagon?

These examples highlight the importance of identifying whether states are more likely to balance or bandwagon and which sources of threat have the greatest impact on the decision. An answer to the questions of when states balance and when they bandwagon is deferred to chapter 5, but several observations can be made here. In general, we should expect balancing behavior to be much more common than band-wagoning, and we should expect bandwagoning to occur only under certain identifiable conditions.

Although many statesmen fear that potential allies will align with the strongest side, this fear receives little support from most of international history. For example, every attempt to achieve hegemony in Europe

---

37. This situation is analogous to Robert Jervis's distinction between the deterrence model and the spiral model. The former calls for opposition to a suspected aggressor, the latter for appeasement. Balancing and bandwagoning are the alliance equivalents of deterring and appeasing. See Robert Jervis, *Perception and Misperception in International Politics* (Princeton, N.J., 1976), chap. 3.

38. The French attempt to contain Germany after World War I was undermined both by the Locarno Treaty (which guaranteed the French border with Germany but failed to provide similar guarantees for France's allies) and by the French adoption of a defensive military doctrine, which made it impossible for France to come to the aid of its allies. See Telford Taylor, *Munich: The Price of Peace* (New York, 1980), pp. 111–12; and Richard D. Challener, *The French Theory of the Nation in Arms* (New York, 1955), pp. 264–65.

since the Thirty Years War has been thwarted by a defensive coalition formed precisely for the purpose of defeating the potential hegemon.[39] Other examples are equally telling.[40] Although isolated cases of band-wagoning do occur, the great powers have shown a remarkable tenden-cy to ignore other temptations and follow the balancing prescription when necessary.

This tendency should not surprise us. Balancing should be preferred for the simple reason that no statesman can be completely sure of what another will do. Bandwagoning is dangerous because it increases the resources available to a threatening power and requires placing trust in its continued forbearance. Because perceptions are unreliable and inten-tions can change, it is safer to balance against potential threats than to rely on the hope that a state will remain benevolently disposed.

But if balancing is to be expected, bandwagoning remains a pos-sibility. Several factors may affect the relative propensity for states to select this course.

Strong versus Weak States

In general, the weaker the state, the more likely it is to bandwagon rather than balance. This situation occurs because weak states add little to the strength of a defensive coalition but incur the wrath of the more threatening states nonetheless. Because weak states can do little to affect the outcome (and may suffer grievously in the process), they must choose the winning side. Only when their decision can affect the out-come is it rational for them to join the weaker alliance.[41] By contrast, strong states can turn a losing coalition into a winning one. And because their decision may mean the difference between victory and defeat, they are likely to be amply rewarded for their contribution.

Weak states are also likely to be especially sensitive to proximate

39. See Dehio, *The Precarious Balance*; Georg Schwarzenberger, *Power Politics* (London, 1941); Hinsley, *Power and the Pursuit of Peace*; and Jack S. Levy, "Theories of General War," unpublished manuscript, 1984. An extensively revised version of this paper can be found in *World Politics*, 37, no. 3 (1985).

40. Prominent recent examples include (1) the enhanced cooperation among the ASEAN states following the U.S. withdrawal from Vietnam and the Vietnamese conquest of Cambodia; (2) the rapprochement between the Unites States and Communist China in the 1970s (and the renewed rivalry between China and Vietnam); (3) the alignment of the Front-Line States against South Africa throughout the 1970s; (4) the formation of a Gulf Cooperation Council in the Persian Gulf following the Iranian revolution. On the South African and Persian Gulf examples, see Mahnaz Z. Ispahani, "Alone Together: Regional Security Arrangements in Southern Africa and the Arabia Gulf," *International Security*, 8, no. 4 (1984). Whatever one thinks of the efficacy of these arrangements, the tendency they illustrate is striking.

41. See Rothstein, *Alliances and Small Powers*, p. 11. This problem is one of collective goods. The weakest states cannot provide for their own security, so they bandwagon with the strongest while hoping others will defend them anyway.

power. Where great powers have both global interests and global capabilities, weak states will be concerned primarily with events in their immediate vicinity. Moreover, weak states can be expected to balance when threatened by states with roughly equal capabilities but they will be tempted to bandwagon when threatened by a great power. Obviously, when the great power is capable of rapid and effective action (i.e., when its offensive capabilities are especially strong), this temptation will be even greater.

The Availability of Allies

States will also be tempted to bandwagon when allies are simply unavailable. This statement is not simply tautological, because states may balance by mobilizing their own resources instead of relying on allied support. They are more likely to do so, however, when they are confident that allied assistance will be available. Thus a further prerequisite for balancing behavior is an effective system of diplomatic communication. The ability to communicate enables potential allies to recognize their shared interests and coordinate their responses.[42] If weak states see no possibility of outside assistance, however, they may be forced to accommodate the most imminent threat. Thus the first Shah of Iran saw the British withdrawal from Kandahar in 1881 as a signal to bandwagon with Russia. As he told the British representative, all he had received from Great Britain was "good advice and honeyed words—nothing else."[43] Finland's policy of partial alignment with the Soviet Union suggests the same lesson. When Finland joined forces with Nazi Germany during World War II, it alienated the potential allies (the United States and Great Britain) that might otherwise have helped protect it from Soviet pressure after the war.[44]

Of course, excessive confidence in allied support will encourage weak states to free-ride, relying on the efforts of others to provide security. Free-riding is the optimal policy for a weak state, because its efforts will contribute little in any case. Among the great powers, the belief that

42. One reason for Rome's durable hegemony in the ancient world may have been the fact that her various opponents found it difficult to coordinate effective opposition against her. See Edward N. Luttwak, *The Grand Strategy of the Roman Empire* (Baltimore, Md., 1976), pp. 192, 199–200. By contrast, when a workable diplomatic system was established during the Renaissance, prospects for European hegemony declined drastically. On this point, see Gulick, *Europe's Classical Balance of Power*, p. 16; Hedley Bull, *The Anarchical Society* (New York, 1977), p. 106 and chap. 7; Garrett Mattingly, *Renaissance Diplomacy* (Boston, 1971), chaps. 13–16; and Harold Nicolson, *Diplomacy* (London, 1963), chap. 1.
43. Quoted in C. J. Lowe, *The Reluctant Imperialists* (New York, 1967), p. 85.
44. See Fred Singleton, "The Myth of Finlandisation," *International Affairs*, 57, no. 2 (1981), especially pp. 276–78. Singleton points out that the Western allies approved the 1944 armistice between Finland and the Soviet Union (which established Soviet predominance there) in 1947.

allies are readily available encourages buck-passing; states that are threatened strive to pass to others the burdens of standing up to the aggressor. Neither response is a form of bandwagoning, but both suggest that effective balancing behavior is more likely to occur when members of an alliance are not convinced that their partners are unconditionally loyal.[45]

Taken together, these factors help explain the formation of spheres of influence surrounding the great powers. Although strong neighbors of strong states are likely to balance, small and weak neighbors of the great powers may be more inclined to bandwagon. Because they will be the first victims of expansion, because they lack the capabilities to stand alone, and because a defensive alliance may operate too slowly to do them much good, accommodating a threatening great power may be tempting.[46]

Peace and War

Finally, the context in which alliance choices are made will affect decisions to balance or bandwagon. States are more likely to balance in peacetime or in the early stages of a war, as they seek to deter or defeat the powers posing the greatest threat. But once the outcome appears certain, some will be tempted to defect from the losing side at an opportune moment. Thus both Rumania and Bulgaria allied with Nazi Germany initially and then abandoned Germany for the Allies, as the tides of war ebbed and flowed across Europe in World War II.[47]

The restoration of peace, however, restores the incentive to balance. As many observers have noted, victorious coalitions are likely to disintegrate with the conclusion of peace. Prominent examples include Austria and Prussia after their war with Denmark in 1864, Britain and France after World War I, the Soviet Union and the United States after World War II,

45. For discussions on the problems of buck-passing, see Posen, *Sources of Military Doctrine*, pp. 63–64 and passim. See also Glenn Snyder's discussion of abandonment in his "Security Dilemma in Alliance Politics," pp. 466–68; and the discussion of the free-rider problem in Olson and Zeckhauser, "Economic Theory of Alliances."

46. King Leopold of Belgium justified Belgium's policy of neutrality after World War I by saying, "An alliance, even if purely defensive, does not lead to the goal [of security] for no matter how prompt the help of an ally might be, it would not come until after the invader's attack which will be overwhelming." Quoted in Rothstein, *Alliances and Small Powers*, pp. 111–12. Urho Kekkonen of Finland argued for accommodation with the Soviet Union in much the same way: "It cannot be in Finland's interests to be the ally of some great power, constantly on guard in its peripheral position on the Russian border and the first to be overrun by the enemy, and devoid of political importance to lend any significance to its word when decisions over war and peace are being taken." See Urho Kekkonen, *A President's View* (London, 1982), pp. 42–43 and passim.

47. For an analysis of Balkan diplomacy during World War II, see "Hungary, Rumania and Bulgaria, 1941–1944," in *Survey of International Affairs, 1939–46: Hitler's Europe*, ed. Arnold Toynbee and Veronica Toynbee (London, 1954), pp. 604–31.

and China and Vietnam after the U.S. withdrawal from Vietnam. This recurring pattern provides further support for the proposition that balancing is the dominant tendency in international politics and that bandwagoning is the opportunistic exception.[48]

Summary of Hypotheses on Balancing and Bandwagoning

Hypotheses on Balancing

1. *General form:* States facing an external threat will align with others to oppose the states posing the threat.
2. The greater the threatening state's aggregate power, the greater the tendency for others to align against it.
3. The nearer a powerful state, the greater the tendency for those nearby to align against it. Therefore, neighboring states are less likely to be allies than are states separated by at least one other power.
4. The greater a state's offensive capabilities, the greater the tendency for others to align against it. Therefore, states with offensively oriented military capabilities are likely to provoke other states to form defensive coalitions.
5. The more aggressive a state's perceived intentions, the more likely others are to align against that state.
6. Alliances formed during wartime will disintegrate when the enemy is defeated.

Hypotheses on Bandwagoning

The hypotheses on bandwagoning are the opposite of those on balancing.

1. *General form:* States facing an external threat will ally with the most threatening power.
2. The greater a state's aggregate capabilities, the greater the tendency for others to align with it.
3. The nearer a powerful state, the greater the tendency for those nearby to align with it.
4. The greater a state's offensive capabilities, the greater the tendency for others to align with it.

---

48. The role of different sources of threat also explains why coalitions possessing overwhelming power may stay together even after their enemies are clearly doomed (but not yet defeated). For example, focusing on aggregate power alone would have led us to expect the Grand Alliance to have disintegrated long before the end of the war (i.e., once the Axis was clearly overmatched). The fact that German and Japanese intentions appeared so malign helps explain why the Allies preserved their alliance long enough to obtain the unconditional surrender of both countries.

5. The more aggressive a state's perceived intentions, the less likely other states are to align against it.
6. Alliances formed to oppose a threat will disintegrate when the threat becomes serious.

Hypotheses on the Conditions Favoring Balancing or Bandwagoning
1. Balancing is more common than bandwagoning.
2. The stronger the state, the greater its tendency to balance. Weak states will balance against other weak states but may bandwagon when threatened by great powers.
3. The greater the probability of allied support, the greater the tendency to balance. When adequate allied support is certain, however, the tendency for free-riding or buck-passing increases.
4. The more unalterably aggressive a state is perceived to be, the greater the tendency for others to balance against it.
5. In wartime, the closer one side is to victory, the greater the tendency for others to bandwagon with it.

BIRDS OF A FEATHER FLOCKING TOGETHER (AND FLYING APART): IDEOLOGY AND ALLIANCE FORMATION

Ideological solidarity (to use Hans Morgenthau's term) refers to alliances that result from states sharing political, cultural, or other traits. According to the hypothesis of ideological solidarity, the more similar two or more states are, the more likely they are to ally. This hypothesis stands in sharp contrast to the hypotheses just considered, which view alliances as expedient responses to external threats. As a result, most realist scholars downplay the importance of ideology in alliance choices.[49]

Yet despite their skepticism, the belief that like states attract has been loudly and frequently proclaimed. Edmund Burke, for example, believed that alliances were the product of a "correspondence in laws, customs, and habits of life" among states.[50] Despite Lord Palmerston's famous claim that England "has no permanent friends; she has only permanent interests," his policy as foreign secretary suggests a belief in

---

49. For scholarly discussions that question the importance of ideology in alliance formation, see Edwin Fedder, "The Concept of Alliance," *International Studies Quarterly*, 12, no. 1 (1968): 86; Morgenthau, *Politics among Nations*, pp. 183–84; and Schwarzenberger, *Power Politics*, pp. 112–14. For a quantitative analysis that supports these assertions, see Holsti, Hopmann, and Sullivan, *Unity and Disintegration in International Alliances*, pp. 61–64.

50. Edmund Burke, *First Letter on a Regicide Peace*, cited in Wight and Butterfield, *Diplomatic Investigations*, p. 97.

the natural affinity of democracies. As he said in 1834: "Our policy ought now to be to form a Western confederacy of free states as a counterpoise to the Eastern League of arbitrary governments. We shall be on the advance, they on the decline, and all the smaller planets in Europe will have a natural tendency to gravitate towards our system."[51]

More recently, Soviet clients such as the late Samora Machel of Mozambique and Colonel Mengistu Haile Mariam of Ethiopia have emphasized the "natural" alignment of socialist states, a concept that Soviet officials also endorse.[52] In the same spirit, Ronald Reagan is fond of describing how the United States and its allies have "rediscovered their democratic values," values that "unite us in a stewardship of peace and freedom with our allies and friends."[53] And as noted in chapter 1, U.S. opposition to leftist movements in the Third World has been based on the same belief, that these groups are naturally inclined to ally with the Soviet Union. Indeed, the so-called Reagan Doctrine, which calls for active support for anti-Communist insurgencies throughout the developing world, is merely the latest manifestation of this general policy.[54]

What is the logic behind such beliefs? Several possibilities can be identified. First, alignment with similar states may be viewed as a way of defending one's own political principles. After all, if statesmen believe their own system of government is inherently good, then protecting states with similar systems must be considered good as well. Second, states with similar traits are likely to fear one another less, because they find it harder to imagine an inherently good state deciding to attack them.[55] Third, alignment with similar states may enhance the legitimacy

---

51. Quoted in Charles K. Webster, *The Foreign Policy of Palmerston* (London, 1951), 1: 390. Palmerston's belief that weak states are prone to bandwagon is also evident in this passage.

52. See U.S. House Committee on Foreign Affairs, *The Soviet Union and the Third World*, pp. 46–48; and U.S. House Committee on Foreign Affairs, *The Soviet Union in the Third World, 1980–85: An Imperial Burden or Political Asset?* 99th Cong., 1st sess., 1985, pp. 201, 231–32. It is worth noting that Machel had largely abandoned his pro-Soviet position by the time of his death in 1986, in an effort to reduce pressure from South Africa and to obtain economic aid from the West.

53. "State of the Union Message," *New York Times*, January 26, 1983.

54. See Richard J. Barnet, *Intervention and Revolution: The United States in the Third World* (New York, 1968); Richard E. Feinberg and Kenneth A. Oye, "After the Fall: U.S. Policy toward Radical Regimes," *World Policy Journal*, 1, no. 1 (1983); Gaddis, *Strategies of Containment*, pp. 96, 136–44, 175–82, 284–88; and Stephen D. Krasner, *Defending the National Interest: Raw Materials Investments and U.S. Foreign Policy* (Princeton, N.J., 1978), pp. 338–42 and passim. On the Reagan Doctrine, see U.S. Senate Committee on Appropriations, *U.S. Policy toward Anti-Communist Insurgencies*, 99th Cong., 1st sess., 1985; and George P. Shultz, "New Realities and Ways of Thinking," *Foreign Affairs*, 63, no. 3 (1985), pp. 710, 712–13.

55. Thus Indian prime minister Jawaharlal Nehru believed that a policy of appeasement would ensure good relations between India and China, because he saw China as an Asian country that, like India, had recently achieved its freedom from imperialist interference.

of a weak regime by demonstrating that it is part of a large, popular movement. Fourth, the ideology itself may prescribe alignment. Marxism-Leninism is perhaps the most obvious example of this possibility.[56]

Many examples can be cited in support of this hypothesis. Australia fought Germany in both world wars, despite the fact that Germany did not pose a direct threat to Australia in either one. According to one account, the colonies' loyalty to Great Britain was "not one of all to one but all to all, to the British ideal and way of life wherever it was to be found."[57] In the nineteenth century, the Holy Alliance that followed Napoleon's defeat and the League of the Three Emperors in 1873 united similar states in opposition to alternative political systems, although questions of power and security also played a role.[58] The Treaty of Munchengratz in 1833 and the Quadruple Alliance of 1834, which divided Europe neatly along ideological lines (notwithstanding occasional rifts within the two coalitions), also offer apt examples.[59]

Birds of a Feather Flying Apart: Divisive Ideologies

The examples just mentioned illustrate how a common ideology can help create effective alliances. Less widely recognized, however, is the fact that certain types of ideology cause conflict and dissension rather than solidarity and alignment. In particular. when the ideology calls for the members to form a centralized movement obeying a single authoritative leadership, the likelihood of conflict among the members is increased. This somewhat paradoxical result may occur for several reasons.

First, because the ideology is a source of legitimacy for each of the

---

As a result, he did not see China as an imminent threat. The Sino-Indian War of 1962 revealed that Nehru had overestimated the power of "Asian solidarity." See Vidya Prakah Dutt, "India and China: Betrayal, Humiliation, Reappraisal," in *Policies toward China: Views from Six Continents*, ed. A. M. Halpern (New York, 1965), pp. 202–9; and Michael Brecher, *Nehru: A Political Biography* (London, 1959), pp. 588–92.

56. For a discussion of the centralizing tenets of Marxism-Leninism and a general history of the World Communist Movement, see Richard Lowenthal, *World Communism: The Disintegration of a Secular Faith* (New York, 1964).

57. See James A. Williamson, *Great Britain and the Commonwealth* (London, 1965), pp. 180–81.

58. The Holy Alliance began with a declaration by the principal European sovereigns that they would refrain from using force against one another. By 1820, England had withdrawn over the issue of intervention against liberal movements, leaving Austria-Hungary, Russia, and Prussia allied against the threat of liberal revolutions. See Nicolson, *Congress of Vienna*, pp. 242–43, 245–51, and chap. 16. On the League of the Three Emperors, see Geiss, *German Foreign Policy*, pp. 29–30; and Craig, *Germany 1866–1945*, pp. 103–4.

59. See Webster, *The Foreign Policy of Palmerston*, 1: 386–410; and Hinsley, *Power and the Pursuit of Peace*, pp. 215–17.

member regimes, they must all acknowledge its validity. But when the ideology calls for a single leader, then the regimes that embrace the ideology must also agree on who will occupy the leading role. In practice, all regimes save the one that emerges on top will be pressed to accept the authoritative guidance of the leading power, even if that power is a foreign party. Thus all member regimes will find their autonomy threatened by the other members of the same movement.[60]

Second, because the authority of the leading group rests on its interpretation of the common ideology, ideological quarrels are likely. They are also likely to be intense, because each faction can defend its own actions only by portraying rivals as traitors or heretics.

The history of international Communism provides a striking example of these problems. According to an authoritative Soviet source, "ideological cohesion on the basis of Marxism-Leninism is the foundation of [Communist] international cohesion."[61] But as several scholars have shown, the cohesion of the Communist International lasted only as long as foreign Communist parties were dependent on Moscow's support. When independent Communist states emerged after World War II, the unchallenged role of the Communist Party of the Soviet Union (CPSU) was a thing of the past.[62] Conflicts between Communist states have been among the world's most virulent, with ideological disputes playing a major role in their origins and evolution. The "natural" cohesion of the movement has survived in Eastern Europe alone, and there largely through the direct presence of Soviet power.

Unifying Ideologies

Significantly, these problems do not afflict either liberal states or monarchies. Because their legitimacy does not rest on an ideology that prescribes transnational unity under a single leader, liberal states do not pose an ideological threat to one another. For a liberal society, legitimacy rests not on relations with other states but on popular elections and the voice of the people. For monarchies, the right to govern is based on the traditional or divine right of kings. Because the principles of monarchical or liberal rule grant legitimate authority over one's own domain but

60. Richard Lowenthal, "Factors of Unity and Factors of Conflict," *The Annals*, 349 (1963): 107; Rothstein, *Alliances and Small Powers*, p. 178; and Liska, *Nations in Alliance*, p. 171.
61. V. V. Zagladin, *The World Communist Movement* (Moscow, 1973), p. 465.
62. See Lowenthal, *World Communism*, pp. 234–35, 247–52, 256; Zbigniew Brzezinski, *The Soviet Bloc; Unity and Conflict* (Cambridge, Mass., 1967), pp. 51–58; and Franz Borkenau, *World Communism: A History of the Communist International* (Ann Arbor, Mich., 1971), pp. 196–207.

imply no such authority over the domain of others, alliances between monarchies or between liberal states are not torn by ideological conflicts. Moreover, such regimes have an interest in collaborating to oppose any movements that do threaten their legitimacy, which provides a further incentive for them to ally with one another.[63] Thus it is not surprising that Russia, Prussia, and Austria-Hungary joined forces to counter liberalism in the 1820s or that the current alliance of industrial democracies has been remarkably stable.[64] And as Michael Doyle has shown, the extraordinary absence of warfare among democratic and republican regimes suggests that their domestic order may reduce conflicts between them as well.[65]

The Importance of Ideological Solidarity

How important is ideological solidarity as a cause of alliances? Under what conditions should we expect ideological factors to exert a strong unifying effect? When will their effect be divisive? Like the balancing and bandwagoning hypotheses, the actual importance of ideological solidarity as a cause of alignment carries important theoretical and practical consequences. If ideology is in fact an important determinant of alliance choices, then identifying friends and foes will be relatively easy. States with similar domestic systems are one's natural allies, and those with different political systems or beliefs should be viewed with suspicion. And this belief has other implications as well. Intervening in the internal affairs of other countries will be more tempting when one believes that domestic characteristics exert a strong impact on a state's international behavior. Moreover, because the ability of one's rivals to draw on support from like-minded states is a function of the power of ideology, the danger of monoliths increases when ideology is an important cause of alignment.[66] When is this likely to be the case? One variable is the type of ideology itself (unifying or divisive). Several other variables should be considered as well.

First, states are more likely to follow their ideological preferences

63. Of course, liberal ideologies can pose a threat to monarchical systems. Thus we would not expect monarchies and democracies to cooperate as a result of ideological solidarity, except against ideologies that both found repugnant or dangerous.

64. See William L. Langer, *Political and Social Upheaval: 1832–1852* (New York, 1969), pp. 290–95; and Walter Alison Philips, *The Confederation of Europe* (London, 1920), pp. 202–3, 208–9, and passim. Of course, military and ideological threats can reinforce one another, as the division of Europe between NATO and the Warsaw Pact illustrates.

65. Michael Doyle, "Liberalism and World Politics," *American Political Science Review*, 80, no. 4 (1986).

66. As noted earlier, this belief underlies U.S. intervention against radical or Marxist regimes in the developing world. See the references in note 54.

when they are already fairly secure. When faced by great danger, however, they will take whatever allies they can get. Winston Churchill captured this idea in his famous statement, "If Hitler invaded Hell, I should at least make a favorable reference to the Devil in the House of Commons"—a sentiment that Franklin D. Roosevelt shared.[67] These views can be compared with earlier British and U.S. attitudes. Until the late 1930s, Germany's weakness made it possible for Britain, France, and the United States to treat the Soviet Union with disdain, a revulsion based largely on ideology and echoed by the Soviets. Only when Nazi Germany began to pose a significant threat did these ideological preferences lose their power.[68] In short, security considerations are likely to take precedence over ideological preferences, and ideologically based alliances are unlikely to survive when more pragmatic interests intrude.

Several interesting implications follow. Any factors that tend to make states more secure should increase the importance of ideological considerations in alliance choices. If Kenneth Waltz is correct that bipolar worlds are the most stable, then the impact of ideology should be greater in a bipolar world. Not only will the bipolar rivalry encourage both superpowers to support third parties freely (giving third parties the option to choose the ideologically most compatible side), but the caution that bipolarity imposes on superpower conduct may permit most other states to follow ideological preferences rather than security requirements.[69] In addition, other factors that make defense easy and conquest difficult should increase the importance of ideology in alliance choices. Thus an underlying cause of the ideological alliances of the 1820s and 1830s may have been the condition of defense dominance that seems to have prevailed during this period.[70] Nuclear weapons may make ideology somewhat more important today for precisely this rea-

---

67. Winston S. Churchill, *The Second World War*, vol. 3: *The Grand Alliance* (Boston, 1950), p. 370. Roosevelt told Ambassador Joseph Davies, "I can't take communism nor can you, but to cross this bridge I would hold hands with the Devil." Quoted in John Lewis Gaddis, *Russia, the Soviet Union, and the United States: An Interpretative History* (New York, 1978), p. 149.

68. See Gaddis, *Russia, the Soviet Union, and the United States*, chaps. 4 and 5.

69. See Kenneth N. Waltz, "The Stability of a Bipolar World," *Daedalus*, 93, no. 3 (1964); and Waltz, *Theory of International Politics*, chap. 8; Glenn Snyder and Paul Diesing, *Conflict among Nations: Bargaining, Decision Making, and System Structure in International Crises* (Princeton, N.J., 1977), pp. 419–29; and Dinerstein, "Transformation of Alliance Systems," p. 593.

70. On this point, see Osgood and Tucker, *Force, Order, and Justice*, pp. 52–53, 78–81; Quester, *Offense and Defense in the International System*, pp. 73–76; Robert Jervis, "Security Regimes," in *International Regimes*, ed. Stephen D. Krasner (Ithaca, 1983), pp. 178–84; and Stanislaw Andrewski, *Military Organization and Society* (Berkeley, Calif., 1968), pp. 68–69. The main reason for defense dominance was the widespread preference for small standing armies among the conservative regimes of that period, which feared the effects of large standing armies on internal stability.

son. Because nuclear deterrence makes it more difficult for great powers to threaten weaker states (and gives the superpowers a strong incentive to moderate the conduct of others as well), third parties need formal alliances less and can pay greater attention to ideological factors when choosing alliance partners.

This situation reveals an important paradox. Ideology is most important when defense is dominant and states are most secure. That is, states must worry most about ideological monoliths in circumstances in which it will also be relatively easy for them to defend themselves. In other words, the conditions under which ideology is a significant cause of alignment are the conditions under which large, ideologically based alliances are the least dangerous.

Second, when weak or unstable regimes rely on ideological arguments to bolster their legitimacy, this reliance may affect their alliance choices. In particular, weak regimes may try to enhance their popularity (and attract external support) by seeking membership in a large and popular movement. By aligning with a larger group, a weak regime may hope to convince its citizens that it is pursuing worthy and widely accepted aims—that it is part of the forces of progress. Cuba's self-propelled entry into the Communist world may provide one example of this type of behavior. By declaring himself to be a Marxist-Leninist, Castro was able to both extract greater Soviet assistance and demonstrate his rejection of imperialist ideas while enjoying the benefits of membership in a large, worldwide movement. Accordingly, we can expect regimes whose legitimacy is precarious to enter ideologically based alliances.

Third, it is worth noting that we may exaggerate the apparent importance of ideology by taking the rhetoric of statesmen too seriously. For both internal and external reasons, statesmen are likely to describe their allies in favorable terms, suggesting that a strong ideological affinity exists. This tactic helps convince adversaries that the alliance is viable and increases the likelihood of public support in both countries. Thus Joseph Stalin received a deliberate whitewashing during World War II, one that transformed the former "Communist tyrant" into the heroic "Uncle Joe."[71]

Moreover, if the leaders of one state believe that ideology determines international alignments, they will view similar states as potential friends and dissimilar ones as potential enemies. Because they will view the former with approval and the latter with suspicion, relations with similar states will generally be cordial and relations with states espous-

71. See Robert Dallek, *Franklin D. Roosevelt and American Foreign Policy: 1932–1945* (London, 1979), pp. 296–98. On the general tendency for allies to exaggerate their level of agreement, see Robert Jervis, "Hypotheses on Misperception," *World Politics*, 20, no. 3 (1968): 463.

ing a different ideology will generally be poor. As a result, those espousing a different ideology are more likely to join forces in opposition. The belief that like states attract can easily be self-fulfilling, even if most states are relatively indifferent to ideological considerations. For both reasons, the tendency for birds of a feather to flock together may be overstated.

Finally, we should not overlook the close relationship between ideological factors and security considerations. Because all states try to minimize domestic opposition (not to mention violent internal upheavals), ideological movements that endanger a particular domestic order can pose every bit as significant a threat as that posed by military power. As a result, many ideological alliances may just be balancing alliances in disguise if they have been formed to oppose the spread of a hostile ideology. The Holy Alliance of Russia, Prussia, and Austria-Hungary is an obvious example. In the same way, weak regimes may bandwagon by altering their ideological positions when a new ideological movement appears to be gaining momentum. The distinction between these hypotheses may not be as sharp as the realist perspective suggests. A central question to consider later is whether contemporary Middle East states have been willing to sacrifice their security in order to gratify their ideological preferences or whether ideology reflects an aspiration that is readily ignored when necessity arises.

Summary of Hypotheses on Ideology and Alliance Formation

1. *General form:* The more similar the domestic ideology of two or more states, the more likely they are to ally.
2. The more centralized and hierarchical the movement prescribed by the ideology, the more conflictive and fragile any resulting alliance will be. Therefore, Leninist movements will find stable alliances more difficult to sustain than will either monarchies or democracies.
3. The more secure a state perceives itself to be, the greater the impact of ideology on alliance choices. Therefore, ideological alignments are more likely in a bipolar world. And therefore, the greater the advantage to the defense in warfare, the greater the impact of ideology on alliance choices.
4. States lacking domestic legitimacy will be more likely to seek ideological alliances to increase internal and external support.
5. The impact of ideology on the choice of alliance partners will be exaggerated; statesmen will overestimate the degree of ideological agreement among both their allies and their adversaries.

[40]

FOREIGN AID AND ALLIANCE FORMATION

According to this set of arguments, the provision of economic or military assistance can create effective allies, because it communicates favorable intentions, because it evokes a sense of gratitude, or because the recipient becomes dependent on the donor. Stated simply, the hypothesis is: the more aid, the tighter the resulting alliance. This hypothesis helps justify most economic and military assistance programs, as well as U.S. concern over Soviet arms shipments and economic aid to various Third World countries. In 1983, for example, U.S. undersecretary of defense Fred C. Ikle warned that Soviet arms assistance to Cuba and Nicaragua threatened to turn Central America into "another Eastern Europe," just as other U.S. officials saw Soviet military aid in other areas as a reliable tool of influence.[72] Regardless of the context, the argument is the same: the provision of military or economic assistance is believed to give suppliers significant leverage over recipients.[73]

As with the other hypotheses examined in this chapter, this belief is not without some basis. Throughout history, states have often provided some form of side payment to attract allies. Louis XIV purchased English neutrality during his campaign for hegemony in Europe by dispensing subsidies to the impoverished court of James II.[74] In World War I, Britain and France obtained the support of various Arab leaders by providing a gold subsidy and by promising them territorial acquisitions after the war. Similar pledges swung Italy to their side as well.[75] Historians generally agree that France's loans to Russia played a role in encouraging the Franco-Russian alliance of 1982.[76] In short, various kinds of foreign aid are frequently part of the process of forging alliances.

To conclude that the provision of aid is the principal cause of align-

72. *New York Times*, March 15, 1983. Former Secretary of Defense Harold Brown explained Soviet arms exports in similar terms: "How else are they going to expand their influence? . . . They're doing what they're good at. . . . When they ship out tanks to the Third World to use against neighbors that increases their political influence." *Washington Post*, December 7, 1980, p. A10.

73. See Hans J. Morgenthau, "A Political Theory of Foreign Aid," *American Political Science Review*, 56, no. 2 (1962): 302–3.

74. See John Wolf, *The Emergence of the Great Powers* (New York, 1962), pp. 18, 26, 103.

75. See Lenczowski, *The Middle East in World Affairs*, p. 81; Howard M. Sachar, *The Emergence of the Middle East: 1914–1924* (New York, 1969), pp. 125–30, 136; Bernadotte Schmitt and Harold M. Vedeler, *The World in the Crucible: 1914–1918* (New York, 1984), pp. 92–94.

76. Jacob Viner, "International Finance and Balance of Power Diplomacy, 1881–1914," in Viner, *International Economics: Studies* (Glencoe, Ill., 1952); George F. Kennan, *The Decline of Bismarck's European Order* (Princeton, N.J., 1978), pp. 342–46; and Fritz Stern, *Gold and Iron: Bismarck, Bleichroder, and the Building of the German Empire* (New York, 1979), pp. 439–47.

ment or a powerful tool of influence, however, may be incorrect. The notion that aid causes alignment ignores the fact that military or economic assistance is offered and accepted only when both parties believe it is in their interest to do so. In particular, offering or accepting aid is one way that states with different capabilities can respond to a common threat. Thus Secretary of State Alexander Haig justified the U.S. security assistance program by saying, "The friendly states we support can themselves help us assure our most vital national interests."[77] This statement suggests that an aid relationship may be more the result of political alignment than a cause of it. For example, no one would claim that the Grand Alliance in World War II was caused by U.S. Lend-Lease aid to Great Britain and Russia. It is more accurate to say that Lend-Lease was a means by which U.S. industrial might could be applied more effectively against the common enemy.[78] Yet those who now assert that Soviet or U.S. military aid can create reliable proxies are in effect making just such a claim; they are focusing solely on the means by which an alliance is implemented and ignoring the common political goals that inspired the relationship in the first place.

Accordingly, when evaluating the importance of economic or military assistance on alliances, we should consider the degree to which such assistance has powerful independent effects on the recipient's conduct and the conditions that will increase the influence that aid brings. If we are worried about Soviet military assistance, for example, we want to know whether or not this assistance will enable Moscow to control aid recipients for its own purposes. Similarly, before the United States provides military aid to an ally, it should consider whether or not this assistance will be used in ways that are consistent with U.S. interests. The question thus becomes: when does foreign aid give suppliers effective political leverage? Several additional hypotheses address this point.[79]

---

77. See Alexander Haig, "Security and Development Assistance," in U.S. Department of State, Bureau of Public Affairs, *Current Policy #264* (Washington, D.C., March 19, 1981), p. 2. The Joint Chiefs of Staff use similar language: "Security Assistance Programs contribute to U.S. national security objectives by assisting allies . . . to meet their defense needs and supporting collective security efforts." See U.S. Joint Chiefs of Staff, *U.S. Military Posture for FY1987* (Washington, D.C., 1986), p. 83.

78. See Gaddis, *Strategies of Containment,* chap. 1; and William H. McNeill, *America, Britain, and Russia: Their Cooperation and Conflict, 1941–1946* (London, 1953), pp. 137–55 and passim.

79. There is an extensive literature on the sources and conditions of economic leverage. Interestingly, writers focusing solely on the phenomena of arms transfers and economic assistance usually assume that aid can produce substantial leverage, whereas writers focusing on the more general subjects of economic leverage and coercion are much less optimistic about the possibility of states achieving significant control over others via direct economic pressure. In evaluating this literature, I have found the following works es-

Monopoly Supply of an Important Asset

The more valuable the asset offered and the greater the degree of monopoly that the supplier enjoys, the more effective the asset will be as an instrument of alliance formation. The logic here is obvious; when aid is especially valuable and when alternatives are nonexistent, recipients will be more willing to follow the donor's preferences in order to obtain assistance. Suppliers will thus have greater leverage. Obviously, if alternative sources are available, leverage will be significantly reduced.

Several implications follow. First, the impact of such aid on alliance choices (and the degree of leverage obtained through foreign aid) will be enhanced when a continuous supply of the commodity in question is needed. Examples include food, hard currency, and military equipment during wartime. Items that are valuable, that are difficult to store, or that require frequent resupply will give the donor greater leverage than will items that can be stockpiled or that are provided on a once-only basis.[80]

Second, military aid may be an especially important source of leverage when the recipients face a significant external threat. In this respect, foreign aid can be one way of balancing against a common foe. It also reinforces the idea that the importance of a given asset will depend on the context in which it is offered (i.e., on the specific circumstances the recipient faces).

Asymmetrical Dependence

Leverage will be enhanced if the supplier enjoys an asymmetry of dependence vis-à-vis the recipient. For example, if a client state faces an imminent threat, but its principal patron does not, then the latter's ability to influence the former's conduct should increase. When dependence is mutual, however, both states must adapt to their partner's interests. In short, when one ally does not need the other very much, its leverage should increase.

Conversely, the more important the recipient is to the donor, the

---

pecially helpful: Ariel Levite and Athanassios Platias, "Evaluating Small States' Dependence on Arms Imports: An Alternative Perspective" (Ithaca, 1983); Albert O. Hirschman, *State Power and the Structure of International Trade* (Berkeley, Calif., 1945), especially pp. 29–40; James A. Caporaso, "Dependence, Dependency, and Power in the Global System: A Structural and Behavioral Analysis," *International Organization*, 32, no. 1 (1978); Klaus Knorr, *The Power of Nations* (New York, 1975); Klaus Knorr, "Is International Coercion Waning or Rising?" *International Security*, 1, no. 4 (1977); Michael Mastanduno, "Strategies of Economic Containment," *World Politics*, 37, no. 4 (1985); and Steven E. Miller, "Arms and Impotence" (paper delivered at the International Institute for Strategic Studies New Faces Conference in Bellagio, Italy, 1979).

80. See Robert E. Harkavy, *Arms Trade and International Systems* (Cambridge, Mass., 1975), p. 101.

more aid it is likely to receive but the less leverage such aid will produce. Patrons will be reluctant to pressure important allies too severely by reducing the level of support. This tendency will be increased by the fact that the provision of aid usually commits the donor's own prestige. A client's threats to realign if its interests are not served will be all the more effective once an ally has invested heavily in the relationship. In fact, large aid programs, far from providing suppliers with effective leverage, may actually indicate that the client has successfully coerced the patron into providing ever-increasing amounts of support.

Asymmetry of Motivation

The relative importance of the issues on which alliance members differ will also affect the amount of leverage that patrons can exert over their clients. Other things being equal, when the recipient cares more about a particular issue, the supplier's ability to influence the recipient is reduced. This reduction occurs because the cost of complying with the patron's wishes may be greater than the cost of renouncing assistance.[81]

Thus even powerful patrons are unlikely to exert perfect control over their clients. Because recipients are usually weaker than suppliers, they have more at stake. They are thus likely to bargain harder to ensure that their interests are protected. In general, therefore, the asymmetry of motivation will favor recipients. As a result, the leverage available from large foreign aid programs will usually be less than donors expect.

Decision-Making Autonomy

Finally, leverage will be enhanced when the patron is politically capable of manipulating the level of assistance provided to the client. Authoritarian governments are likely to be better at using foreign aid to influence their allies' policies, because they face fewer internal obstacles to a decrease in assistance. By contrast, a state whose domestic political process is easily hamstrung by conflicting interest groups may find it difficult to make credible threats to reduce support in order to control the behavior of even heavily dependent client states.[82]

These four conditions will largely determine the independent impact

81. This formulation is similar to the one employed by Klaus Knorr in "Is International Coercion Waning or Rising?" pp. 102–10. On the conditions favoring successful coercion, consult Alexander L. George, David Hall, and William Simons, *The Limits of Coercive Diplomacy: Laos, Cuba, Vietnam* (Boston, 1971), pp. 216–20.

82. See Stephen D. Krasner's discussion of policy making in a "weak state" in *Defending the National Interest*, chap. 3; and Mastanduno, "Strategies of Economic Containment," pp. 519–20, 522–24.

of foreign aid on international alliances. When they are considered in light of the hypotheses we have already examined, several additional hypotheses can be inferred.

First, foreign aid can also affect alliance choices by providing a clear and credible signal that a powerful state does not have aggressive intentions. A generous offer of military assistance may be worth a thousand friendly words, for great powers are unlikely to try to increase the military capabilities of those toward whom they harbor aggressive intentions.

Second, the more that leaders of a supplier regime embrace the bandwagon hypothesis, the more easily clients will be able to defy attempts at pressure and extract additional assistance. When statesmen fear bandwagoning, they fear the cascading effects that even a single defection might produce. In such circumstances, patrons are willing to invest large sums to prevent the loss of even a minor ally. As a result, they find their potential leverage evaporating still further. In the same way, when statesmen believe ideology is extremely important, they place a high value on preserving ideologically similar regimes. Their reluctance to endanger these allies by reducing aid (even when this might make the allies more compliant) further reduces the impact of foreign assistance.[83]

Third, the provision of aid may often be self-defeating. After all, if the assistance is valuable enough to be appreciated, it is likely to leave the recipient better off than before. As the client's capabilities improve, it will be better equipped to resist the patron's blandishments or counter subsequent pressure. The link between aid and influence is weakened even more.

Taken together, these propositions suggest that foreign aid plays a relatively minor role in alliance formation. It encourages favorable perceptions of the donor, but it provides the patron with effective leverage only under rather rare circumstances. These conditions are instructive in themselves; aid is most likely to create reliable proxies when the recipients are so vulnerable and dependent that they are forced to follow the patron's wishes even when those wishes conflict with their own. Ironically, foreign aid is likely to be useful in manipulating allies that don't matter very much or in influencing more consequential states only on matters that are of vital importance to the patron. There is ample evidence for this observation; although Great Britain financed and equipped the coalition that defeated Napoleon, her efforts produced an unruly coalition in which British leverage was at best erratic. Much the

83. On these points, see Robert O. Keohane, "The Big Influence of Small Allies," *Foreign Policy*, no. 2 (Spring 1971).

same lesson can be drawn from the U.S. experience with Lend-Lease in World War II.[84]

Summary of Hypotheses on Foreign Aid and Alliance Formation

1. *General form:* The more aid provided by one state to another, the greater the likelihood that the two will form an alliance. The more aid, the greater the control by the donor over the recipient.
2. Foreign aid is a special form of balancing behavior. Therefore, the greater the external threat facing the recipient, the greater the effect of aid on alignment.
3. The greater the donor's monopoly on the commodity provided, the greater its leverage over the recipient.
4. The greater the asymmetry of dependence favoring the donor, the greater its leverage over the recipient.
5. The greater the asymmetry of motivation favoring the donor, the greater its leverage over the recipient. Because the recipient's security is usually more precarious, however, asymmetry of motivation will usually favor the recipient.
6. The weaker the domestic political decision-making apparatus of the donor, the less leverage it can exert on the recipient.

TRANSNATIONAL PENETRATION AND ALLIANCE FORMATION

A final set of hypotheses concerns the effects of *transnational penetration*, which I define as the manipulation of one state's domestic political system by another.[85] This penetration may take at least three forms: (1) Public officials whose loyalties are divided may use their influence to move their country closer to another. (2) Lobbyists may use a variety of means to alter public perceptions and policy decisions regarding a potential ally. (3) Foreign propaganda may be used to sway elite and mass attitudes. These hypotheses predict that alliances can be readily formed by manipulation of foreign governments through these indirect avenues of influence.

Although penetration has received relatively little attention in recent

84. See Robert Sherwig, *Guineas and Gunpowder: British Foreign Aid in the Wars with France, 1793–1815* (Cambridge, Mass., 1969), pp. 311–13, 350–55; and McNeill, *America, Britain, and Russia.*
85. For careful distinctions among different types of penetration, see Karen Dawisha, "Soviet Cultural Relations with Iraq, Syria and Egypt, 1955–1970," *Soviet Studies*, 27, no. 3 (1975).

scholarly research, examples are easy to find.[86] The Turkish decision to ally with Germany in World War I was due in part to the influence of Liman von Sanders, a German officer serving as inspector-general of the Turkish army.[87] During the war itself, Britain conducted an effective propaganda campaign in the United States, and it played an important role in the U.S. decision to intervene.[88] During the 1950s, the China Lobby exerted a substantial influence over U.S. policy in the Far East—and especially the alliance with Taiwan—by manipulating public opinion and influential U.S. officials.[89] Finally, the belief that penetration is an effective tool of alliance building has inspired the political indoctrination programs that accompanied U.S. military training and educational assistance to various developing countries, as well as U.S. concern over similar Soviet programs.[90]

As with foreign aid, however, the true causal relationship between transnational penetration and international alliances is often unclear. In particular, widespread contacts between two states (in the form of educational assistance, military training, and the like) are as likely to be the result of common interests and a close alliance as they are to be the cause of them. The observed association may well be partly spurious; both extensive contacts and alignment may be the result of some other cause (e.g., an external threat). Once again, therefore, we should consider the circumstances under which penetration will have the greatest independent effect on alliance formation. When is it more likely to alter alliance choices rather than merely reflect preexisting preferences?

Open versus Closed Societies

First, penetration will be more effective against open societies. When power is diffuse, when state and society are more accessible to propaganda from abroad or to lobbyists representing foreign interests, or

86. Exceptions include K. J. Holsti, *International Politics: A Framework for Analysis* (Englewood Cliffs, N.J., 1967), chap. 8; Andrew M. Scott, *The Revolution in Statecraft: Informal Penetration* (New York, 1965); and Nicholas O. Berry, "The Management of Foreign Penetration," *Orbis*, 17, no. 3 (1973).

87. Schmitt and Vedeler, *The World in the Crucible*, pp. 98–102; and A. J. P. Taylor, *The Struggle for Mastery in Europe: 1848–1918* (London, 1952), pp. 508–11, 533–34.

88. See Horace C. Peterson, *Propaganda for War: The British Campaign against American Neutrality, 1914–1918* (Norman, Okla., 1939).

89. See Ross Y. Koen, *The China Lobby in American Politics* (New York, 1974); and Stanley Bachrack, *The Committee for One Million: "China Lobby" Politics* (New York, 1976).

90. Miles D. Wolpin, "External Political Socialization as a Source of Conservative Military Behavior in the Third World," in *Militarism in Developing Countries*, ed. Kenneth Fidel (New Brunswick, N.J., 1975); Anthony Cordesman, "U.S. and Soviet Competition in Arms Exports and Military Assistance," *Armed Forces Journal International*, 118, no. 12 (1981): 66–67; and U.S. Department of Defense, *Soviet Military Power* (Washington, D.C., 1983), pp. 86–90.

when censorship is rare, transnational penetration is more likely to work. Thus we would expect a democratic state such as the United States to be more susceptible to penetration than an authoritarian regime such as the Soviet Union.

Ends and Means

The effectiveness of penetration will also depend on the ends sought by the state intending to penetrate another state. In particular, if one state seeks to encourage alignment solely by manipulating public and elite attitudes in another country, this effort is unlikely to be viewed as a direct threat to the independence of the state in question. However, if realignment is sought by the subversion of one regime (e.g., through hostile propaganda or support for dissident groups), then the target regime will probably react negatively toward the state directing the campaign.

The means employed may make a difference as well. If the means are viewed as legitimate, the likelihood of a hostile backlash is reduced. For example, attempts to coopt or indoctrinate foreign troops through a military training program are likely to be viewed with suspicion, whereas lobbying efforts by accredited representatives in a democratic society are more likely to be seen as politics as usual.[91]

These two conditions are closely related. The more open a given political system, the greater the range of activities that will be viewed as legitimate avenues of influence and the less the effort required to effect a change. By contrast, altering the behavior of a highly centralized, authoritarian regime may require either coopting or removing the top leadership itself. Needless to say, efforts to do this are likely to lead to suspicion and hostility rather than amity and alliance. Thus, when penetration does contribute to alliance formation, it will generally be where the means are perceived as legitimate and where other important incentives for the alliance already exist.

Taken together, these conditions imply that penetration will be an important cause of alliance formation only in rather rare circumstances. Two possibilities can be identified. First, states that lack established government institutions may be more vulnerable to pressure, especially if they are forced to rely on foreigners to provide essential skills. Such states will usually be weak and relatively unimportant. Second, and conversely, penetration may also be relatively effective against the largest powers, because their attention is divided and because foreign

91. Even democracies can be sensitive to overt foreign manipulation. Thus the China Lobby tried to prevent careful scrutiny of all its activities. See Bachrack, *Committee for One Million.*

elites can readily acquire expertise on how to manipulate the system, especially if they received part of their education in the country in question. In both cases, however, penetration will be most effective when it serves to reinforce other motives for alignment—that is, when lobbyists or propagandists are preaching to the converted.

Summary of Hypotheses on Penetration and Alliance Formation

1. *General form:* The greater one state's access to the political system of another, the greater the tendency for the two to ally.
2. Penetration is more effective against open societies.
3. Penetration is more effective when the objectives are limited. Therefore, the more intrusive the act of penetration, the greater the probability that it will have a negative effect on alignment.
4. Penetration is most effective when other causes contribute to the alliance.

CONCLUSION

The hypotheses examined in this chapter imply very different worlds. If balancing is the norm, if ideology exerts little effect or is often divisive, and if foreign aid and penetration are rather weak causes, then hegemony over the international system will be extremely difficult to achieve. Most states will find security plentiful. But if the bandwagoning hypothesis is more accurate, if ideology is a powerful force for alignment, and if foreign aid and penetration can readily bring reliable control over others, then hegemony will be much easier (although it will also be rather fragile).[92] Even great powers will view their security as precarious.

Because the implications of each hypothesis are different, it is important to determine which of the hypotheses presented here offers the best guide to state behavior. The next task, therefore, is to assemble a body of evidence that will enable us to perform this assessment.

92. If bandwagoning is common, a dominant position may be fragile because a few small defeats may cause a flood of defections. Once allies have concluded that the dominant power's fortunes are waning, the bandwagoning hypothesis predicts that they will quickly realign. The fortunes of the great powers are thus highly elastic in a bandwagoning world, because small events anywhere will have major consequences.

[3]

From the Baghdad Pact
to the Six Day War

This chapter and the next describe the principal alliances in the Middle East from 1955 to 1979. The purpose is to provide the historical background for the analysis in chapters 5 to 7 by identifying the most important causes for the various alliances.

Middle East diplomacy from the Baghdad Pact to the Six Day War was dominated by three interrelated themes. The first was the repeated failure of Gamal Abdel Nasser's various efforts to translate his own charisma and Egypt's regional stature into permanent hegemony in the Arab world. Relying on propaganda, subversion, and the astute manipulation of the ideology of Arab unity, Nasser repeatedly sought to entice or intimidate the other Arab states into accepting Egypt's leadership. These efforts ultimately failed because Nasser's targets were able to form alliances against him (their occasional efforts at appeasement notwithstanding) and because the pan-Arab ideology that Nasser invoked in fact caused more conflict than cooperation. Put simply, the harder Nasser tried to force the other Arab states to accept his predominance, the more resistance he faced.

A second theme is the steady growth of superpower commitments in the Middle East. Although both the United States and the Soviet Union made a number of blunders during this period, Egypt, Syria, North Yemen, and (to a lesser degree) Iraq were informally allied with the Soviet Union by 1967. The United States, in turn, had established important security ties with Israel, Jordan, and Saudi Arabia. The super-

[50]

powers and their regional clients were united by different but usually compatible aims; the superpowers sought to balance each other, and their clients sought outside support to counter threats from other regional states.

A final theme is the persistence of the Arab-Israeli conflict and the inability of the Arab states to form an effective alliance against the so-called Zionist entity. Although the ideology of Arab solidarity helped sustain a broad Arab coalition against Israel (especially during crises), the fact that the Arab states were equally suspicious of one another helped turn the conflict with Israel into another arena of inter-Arab rivalry. As the Six Day War revealed, the largely symbolic efforts of the Arab states to prove their anti-Israel credentials (while discrediting those of their rivals) were a poor basis on which to build an effective alliance against anyone. Thus it is not surprising that these states relied heavily on superpower support. If balancing with other regional powers was difficult or risky, then obtaining support from a great power outside the region was the only alternative.

THE SETTING AND THE PLAYERS

The security environment in the Middle East after World War II was the product of four main developments. First, the imperial order established by the French and British was rapidly decaying, as the colonial powers relinquished control over the areas they had inherited from the Ottoman Empire after World War I.[1]

The decline in British and French influence was due primarily to a second major trend: the resurgence of nationalism throughout the Middle East. Beginning in the nineteenth century, this "Arab awakening" was forged in the struggle against the foreign powers that had long dominated the region. By 1950, a variety of political movements espousing nationalist ideas had emerged throughout the region.[2]

The Arab nationalists shared several key beliefs. Virtually all the nationalists were hostile to "imperialist" activity and were committed to promoting economic development and a more equitable distribution of

1. For an account of the decline in British and French hegemony in the Middle East, see Howard M. Sachar, *Europe Leaves the Middle East* (New York, 1972).

2. See George Antonius's classic *The Arab Awakening: The Story of the Arab Movement* (New York, 1946). For developments since World War II, see Patrick Seale, *The Struggle for Syria: A Study of Arab Politics, 1945–1958* (London, 1965); Robert W. McDonald, *The League of Arab States: A Study in the Dynamics of Regional Organization* (Princeton, N.J., 1965); Sylvia Haim, "Introduction," in *Arab Nationalism: An Anthology*, ed. Sylvia Haim (Berkeley, Calif., 1962); and Hisham B. Shirabi, *Nationalism and Revolution in the Arab World* (New York, 1966).

wealth. Moreover, because the division of the Arabs was seen as the artificial result of foreign domination, a desire to restore the political unity of the Arab world became an influential theme of the nationalist movement.[3]

Third, the establishment of Israel and its subsequent victory in the 1948 war created an enduring source of conflict. Not only had the various Arab states suffered a humiliating defeat, but as many as 700,000 Arab refugees had fled Palestine during the war. For the Arabs, an alien presence on land that had been in Arab hands for centuries presented a direct challenge to the nationalist sentiment now present in the Arab world. Thus, from 1948 onward, loyalty to the ideal of Arab nationalism meant strict opposition to Israel. Moreover, the Arab defeat helped discredit the traditional Arab ruling elites and reinforced the belief that Arab unity was necessary to restore Palestine and preserve Arab independence.[4]

Finally, Soviet and U.S. interest in the region was growing rapidly. The United States had already begun to assume Britain's traditional role in the Eastern Mediterranean, and both superpowers played key roles in the creation of Israel. After the 1948 war, the United States sought a neutral position on the Arab-Israeli conflict and devoted its efforts to promoting a new pro-Western security system in the region.[5] As for the Soviet Union, a growing awareness that Arab nationalism was now the major force opposing "imperialism" encouraged a shift toward the

3. On the ideology of pan-Arabism, see Fayez Sayegh, *Arab Unity* (New York, 1958); Israel Gershoni, *The Emergence of Pan-Arabism in Egypt* (Tel Aviv, 1981); Haim, *Arab Nationalism*; and Leonard Binder, *The Ideological Revolution in the Middle East* (New York, 1964), chap. 6.

4. The events surrounding the establishment of Israel and its victory in the 1948 war are described in Nadav Safran, *Israel: The Embattled Ally* (Cambridge, Mass., 1981); and Fred J. Khouri, *The Arab-Israeli Dilemma* (Syracuse, N.Y., 1976). For a pro-Arab perspective, see David Hirst, *The Gun and the Olive Branch* (London, 1978), chaps. 4 and 5. The Arab departure from Palestine triggered a lengthy and bitter debate over whether it was provoked by the Israelis or incited by the various Arab leaders. The true story now appears to lie squarely in between. Many Arabs left voluntarily; many others were driven out by terror and intimidation. See, for example, the sections by Abba Eban and Erskine B. Childers in *The Israel-Arab Reader*, ed. Walter Z. Laqueur (New York, 1969), pp. 143–64. For an assessment of the debate, see Nadav Safran, *From War to War: The Arab-Israeli Confrontation, 1948–1967* (New York, 1969), pp. 34–35.

5. On U.S. commitments in the Near East, see Kuniholm, *The Origins of the Cold War in the Near East.* The main objectives of U.S. Middle East policy prior to 1954 are illustrated by the Tripartite Declaration of 1950, in which the United States, Great Britain, and France agreed to voluntary restrictions on arms shipments to the region and called for the formation of a Middle East Defense Command to provide for regional security and a continuing great power presence in the region. See Paul Jabber, *Not by War Alone* (Berkeley, Calif., 1981), pp. 63–81; and Robert W. Stookey, *America and the Arab States: An Uneasy Encounter* (New York, 1975), pp. 128–29.

Arabs.[6] After many years of ignoring the Middle East, the Soviet Union and the United States were poised for a more active role.

The Cast of Characters

Egypt

With 30 percent of the population of the Arab world, Egypt was easily the most powerful Arab state. Its size gave it considerable military potential, and Cairo was also a major educational and cultural center. Egypt's geographic position—in the center of the Arab world and guarding the Suez Canal—also increased its power relative to that of its neighbors.[7]

A watershed in modern Egyptian history was the Free Officers coup against King Farouk in 1952. The new regime—a military dictatorship soon dominated by Nasser—was dedicated above all to maintaining Egypt's freedom from foreign influence and to improving social and economic conditions at home.

Nasser's early successes increased his ambitions considerably. In particular, preserving his own leadership of the Arab revolution, whether through formal unity or through some other mechanism, became the cardinal principle of Nasser's foreign policy. As part of his revolutionary plans, Nasser began an ambitious program of socialist economic development in the early 1960s. Neither campaign achieved its aims—for reasons that will become clear as we proceed—and many of his foreign and domestic policies were eventually abandoned by his successors.[8]

6. For accounts of Soviet foreign policy in the early 1950s, see Aryeh Yodfat, *Arab Politics in the Soviet Mirror* (New Brunswick, N.J., 1973), pp. 1–6; Ya'acov Roi, *Soviet Decisionmaking in Practice: The USSR and Israel, 1947–1954* (New Brunswick, N.J., 1980), pp. 401–11; Walter Z. Laqueur, *The Soviet Union and the Middle East* (New York, 1959), chaps. 4–6, especially pp. 156–58; Ya'acov Roi, *From Encroachment to Involvement: A Documentary History of Soviet Foreign Policy in the Middle East, 1945–1973* (New Brunswick, N.J., 1974), pp. 71–79, 82–94, 101–5, 111–24, 127–30, 135–43. The first concrete signs of the shift in Soviet policy was a Soviet veto of a U.N. Security Council resolution condemning Egypt's blockade of Israeli shipping in March 1954 and the raising of the Soviet and Egyptian legations to embassy status at roughly the same time. See Sachar, *Europe Leaves the Middle East*, pp. 602–3.

7. In the 1950s, Egyptian defense expenditures were more than twice those of any other Arab country. See Adeed Dawisha, *Egypt in the Arab World* (London, 1976), chap. 7.

8. For descriptions or analyses of Egyptian politics, economics, and society, see John Waterbury, *The Egypt of Nasser and Sadat: The Political Economy of Two Regimes* (Princeton, N.J., 1983); P. J. Vatikiotis, *The Modern History of Egypt* (New York, 1969); P. J. Vatikiotis, *Nasser and His Generation* (New York, 1978); Lenczowski, *Middle East in World Affairs*, chap. 12; Derek Hopwood, *Egypt: Politics and Society 1945–1981* (London, 1982); and R. Hrair Dekmejian, *Egypt under Nasir: A Study in Political Leadership* (Albany, N.Y., 1971).

During his lifetime, however, Nasser was the dominant political figure in the Arab world.

Syria

The postwar history of Syria is intertwined with that of the Ba'th Party. Founded in 1941, the Ba'th is an avowedly transnational party with branches throughout the Arab world. Ba'th ideology stressed the goals of unity, freedom, and socialism, and its leaders were among the foremost advocates of an Arab union.

Syria received full independence from France in 1945, but its parliamentary system soon fell victim to a series of military coups. A gradual move to the left increased both Ba'th and Communist influence, and the Ba'th led the country into union with Egypt in 1958 partly to overcome its Communist rivals. The union collapsed in 1961, and the Ba'th seized permanent control two years later. At the same time, a bitter factional dispute arose between the Syrian and Iraqi wings of the party, a rift that has divided Damascus and Baghdad ever since. An extreme leftist faction rose to power in 1966, but it was ousted in 1970 by a somewhat more moderate group led by Hafez el-Assad.

Syria's status rests not only on the steady growth of its military power but also on its image as the cradle of Arab nationalism. In addition to its public commitment to the Palestinian cause, Syrian foreign policy includes several revisionist goals, among them the creation of a Greater Syria encompassing parts of Lebanon, Jordan, and Israel.[9]

Iraq

Iraq was Egypt's major Arab rival after World War II. Although blessed with substantial resources and a large population, Iraq's regional influence was reduced by its geographic isolation and pro-Western orientation. Partly as a reward for the help that Sherif Hussein, head of the Hashemite dynasty, had given Britain during World War I, the British granted the Iraqi throne to Hussein's son Feisal in 1921. Formal independence came a decade later, although the British occupied Iraq in 1941 to oust an anti-British government and restore Iraq's conservative, pro-British leaders.

Under Feisal II, Iraq maintained its links with Britain while unsuc-

9. Basic analyses of Syria and the Ba'th include Seale, *Struggle for Syria;* Itamar Rabinovich, *Syria under the Ba'th: The Army-Party Symbiosis* (New York, 1974); Nikalaos Van Dam, *The Struggle for Power in Syria: Sectarianism, Regionalism, and Tribalism in Politics, 1961–1978* (New York, 1979); Tabitha Petran, *Syria* (New York, 1972); John F. Devlin, *The Ba'th Party: A History from Its Origins to 1966* (Stanford, Calif., 1968); Gordon H. Torrey, *Syrian Politics and the Military, 1945–1958* (Columbus, Ohio, 1964); and Kamal S. Abu-Jaber, *The Arab Ba'th Socialist Party: History, Ideology, and Organization* (Syracuse, N.Y., 1966).

cessfully pursuing its traditional ambitions in Syria.[10] The monarchy was overthrown in 1958, beginning a decade of unstable military rule. Domestic stability was finally achieved by the Iraqi wing of the Ba'th Party, which seized power in 1968 and has maintained a rigid dictatorship ever since. Each regime since the revolution has proclaimed some form of socialism, but only the Ba'th has actually implemented an extensive program of socialist economic development.[11]

Jordan

The Hashemite kingdom of Jordan is another British creation. After setting up the Hashemite monarchy in Iraq, Britain gave Transjordan to Feisal's elder brother, Abdullah. British influence was considerable until the mid-1950s, through extensive subsidy payments and its role in training Jordan's Arab Legion.

These troops fought well in the 1948 war, and Abdullah acquired the West Bank (and a large Palestinian population) at this time. His efforts to reach a peace settlement with Israel led to his assassination in 1950, and his grandson, Hussein, became king in 1953 at the age of eighteen. In spite of internal challenges and external threats, Hussein has maintained his throne for over three decades, Jordan's weakness and vulnerability notwithstanding. As with Saudi Arabia, Hussein's foreign policy has generally been extremely cautious, and Hussein has relied on a combination of Western support and skillful appeasement to contain threats to his fragile regime.[12]

Saudi Arabia

Unlike the other Middle East states, Saudi Arabia was never under direct colonial rule. The kingdom is the creation of Abdul Aziz ibn Saud,

10. Feisal's father, Sherif Hussein, had sought to bring Syria, Iraq, and Transjordan under Hashemite rule by dividing them between his two sons, Feisal and Abdullah. This plan was stymied by the French desire to maintain control in Syria. Feisal ended up with Iraq, and Abdullah eventually became king of Jordan. Both Hashemite monarchies thus harbored designs on Syria, which they believed was rightfully theirs. See Majid Khadduri, "The Scheme of Fertile Crescent Unity: A Study in Inter-Arab Relations," in *The Near East and the Great Powers*, ed. R. N. Frye (Cambridge, Mass., 1951).

11. On events in Iraq, consult Majid Khadduri, *Independent Iraq* (London, 1968); *Socialist Iraq: A Study in Iraq's Politics since 1968* (Washington, D.C., 1978); Hanna Batatu, *The Old Social Classes and Revolutionary Movements of Iraq: A Study of Iraq's Old Landed and Commercial Classes and of Its Communists, Ba'thists, and Free Officers* (Princeton, N.J., 1978); Christine Moss Helms, *Iraq: Eastern Flank of the Arab World* (Washington, D.C., 1984); and Edith Penrose and E. F. Penrose, *Iraq: International Relations and National Development* (London, 1978).

12. On Jordan, see P. J. Vatikiotis, *Politics and the Military in Jordan: A Study of the Arab Legion, 1921–1957* (London, 1967); Aqil Abidi, *Jordan: A Political Study 1948–1957* (New Delhi, 1965); Anne Sinai and Allen Pollock, *The Hashemite Kingdom of Jordan and the West Bank* (New York, 1977); and Naseer H. Aruri, *Jordan: A Study in Political Development (1921–1965)* (The Hague, Netherlands, 1972).

who completed his conquest of the Arabian Peninsula by 1932. A rival of the Hashemites, ibn Saud relied on British (and later U.S.) support to protect his vast but sparsely populated realm. Ties with the United States were enhanced further by the role U.S. companies played in developing Saudi Arabia's enormous petroleum reserves.[13]

The kingdom is a traditional monarchy ruled by ibn Saud's extended network of descendants. As a result, a dominant concern throughout the postwar period has been the maintenance of domestic stability in an era of rapid social change. That goal has so far been achieved, although the Saudis faced several serious challenges in the past. Saudi Arabia's influence is derived from the country's oil wealth and its control of the Islamic holy sites in Mecca and Medina. Given the limited capabilities and numerous internal and external vulnerabilities of the country, its foreign policy has been largely defensive and reactive.[14]

The Yemens

The Yemeni people are divided into two states, and relations between them have alternated between overt hostility and unfulfilled aspirations for formal unity. From 1948 to 1962, North Yemen was a primitive tribal monarchy under Imam Ahmed. The Imamate was overthrown by a group of Nasserist army officers in September 1962, and the coup led to an extended civil war that brought in Egypt and Saudi Arabia on opposing sides. The war was finally settled in 1970, and a series of moderate military governments has ruled since then.

To the south, the People's Democratic Republic of Yemen (PDRY) is the only Marxist regime in the Arab world. After a lengthy revolutionary struggle, South Yemen gained independence from Britain in 1968. The regime has grown increasingly radical since independence, a process punctuated by violent quarrels between contending factions. South Yemen's support for revolutionary movements throughout the Arabian Peninsula has marred its relations with Saudi Arabia, and this poor and weak state has been heavily dependent on Soviet economic and military aid throughout its brief history.[15]

13. See Aaron D. Miller, *Search for Security: Saudi Arabian Oil and American Foreign Policy, 1939–49* (Chapel Hill, N.C., 1980).

14. Basic works on Saudi Arabia are David Holden and Richard Johns, *The House of Saud* (New York, 1981); William B. Quandt, *Saudi Arabia in the 1980s: Foreign Policy, Security, Oil* (Washington, D.C., 1981); Robert Lacey, *The Kingdom* (New York, 1981); Adeed Dawisha, "Saudi Arabia's Search for Security," *Adelphi Paper #168* (London, 1979); and especially Nadav Safran, *Saudi Arabia: The Ceaseless Quest for Security* (Cambridge, Mass., 1985).

15. On the Yemens, see Manfred Wenner, *Modern Yemen* (Baltimore, Md., 1967); Robert W. Stookey, *Yemen: The Politics of the Yemen Arab Republic* (Boulder, Colo., 1978); Robert W. Stookey, *South Yemen: A Marxist Republic in Arabia* (Boulder, Colo., 1982); J. E. Petersen, *Yemen: The Search for a Modern State* (London, 1980); and B. R. Pridham, ed., *Contemporary Yemen: Politics and Historical Background* (New York, 1984). On Soviet relations with the two

Lebanon

Weak and ethnically divided, Lebanon has played a minor role in the events examined here. Lebanon received full independence from France in 1945, a decision that angered those Syrian nationalists who saw Lebanon as rightfully theirs. At that time, the state was inhabited by roughly equal numbers of Christians and Moslems, and political stability in Lebanon rested on a fragile accord dividing power between the two religious groups. To satisfy both, Lebanon was committed to strict neutrality. As is all too well known, this precarious arrangement gradually collapsed in the 1970s, leading to an interminable civil war exacerbated by repeated foreign (e.g., Syrian and Israeli) intervention.[16]

Israel

The state of Israel is a parliamentary democracy with significant religious influence and its own form of welfare-state socialism. Following its creation in 1947—the result of Zionist efforts over many decades and support from both superpowers—Israel initially adopted a policy of nonalignment. By the early 1950s, however, this policy had shifted to an explicitly pro-Western stance, largely in response to growing tensions with the Soviet Union.

Military security has been a major concern. Since the founding of the state, Israel has successfully translated its various assets (including support from France and the United States) into regional military superiority. Thus, despite its small size and population, Israel has been the foremost military power in the Middle East throughout much of the period examined here. Employing a doctrine of preemption and reprisal against its adversaries, Israel simultaneously sought international recognition and a peace settlement with the Arabs. And like several of its neighbors, Israel was willing to try more ambitious actions as well.[17]

Summary

By the early 1950s, the stage was filled with a diverse cast of characters seeking often incompatible objectives. The existing regional rivalries

---

Yemens, see Aryeh Yodfat, *The Soviet Union and the Arabian Peninsula: Soviet Policy towards the Persian Gulf and Arabia* (New York, 1983); and Mark N. Katz, *Russia and Arabia: Soviet Foreign Policy toward the Arabian Peninsula* (Baltimore, Md., 1986).

16. For basic descriptions of Lebanese politics, see Michael Hudson, *The Precarious Republic: Political Modernization in Lebanon* (New York, 1968); Leonard Binder, ed., *Politics in Lebanon* (New York, 1966); and Leila Meo, *Lebanon: Improbable Nation* (Bloomington, Ind., 1965). For accounts of the civil war, see Itamar Rabinovich, *The War for Lebanon: 1970–1985* (Ithaca, 1986); and Walid Khalidi, *Conflict and Violence in Lebanon* (Cambridge, Mass., 1979).

17. Basic accounts of Israeli politics and foreign policy include Howard M. Sachar, *A History of Israel: From the Rise of Zionism to Our Time* (New York, 1979); Safran, *Israel*; and Michael Brecher, *The Foreign Policy System of Israel* (New Haven, Conn., 1972). A good introduction to Israeli military doctrine is Michael Handel, *Israel's Political-Military Doctrine* (Cambridge, Mass., 1973).

were exacerbated by the fact that many of the new states were undergoing rapid social change and faced serious problems of domestic legitimacy.[18] This situation raised the stakes considerably, because foreign successes could yield great benefits and foreign challenges threatened total defeat. With this rough sketch as background, we can now consider the first round of alliances, beginning with the Baghdad Pact.

THE BAGHDAD PACT AND THE RISE OF NASSER'S EGYPT

Iraqi-Egyptian Rivalry

The first wave of postwar alliances in the Middle East began in 1955 with the ill-fated Baghdad Pact. This alliance was the product of the complementary objectives of Great Britain, the United States, and Iraq. As originally conceived by Iraqi prime minister Nuri al-Said, the pact would be a multilateral alliance binding the Arab League to Turkey (already a NATO member), Great Britain, and (informally) the United States. For the United States and Great Britain, the pact offered the hope that they could retain their dwindling influence throughout the Middle East while helping defend Western interests against Soviet pressure.[19] For Iraq, the plan was seen as a way to obtain protection against the Soviet Union and to enhance Iraq's position within the Arab world.[20]

Unfortunately for these ambitions, the proposal attracted immediate opposition from several other Arab states, especially Egypt. Nasser's opposition to the pact was based on several concerns.

First, Nasser believed that the pact was merely another scheme by which the great powers could interfere in Arab affairs.[21] As he told the British, a defense pact between Egypt and the West "would not be an

18. For analyses of social change in the Middle East and its effects on political life, see Manfred Halpern, *The Politics of Social Change in the Middle East and North Africa* (Princeton, N.J., 1963), especially chap. 10; Daniel Lerner, *The Passing of Traditional Society: Modernizing the Middle East* (New York, 1964); and Michael Hudson, *Arab Politics: The Search for Legitimacy* (New Haven, Conn., 1977).

19. Nuri's plan was especially appealing to Britain because it would ally Britain with the entire Arab League, thus providing an avenue of influence far beyond Iraq itself. More limited schemes (such as John Foster Dulles's proposal for a Northern Tier alliance of Turkey, Iraq, Iran, Pakistan, and the West) were less appealing to Britain because they lacked this essential feature. See Seale, *Struggle for Syria*, pp. 189–92.

20. See Lenczowski, *Middle East in World Affairs*, pp. 283–84; and Khadduri, *Independent Iraq*, pp. 346–50. The Iraqi prime minister told one Egyptian emissary that Iraq needed external support because "[Iraq's] borders were close to the [Soviet] Caucasus, only some 300 or 400 miles," but most accounts agree that Nuri also viewed the Pact as a way to increase Iraq's power within the Arab world. See Seale, *Struggle for Syria*, pp. 199–201.

21. In January 1954, Egypt had announced that its foreign policy would seek (among other things) "the establishment of an Arab bloc, free from imperialist interference, to protect the interests of Islamic, Asiatic, and African peoples." Quoted in Seale, *Struggle for Syria*, p. 195.

alliance—merely subordination."[22] Having finally succeeded in ousting British troops from Egypt (through a formal agreement on evacuation of the British base at Suez), Nasser and his associates were understandably reluctant to enter an alliance that might give the great powers an excuse to return.

Second, Nasser did not believe that the Soviet Union was a significant threat. As he told John Foster Dulles, the Soviet Union had never threatened Egypt before and was "thousands of miles away." Because the Egyptians did not share British or Iraqi concerns about the Soviet Union, their suspicions that the Baghdad Pact was directed at them increased.[23]

Third, the Iraqi plan threatened to leave Egypt isolated within the Arab world. If the rest of the Arab League joined the pact, the combination of Arab collaboration and military support from Great Britain could make Iraq the dominant Arab power. Thus the clash over the Baghdad Pact was merely another round in the postwar rivalry between the two most powerful Arab states.[24]

In short, the issue was whether Nuri's plan for a regional security scheme linked to Great Britain and the United States would attract greater support than Nasser's alternative, a unified and nonaligned Arab bloc. The rivalry between Egypt and Iraq thus became a competition for allies within the Arab world. Given the symbolic importance of Arab solidarity, placing one's rival in the minority by attracting greater allied support was a very effective tactic.

Egypt won the contest handily. Even before the treaties linking Iraq, Turkey, and Britain were signed in February and April 1955, a combination of Egyptian propaganda, Saudi bribery, and adroit Egyptian diplomacy had convinced Syria to reject the pact.[25] Aided by a flare-up in border violence with Israel, Egypt countered Iraq by forming a unified military command with Syria and Saudi Arabia, and a series of bilateral defense treaties was signed in October 1955. Iraq's bid for leadership had thus been matched by a countervailing Arab coalition.[26] Yemen joined

22. Quoted in J. C. Hurewitz, *Middle East Politics: The Military Dimension* (New York, 1969), pp. 87–88.

23. On Nasser's relaxed appraisal of the Soviet Union, see Stookey, *America and the Arab States*, pp. 128–29; Mohamed Heikal, *The Cairo Documents* (New York, 1971), p. 40; and Erskine B. Childers, *The Road to Suez* (London, 1962), pp. 120–21.

24. On these points, see Seale, *Struggle for Syria*, pp. 23, 196–97, 211–12; Stephens, *Nasser*, pp. 147–51; and Keith Wheelock, *Nasser's New Egypt* (New York, 1960), pp. 218–21.

25. The pro-Iraqi cabinet of Faris al-Khuri collapsed in January 1955 and was replaced by a leftist coalition led by Sabri al-Asali, who quickly proclaimed Syria's opposition to foreign military pacts and its support for the Egyptian line. See Seale, *Struggle for Syria*, pp. 217–22.

26. Seale, *Struggle for Syria*, pp. 223–24. Although the Egyptian-Syrian-Saudi alliance had little military significance, its political implications were weighty. In particular, it was a decisive rejection of Nuri's plans to link the Arab League to the Western powers and a solid endorsement of Nasser's own proposal for a unified, independent Arab policy.

the new alignment shortly thereafter, as the Imam was eager to gain Arab backing for his campaign against British rule in South Arabia.[27]

Egyptian motives have already been considered. What of Iraq's other opponents? Saudi Arabia's opposition to the Baghdad Pact was based on the Saudis' traditional rivalry with the Hashemites in Iraq, a feud with Great Britain over disputed claims to the Buraimi Oasis, and a desire to defuse revolutionary sentiment in Saudi Arabia itself.[28] Syria's decision was based on the broad appeal of a neutralist, pan-Arab policy in postcolonial Syria; the lingering suspicion that Iraq still harbored revisionist aims toward Syria; the triumph of a leftist coalition strongly opposed to close ties with the West; and Egypt's promotion of these trends through its propaganda and personal diplomacy.

The final step in Nasser's campaign against the Baghdad Pact was the neutralization of Lebanon and Jordan. Both were under considerable pressure from Britain to join the pact, but the Lebanese government soon declared it would await Jordan's decision. The British offered Hussein increased financial subsidies if he accepted Nuri's plan, and Hussain was leaning toward alignment with Iraq by the fall of 1955.[29] Jordan's flirtation with the Baghdad Pact prompted a vicious Egyptian propaganda campaign over Radio Cairo, and the subsequent riots in the Jordanian capital brought down the cabinet in December 1955 and again in January 1956. Hussein quickly announced that he would remain neutral, and he appeased nationalist sentiment by dismissing General John Glubb, the British commander of the Arab Legion.[30] Thus Iraq was effectively isolated by the beginning of 1956, and Egypt was now the leader of a broad Arab coalition.

27. The poor and extremely backward Imamate of Yemen had remained neutral on the inter-Arab scene through 1955. The decision to enter a formal alliance with Egypt and Saudi Arabia in early 1956 also reflected Saudi Arabia's traditional influence in Yemen and the activities of Imam Ahmed's son, Badr, who was reportedly a profound admirer of Nasser. One effect of this loose alliance (which would have considerable impact some years later) was the dispatching of Yemeni military officers for training and political indoctrination in Egypt. Yemen signed a friendship treaty with the Soviet Union in 1955, also based on Imam Ahmed's desire to pressure Great Britain. On these points, see Wenner, *Modern Yemen*, pp. 176–77; Lenczowski, *Middle East in World Affairs*, pp. 617–22; and Ali Abdel Rahman Rahmy, *The Egyptian Policy in the Arab World: The Intervention in Yemen, 1961–1967 Case Study* (Washington, D.C., 1983), pp. 56–59.

28. See Holden and Johns, *House of Saud*, pp. 184–87; Lenczowski, *Middle East in World Affairs*, pp. 590–92; and Dawisha, "Saudi Arabia's Search for Security," p. 2.

29. In his memoirs, Hussein claims to have consulted Nasser prior to entering negotiations with the British on joining the pact, and he states that he received Nasser's approval. See Hussein, King of Jordan, *Uneasy Lies the Head* (New York, 1962), pp. 108–10. Kennett Love argues that Hussein's declaration of neutrality in November 1955 was a smokescreen masking his plans to join the pact shortly thereafter. See his *Suez: The Twice-Fought War* (New York, 1969), pp. 202–3.

30. Hussein denies that either foreign pressure or domestic instability prompted his dismissal of Glubb, which is hardly surprising. See Hussein, *Uneasy Lies the Head*, chap. 9, especially p. 130. See also Lenczowski, *Middle East in World Affairs*, pp. 481–83; Dawisha, *Egypt in the Arab World*, p. 14; and Childers, *Road to Suez*, pp. 142–43, 145.

Arab-Israeli Tensions

The conflict over the Baghdad Pact quickly spilled into the Arab-Israeli conflict. Israel now felt threatened by several developments: (1) The British withdrawal from Suez removed an important buffer between Egypt and Israel. (2) Nasser was beginning to place greater pressure on Israel in order to enhance his image as the Arab leader most devoted to the Palestinian cause. (3) The formation of the Egyptian-Syrian-Saudi alignment increased Israel's fears of Arab encirclement.[31] Israel's response was predictable. It intensified reprisal raids against its neighbors (including a major raid against the Egyptian town of Gaza in February 1955), renewed efforts to reach a modus vivendi with Egypt, and intensified its search for great power support.[32] It was most successful in accomplishing the last goal; by 1954 Israel and France had established a tacit alliance that would last for almost a decade.[33]

These Israeli responses encouraged Egypt to seek great power support as well. Nasser had already sought arms from Britain and the United States without success, and the Gaza raid had exposed the Egyptian army's inability to defend Egypt's borders successfully.[34] In April 1955, Nasser began negotiations for military aid from the Soviet Union,

31. In the period 1954–1956, Egypt gradually intensified the naval and air blockade against Israel, began providing passive and active support for fedayeen attacks against Israeli settlements, and executed several Israelis caught conducting a sabotage mission in Cairo. On these points, see Michael Brecher, *Decisions in Israel's Foreign Policy* (New Haven, Conn., 1975), pp. 254–55; Love, *Suez*, pp. 71–72; and Childers, *Road to Suez*, p. 130.

32. On Israel's policy of reprisal, see Jonathan Shimshoni, "Conventional Deterrence: Lessons from the Middle East" (diss., Princeton University, 1985), chaps. 2, 3, and 4. Israeli motives for the Gaza raid—in which thirty-nine Egyptians were killed and another thirty wounded—are still disputed. Israel may have been seeking to reduce Nasser's prestige in the Arab world and in Egypt itself, to retaliate for the execution of a group of Israeli spies or for earlier fedayeen attacks, or to force Egyptian concessions at the risk of provoking a major war. Alternatively, Israel may not have been seeking any specific aim other than the dissuasion of Egyptian support for fedayeen attacks, and the high casualties inflicted during the Gaza raid may have been an unintended consequence of the "fog of war." For varying accounts, see Brecher, *Decisions in Israel's Foreign Policy*, pp. 254–55, especially note 1; Ernest Stock, *Israel on the Road to Sinai* (Ithaca, 1967), pp. 70–75; Livia Rokach, *Israel's Sacred Terror* (Belmont, Mass., 1980), pp. 42–44; Love, *Suez*, p. 86 and chap. 1; and Childers, *Road to Suez*, p. 132.

33. Unable to obtain a substantial U.S. commitment, Israel established a covert arms supply agreement with France as early as 1952. The search for armaments intensified in 1954, and French deliveries of jet aircraft, tanks, and other equipment began in earnest in late 1955 and 1956. See Sylvia Kowitt Crosbie, *A Tacit Alliance: France and Israel from Suez to the Six Day War* (Princeton, N.J., 1974), pp. 35–70, especially pp. 42–44.

34. On Nasser's attempts to obtain arms from the West, see Townsend Hoopes, *The Devil and John Foster Dulles* (Boston, 1971), pp. 323–24; Gail C. Meyer, *Egypt and the United States: The Formative Years* (Cranbury, N.J., 1980), pp. 120–22; and Stephens, *Nasser*, pp. 157–59. Having taken an ambitious stand as an Arab leader, Nasser undoubtedly felt that the Gaza raid jeopardized his prestige. Moreover, the Egyptian army was demoralized by the raid and could best be mollified by a great improvement in its equipment. Thus, regardless of Israel's motives behind Gaza (and the other reprisal actions), the effect was to encourage Nasser to seek outside support.

and he accepted a Soviet offer to provide Egypt with arms in September. With one stroke Egypt had destroyed the Western monopoly on arms to the Middle East and greatly increased its potential military power. Even more important, this display of independence enhanced Nasser's already considerable prestige in the Arab world.[35]

Egypt's Syrian ally also was moving toward the Soviet Union. Facing overt Turkish and Iraqi pressure to join the Baghdad Pact, and involved in an intermittent border conflict with Israel, the Syrians had already received modest Soviet arms shipments in 1954. Diplomatic support from the Soviet Union helped Syria resist continued pressure from its neighbors in March 1955, and an especially fierce Israeli raid in December removed any lingering doubts about Syria's need for additional Soviet support.[36]

SUPERPOWER COMPETITION AND THE SINAI WAR

The Suez Crisis

The sudden entry of the Soviet Union into the Middle East arena triggered a series of U.S. responses. The United States initially sought to counter Soviet support for Egypt and Syria by offering to assist Egypt in its plans to construct the Aswan High Dam.[37] At the same time, however, the Soviet arms deal increased U.S. suspicions that Nasser had strong pro-Communist leanings. When Egypt insisted on more favorable terms for financing the dam by threatening to accept Soviet aid, and

35. On the arms deal, see Mohamed Heikal, *The Sphinx and the Commissar* (New York, 1976), pp. 56–63; Hoopes, *Devil and John Foster Dulles*, pp. 323–38; and Stephens, *Nasser*, pp. 157–61. For an alternative interpretation, see Uri Ra'anan, *The USSR Arms the Third World: Case Studies in Soviet Foreign Policy* (Cambridge, Mass., 1969). Michael Brecher summarizes and evaluates the various accounts in *Decisions in Israel's Foreign Policy*, pp. 257–58, note 1. On the effects of the arms deal on Nasser's stature, see Bernard Lewis, *The Middle East and the West* (New York, 1964), p. 132.

36. The Soviets threatened to provide direct military assistance to Syria in March 1955, during Turkish and Iraqi maneuvers on the Syrian border. The Israeli raid in December was probably intended to discredit the emerging Arab alliance network and to deter Jordan from joining it. On these events, see Seale, *Struggle for Syria*, pp. 219–20, 233–34; Roi, *From Encroachment to Involvement*, p. 136; N. Bar-Ya'acov, *The Israel-Syrian Armistice: Problems of Implementation, 1949–1966* (Jerusalem, 1967), pp. 219–26; Wynfred Joshua and Stephen Gibert, *Arms for the Third World* (Baltimore, Md., 1969), pp. 11–13; and Stockholm International Peace Research Institute (SIPRI), *The Arms Trade with the Third World* (New York, 1971), pp. 546–47.

37. See Herbert Finer, *Dulles over Suez: The Theory and Practice of His Diplomacy* (Chicago, 1964), pp. 36–37; Hoopes, *Devil and John Foster Dulles*, pp. 330–31; Meyer, *Egypt and the United States*, pp. 123–26, 130–36; Stookey, *America and the Arab States*, pp. 130–40; and William J. Burns, *Economic Aid and American Policy toward Egypt, 1955–1981* (Albany, N.Y., 1985), pp. 36–39, 45–46. For a description of the dam's importance to Egypt, see Childers, *Road to Suez*, pp. 151–55.

when Nasser formally recognized Communist China in May 1956, Secretary of State Dulles decided to withdraw the U.S. offer.[38] It was a fateful step. Nasser responded by nationalizing the Suez Canal in July, and he announced that Egypt would use toll revenues from the canal to finance the dam.[39]

This bold move increased Nasser's prestige even more, but it also brought his principal adversaries together against him. The French were already hostile, blaming Egypt for the continued rebellion in Algeria.[40] The British were incensed by Nasser's opposition to the Baghdad Pact and his propaganda attacks against Jordan. Nationalization of the canal was the last straw for both. Although Egypt offered full compensation for the Suez Canal Company shareholders, the image of Nasser as an Arab Hitler was now firmly planted in the minds of the French and British leaders. They began to plan military operations to retake the canal and to bring about Nasser's downfall.[41]

The Sinai War

Israel joined the Anglo-French coalition in August 1956. The events of the past two years—Britain's withdrawal from Suez, the expanded Arab blockade, the rising level of fedayeen activity, the Soviet-Egyptian arms deal, and the tripartite alliance of Egypt, Syria, and Saudi Arabia—had already led the Israelis to begin planning for offensive action on their own.[42] The canal crisis provided a golden opportunity. Arms shipments

38. The decision to withdraw the offer was based on Nasser's continued relationship with the Soviet Union, his reluctance to make major concessions on the Palestine issue in exchange for Western assistance, and his decision to recognize Red China. Dulles apparently believed that the Soviet Union would be unable to complete the dam. This failure, he thought, would undermine Soviet standing in the Arab world and teach Nasser not to play the two superpowers off against each other. See Burns, *Economic Aid and American Policy*, chap. 3; Hoopes, *Devil and John Foster Dulles*, pp. 336–42; Childers, *Road to Suez*, pp. 149–50, 152–55, 163–70; Love, *Suez*, chap. 10, especially pp. 337–58; and Meyer, *Egypt and the United States*, pp. 138–46. For testimony that Nasser would have preferred Western aid, see Heikal, *Cairo Documents*, pp. 58–59.

39. Stephens, *Nasser*, pp. 192–97; and Heikal, *Cairo Documents*, pp. 66–69.

40. As a former French governor general of Algeria put it, Nasser was "the head of the octopus whose tentacles are strangling French North Africa." Quoted in Love, *Suez*, p. 129. The Soviet arms deal greatly increased French fears, as the deal would enable Egypt to give greater aid to the Algerian rebels. See also Childers, *Road to Suez*, pp. 171–75; Safran, *From War to War*, pp. 50–51; and Brecher, *Decisions in Israel's Foreign Policy*, pp. 262–64.

41. See Donald Neff, *Warriors at Suez* (New York, 1981), pp. 182, 275–77; Hugh Thomas, *Suez* (New York, 1966), pp. 20, 36–37, 48, 52, 57, 63, 70, 163. For a critique of the Hitler image, see Childers, *Road to Suez*, pp. 199–204.

42. See Moshe Dayan, *Diary of the Sinai Campaign* (New York, 1966), chap. 1; Brecher, *Decisions in Israel's Foreign Policy*, pp. 229–31, 258–59; and Avi Shlaim, "Conflicting Approaches to Israel's Relations with the Arabs: Ben-Gurion and Sharett, 1953–56," *MEJ*, 37, no. 2 (1983).

from France increased Israel's capabilities further, the French agreed to provide air cover for Israel's cities, and an Israeli invasion of Sinai (aimed at seizing the Straits of Tiran and lifting the Egyptian blockade in the Gulf of Aqaba) would provide a pretext justifying Anglo-French intervention "to protect the canal."[43] The final plans were approved on October 25, and the attack commenced on the 29th.

Although it succeeded militarily, the attack on Egypt failed to achieve its main objectives. Nasser did not fall, as Egypt's attackers had hoped. Syria supported its ally by cutting the oil pipeline from Iraq, which helped trigger a severe oil shortage in Britain and France. Most important of all, the United States quickly brought strong diplomatic and economic pressure to bear against the belligerents. Despite his concerns about Nasser, President Eisenhower remained convinced that using military force would only undermine the Western position further.[44] Moreover, he was angered by British, French, and Israeli duplicity in staging the attack. Britain and France left the Canal Zone in December, largely in response to U.S. pressure. After much haggling, Israel withdrew from Sinai and Gaza in March 1957. Although Israel had failed to topple Nasser, acquire additional territory, or force a formal peace settlement, it did obtain a U.S. pledge to guarantee free passage to Israeli ships through the Straits of Tiran. The Sinai campaign also fostered an image of Israeli military superiority that would encourage moderate Arab behavior for the next ten years.[45]

Aftermath

The Suez affair was a watershed in several respects. The Soviet Union quickly swung to Egypt's side; Soviet propaganda supported Egypt through the crisis, and Soviet Premier Bulganin sent threatening notes to Great Britain and France as a further display of support for Egypt.

43. For accounts of the Anglo-French-Israeli agreement to attack Egypt, see Brecher, *Decisions in Israel's Foreign Policy*, pp. 247–48, 268–74; Stock, *Israel on the Road to Sinai*, pp. 201–3; Crosbie, *Tacit Alliance*, p. 73; Thomas, *Suez*, pp. 86–88, 112–14; Childers, *Road to Suez*, pp. 174–75, 227–30, 233–43; Love, *Suez*, pp. 433–34, 450–51, 459–73; and Neff, *Warriors at Suez*, pp. 295–96, 309–10, 323–26, 342–48.

44. On this point, see Dwight D. Eisenhower, *The White House Years, 1956–61: Waging Peace* (Garden City, N.Y., 1965), pp. 36–40 and passim, especially apps. C and D.

45. For a description of the economic and political pressures that led to British and French withdrawal, see Thomas, *Suez*, pp. 130, 146–49; and Richard Neustadt, *Alliance Politics* (New York, 1970), chap. 2, especially pp. 24–29. On the impact of the petroleum cutoff, see Love, *Suez*, p. 651. Syria reportedly offered to attack Israel during the war, but as Egyptian troops were already evacuating the Sinai, Nasser told Syria to refrain. See Seale, *Struggle for Syria*, p. 262. On the Israeli withdrawal and the U.S. pledge, see Brecher, *Decisions in Israel's Foreign Policy*, pp. 297–98; Eisenhower, *Waging Peace*, pp. 183–89; and Neff, *Warriors at Suez*, pp. 365–66, 415–16.

Soviet aid increased after the war; Egypt reportedly received $150 million worth of Soviet arms in 1957–1958, including seven hundred MIG-17s, additional artillery, and several naval vessels.[46]

Soviet ties with Syria expanded as well; a new arms package was signed in December 1956, Soviet Foreign Minister Shepilov and Syrian President Quwatli exchanged visits in June and October, and a host of cultural and economic contacts were underway. This growing alliance between Moscow and Damascus was due partly to broad ideological compatibility. More important than that, however, was the fact that Syria faced considerable overt and covert pressure from Turkey, Iraq, Great Britain, and the United States, all of whom still hoped to pressure Syria into joining the Baghdad Pact.[47]

Finally, Nasser's successful defiance of Britain and France sent his prestige soaring, with far-reaching effects on inter-Arab relations. As noted, Jordan had been facing continued pressure to renounce the Anglo-Jordanian treaty and the British subsidy. Before Suez, Hussein had tried to preserve his independence by straddling the fence; he had therefore signed a series of defense agreements with Saudi Arabia, Lebanon, Egypt, *and* Iraq in May 1956. In September he at last agreed to enter a military agreement with Egypt and Syria. At the same time, however, he also sought to preserve Jordan's ties with Iraq.[48]

The Suez crisis and the Sinai war made accommodation with Egypt a

46. The Soviets threatened to send volunteers to aid Egypt, and Bulganin's letter made oblique references to nuclear weapons. The Soviets were careful in showing their support, however; their threats were delivered after the U.S. position was clear and movement toward a ceasefire had begun. They also evacuated a number of Soviet aircraft and personnel from Egypt during the fighting. On these points, see Roi, *From Encroachment to Involvement*, pp. 184–85, 189–91; Jon Glassman, *Arms for the Arabs: The Soviet Union and War in the Middle East* (Baltimore, Md., 1975), pp. 16–20; Peter Mangold, *Superpower Intervention in the Middle East* (New York, 1978), p. 116; Oles M. Smolansky, *The Soviet Union and the Arab East under Khrushchev* (Lewisburg, Pa., 1974), pp. 45–51; Heikal, *Sphinx and Commissar*, pp. 70–71; and Heikal, *Cairo Documents*, p. 133. On Soviet aid to Egypt after Suez, see Glassman, *Arms for the Arabs*, p. 23; George Lenczowski, *Soviet Advances in the Middle East* (Washington, D.C., 1971), p. 247; and SIPRI, *Arms Trade with the Third World*, pp. 547, 522.

47. See Seale, *Struggle for Syria*, pp. 255–57 and chap. 20; Charles McLane, *Soviet-Middle East Relations* (London, 1973), pp. 90–94; Joshua and Gibert, *Arms for the Third World*; Lenczowski, *Middle East in World Affairs*, pp. 342–43; and Wilbur Crane Eveland, *Ropes of Sand: America's Failure in the Middle East* (New York, 1980), pp. 169–70, 180, 196–97, and chaps. 19 and 23.

48. Hussein signed an agreement for economic unity with Syria in August, held talks with an Iraqi military delegation in September, and sent his foreign minister to Iraq in early October. On these various measures, see "Chronology," *MEJ*, 10, no. 3 (1956): 80–81; and 11, no. 3 (1957): 289; Love, *Suez*, pp. 448–50; Lenczowski, *Middle East in World Affairs*, p. 287; Vatikiotis, *Politics and the Military in Jordan*, pp. 124–25; Abidi, *Jordan*, chap. 6, especially pp. 137–45; and Sinai and Pollock, *Hashemite Kingdom of Jordan*, p. 150. In general, Hussein's policy prior to the Suez war was to express his firm support for Arab solidarity while avoiding definitive commitments to any particular group.

matter of necessity for Hussein. When new elections on October 21 brought a group of pro-Nasser politicians into the cabinet, Jordan moved steadily toward alliance with Egypt, Syria, and Saudi Arabia. Hussein signed a defense treaty with Egypt and Syria on October 24; he broke relations with France and offered Nasser his support during the war; the Jordanian parliament voted to abrogate the existing defense treaty with Britain in November; and the new prime minister, Suleiman Nabulsi, began negotiating with the other Arab states for a replacement of the British subsidy. At a summit meeting in Cairo on January 19, 1957, Jordan agreed to sign the Arab Solidarity Pact, thereby joining Syria and Saudi Arabia in Egypt's alliance network.[49]

In the words of one scholar, this was "Nasser's high tide."[50] Iraq's bid for leadership had been thwarted, Western influence had been reduced, and both Egypt and Syria had broken the Western monopoly on military and economic aid by opening ties with the Soviet Union. Israel's victory in the Sinai had been neutralized as well. Most important of all, Nasser had succeeded in bringing Syria, Jordan, Saudi Arabia, and Yemen into formal alignment with Egypt, greatly enhancing Egypt's stature in the region and the world.

Nasser's success is revealing. His ability to defy Western pressure was a direct result of the superpower competition: the more the superpowers sought to balance one another, the greater Egypt's freedom of action became. Nasser's ability to marshal opposition to the Baghdad Pact reflected a similar dynamic; because Syria and Saudi Arabia feared Iraqi ambitions (and because Western influence was increasingly unpopular), they chose to forego the Baghdad Pact in favor of an all-Arab alliance with Egypt. Finally, Nasser successfully exploited these nationalist beliefs in order to intimidate more vulnerable states, such as Jordan, into acknowledging his leadership. Thus Nasser's high tide reflected his own tactical skill, considerable luck, and a set of favorable international circumstances.

Unfortunately for Nasser, this dominant position quickly eroded. The reason is simple; Nasser's initial success removed several of the advantages he had previously enjoyed. Support from the Soviet Union increased the U.S. interest in containing him more effectively, and his

49. Syrian and Saudi Arabian troops were dispatched to Jordan during the Suez war. Iraq also sent a contingent of troops, but it was quickly withdrawn at the request of the Jordanian cabinet, indicating that the new government was already leaning toward Egypt and its other allies. In exchange for signing the Arab Solidarity Pact, Jordan received a pledge from the other members that they would replace the British subsidy, which paid 12.5 million Egyptian pounds annually. On these points, see Lenczowski, *Middle East in World Affairs*, pp. 483–85; and Abidi, *Jordan*, pp. 145–51.

50. Adeed Dawisha, *Egypt in the Arab World* (London, 1976), p. 16.

dominant regional position now made him a greater threat than Iraq to his neighbors.

THE EISENHOWER DOCTRINE AND REGIONAL REALIGNMENT

The reaction against Egypt's ascendancy was encouraged by the United States. Although U.S. opposition to the Anglo-French invasion brought a brief improvement in relations with Egypt, the United States still sought to counter what it saw as a growing Soviet role in January 1957. Arguing that "the existing vacuum in the Middle East must be filled by the U.S. before it is filled by Russia," President Eisenhower obtained a congressional resolution authorizing him "to use armed force to assist any nation or group of such nations requesting assistance . . . against any nations controlled by international communism." At the same time, the Eisenhower Doctrine authorized $200 million in economic and military assistance to help friendly states in the Middle East increase their security and welfare.[51]

The Eisenhower Doctrine revealed both the administration's preoccupation with the Soviet Union and its lingering concern over Nasser's aims and sympathies. Although U.S. policy-makers were aware of Nasser's hostility to Communism in Egypt itself, the new initiative reflected the overriding concern that the Soviet Union might exploit the decline in British and French influence to "seize the oil, to cut the Canal and pipelines, and thus seriously weaken Western civilization."[52] An image of Egypt and Syria as Soviet satellites was growing, and U.S. policy now focused on limiting the influence of these two regimes.[53]

Reaction to the Eisenhower Doctrine was mixed. Predictably, both Nasser and the Soviet Union denounced it as a revival of imperialism. Just as predictably, the Baghdad Pact states expressed their approval, as

---

51. See Eisenhower, *Waging Peace*, p. 178 and passim; and Alexander L. George and Richard Smoke, *Deterrence in American Foreign Policy: Theory and Practice* (New York, 1974), p. 313, especially note 8. For a brief critique of the doctrine, see Brown, *International Politics and the Middle East*, pp. 176–79.

52. See Eisenhower, *Waging Peace*, p. 178. Secretary of State Dulles remarked that "the leaders of International Communism will take every risk that they dare in order to win the Middle East." Quoted in Seale, *Struggle for Syria*, p. 285. See also George and Smoke, *Deterrence in American Foreign Policy*, pp. 313–16.

53. Among other things, the United States declined to send emergency food and medical supplies to Egypt after the Suez war and refused to unfreeze the Egyptian assets it had seized after nationalization of the canal. The Soviet Union eventually sent the desired supplies. See Stookey, *America and the Arab States*, p. 148; Burns, *Economic Aid and American Policy*, pp. 108–11; and George and Smoke, *Deterrence in American Foreign Policy*, pp. 317–18.

did the pro-Western government of Lebanon. A presidential emissary, James Richards, succeeded in giving away roughly $120 million in aid during a goodwill tour of the region in March 1957, but there was no immediate stampede to enlist in Washington's anti-Communist crusade.[54]

The Kings' Alliance

The doctrine's greatest impact, however, was on Nasser's reluctant allies in Saudi Arabia and Jordan. Hussein's alliance with Egypt was largely a response to Egyptian threats, and the Saudi monarchy now saw Nasser's growing influence and aggressive tactics as a source of considerable danger. Indeed, Egypt was implicated in plots against both monarchies early in 1957. With Egypt presenting a more imminent threat and with the United States offering increased great power support, realignment against Nasser was in order.[55]

The first step came with King Saud's visit to the United States in February. Seeking to use Saud "as a counterweight to Nasser," Eisenhower held extensive discussions with the Saudi king.[56] The results were encouraging; Saud renewed the U.S. lease on Dhahran airfield and made a vague statement of support for the Eisenhower Doctrine. Even more important, a secret meeting between Saud and Iraqi crown prince Abdul Illah began a rapprochement between the two dynasties. Additional military training programs were implemented later that year, and a U.S. jet training squadron made a goodwill visit to Saudi Arabia in May.[57]

Jordan was next to abandon Egypt. Hussein had agreed to join the Egyptian alliance network in January 1957, and Jordan's pro-Egyptian

54. On Richards's trip, see William C. Polk, *The Arab World* (Cambridge, Mass., 1981), p. 331; and Charles D. Cremeans, *The Arabs and the World: Nasser's Arab Nationalist Policy* (New York, 1963), pp. 157–58.

55. Eisenhower was obviously aware of conservative Arab suspicions of Nasser, as letters written to British prime minister Anthony Eden during the Suez crisis reveal. As Eisenhower wrote on September 2, 1956: "We have friends in the Middle East who tell us they would like to see Nasser's deflation brought about. . . . But [they feel] that the Suez is not the issue on which to attempt to do this by force. Under those circumstances, because of the temper of their populations, they say they would have to support Nasser even against their better judgement." And on September 8: "Unless it can be shown to the world that he is an actual aggressor, then I think all Arabs would be forced to support him, even though some of the ruling monarchs might very much like to see him toppled." See Eisenhower, *Waging Peace*, pp. 667, 669. On the plots against Jordan and Saudi Arabia, see Tawfiq Y. Hasou, *The Struggle for the Arab World* (London, 1985), p. 61.

56. See Eisenhower, *Waging Peace*, pp. 115–16 and passim.

57. See Holden and Johns, *House of Saud*, pp. 192–95; "Chronology," *MEJ*, 11, no. 3 (1957): 304; and Safran, *Saudi Arabia*, pp. 82–84. Safran calls the meeting between Saud and Abdul "of substantial consequence."

cabinet moved to recognize Communist China in March. King and cabinet were clearly divided by this time; when Hussein indicated his interest in U.S. assistance "if offered without political strings," the opposition responded with a petition of protest. The showdown came in April; Hussein dismissed Prime Minister Nabulsi and declared that Jordan was threatened by "international communism." The United States sent a $10 million aid package and a variety of military equipment, and King Saud ordered a contingent of Saudi troops in Jordan to obey Hussein's commands in the contest with his domestic opposition. Iraq massed troops on the border to deter Syrian intervention, and the Syrian forces stationed in Jordan since the Suez war were ordered to leave.[58]

The conservative alliance against Egypt was completed by an agreement between the Hashemite kingdoms of Jordan and Iraq. A June 1957 summit between Feisal of Iraq and Hussein led to a mutual defense pact between the two Hashemite kingdoms and was followed by an exchange of visits between Feisal and King Saud. The Kings' Alliance now brought the three Arab monarchies into a tacit alignment against Egypt, with the active support of the United States.[59]

Egypt's first bid for dominance of the Arab world—however improvised it was—had been thwarted. Although Nasser's use of Arab nationalist propaganda and his exploitation of the East-West rivalry had won Egypt some noteworthy diplomatic victories, his successes after 1955 had alarmed both his early supporters (e.g., Saudi Arabia) and his more reluctant partners (e.g., Jordan). Once alternative arrangements (which the Eisenhower Doctrine provided) were available, even such traditional rivals as Iraq and Saudi Arabia found alignment against Nasser a more prudent policy.

These developments left the Middle East sharply polarized. The Soviet Union continued to support Syria and Egypt and condemned the Eisenhower Doctrine as "a policy of creating closed aggressive military blocs."[60] Egypt and Syria, in turn, saw the new U.S. initiative as a threat to their own freedom of action. In the eyes of the Arab nationalists, the

---

58. The United States also ordered the Sixth Fleet to move closer to Jordan and was apparently prepared to intervene militarily in support of Hussein. On these events, see Abidi, *Jordan*, pp. 152–67; George and Smoke, *Deterrence in American Foreign Policy*, pp. 330–31; Seale, *Struggle for Syria*, pp. 289–90; Lenczowski, *Middle East in World Affairs*, p. 487; and John C. Campbell, *Defense of the Middle East: Problems of American Policy* (New York, 1963), pp. 127–29.

59. See Holden and Johns, *House of Saud*, pp. 194–95; and Lenczowski, *Middle East in World Affairs*, p. 288.

60. See Roi, *From Encroachment to Involvement*, pp. 212, 226, and passim. Egypt and Syria received small Soviet military training missions at this time, and both countries roundly condemned the Kings' Alliance. See Glassman, *Arms for the Arabs*, p. 23; Lenczowski, *Soviet Advances in the Middle East*, p. 144; and SIPRI, *Arms Trade with the Third World*, pp. 547, 522.

United States was now seeking to replace Britain and France as imperialist overseer of the Middle East. Continued alignment with the Soviet bloc was their predictable response.[61]

The Syrian Crisis

These developments were reinforced by a sudden crisis in Syria. In the summer of 1957, the Eisenhower administration became convinced that Syria was "going Communist." This belief was based on Syria's growing ties with the Soviet Union, the presence of allegedly pro-Soviet figures within the Syrian cabinet, and Syria's expulsion of three U.S. diplomats in August. Ignored amid the alarm was the fact that these developments were partly the result of Iraq's continued efforts to subvert the Syrian regime, a campaign that enjoyed both British and U.S. support.[62]

At this point, the United States pressed Iraq, Turkey, and Jordan to mobilize their armed forces on the Syrian border. But far from causing the Syrian government to collapse or concede, these threats merely gave the Soviet Union another opportunity to come to Syria's side.[63] Iraq, Turkey, and Jordan backed away at this point, and King Saud began a successful effort to mediate the largely artificial crisis.[64] Viewing Saud's intervention as a threat to his own influence in Syria, Nasser countered by dispatching Egyptian troops to "defend" Egypt's principal Arab ally. This effort made Saud's mediation seem timid by comparison. Along with the rapidly growing contacts between the Egyptian and Syrian armies, Egypt's symbolic defense of Syria helped preserve Nasser's pop-

61. See Stookey, *America and the Arab States*, pp. 148–51; Stephens, *Nasser*, pp. 257–58.
62. U.S. officials had approved plans for a covert plot to overthrow the leftist government of Syria in 1956. For accounts of the Syrian crisis, see George and Smoke, *Deterrence in American Foreign Policy*, pp. 332–33; Seale, *Struggle for Syria*, pp. 291–96; Karen Dawisha, *Soviet Foreign Policy toward Egypt* (New York, 1979), pp. 16–17, especially note 28; Laqueur, *The Soviet Union and the Middle East*, pp. 250–54; Smolansky, *Soviet Union and Arab East*, pp. 65–66; and Eveland, *Ropes of Sand*. Eisenhower's own account is especially revealing regarding U.S. perceptions. See *Waging Peace*, pp. 196–203.
63. Soviet premier Bulganin and foreign minister Gromyko made public statements supporting Syria, and two Soviet warships visited the Syrian port of Latakia as a signal of the Soviet commitment. See Seale, *Struggle for Syria*, p. 303; Smolansky, *Soviet Union and Arab East*, pp. 68–69; and James M. McConnell, "Doctrine and Capabilities," in *Soviet Naval Diplomacy*, ed. Bradford Dismukes and James M. McConnell (New York, 1979), pp. 7–8.
64. After talks with Syrian leaders in Damascus, Saud and Iraqi premier 'Ali Jawdat al-Ayubi announced "complete understanding" with Syrian president Quwatli. King Hussein declared that he had "no intention" of intervening in Syria, and Saud sought to reassure the United States about the lack of Communist influence in Syria. See Seale, *Struggle for Syria*, p. 303; and George and Smoke, *Deterrence in American Foreign Policy*, pp. 335–36.

Table 1. Middle East alliances, 1955-1957

Alliance	Interpretation
Baghdad Pact (1955-1958)	Iraq allies with Britain and United States to balance Soviet Union and Egypt, United States and Britain seek to contain Soviet expansion in the Middle East.
Arab Solidarity Pact (1955-1956)	Egypt allies with Syria and Saudi Arabia against the Baghdad Pact, Yemen joins to pressure Britain over Aden, Jordan to appease Nasser. Some bandwagoning by Saudi Arabia and Yemen too.
Soviet Union-Egypt (1955-1974)	Egypt seeks great power ally to counter Baghdad Pact and Israel, Soviet Union to counter Baghdad Pact and United States. Alliance expands greatly during 1960s.
Soviet Union-Syria (1955-1958)	Syria seeks support against Iraq, Turkey, and Israel. Soviet Union seeks to counter Baghdad Pact and United States. Some ideological affinity as well.
Soviet Union-Yemen (1955-1961)	Imam seeks aid against Britain over Aden, Soviet Union supports Yemen to weaken British influence.
Suez War Coalition (1956)	Britain, France, and Israel ally to defeat or depose Nasser in Egypt.
Kings' Alliance (1957-1958)	Arab monarchies of Iraq, Jordan, and Saudi Arabia ally against threat from Nasser.
United States-Saudi Arabia (1957-present) United States-Jordan (1957-present) United States-Lebanon (1957-1958)	Eisenhower Doctrine encourages pro-Western Arab states to balance against the threat from Egypt and Soviet Union.

ularity and prestige there.[65] Egypt and Syria were closer than ever, and closer to Moscow, and the disparities between Washington's Cold War images and the other actors' largely regional concerns had been clearly revealed.

The first round of Middle East alliances is summarized in Table 1.

The United Arab Republic: A Second Bid for Hegemony?

Given the U.S. fear that Nasser was a tool of Soviet influence, it is ironic that Egypt's next bid for regional dominance was caused in part

65. Seale, *Struggle for Syria*, pp. 305–6; and Heikal, *Sphinx and Commissar*, p. 77.

by Nasser's own opposition to Communism. This phase began with the first serious attempt to implement the cherished dream of Arab unity. In the aftermath of the Syrian crisis, the Syrian government split between rival Ba'th and Communist factions. Fearing a possible Communist take-over, Ba'thist officers in the Syrian army requested mediation by the head of the Syrian-Egyptian joint military command, General Abdel Hakim Amer, and a Syrian military delegation flew to Cairo in January 1958 to persuade Nasser to lead a union of Syria and Egypt. Nasser reluctantly agreed, but he insisted on being given sole control over both countries. Although union with Syria was not his idea, he was prepared to use it to serve his own ends.[66]

The United Arab Republic and the Iraqi Revolution

The formation of the United Arab Republic (UAR) "was greeted with almost universal enthusiasm by public opinion throughout the Arab world."[67] The other Arab states responded quickly. Yemen joined the UAR in March, (although its inclusion was a largely cosmetic gesture).[68] Jordan and Iraq formed their own Federal Union in February, designed to counter Nasser while appearing equally supportive of pan-Arab senti-ment. The defensive motives that inspired the Federal Union were re-vealed by Hussein's comment that "Jordan has found someone to pro-tect her" and by the Iraqi foreign minister's accusation that the UAR "was an artificial creation based on propaganda and personal interests."[69] King Saud made an even more drastic attempt to sabotage the UAR by offering a bribe to the head of Syrian military intelligence to assassinate Nasser. The Syrian official exposed the offer immediately, and this debacle soon forced Saudi Arabia to shift to a pro-Egyptian policy.[70]

Conservative opposition to the UAR proved short-lived, enhancing Nasser's prestige and influence even more. On July 14, 1958, a group of

66. Nasser's decision to accept the Syrian offer was based on (1) his own opposition to Communism, (2) his awareness that Syria's internal problems reduced Syria's reliability as an ally, and (3) his recognition that this acceptance would enhance his pan-Arab creden-tials still further. For accounts of the decision to unify the two countries, see Seale, *Struggle for Syria*, chap. 22, especially pp. 317–22; Torrey, *Syrian Politics and the Military*, pp. 374–81; Malcolm Kerr, *The Arab Cold War: Gamal 'Abdel Nasser and His Rivals* (London, 1971), pp. 7–12; Heikal, *Sphinx and Commissar*, pp. 86–87; and Dawisha, *Egypt in the Arab World*, pp. 19–20.

67. Dawisha, *Egypt in the Arab World*, p. 21.

68. See Wenner, *Modern Yemen*, pp. 185–86, especially note 29; and Rahmy, *Egyptian Policy in the Arab World*, pp. 59–61.

69. Quoted in "Chronology," *MEJ*, 12, no. 2 (1958): 180; and Dawisha, *Egypt in the Arab World*, p. 21.

70. See Holden and Johns, *House of Saud*, p. 208; Eveland, *Ropes of Sand*, p. 273; Ste-phens, *Nasser*, pp. 261–62; and Safran, *Saudi Arabia*, pp. 85–86.

Iraqi army officers overthrew the monarchy and declared a republic based on the model of the "Egyptian revolution."[71] Nasser endorsed the revolution and offered military aid, and one of the leaders of the coup, Colonel Abdel Salam Aref, signed an agreement for military, economic, and cultural cooperation between Egypt and Iraq. Jordan's protector had vanished overnight, and Nasser had apparently gained another ally.[72]

Saudi Arabia moved quickly to appease Egypt. After his plot to kill Nasser was exposed, King Saud was replaced by Crown Prince Feisal (although Saud remained the titular head of the royal family). Feisal announced first that Saudi Arabia would remain neutral in the contest between the UAR and the Iraqi-Jordanian Federal Union, and the Nasserist slogan of "positive neutrality" reappeared in Saudi public statements. To demonstrate their independence from the United States, the Saudis refused to permit U.S. flights to Jordan during the tensions that followed the Iraqi revolution, and they repeated their claim that the Dhahran airfield was not a U.S. base. Nasser and Feisal proclaimed their "complete agreement and reaffirmation of friendship and brotherhood" at a summit meeting in August 1958, and the Saudi deputy foreign minister described the two countries as "allies whose policy is first to promote Arab interests."[73]

Jordan, by contrast, continued to rely primarily on its Western allies, Having overcome his internal opponents the year before, Hussein was most concerned about external threats after the coup in Iraq. At this time, the United States began petroleum shipments to Jordan (whose supplies had been cut off by the new regime in Baghdad) and the British sent a contingent of paratroopers to Jordan.[74] Jordan and Egypt would remain bitterly opposed for most of the next decade, notwithstanding several tactical shifts.

71. The new regime withdrew from the union with Jordan and proclaimed a policy of neutralism in accordance with the principles of the Bandung Conference. Inspired by Nasser's example, the leaders of the coup had sought his advice some months before the actual revolt. According to Heikal, Nasser had rebuffed their overtures, claiming that a coup that required external support would not succeed in any case. After the coup, Nasser did request that the Soviets stage a military demonstration near the border to deter Western intervention, a request that the Soviets complied with reluctantly. See Heikal, *Cairo Documents*, pp. 132–35.

72. See Majid Khadduri, *Republican Iraq* (London, 1969), chap. 3; and Lenczowski, *The Middle East in World Affairs*, pp. 289–90. For a detailed description of the Free Officers' Movement in Iraq, see Batatu, *Old Social Classes and Revolutionary Movements*, chap. 41, especially pp. 766–67, 776, 795–802.

73. On the transfer of power to Feisal and his policy of appeasement, see Safran, *Saudi Arabia*, pp. 87–90. See also Holden and Johns, *House of Saud*, p. 204; and "Chronology," *MEJ*, 12, no. 4 (1958): 443.

74. Mangold, *Superpower Intervention in the Middle East*, pp. 106–7; Hussein, *Uneasy Lies the Head*, pp. 201–3; and "Chronology," *MEJ*, 12, no. 4 (1958): 430–31.

The Lebanese Crisis

Although the effort to contain Nasser by supporting his regional opponents had been initially successful, the main instruments of this policy—the Baghdad Pact and the Kings' Alliance—were shattered by the Iraqi revolution. As a result, the fear that Western interests were at risk once again grew in Washington.[75]

The immediate result was the forceful U.S. response to the Lebanese crisis. In 1957, Lebanese president Camille Chamoun had been the first Arab leader to endorse the Eisenhower Doctrine. Not only did this endorsement violate the neutralist premises that underlay the delicate political balance within Lebanon, but Chamoun's illegal efforts to secure his own reelection undermined his domestic support even further.[76] By May 1958, the situation had deteriorated to a full-scale civil war, with Chamoun accusing the UAR of interference. As the struggle continued through July, Eisenhower became convinced that "Communists were principally responsible for the trouble. . . . [T]he time had come to act."[77] Eisenhower ordered U.S. marines to intervene on July 15, a U.S. envoy arranged for Chamoun's replacement, and order was restored by late 1958. Lebanon returned to its previous policy of neutrality, and the alleged Nasserist threat to Lebanon seemed to have been thwarted.

Arab Factionalism Resurgent

Such fears, in any case, were almost certainly exaggerated. Nasser's ascendance at the end of 1958 proved just as evanescent as his earlier ascendance following the Suez crisis. Once again, the main challenge came from Iraq, where the new revolutionary regime quickly split over the issue of relations with Egypt. A rift between Abdel Salam Aref and Abdel Karim Qassem (the leading figures in the Revolutionary Com-

---

75. In his memoirs, Eisenhower reports his feeling that "this sombre turn of events could . . . result in the complete elimination of Western influence in the Middle East." See Eisenhower, *Waging Peace*, p. 269. Dulles believed that if the Iraqi coup were Communist-inspired, it would mean the Soviets had "leapfrogged the Northern Tier." He also believed that a Nasserist coup would be just as bad; it would mean that the pro-Western countries (Lebanon, Jordan, and Israel) "were now completely surrounded." See George and Smoke, *Deterrence in American Foreign Policy*, pp. 338–39. The following year CIA director Allen Dulles stated that the situation in Iraq was "the most dangerous in the world today." Quoted in "Chronology," *MEJ*, 13, no. 3 (1959): 292.

76. Lebanon's National Covenant established that the leadership of Lebanon would be divided between the Christian and Moslem populations. It also stated that Lebanon would remain neutral and that neither confessional group would seek external support for its faction. For details, see Hudson, *Precarious Republic*, pp. 44–45; and Fahim I. Qubain, *Crisis in Lebanon* (Washington, D.C., 1961), pp. 17–18. For other accounts of the Lebanese crisis, see George and Smoke, *Deterrence in American Foreign Policy*, pp. 338–55; and Barnet, *Intervention and Revolution*, chap. 7.

77. Eisenhower, *Waging Peace*, pp. 266, 270.

mand Council) led first to Aref's arrest, then to his exile, and finally to a rapidly escalating quarrel with Egypt.[78] In particular, Qassem challenged Nasser's claim to leadership in the Arab world and emphasized independent Iraqi sovereignty rather than formal Arab unity. Egyptian support for an abortive coup against Qassem merely made matters worse, as did Qassem's reliance on Communist support at a time when the Syrian Communist Party was challenging Nasser's leadership in Syria.[79] As a result, "by the end of the year, relations between Iraq and the UAR were even worse than they had been in the days of the old regime."[80]

The emergence of the Egyptian-Iraqi rivalry created a serious problem for the Soviet Union. To begin with, the Soviets were hardly enthusiastic about the formation of the UAR. Although their relations with Egypt were not immediately affected—Nasser visited the Soviet Union for seventeen days in April 1958 and obtained a Soviet commitment to build the Aswan High Dam—Syria's union with Egypt eliminated the once-powerful Syrian Communist Party as a serious political force. Moreover, the Soviets remained ambivalent about the entire concept of Arab unity. From a Soviet perspective, the prospect of a unified Arab state on the Soviet southern border could be seen only as a threatening possibility.[81] Yet the Soviets faced an obvious dilemma: any efforts to oppose the union (or to question Nasser's policies) jeopardized the Soviet Union's prized relationship with Egypt.

In sharp contrast to the Soviet Union's lukewarm attitude toward the UAR, the Soviets greeted the Iraqi revolution with enthusiasm. For them, the collapse of the West's principal regional ally was a most welcome development. At Nasser's request, they staged military maneuvers in the Caucasus to discourage Western intervention, and an agreement for Soviet economic aid to Iraq was signed at the end of the year.[82]

78. On the rift between Aref and Qassem, see Khadduri, *Republican Iraq*, pp. 86–98; and Batatu, *Old Social Classes and Revolutionary Movements*, pp. 815–18 and passim.

79. See Batatu, *Old Social Classes and Revolutionary Movements*, chap. 43. Qassem relied on Communist support largely because his internal position was threatened by a combination of Ba'thist and Nasserist forces in Iraq.

80. See Kerr, *Arab Cold War*, pp. 17–18. Over the next two years, Egyptian-Iraqi enmity reached impressive levels even by Arab standards. Nasser labeled Qassem the "divider of Iraq" and accused him of "inferiority complexes." Iraqi officials, in turn, began referring to Nasser as "mangy," "the filthy one," "Gamal the Butcher," and so on. See Dawisha, *Egypt in the Arab World*, pp. 25–28, 178–79; *MER 1960*, p. 144; and "Chronology," *MEJ*, 14, no. 1 (1960): 70.

81. See Heikal, *Cairo Documents*, pp. 124–27; Roi, *From Encroachment to Involvement*, pp. 250–54; Dawisha, *Soviet Foreign Policy towards Egypt*, p. 19; Smolansky, *Soviet Union and Arab East*, pp. 79–80; and Walter Z. Laqueur, *The Struggle for the Middle East: The Soviet Union in the Mediterranean, 1958–1968* (New York, 1968), p. 84.

82. The Soviets went to some lengths to make clear to Nasser that these maneuvers were only symbolic. See Heikal, *Cairo Documents*, pp. 132–35. On the development of

And given the prominent place occupied by the Iraqi Communist Party after the revolution, a warm Soviet response was hardly surprising.

The rift between Nasser and Qassem thus presented the Soviets with the difficult challenge of trying to preserve good relations with both. When this effort proved impossible, the Soviets tilted toward Iraq, largely because of the greater role of the Communist party there. Communist influence in Iraq stood in sharp contrast to the situation in the UAR, where Nasser had rigidly suppressed the Egyptian and Syrian Communist parties. After an attempted Ba'thist uprising in March 1959, Soviet support for Iraq increased still further. Already the beneficiaries of a large arms deal in November 1958, Iraq received a $500 million loan at this time.[83]

Soviet relations with Egypt, by contrast, had soured. The issue was the role of Communism in the Middle East, and the dispute flared intermittently over the next several years. The rift began when Nasser learned of a Syrian Communist Party manifesto protesting the "lack of democratic freedoms" in the UAR. In his reply, Nasser accused the Arab Communists of "undermining Arab unity." Khrushchev termed Nasser's attacks on Arab Communists a "reactionary undertaking" and a "campaign against progressive forces." By March 1959, Nasser's views were termed "outright slander," and Khrushchev referred to Nasser as a "hotheaded young man." Nasser then denounced Arab Communists as "foreign agents" and "first-class opportunists" and declared them guilty of "atheism and dependence."[84]

In spite of these polemics, however, Soviet-Egyptian cooperation was not suspended. Construction of the Aswan Dam continued, along with several other Soviet-sponsored projects. Yet another arms deal (worth roughly $120 million) was delivered in 1959, and the Soviets reportedly helped build a number of airfields and naval facilities in Egypt at this time.[85] Thus important elements of Soviet-Egyptian cooperation remained intact.

This cooperation did not mean that all was well between Moscow and Cairo. Although the subsequent decline in Soviet relations with Iraq removed one important obstacle, Nasser's opposition to Communism still rankled his Soviet patrons. In May 1961 Khrushchev lectured a

Soviet ties to Iraq, see Roi, *From Encroachment to Involvement*, pp. 258–62; Smolansky, *Soviet Union and Arab East*, pp. 102–9; and Yodfat, *Arab Politics in the Soviet Mirror*, pp. 146–48.

83. See Smolansky, *Soviet Union and Arab East*, p. 121; Laqueur, *Struggle for the Middle East*, p. 96; and SIPRI, *Arms Trade with the Third World*, p. 556.

84. For these statements, see Roi, *From Encroachment to Involvement*, pp. 275–78; and McLane, *Soviet–Middle East Relations*, p. 30. For further discussion, see Batatu, *Old Social Classes and Revolutionary Movements*, pp. 861–65.

85. See Lenczowski, *Soviet Advances in the Middle East*, p. 146; Glassman, *Arms for the Arabs*, p. 24; and SIPRI, *Arms Trade with the Third World*, p. 523.

visiting Egyptian delegation on the follies of this policy, telling the group: "I feel that some of those present here are going to be communists in the future, because life imposes itself on man." After the delegation's return to Egypt, its leader, Anwar Sadat, published a lengthy reply to Khrushchev's remarks. Although basic strategic interests still united the two countries, this prolonged dispute reveals that the Soviet-Egyptian alliance was marred by serious ideological differences.[86]

Soviet hopes for Iraq, meanwhile, had proven to be illusory. Khrushchev had at one point claimed that Iraq was establishing a "more advanced system" than Egypt, and the Soviets had rapidly expanded their aid and trade commitments with Baghdad. Despite these gestures, however, Qassem began to move away from the Soviet Union in the latter half of 1959.[87] After using the Iraqi Communist Party to overcome his other domestic rivals, Qassem moved to curtail its activities as well, prompting repeated criticisms in the Soviet press.[88] Throughout 1960 Qassem emphasized his opposition to Communism and the purely instrumental nature of Iraqi relations with the Soviet Union, and his warnings about the dangers of Soviet influence in Iraq brought predictable condemnation from Moscow. Economic and military aid continued, however, and a complete break between the two countries was avoided.[89]

These developments encouraged the United States to abandon the policy of confrontation embodied by the Eisenhower Doctrine in favor of a more conciliatory approach. Support for King Hussein continued, based on the belief that Jordan was "firmly committed to the free world" and was "a keystone in the preservation of the existing equilibrium in the Middle East."[90] Relations with Saudi Arabia remained cordial, although the Saudi policy of appeasing Nasser led the Saudis to limit military cooperation with the United States to a very discreet level.[91]

---

86. For the text of Khrushchev's remarks and Sadat's reply, see Roi, *From Encroachment to Involvement*, pp. 337–44.

87. Khrushchev's statement is quoted in Dawisha, *Soviet Foreign Policy towards Egypt*, p. 23. See also Batatu, *Old Social Classes and Revolutionary Movements*, pp. 863–64.

88. See Smolansky, *Soviet Union and Arab East*, pp. 158–62.

89. During a visit by Soviet Deputy Premier Anastas Mikoyan in April 1960, Qassem complained about the quality of Soviet aid and announced to a crowd, "We are no communist country; . . . we are a free democracy." He assured another audience that "friendship with the Soviet Union was based on mutual benefit." When his attacks on Communism increased in 1961, Soviet commentators accused him of the "massive repression of genuine patriots" and claimed that "reactionaries were once more rampant" in Iraq. However, the Soviets continued work on various economic projects, and the leaders of both countries called for "further strengthening of Soviet-Iraqi ties" on the anniversary of the 1958 revolution. See *MER 1960*, p. 71; and Smolansky, *Soviet Union and Arab East*, pp. 167–75.

90. See *MER 1960*, p. 105. Jordan received a total of $235.2 million in economic and military assistance between 1958 and 1961. See AID, *U.S. Overseas Loans and Grants* (Washington, D.C., various years).

91. Preoccupied with internal matters during this period, the kingdom continued to

The principal change was an explicit opening to Nasser, beginning at the end of the Eisenhower administration and expanding further under President Kennedy. Now aware that Arab nationalism was largely hostile to Soviet Communism, the United States began to grant assistance more widely, "to provide these countries with an alternative to large-scale Communist aid."[92] After a two-year hiatus, the UAR received almost $250 million in economic assistance between 1958 and 1961. Kennedy continued these policies by increasing the aid totals and by appointing John S. Badeau, former president of the American University in Cairo, as ambassador to Egypt in 1961.[93] The result was a marked—but ultimately temporary—improvement in the U.S. position throughout the Arab world.

Another Setback for Nasser: The Collapse of the UAR

The momentum toward Arab unity produced by the formation of the UAR and the Iraqi revolution had been effectively dissipated by Qassem's emphasis on Iraqi interests over Arab unity. Although the Egyptian-Iraq split enabled Saudi Arabia to move away from Egypt slightly, Iraq was largely isolated during most of Qassem's rule. Given Qassem's often capricious rule and his own revolutionary aims, neither Nasser nor the conservative regimes in Jordan and Saudi Arabia saw Iraq as an especially desirable ally at this time. Indeed, Jordan and Saudi Arabia increasingly sought a neutral position between Egypt and Iraq, as it was simply unclear which posed the greater threat.[94]

---

receive modest levels of U.S. military assistance and training while the United States continued to use Dhahran airfield. See "Chronology," *MEJ*, 14, no. 4 (1960): 449. After the profligate rule of King Saud, Saudi Arabia faced a serious fiscal crisis, along with a continued struggle for power between Feisal and Saud. See Holden and Johns, *House of Saud*, pp. 199–202, 204–9; and Helen Lackner, *A House Built on Sand: A Political Economy of Saudi Arabia* (London, 1978), pp. 59–64.

92. *MER 1960*, p. 105.

93. AID, *Overseas Loans and Grants*; "Chronology," *MEJ*, 14, no. 2 (1960): 199. For a summary of Kennedy's policies, see John S. Badeau, *The American Approach to the Arab World* (New York, 1968); and Mordechai Gazit, *President Kennedy's Policy toward the Arab States and Israel* (Tel Aviv, 1983). See also Heikal, *Cairo Documents*, pp. 149–50 and chap. 6.

94. Saudi Arabia had adopted a largely pro-Egyptian position in 1958, whereas Hussein had maintained a delicate balancing act. In October 1958, however, Feisal declared that Saudi Arabia would now follow an "independent" policy of "neutrality and Arab nationalism." Saudi policy shifted frequently during this period, in part because of a continued struggle for power between Feisal and Saud. Jordan shifted between Baghdad and Cairo on several occasions, moving to favor one side or the other as the fortunes of each waxed and waned. Thus Qassem's rise led to a détente between Jordan and Egypt in August 1959, which ended when Egyptian agents assassinated the Jordanian foreign minister in 1960. Hussein then tilted toward Iraq and received a pledge from Qassem that

Iraq's isolation increased in the summer of 1961, when the Arab League acted with unusual unanimity to prevent an Iraqi invasion of Kuwait. Following Britain's declaration of Kuwait's independence in June, Qassem announced that Iraq intended to annex the sheikhdom. British troops quickly returned, the Arab League condemned Iraq's action, and the British forces were then replaced by a contingent of troops from Jordan, Saudi Arabia, and the UAR. Qassem quickly backed down, and the Arab forces were withdrawn in February 1962.[95] Once again, even unlikely allies showed a willingness to act together when their interests were threatened.

At first glance, Egypt's situation in the summer of 1961 still appeared extremely favorable. Egypt had established the first formal union between two Arab states, was enjoying seemingly cordial relations with Saudi Arabia and slightly improved relations with Jordan, had successfully isolated its Iraqi rival, and was now receiving considerable support from both superpowers. Once again, however, this apparently strong position dissolved quickly. On September 28, 1961, a group of military officers staged a coup against the UAR regime in Damascus. Angered by political and economic conditions in Syria and by Egyptian domination of the political system, the new regime withdrew from the union, declared a policy of nonalignment, and announced that Syria would rejoin the Arab League as an independent state.

The international repercussions were immediate. Jordan, Saudi Arabia, and Turkey recognized the new Syrian regime the following day, and the superpowers followed suit the following week. Syria and Iraq signed an economic agreement in November, and the détente between Saudi Arabia, Jordan, and Egypt collapsed. Even the Imam of Yemen saw the collapse of the UAR as the opportunity to abandon his ties with Egypt. Nasser responded by breaking relations with Jordan, blaming the secession on "reactionary" elements within Syria, and by accusing Saud, Hussein, and Imam Ahmed of being "agents of imperialism and reaction."[96] Nasser's second bid for hegemony was over, and a new approach was needed (see Table 2).

"any aggression against Jordan shall be considered as aggression against Iraq." On these events, see Safran, *Saudi Arabia*, p. 90; "Chronology," *MEJ*, 13, no. 4 (1959): 424, 433, 441; and 15, no. 1 (1961): 52–53; Kerr, *Arab Cold War*, p. 97; *MER 1960*, pp. 148–55, 158–61.

95. Brief accounts of the Kuwait crisis can be found in Lenczowski, *Middle East in World Affairs*, pp. 298–99; and Kerr, *Arab Cold War*, pp. 20–21. The Egyptian troops were withdrawn before the others, following the Syrian secession from the UAR.

96. For a summary of the problems that afflicted the UAR, see Kerr, *Arab Cold War*, pp. 23–25. On the effects of the collapse, see Lenczowski, *Middle East in World Affairs*, p. 625; Hasou, *Struggle for the Arab World*, pp. 115–19; Wenner, *Modern Yemen*, p. 188; and "Chronology," *MEJ*, 16, no. 1 (1962): 83; and no. 2 (1962): 212.

Table 2. Middle East alliances, 1958-1961

Alliance	Interpretation
United Arab Republic (1958-1961)	Egypt and Syria unite under Nasser to fulfill pan-Arab ideology and prevent a Communist takeover in Syria.
Iraq-Jordan (1958)	A Federal Union is formed to balance against the UAR. It collapses after the Iraqi revolution in July 1958.
Egypt-Saudi Arabia (1958-1961)	Saudi Arabia bandwagons with Egypt to appease Nasser after the attempt to assassinate him fails.
Egypt-Iraq (1958)	A brief agreement is made to unite Iraq with the UAR. It ends when Qassem ousts Aref from leadership.
Soviet Union-Iraq (1) (1958-1959)	Soviets support Iraq to deter U.S. and British intervention because of the prominent role of the Iraqi Communist Party (ICP). Qassem seeks to balance Egypt and appease the ICP, but moves away from the Soviet Union once his position in Iraq is secure.
Kuwait Intervention (1961)	Saudi Arabia, Jordan, and Egypt send troops to Kuwait to deter Iraq's plans to annex the sheikhdom. Egypt withdraws after the collapse of the UAR in 1961.

NASSER'S NEW APPROACH

From 1954 to 1956 Egypt had exploited superpower rivalries and resurgent Arab nationalism to form an Arab alliance against the Baghdad Pact. This alliance—directed against Iraq and "Western imperialism"—collapsed when Nasser's ambitions and prestige became a greater threat than Iraq to the other Arab states. Nasser's second effort, equally improvised, exploited his undiminished personal prestige in the service of formal union with Syria. Here too, the effort failed when Nasser's opponents found alternative alignments preferable and when the union proved unpopular and unworkable in Syria.

Nasser's response was typical. He again sought to use his status as leader of the Arab revolution to challenge his opponents. After 1961 Nasser placed renewed emphasis on revolutionary ideology in both domestic and foreign policy. In the domestic arena, a new ideological platform (known as the National Charter) was drafted and a new mass party was created to replace the ineffective National Union.[97] In foreign

97. Nasser had already begun to make major changes in Egyptian economic, social, and

policy, Nasser initiated a new campaign against conservative forces in the Middle East.

The rationale for this policy was straightforward. The collapse of the UAR was attributed to continued opposition from "reactionary forces". Accordingly, Nasser and his associates now argued that true Arab unity could be achieved only if all Arab states had compatible (i.e., revolutionary) political systems. In effect, Nasser's foreign policy was now premised on the belief that ideological considerations were the most important factors in identifying friends and enemies. The new formula shifted blame for the break-up of the UAR onto others and justified Nasser's attacks on the conservative Arab regimes, all in the name of Arab unity.[98] The result was to divide the Middle East into two distinct groups, with inevitable effects on relations between the regional states and the superpowers as well.

The new policy took several forms. First, Egyptian propaganda continually attacked the secessionist regime in Syria, and Egypt gave ideological and material support to the pro-Nasser groups still contending for power there.[99] In the same way, Jordan, Saudi Arabia, and, to a lesser degree, Iraq became the targets of hostile propaganda over Radio Cairo. Nasser's enemies responded by isolating Egypt: Syria and Iraq tried to enhance their own pan-Arab credentials by negotiating an agreement for military and political cooperation in April, and Jordan and Saudi Arabia took the offensive against Nasser within the Arab League. Egypt's isolation was virtually complete by the summer of 1962.[100] The

---

political life in early 1961, including the nationalization of the Egyptian banks. However, these changes became much more extensive after the collapse of the UAR. For analyses of these programs, see Dekmejian, *Egypt under Nasir*, pp. 52–60; Vatikiotis, *Nasser and His Generation*, pp. 211–20; Raymond W. Baker, *Egypt's Uncertain Revolution under Nasser and Sadat* (Cambridge, Mass., 1978), chap. 2 and pp. 101–8; Hopwood, *Egypt: Politics and Society*, pp. 90–95; Stephens, *Nasser*, pp. 344–45; and Waterbury, *Egypt of Nasser and Sadat*, pp. 312–32.

98. As Nasser put it in a 1962 speech: "These [conservative] puppets should not be confused with the Arab peoples but as long as they are in power, there can be no real unity." Quoted in Rahmy, *Egyptian Policy in the Arab World*, pp. 33–35.

99. The Syrians brought a protest before the Arab League in July 1962, claiming that Egypt was actively attempting to subvert the government in Syria. Although the defection of the Egyptian military attaché (who was allegedly responsible for some of these activities) lent credence to the Syrian claims, the league refused to condemn Egypt's actions. After bitter debates between the Egyptian and Syrian delegations, the meeting collapsed when the Egyptians threatened to withdraw from the league. Egypt proceeded to boycott meetings of the Arab League for the rest of the year. For details, see "Chronology," *MEJ*, 16, no. 4 (1962): 502; *New York Times*, June 19, 1962, and July 29–30, 1962; *London Times*, August 29–31, 1962; Kerr, *Arab Cold War*, pp. 38–39; and Petran, *Syria*, pp. 160–61.

100. See "Chronology," *MEJ*, 16, no. 3 (1962): 366; Uriel Dann, *Iraq under Qassem: A Political History, 1958–1963* (New York, 1969), pp. 348–49; Kerr, *Arab Cold War*, pp. 33, 35; Stephens, *Nasser*, pp. 379–80, 348–49; Dawisha, *Egypt in the Arab World*, pp. 36–37; and Anthony Nutting, *Nasser* (London, 1972).

stage was thus set for Nasser's next move: intervention in the Yemen civil war.[101]

Egyptian relations with Yemen had been growing for some time. No more than a nominal member of Nasser's earlier alliances, Imam Ahmed had severed his ties with Nasser after the Syrian secession.[102] In the meantime, however, a number of Yemeni military officers had acquired strong pro-Egyptian sympathies after receiving military training from Egyptian instructors. On September 27, 1962, following Ahmed's death, a group of these officers staged a coup against Ahmed's son, Badr. Badr escaped to the countryside and began rallying loyal tribes to his side, which in turn led to a full-scale civil war.[103]

To further his avowed revolutionary goals and to threaten Saudi Arabia, Nasser moved quickly to support the revolutionary government. Approximately fifteen thousand troops were sent to assist the republican regime, and Egyptian planes attacked rebel positions and a number of towns in Saudi Arabia.[104] In response, Jordan and Saudi Arabia signed a series of mutual defense treaties in November 1962, and both began providing support to the royalist forces. Thus once Nasser began an ideologically inspired campaign, his targets joined forces to counter the threat. Relations between Cairo and Amman and Riyadh would be especially hostile for the next two years.[105]

Encore for Arab Unity?

Egypt's isolation did not last long. Domestic politics in Syria and Iraq intervened once again, setting off a dizzying series of internal maneuvers that continued until 1966. On February 8, 1963, Iraqi Premier Qassem was ousted and executed in a Ba'thist military coup. The new

101. See Malcolm Kerr, "Regional Arab Politics and the Conflict with Israel," in *Political Dynamics in the Middle East*, ed. Paul Y. Hammond and Sidney S. Alexander (New York, 1972), p. 50.

102. He did so by publishing a poem mocking Egyptian leadership (and Nasser). Given Yemen's feudal social structure and extremely backward economy, close ties with Egypt were probably embarrassing to Nasser anyway at this point. See Rahmy, *Egyptian Policy in the Arab World*, pp. 63–65.

103. For accounts of the Yemen war, see Rahmy, *Egyptian Policy in the Arab World;* Dana Adams Schmidt, *Yemen: The Unknown War* (London, 1968); Edgar O'Ballance, *The War in the Yemen* (London, 1971); and Wenner, *Modern Yemen*, chap. 8.

104. "Chronology," *MEJ*, 17, no. 1 (1963): 132–34, 141–43; Wenner, *Modern Yemen*, p. 198. The speed with which Nasser intervened has led many to suspect that he helped arrange the coup against Badr. For a dissenting view, see Nutting, *Nasser*, pp. 320–22.

105. "Chronology," *MEJ*, 17, no. 1 (1963): 117; Wenner, *Modern Yemen*, p. 205; Holden and Johns, *House of Saud*, pp. 225–29; and Dawisha, *Egypt in the Arab World*, pp. 37–40. The Saudis broke diplomatic relations after the bombing attacks, sought arms from Pakistan and diplomatic support from Iran, and began to press the United States for a greater security commitment.

leader, however, was the non-Ba'thist Abdel Salam Aref, Qassem's former partner in the 1958 revolution.[106] One month later, a coup in Syria brought another Ba'th-led regime to power. Still pressed by Nasserist forces within Syria, the new regime quickly expressed its interest in another union with Egypt.[107] With two avowedly revolutionary socialist states now seeking to unite with Egypt (and with the "progressive regime" in Yemen fighting a "war of liberation"), "Nasser's refusal to compromise with reactionaries and separatists had seemingly been vindicated."[108]

Vindication, however, did not mean success. Representatives from Syria, Iraq, and Egypt met in Cairo in March and April 1963 to discuss plans for a new tripartite union. The talks were probably doomed from the start, as each state sought different (and ultimately irreconcilable) goals. For Egypt, Nasser sought to prevent a union between Syria and Iraq that would exclude Egypt and to ensure that Egypt would dominate any union that might emerge. Syria and Iraq, in turn, sought to enhance their precarious domestic positions by uniting with Egypt, thereby demonstrating their own pan-Arab convictions and obtaining the domestic political benefit of Nasser's blessing. Because they needed him more than he needed them, it is not surprising that the final agreement for a tripartite union conformed to Egypt's desires rather than theirs.[109]

Although at best a stillborn alliance, the Tripartite Unity Agreement was an extremely revealing event. As in 1958, the civilians in the Syrian Ba'th wanted a union with Egypt to fulfill their own ideological visions and to defuse their domestic opponents (including the Syrian army) by allying with the charismatic figure of Gamal Abdel Nasser. The abortive

106. On the coup in Iraq, see Dann, *Iraq under Qassem*, pp. 358–60, 369–70; Khadduri, *Republican Iraq*, pp. 189–96; and Batatu, *Old Social Classes and Revolutionary Movements*, chaps. 52 and 53, especially pp. 974–81.

107. The coup in Syria originated in the increasingly powerful Military Committee, a group of Ba'th military officers in Syria. The struggle between the civilian and military wings of the party (and the related contest between the Iraqi and Syrian branches) would exert a tremendous impact on the subsequent fortunes of and policies adopted by the Ba'th. Among other things, the civilian leadership continued to seek a union with Egypt as a means of enhancing its position vis-à-vis the Military Committee, which was opposed to formal unity. On these events, see Lenczowski, *Middle East in World Affairs*, pp. 347–48; Rabinovich, *Syria under the Ba'th*, pp. 53–56; Devlin, *Ba'th Party*, pp. 237–39; and Batatu, *Old Social Classes and Revolutionary Movements*, p. 1015.

108. Kerr, *Arab Cold War*, p. 43.

109. Malcolm Kerr provides a fascinating analysis of these discussions in his *Arab Cold War*, chap. 3. For an abridged transcript from Egyptian sources, see *Arab Political Documents 1963* (Beirut, 1964), pp. 75–217. See also Devlin, *Ba'th Party*, pp. 240–47; and Rabinovich, *Syria under the Ba'th*, pp. 52–56. The final agreement called for a federal union of the three countries after twenty-five months preparation—a lifetime by the standards of these regimes—and granted the president (Nasser, of course) both the right to restrict the powers of his regional vice-presidents and extensive veto powers over the regional parliaments.

[83]

agreement was thus the product of bandwagoning by Syria and (to a lesser degree) Iraq as well as the lingering impact of the Ba'th's pan-Arab ideology and the ultimately counterproductive effects of Nasserist penetration in Syria. Given its members' contradictory goals (i.e., the Syrians sought to gain Nasser's support without giving him power, but Nasser would not provide the former without the latter), the rapid demise of the much-heralded union was virtually inevitable.

In any case, the tripartite union collapsed almost immediately. The Military Committee of the Syrian Ba'th was opposed from the start, and its purge of Nasserist officers in the Syrian army produced the first cracks in the union agreement.[110] Several attempted coups by Nasser's supporters in Syria and their continued repression by the Syrian military led to a decisive break in July; Syrian president Luay al-Atasi (a non-Ba'thist) was forced from office and replaced by the head of the Ba'th Military Committee, Amin al-Hafez. The new government resumed harsh propaganda attacks against Egypt, and Nasser responded in kind over Radio Cairo. Nasser then canceled the April unity agreement.[111]

Nasser's hostility toward the Ba'th now drove Syria and Iraq together. The two Ba'th regimes signed agreements for economic and military cooperation in September and October, the Ba'th National Congress (containing representatives from both Syria and Iraq) passed a resolution calling for "full federal unity," and steps were taken to unify the Syrian and Iraqi armed forces at this time. The unification was not merely symbolic; a Syrian brigade was sent to Iraq to aid the government's campaign against the Kurdish insurgents.[112]

Revolutionary ideology having proved a poor basis for cooperation, Nasser initiated a sudden détente with the conservative Arab monarchies. King Hussein of Jordan responded eagerly. Earlier in 1963, Nasser's propaganda had incited new upheavals in Jordan, which Hussein had put down by once again calling upon U.S. aid.[113] Moreover,

110. See Batatu, *Old Social Classes and Revolutionary Movements*, p. 1015; Rabinovich, *Syria under the Ba'th*, pp. 56–57, 63; Devlin, *Ba'th Party*, pp. 283–84.

111. See Kerr, *Arab Cold War*, pp. 88–89; Rabinovich, *Syria under the Ba'th*, pp. 52–54, 66–72; and Devlin, *Ba'th Party*, p. 282. Nasser now described the Ba'thists in Syria as "fascists, opportunists, and secessionists," to whom unity meant "domination, terrorism, murder, blood, and the gallows." Quoted in Stephens, *Nasser*, p. 408.

112. See "Chronology," *MEJ*, 18, no. 1 (1964): 85, 103; and "Resolutions of the Sixth National Congress of the National Command of the Arab Ba'th Socialist Party," *Arab Political Documents 1963*, p. 93. In Ba'th parlance, National Command refers to the transnational party structure throughout the Arab world; the organization in each separate state is a Regional Command. See also Rabinovich, *Syria under the Ba'th*, pp. 73–74; and Kerr, *Arab Cold War*, pp. 92–94.

113. "Chronology," *MEJ*, 17, no. 3 (1963): 300–301; Abu-Jaber, *Arab Ba'th Socialist Party*, p. 71; *New York Times*, April 21, 1963, and May 2, 1963; *New York Herald Tribune*, April 23, 1963.

Hussein had every reason to fear a Ba'thist union of Syria and Iraq—which would certainly be hostile to Jordan—and thus to welcome Nasser's help if he could get it. Now preoccupied by his own struggle with Syria and Iraq, Nasser agreed to cease his attacks on Jordan. In exchange, Hussein released former Prime Minister Nabulsi from jail and allowed Egyptian journals to circulate inside Jordan once again. Although only temporary, the détente illustrates the alarm Nasser must have felt at the prospect of a Ba'thist union between Syria and Iraq as well as the value Hussein placed on deflecting Nasser's opposition elsewhere.[114]

Nasser's precautions proved unnecessary. The continued struggle for power within Syria and Iraq soon led to a rift in the transnational organization of the Ba'th Party itself.[115] In Iraq, Aref abandoned his erstwhile Ba'thist partners and used his own supporters in the Iraqi army to suppress the independent Ba'thist national guard. The unity movement between Iraq and Syria collapsed immediately, much to Nasser's relief.[116]

Thus another attempt at Arab unity had come to an end. Despite their public commitment to pan-Arabism, the progressive regimes in Egypt, Syria, and Iraq were ultimately unwilling or unable to implement the ideological vision that they all claimed to share. More than that, they found it impossible either to form effective military alliances—even to challenge Israeli occupation of "Arab" territory—or to implement the most rudimentary agreements for economic or military cooperation. By the end of 1963, the record of pan-Arabism was a dismal one.

The Cairo Summit

Following the failure of the latest round of unity experiments, both Egypt and Iraq reverted to more moderate policies. By contrast, Syrian foreign and domestic policy began a steady evolution toward a more radical stance.

The result was an expanded, largely tacit alignment within the rest of

114. Abu-Jaber, *Arab Ba'th Socialist Party*, p. 76; Kerr, *Arab Cold War*, p. 93.

115. The split within both the Syrian and Iraqi wings of the Ba'th resulted from differences between an increasingly powerful radical faction (espousing vague Marxist notions and less interested in the traditional goals of Arab unity) and a more moderate, reformist group. The radicals eventually triumphed in Syria, whereas the split in Iraq gave Aref the excuse to remove the Ba'th from power completely. For details, see Rabinovich, *Syria under the Ba'th*, chap. 4; Khadduri, *Republican Iraq*, pp. 207–14; Devlin, *Ba'th Party*, pp. 259–76; and Batatu, *Old Social Classes and Revolutionary Movements*, chap. 55, especially pp. 1016–26.

116. On the origins and effects of Aref's ouster of the Ba'th, see Khadduri, *Republican Iraq*, pp. 215–17; Penrose and Penrose, *Iraq*, pp. 309–11; Kerr, *Arab Cold War*, pp. 93–95; and Batatu, *Old Social Classes and Revolutionary Movements*, pp. 1025–26 and passim.

the Arab world. When the Syrians began to attack Egypt's measured policies as too moderate, Nasser followed the same tactic he had used against the Syrian-Iraqi alliance several months earlier: he quickly mended fences with the other Arab states.

The immediate issue was how to respond to Israel's water project on the Jordan River, which threatened to divert part of the water supply away from Jordan and Syria. The Syrians accused Nasser of failing to halt the project—a telling criticism given Nasser's claim to be the leading defender of the Arab cause—and they began calling for a military response. Still respectful of Israel's military power and already bogged down in Yemen, Nasser had no desire to heed Syria's call to arms. Accordingly, Nasser called for a summit meeting to fashion a joint Arab response to the Israeli action.[117]

The summit convened in Cairo in January 1964. Its chief product was a series of innocuous measures against Israel, including the establishment of a unified military command and a decision to create the Palestine Liberation Organization (PLO) as an additional means of carrying on the struggle against Israel.[118] These resolutions, however, served less as a means of confronting Israel than as a way of deflecting Syria's criticisms. Neither Nasser nor the Arab monarchies wanted a war with Israel at this time, yet none could afford to be seen as lacking devotion to the Palestinian cause.

Nasser's success in isolating the Syrians was demonstrated by several subsequent developments. Jordan and Egypt resumed diplomatic relations in January 1964, and Hussein recognized the republican regime in Yemen in July.[119] Although still wary of each other, Egypt and Saudi Arabia began negotiations to settle the civil war in Yemen.[120] Finally, Egypt and Iraq announced plans for a federal union between their two countries in February 1964.[121]

117. For a summary of the Jordan waters dispute, see Safran, *Israel*, p. 385.
118. The summit also approved a plan for diverting part of the Jordan River away from the Israeli water project, and the wealthy oil states agreed to help strengthen the military capabilities of Egypt, Syria, and Jordan. For details, see Kerr, *Arab Cold War*, chap. 5; and Dawisha, *Egypt in the Arab World*, pp. 43–45.
119. Hussein visited Cairo for talks with Nasser in March and August 1964, and Egyptian vice-president Amer visited Amman in July, praising the "mutual sincerity" of Egyptian-Jordanian relations. See "Chronology," *MEJ*, 18, no. 4 (1964): 466.
120. Feisal and Nasser signed an agreement ending the Yemen war in September 1964, but the effort failed when the various Yemeni factions refused to abide by it. See Dawisha, *Egypt in the Arab World*, p. 44; Wenner, *Modern Yemen*, pp. 214–16; and Rahmy, *Egyptian Policy in the Arab World*, pp. 138–39.
121. The Egyptian-Iraqi federal union was a relatively modest arrangement. The two countries agreed to unify their armed forces—a favorite measure in Arab unity schemes—and conducted joint military exercises in September 1964. Aref reportedly sought "Egyptian support against the Ba'th Party in Syria and against the return of the Ba'th Party in Iraq." However, several attempted coups by Nasserist groups in Iraq convinced Aref to avoid too close an association with Egypt, although the two countries remained loosely

Syria's response, however, was the most interesting of all. Still lacking domestic legitimacy, the Ba'th was unwilling to accept complete isolation. So while it condemned the other Arab states—and especially Nasser—its members continued to attend the summit meetings in order to show their own devotion to Arab solidarity.

In short, once Egypt adopted a less aggressive posture, relations improved with everyone save the Syrians, whose ideological extremism, hostile propaganda, and calls for war with Israel succeeded only in alarming their neighbors and increasing their isolation in the Arab world.[122]

Nasser's tactics worked in part because Syria's extremism and bellicosity was even more threatening to Saudi Arabia and Jordan than to Egypt, especially once Nasser's new-found moderation made it less dangerous to cooperate with him. The period of amity ushered in by the Cairo summit can be viewed either as an attempt to balance against the Syrians or as an effort by the conservative Arab states to bandwagon with (i.e., appease) Egypt as long as Nasser remained on good behavior.

The End of Inter-Arab Détente

This rapprochement between Egypt and the conservative Arabs deteriorated by the end of 1965, resulting in a new pattern of inter-Arab alignments.[123] Several events were responsible. First, efforts to settle the Yemeni civil war failed when neither Saudi Arabia nor Egypt could persuade its clients to lay down their arms and settle their differences.[124] Second, the Saudis began their own ideological offensive against Egypt in late 1965, when Feisal convened a conference of Islamic states in Riyadh. By emphasizing traditional Islamic values (in contrast to Nasser's quasi-socialist ideology), the so-called Islamic Pact was obviously directed against Egypt.[125] Finally, yet another coup d'état in Syria in February

aligned until after the Six Day War. See "Chronology," *MEJ*, 18, no. 3 (1964): 328–39, 349; Khadduri, *Republican Iraq*, pp. 222–24, 231–36, 242–46, 278–81; Batatu, *Old Social Classes and Revolutionary Movements*, pp. 1031–34; and Kerr, *Arab Cold War*, pp. 123–24.

122. On these points, see Kerr, *Arab Cold War*, pp. 101–5.

123. Additional summits were held in Alexandria in September 1964 and Casablanca in September 1965. At the latter summit, the participants signed the so-called Arab Solidarity Agreement, prohibiting propaganda attacks against each other. It would prove effective for less than a year. On these meetings, see Lenczowski, *Middle East in World Affairs*, pp. 753–54; and *Arab Political Documents 1965*, pp. 343–45.

124. See Kerr, *Arab Cold War*, pp. 108–9; and Wenner, *Modern Yemen*, pp. 221–25. Egypt began a new offensive in Yemen in February 1966. It was no more successful than the earlier campaigns.

125. The revelation that Feisal had consulted the Shah of Iran (one of Nasser's bitterest enemies) in preparing the conference encouraged this interpretation, as did Feisal's decision to move closer to the United States at this time. See Dawisha, *Egypt in the Arab World*, pp. 46–47; Safran, *Saudi, Arabia*, pp. 119–21; Holden and Johns, *House of Saud*, pp. 249–50; Kerr, *Arab Cold War*, pp. 109–12; Lackner, *House Built on Sand*, pp. 115–16; and Shahram Chubin and Sepehr Zabih, *The Foreign Relations of Iran* (Berkeley, Calif., 1974), pp. 145–49.

1966 ousted the old guard of the Ba'th Party for good, demolished the international structure of the Ba'th Party completely, and gave a radical faction (subsequently dubbed the neo-Ba'th) undisputed power. Abandoning the traditional goal of Arab unity, the new leaders proclaimed a radical socialist platform at home and a commitment to violent revolutionary activity abroad, including a "people's war" against Israel. As a result, border violence between Syria and Israel increased sharply, with the Syrians providing increasing support to the military wing of the PLO.[126]

These developments restored the sharp ideological divisions of several years before. Egypt and Syria abandoned overt hostility and moved together once again, which led to a formal defense treaty in November 1966. At the same time, Egypt renewed its propaganda war against Jordan and Saudi Arabia.[127] Significantly, because the neo-Ba'th regime placed little weight on pan-Arab ideals, relied largely on military force to stay in power, and thus was not vulnerable to Egyptian propaganda, Nasser was forced to adopt Syria's extreme positions in order to maintain his own revolutionary status (and to retain some influence in Syrian actions).[128] Thus the tactics that had worked against Syria and Iraq in 1963 were of no use against the neo-Ba'th; indeed, the neo-Ba'th regime had greater leverage over Nasser because its more radical position threatened the foundation of his political power—his status as head of the Arab revolution. By the end of 1966, the Arab world was again split between a radical and a conservative camp.

To summarize: Inter-Arab politics between 1961 and 1966 reveals the relative weakness of ideological factors as a cause of effective Arab alliances, despite the considerable emphasis placed on ideological distinctions throughout this period. Although conservative and revolutionary regimes occasionally lined up against one another (most notably in the conflict over Yemen), the "progressive states" were often just as hostile to each other (as the conflict between Egypt and Syria showed) and

126. On the neo-Ba'th takeover in Syria and its effects, see Rabinovich, *Syria under the Ba'th*, chap. 8, especially pp. 207–8; Devlin, *Ba'th Party*, pp. 314–15; and Ya'acov Bar-Siman-Tov, *Linkage Politics in the Middle East: Syria between Domestic and External Conflict, 1961–70* (Boulder, Colo., 1983), pp. 147–52.

127. Increased PLO activity in Jordan forced Hussein to take measures to control the PLO, which in turn provoked widespread criticism from Egypt and Syria. Nasser likened Hussein to the pet dog of the Saudis and dubbed him the "adulterer of Jordan." See Sinai and Pollock, *Hashemite Kingdom of Jordan*, p. 152; Kerr, *Arab Cold War*, pp. 114–17; and William B. Quandt, Ann Mosely Lesch, and Fuad Jabber, *The Politics of Palestinian Nationalism* (Berkeley, Calif., 1972), pp. 163–75.

128. See Kerr, *Arab Cold War*, pp. 121–22; Dawisha, *Egypt in the Arab World*, p. 48; and Stephens, *Nasser*, pp. 461–62. Nasser's renewed interest in alignment with "revolutionary" Syria was also encouraged by his belief that imperialism was by then engaged in a deliberate assault on Third World nationalism, a conclusion based on the recent ousters of leaders such as Nkrumah, Ben Bellah, Sekou-Touré, and Sukarno, as well as on the U.S. involvement in Vietnam.

ready to cooperate with the "forces of Arab reaction" when necessary (as the various Arab summits revealed). Indeed, the collapse of the UAR and the Tripartite Unity Agreement demonstrated that the ideology of pan-Arabism was as much a source of division as it was a basis for cooperation. In short, inter-Arab relations in this period revealed that a shared ideology was no guarantee of stable cooperation and that radically different ideological views were not a barrier to diplomatic coordination. These alignments are summarized in Table 3.

SUPERPOWER POLICY IN A POLARIZED CONFLICT

The ideological conflicts that bedeviled inter-Arab politics also affected relations between the two superpowers and states in the Middle

Table 3. Inter-Arab alliances, 1962-1966

Alliance	Interpretation
Egypt-Yemen Republic (1962-1967)	As part of its campaign against Arab reaction, Egypt intervenes to aid Yemeni revolutionaries fighting against the royalist forces and Saudi Arabia.
Saudi Arabia-Jordan (1962-1964)	Arab monarchies ally to counter Egypt's intervention in the Yemen civil war.
Tripartite Unity Pact (1963)	Egypt and the Ba'th regimes of Syria and Iraq establish a formal union to promote the pan-Arab ideal. The union collapses almost immediately, and Syria and Egypt are now hostile.
Syria-Iraq (1963)	The Ba'th regimes implement military unification to fulfill their ideology and to balance against Egypt. The effort ends when Aref ousts the Ba'th regime in Iraq.
Egypt-Iraq (2) (1964-1967)	The coup against the Iraqi Ba'th leads to the Unified Political Command between Egypt and Iraq, based on pan-Arabism and the desire to isolate Syria. A very limited degree of cooperation is achieved.
Cairo Summit (1964-1965)	A rapprochement occurs between Egypt and the conservative Arab monarchies, intended to isolate Syria and develop a common policy against Israel.
Egypt-Syria (1966-1967)	A neo-Ba'th coup in Syria leads to more radical policies. Syria seeks Egyptian support against Israel; Nasser agrees in order to preserve his prestige and restrain Syria. Both attack Saudi Arabia and Jordan for being pro-imperialist.

East. As the level of conflict within the region increased—among the Arab states themselves and between the Arab states and Israel—both superpowers expanded their commitments to their regional allies. Thus, by the Six Day War, the Middle East was effectively divided between the two superpowers. Moreover, unlike the shifting arrangements within the Arab world itself, the division between the superpowers took place along ideological lines.

Soviet Policy in the 1960s

In the broadest terms, the gradual leftward shift in Egypt and Syria (and, to a much lesser degree, Iraq) encouraged increased Soviet support for these states. At the same time, intensification of the Arab-Israeli conflict and the growing rivalry between the superpowers in the Third World as a whole provided an even more powerful incentive for the Soviet Union to support its Middle Eastern allies more generously.

After some initial reservations, the Soviets viewed Nasser's ideological offensive in 1961–1962 favorably.[129] Trade and aid continued to expand, and the Soviet Union began to supply advanced MIG–21 and TU–16 aircraft to counter Israel's acquisition of the French Mirage III.[130] Even more important, the Soviets moved quickly to support Egypt's intervention in Yemen. Military aid increased in both quality and quantity, and Soviet pilots reportedly flew the transport planes ferrying equipment from Egypt to Sana.[131]

Soviet-Egyptian relations expanded further the following year. Nasser declared an amnesty for Egypt's Communists and invited them to join the Arab Socialist Union instead. Khrushchev paid a successful visit to Egypt in May and awarded both Nasser and Vice-President Amer medals declaring them "Heroes of the Soviet Union." He also agreed to provide an additional $227 million in economic aid.[132] After Khru-

129. Soviet commentators were quick to point out that Nasser's policies were not true socialism, and they continued to condemn Nasser's repression of the Egyptian Communists. Although the Egyptians continued to reject these criticisms, the level of discord was well below the level reached between 1959 and 1961. See Yodfat, *Arab Politics in the Soviet Mirror*, p. 65; Smolansky, *Soviet Union and Arab East*, p. 211; and Dawisha, *Soviet Foreign Policy towards Egypt*, pp. 30–32.

130. See SIPRI, *Arms Trade with the Third World*, p. 530; Glassman, *Arms for the Arabs*, pp. 25, 30, 34; and Crosbie, *Tacit Alliance*, pp. 109, 154.

131. A major arms deal worth between $200 million and $500 million was signed in June 1963. For the first time, the deal included front-line Soviet equipment (rather than obsolescent systems)—for example, T–54/55 tanks and the MIG–21. See Glassman, *Arms for the Arabs*, pp. 24–25; Joshua and Gibert, *Arms for the Third World*, pp. 23–24; and Lenczowski, *Soviet Advances in the Middle East*, p. 148.

132. On Khrushchev's visit to Egypt, see Dawisha, *Soviet Foreign Policy towards Egypt*, pp. 32–33; Roi, *From Encroachment to Involvement*, pp. 376–400; and Nikita S. Khrushchev, *Khrushchev Remembers*, ed. Strobe Talbott (Boston, 1970), p. 360.

shchev's ouster, his successors sent Deputy Premier A. N. Shelepin to Cairo to reassure the Egyptians that the change of leadership would not alter Soviet policy in the region. And the supply of Soviet arms continued unabated.[133]

These trends did not change significantly until after the Six Day War. Military delegations exchanged visits in January and May 1965, and the Soviets apparently made an unsuccessful request for naval facilities at this time.[134] Despite this setback, a major arms deal (reportedly worth $310 million) was completed in July. Following the voluntary dissolution of the Egyptian Communist Party, Nasser and Kosygin exchanged visits in August 1965 and May 1966, and Kosygin reportedly urged Nasser to create a united front against imperialism by cooperating with the neo-Ba'th regime in Syria.[135] Egypt continued to receive more advanced Soviet weaponry, and a Soviet naval flotilla made an extended port visit to Alexandria in August 1966. Thus, by the beginning of 1966, Soviet-Egyptian relations had reached an unprecedented level of amity and cooperation.

Several things contributed to the expansion of Soviet-Egyptian relations in this period. First, both countries were responding to what they perceived as hostile U.S. activity in the Third World in general and the Middle East in particular.[136] Second, Soviet doctrine regarding the Third World was evolving steadily throughout the 1960s (largely as a result of the Sino-Soviet rivalry), and greater support for nationalist leaders such as Nasser was now receiving ideological justification.[137] Third, Egypt's

133. Nasser was reportedly alarmed by Khrushchev's ouster, saying, "Now we have to start all over again." Quoted in Heikal, *Cairo Documents*, pp. 157–58. Both SIPRI, *Arms Trade with the Third World*, and Glassman, *Arms for the Arabs*, report no new arms deal after May 1964; but Laqueur, *Struggle for the Middle East*, p. 72, claims a further agreement was reached during Vice-President Amer's visit to Moscow in November, although he provides no source for this claim. What is more likely is that the November visit merely reaffirmed agreements already reached back in May. See also Dawisha, *Soviet Foreign Policy towards Egypt*, p. 34; and Roi, *From Encroachment to Involvement*, p. 413.

134. See Richard B. Remnek, "The Politics of Soviet Access," in Dismukes and McConnell, *Soviet Naval Diplomacy*, pp. 366–69; and Glassman, *Arms for the Arabs*, p. 26.

135. On the Communist decision to disband the party, see Dawisha, *Soviet Foreign Policy towards Egypt*, p. 35; and Shimon Shamir, "The Marxists in Egypt: The 'Licensed Infiltration' Doctrine in Practice," in *The USSR and the Middle East*, ed. Michael Confino and Shimon Shamir (New York, 1973), pp. 293–319. For accounts of Nasser's visit to the Soviet Union, see Heikal, *Sphinx and Commissar*, pp. 143–47; and Roi, *From Encroachment to Involvement*, pp. 413–19. On Kosygin's visit and advice to Nasser, see Roi, *From Encroachment to Involvement*, pp. 436–37; Dawisha, *Soviet Foreign Policy towards Egypt*, pp. 36–38; and "Chronology," *MEJ*, 20, no. 3 (1966): 383.

136. As already mentioned, the Kennedy administration began by trying to establish better relations with Egypt. By 1965, however, relations had deteriorated to the point that Nasser saw the United States as particularly hostile.

137. The shift in Soviet thinking on Third World leaders began in 1961, when the program of the 22nd Party Congress praised the emergence of "national democracies" in

quasi-socialist reforms and the more tolerant policy taken toward the Egyptian Communist Party may have made closer ties less disquieting to both parties. Finally, Soviet relations with Syria and Iraq (the Soviet Union's principal Middle Eastern alternatives) were at best problematic throughout much of this period. Facing greater challenges from other regional powers and the United States, and with fewer diplomatic options than before, Egypt and the Soviet Union chose to rely even more on each other.

After the earlier flirtation with Qassem, Soviet relations with Iraq deteriorated steadily until 1964. After ousting Qassem in 1963, the Ba'th regime unleashed a ruthless campaign against its traditional rivals in the Iraqi Communist Party.[138] In a rare display of displeasure, the Soviets suspended economic aid and denounced these actions as "barbarous torture."[139]

It is therefore no surprise that the Soviets, like Nasser, viewed Aref's removal of the Ba'th later in the year with relief. Relations improved considerably after this event, despite occasional disputes over Iraq's treatment of its Kurdish minority and the continued repression of the Iraqi Communist Party.[140] Although Soviet arms shipments were renewed in 1964, Iraq's rather mild socialist policies and otherwise independent stance made Iraq the least important of the Soviet Union's Middle East clients throughout the 1960s.[141]

As for Syria, the Soviet Union followed a wait-and-see policy during

---

the developing world who "open vast prospects for the peoples of the economically underdeveloped countries." By 1964, Soviet scholars were writing of "revolutionary democrats" (such as Nasser) following the "non-capitalist path to development," who could now begin the transition to socialism. Soviet support for such regimes (even where the local Communist party was weak or repressed) was thus receiving greater theoretical approval. For discussions on these points, see Roi, *From Encroachment to Involvement*, pp. 347–53, 376–78; Mark N. Katz, *The Third World in Soviet Military Thought* (Baltimore, Md., 1982), pp. 27–28; Richard Lowenthal, *Model or Ally? The Communist Powers and the Developing Countries* (London, 1977), pp. 221–29; and Morton Schwartz, *The Failed Symbiosis: The USSR and Leftist Regimes in Less Developed Countries* (Santa Monica, Calif., 1973), pp. 7–10.

138. Batatu, *Old Social Classes and Revolutionary Movements*, chap. 53; and Smolansky, *Soviet Union and Arab East*, pp. 229–36.

139. Smolansky, *Soviet Union and Arab East*, pp. 235–36; SIPRI, *Arms Trade with the Third World*, p. 557; and Roi, *From Encroachment to Involvement*, pp. 361–63.

140. See Smolansky, *Soviet Union and Arab East*, pp. 240–42; and Khadduri, *Republican Iraq*, pp. 272–73.

141. According to several reports, Aref and Khrushchev engaged in a lengthy shouting match on the subject of Arab unity and Communism during Khrushchev's visit to Cairo. This dispute probably contributed to the restraint in Soviet-Iraqi ties. See Heikal, *Cairo Documents*, pp. 155–56. By 1967, the Soviets often (but not always) referred to Iraq as a progressive state, although they universally used this label for both Egypt and Syria. On these points, see Joshua and Gibert, *Arms for the Third World*, p. 17; "Chronology," *MEJ*, 18, no. 4 (1964): 464; Laqueur, *Struggle for the Middle East*, pp. 101–4; Penrose and Penrose, *Iraq*, pp. 342–43; Khadduri, *Republican Iraq*, pp. 219–21; Yodfat, *Arab Politics in the Soviet Mirror*, pp. 180–81; and Lenczowski, *Soviet Advances in the Middle East*, pp. 137–39.

the turbulent period after Syria's secession from the UAR. The Ba'thist seizure of power in March 1963 was viewed with great suspicion, reflecting the Soviet Union's long-standing opposition to Arab unity (which the Ba'th had long espoused) and the anti-Communist policies of the Ba'th in Iraq.[142]

As the Syrian Ba'th grew increasingly radical, however, both countries sought closer ties. The socialist decrees enacted by the al-Hafez regime in January 1965 encouraged a Soviet reassessment, and a host of economic agreements between Syria and a number of Warsaw Pact countries were signed in September and October.[143] It was the neo-Ba'thist coup in February 1966, however, that brought Syria and the Soviet Union into their closest alignment to date. The new regime brought two Communists into the cabinet, proclaimed a policy of radical socialist transformation, and openly praised Soviet leadership of the world's socialist countries. For their part, the Soviets agreed to build a long-delayed dam on the Euphrates River and to provide large-scale military and economic assistance.[144] Diplomatic support increased as well; the Soviets vetoed several U.N. Security Council Resolutions condemning Syria's support for PLO attacks against Israel, and both states condemned "imperialist" and "Zionist" policies in the Middle East.[145] The consolidation of Soviet-Syrian relations, along with the formal defense treaty between Syria and Egypt signed in November 1966, would be a key factor leading to the Six Day War.

America's Expanding Commitments

The consolidation of Soviet ties in the Middle East was mirrored by the United States. As noted earlier, the Kennedy administration expanded Eisenhower's campaign to improve U.S. relations throughout the region. Rejecting the simple Cold War conceptions that had determined U.S. policy in the mid-1950s, the Kennedy administration now sought closer ties with all states in the region, not just traditional friends

---

142. See Roi, *From Encroachment to Involvement*, pp. 361–63. The Soviets agreed to build several agricultural centers in June 1962 and entertained visiting Syrian military delegations in September and November. These steps may have been inspired by reports of Chinese offers to provide economic aid to Syria at this time. See Lenczowski, *Soviet Advances in the Middle East*, p. 111; and McLane, *Soviet–Middle East Relations*, pp. 90–91, 95.

143. See Yodfat, *Arab Politics*, pp. 124–32; Roi, *From Encroachment to Involvement*, pp. 401–2; "Chronology," *MEJ*, 19, no. 2 (1965): 210; no. 3 (1965): 350; 20, no. 1 (1966): 87–88.

144. See Roi, *From Encroachment to Involvement*, pp. 419–24; SIPRI, *Arms Trade with the Third World*, p. 548; and *The Military Balance 1967–68* (London, 1967), p. 53.

145. See Khouri, *The Arab-Israeli Dilemma*, pp. 229–33; and Roi, *From Encroachment to Involvement*, pp. 432–34.

of the United States.[146] Unfortunately, persistent regional rivalries and the expanded Soviet presence ultimately undermined these efforts. By 1966, in fact, U.S. commitments to traditional allies had increased whereas relations with Egypt, Syria, and Iraq were as bad as ever.

The Kennedy initiatives focused on Egypt. Kennedy appointed a pro-Arab ambassador as his representative to Cairo, made several statements expressing his support for an even-handed approach to the Arab-Israeli dispute, and began a personal correspondence with Nasser.[147] In addition, U.S. economic aid to Egypt doubled between 1961 and 1962, totaling $394 million for the period 1962–1964.[148]

Of even greater importance was the administration's decision to formally recognize the republican regime in Yemen. Anticipating a rapid republican victory and fearing that any delay might provide the Soviets with another regional ally, Kennedy decided to extend recognition despite Saudi Arabia's vehement opposition. At the same time, he sent a U.S. team to begin a mediation effort aimed at ending the civil war. Although the effort failed to produce a settlement, these measures prevented the decision to recognize Yemen from disrupting ties with Saudi Arabia too severely.[149]

While pursuing better relations with Egypt, the United States also sought to maintain or enhance its existing security relations in the region. Thus recognition of Yemen was coupled with a loan of nine F-86 fighter planes to Saudi Arabia and a visit by a squadron of U.S. fighters in the fall of 1962, along with a port visit by a U.S. destroyer the following year. In addition, Kennedy sent a letter to Prince Feisal in October 1962 that promised "full American support for the maintenance of Saudi Arabian [territorial] integrity." After Egypt bombed several Saudi border towns in December and January, the United States also agreed to station a squadron of aircraft to fly air defense patrols in the area. Thus the rapprochement with Egypt was balanced by increased support to Nasser's main conservative opponent.[150]

---

146. For accounts of Kennedy's approach to the Third World in general and the Middle East in particular, see Gaddis, *Strategies of Containment*, pp. 223–25; Brown, *Faces of Power*, pp. 198–204; Badeau, *American Approach to the Arab World*, pp. 26–33 and chap. 5; Gazit, *President Kennedy's Policy*; and Steven L. Spiegel, *The Other Arab-Israeli Conflict: Making America's Middle East Policy from Truman to Reagan* (Chicago, 1985), chap. 4.

147. On the Nasser-Kennedy correspondence, see Heikal, *Cairo Documents*, chap. 6; and Spiegel, *Other Arab-Israeli Conflict*, pp. 101–2.

148. AID, *Overseas Loans and Grants*.

149. On U.S. policy in the Yemen war, see Spiegel, *Other Arab-Israeli Conflict*, pp. 102–6; Wenner, *Modern Yemen*, pp. 199–203, 206–7; Stookey, *America and the Arab States*, pp. 180–85; and Gazit, *President Kennedy's Policy*, pp. 23–24. For a defense of the decision to recognize the republican regime, see Badeau, *American Approach to the Arab World*, chap. 7, especially pp. 132–48. For a critique, see Holden and Johns, *House of Saud*, pp. 232–33.

150. See Holden and Johns, *House of Saud*, p. 233; Wenner, *Modern Yemen*, p. 204; Mangold, *Superpower Intervention in the Middle East*, p. 85; and Spiegel, *Other Arab-Israeli Conflict*, p. 104.

U.S. support for Jordan grew as well. Economic and military aid increased to an average of $57 million per year between 1962 and 1964. Even more important, when Egyptian and Syrian propaganda led to riots in Jordan in the spring of 1963, the United States placed its forces in the region on alert and pressed Egypt and Syria into moderating their attacks on Hussein. At the same time, however, the United States remained reluctant to sell advanced arms to Jordan, which led Hussein to establish diplomatic relations with the Soviet Union later in 1963. Although this ploy had no immediate effect on U.S. policy, it would pay off handsomely over the next several years.[151]

Finally, the U.S. commitment to Israel increased significantly under Kennedy. In the 1950s the United States had resisted a number of Israeli requests for a formal security treaty. But in 1962 Kennedy made several informal statements indicating his belief that the two countries were allies even in the absence of a formal agreement. In the same year Kennedy also informed Ben-Gurion that the United States would support Israel's right to complete its water project on the Jordan River in accordance with the Johnston Plan.[152] And most significant of all, an agreement was signed in June 1963 for the sale of HAWK air defense missiles, the first major weapons system provided to Israel by the United States. And this would be only the beginning.[153]

The expansion of security ties between the United States and Israel at this time—in effect the beginning of the U.S.-Israeli military alliance—was the result of several factors. For the Israelis, the continued acquisition of Soviet arms by their regional adversaries, the various efforts at Arab union, and a gradual increase in border violence provided ample grounds for seeking greater external support.[154] For the United States,

151. On U.S. aid to Jordan, see AID, *Overseas Loans and Grants.* On other measures of U.S. support, see "Chronology," *MEJ,* 17, no. 3 (1963): 300–301; 17, no. 4 (1963): 429; and 18, no. 1 (1964): 89; and Mangold, *Superpower Intervention in the Middle East,* p. 107.

152. In May 1963 Myer Feldman, a close aide to Kennedy, reportedly stated that the United States "did not intend to sit on the sidelines" in an Arab-Israeli war. See "Chronology," *MEJ,* 17, no. 3 (1963): 299. In December 1962 Kennedy told Golda Meir privately that he believed the United States "had a special relationship" with Israel and that "in case of an invasion the U.S. would come to the support of Israel." See Spiegel, *Other Arab-Israeli Conflict,* pp. 106–7; and Gazit, *President Kennedy's Policy,* pp. 46–48. The Johnston Plan was a distribution scheme for the waters of the Jordan River valley devised by U.S. mediator Eric Johnston and experts from the Tennessee Valley Authority in 1953. Despite prolonged negotiations, the plan was never implemented, because of Arab reluctance to recognize Israel's existence implicitly. See Bar-Ya'acov, *Israel-Syrian Armistice,* pp. 130–35.

153. The decision to offer the HAWK was made in September 1962, the final agreement was reached in June 1963, and the missiles were delivered in 1964. See "Chronology," *MEJ,* 17, no. 1 (1963): 116; no. 4 (1963): 427.

154. Israeli leaders were also concerned about reports that Egypt was developing a surface-to-surface missile capability (with the aid of German scientists) and about the gradual decline in Israel's relations with France. On Israeli security perceptions in the early 1960s, see Shlomo Aronson, *Conflict and Bargaining in the Middle East: An Israeli Perspective* (Baltimore, 1978), pp. 39–45; and Safran, *Israel,* pp. 373–74. On the increase in border

the decision to increase the commitment to Israel was due to (1) the desire to maintain a regional balance of power given growing U.S. support for its Arab clients and Soviet support for Egypt, (2) the enhanced role of pro-Israeli forces within the Kennedy administration, (3) the need to minimize domestic opposition to the rapprochement with Nasser, (4) Kennedy's own sympathies for the Jewish state, (5) the effort to persuade Israel to respond favorably to U.S. initiatives for a permanent peace settlement, and (6) a desire to dissuade Israel from developing its own nuclear weapons capability. Thus the growth in the U.S. commitment to Israel at this time was understandable.[155]

Because Kennedy sought good relations with both sides in the major regional conflicts (Arabs versus Israel, conservatives versus revolutionaries), his approach was obviously a delicate one. Although the United States successfully squared the diplomatic circle until Kennedy's death in November 1963, the effort to develop cordial relations with the progressive Arab states deteriorated steadily thereafter.

Relations with Egypt suffered the most obvious decline. The prolonged war in Yemen tarnished Nasser's image as a benign nationalist leader and posed a continued threat to Saudi Arabia, a traditional U.S. ally. Egypt's support for the Congolese rebels and Nasser's flirtation with China, Cuba, and the Viet Cong hardly helped, and a series of minor but annoying events led to growing resentment within the United States.[156] Moreover, Egypt's growing ties with the Soviet Union made further efforts to wean Cairo away from Moscow appear futile.[157] Not only was President Lyndon Johnson personally sympathetic to Israel, but the U.S. Congress now began placing restrictions on U.S. aid to Egypt as a form of pressure on Nasser.[158] In response, Nasser an-

violence (much of it connected with the dispute over the Jordan waters), see Khouri, *Arab-Israeli Dilemma*, pp. 219–29; and Barry M. Blechman, "Impact of Israel's Reprisals on the Behavior of Bordering Arab Nations Directed at Israel," *Journal of Conflict Resolution*, 16, no. 2 (1972): 163, 165.

155. On these points, see Spiegel, *Other Arab-Israeli Conflict*, pp. 106–10; and Gazit, *President Kennedy's Policy*, pp. 30–55.

156. In late 1964 a group of demonstrators protesting U.S. policy in the Congo burnt down the U.S. Information Agency library in Cairo. Shortly thereafter, Egypt shot down a private U.S. plane that had strayed over Egyptian airspace. See Stephens, *Nasser*, p. 418; and Burns, *Economic Aid and American Policy*, pp. 152–54, 157–60.

157. According to Steven Spiegel, Egypt's continued pressure on Saudi Arabia and Jordan and its steady acquisition of Soviet arms led the United States first to provide greater military support for its Arab allies and then, to preserve a balance of power, to offer similar aid to Israel. The dominant motive, however, was the desire to balance Soviet arms supplies to the Middle East. See Spiegel, *Other Arab-Israeli Conflict*, pp. 132–36.

158. U.S. aid to Egypt declined from a high of $200.5 million in 1962 to $97.6 million in 1965 and was completely cut off in 1967. See AID, *Overseas Loans and Grants*. On Johnson's sympathies for Israel and the importance of pro-Israeli forces within his administration, see Spiegel, *Other Arab-Israeli Conflict*, pp. 120–24, 128–30.

nounced that "whoever does not like our policy can go drink up the Red Sea. . . . [W]e cannot sell our independence."[159]

This reaction reflected Nasser's renewed suspicions of the United States. By 1966, the growing U.S. commitment to his regional enemies, combined with the expanded U.S. role in Vietnam and the ouster of nationalist leaders in Ghana, Indonesia, and Algeria, convinced Nasser that "imperialism" was reviving its campaign against "progressive forces." Closer ties with Moscow and renewed hostility toward the United States were the logical response. Thus, by the end of 1966, the campaign to improve U.S. relations with the progressive Arab states had come to an unhappy end.[160]

The decline in relations with Egypt was matched (and in part caused) by the expansion of U.S. ties to Saudi Arabia, Jordan, and Israel. In Saudi Arabia, the continued threat from Egypt led the kingdom to undertake a major program of defense modernization in conjunction with the United States and Great Britain.[161] King Feisal visited Washington in May 1966, and President Johnson reportedly refrained from the public pledge of a U.S. commitment only at Feisal's request, to preserve a public image of Saudi neutrality.[162] The December 1965 arms package was supplemented by another agreement (reportedly worth over $100 million) in September 1966.[163]

Jordan received similar treatment as well. Egypt and Syria had been pressing Jordan to acquire Soviet arms, and Hussein began to hint that he might do so if Western support were not available. The United States responded by beginning negotiations for advanced jet aircraft in 1964 and by donating tanks and armored personnel carriers in 1965. An agreement for the sale of F-104 jet fighters was announced in April 1966,

---

159. Quoted in William B. Quandt, "United States Policy in the Middle East," in Hammond and Alexander, *Political Dynamics in the Middle East,* p. 518.

160. On the deterioration of U.S.-Egyptian relations, see Spiegel, *Other Arab-Israeli Conflict,* pp. 103–6, 122–24; Burns, *Economic Aid and American Policy,* chap. 6; Stephens, *Nasser,* pp. 417–19, 421–22; Stookey, *America and the Arab States,* pp. 196–97; and Dawisha, *Egypt in the Arab World,* p. 47. For an Egyptian view, see Heikal, *Cairo Documents,* chap. 7.

161. In December 1965, Saudi Arabia, the United States, and Great Britain announced that the Saudis would purchase a modern air defense system, including British Lightning fighters and a U.S. radar system linked to the HAWK air defense missiles. British and U.S. technicians would run the system, and the deal marked the entry of the U.S. Army Corps of Engineers into the Saudi kingdom. Over the next several years, the corps would undertake a wide variety of military construction projects on the Saudis' behalf. For details, see Holden and Johns, *House of Saud,* pp. 243–46; Safran, *Saudi Arabia,* pp. 200–202 and passim; SIPRI, *Arms Trade with the Third World,* pp. 562–64; Quandt, *Saudi Arabia in the 1980s,* p. 52; and U.S. House Committee on International Relations, *Military Sales to Saudi Arabia, 1975,* 94th Cong., 1st sess., 1976.

162. Holden and Johns, *House of Saud,* p. 247.

163. "Chronology," *MEJ,* 21, no. 1 (1967): 78; and U.S. House Committee on International Relations, *Military Sales to Saudi Arabia.*

and State Department sources reported that the principal motive behind the sale was U.S. concern that Hussein might seek Soviet support if the deal were denied.[164]

Finally, the United States balanced the support given its Arab clients by providing increasing military aid to Israel. Indeed, arms sales to Israel were explicitly linked to Israel's acquiescence in the U.S. effort to support its Arab clients.[165] The United States transferred two hundred M–48 tanks from West Germany in 1964, and an agreement for the sale of Skyhawk fighter-bombers was reached at this time (although it was not revealed publicly until 1966).[166] Although the growing relationship was not without strains, U.S. involvement in Israeli security was now greater than ever.[167]

To summarize: By the beginning of 1967, several powerful trends had combined to divide the Middle East into two rival camps. Egypt's and Syria's increasingly radical postures had greatly increased the level of conflict among the various Arab regimes. Arab-Israeli violence had increased as well, as the progressive Arab states (especially Syria) tried to enhance their positions in the Arab world by attacking Israel. With virtually all the regional powers facing greater threats from one another, a renewed search for allies—and especially for greater superpower support—was to be expected. Thus by 1967 the Soviet Union was openly supporting the revolutionary Arab regimes in Egypt, Syria, and (to a lesser degree) Iraq while providing significant material aid to the republican forces in Yemen. The United States, in turn, had increased its own commitments to Jordan and Saudi Arabia and was now actively involved in Israel's security planning as well. These commitments are

---

164. See SIPRI, *Arms Trade with the Third World*, pp. 539–41; Stookey, *America and the Arab States*, p. 197; and Spiegel, *Other Arab-Israeli Conflict*, pp. 132–33. According to AID, *Overseas Loans and Grants*, U.S. military aid to Jordan increased from $3.7 million in 1965 to $19.3 million in 1966, with economic aid at even higher levels. Despite the agreement, the F–104s were not delivered until April 1968.

165. See Yitzhak Rabin, *The Rabin Memoirs* (Boston, 1979), pp. 64–66.

166. To disguise the level of U.S. involvement, the tanks were provided by West Germany (which then received replacements from the United States). When the Germans suspended the arrangement in 1965, the United States completed the deliveries on its own. See SIPRI, *Arms Trade with the Third World*, pp. 532, 535; Sachar, *History of Israel*, pp. 562–67; and Bernard Reich, *Quest for Peace: United States–Israel Relations and the Arab-Israeli Conflict* (New Brunswick, N.J., 1977), p. 42.

167. The problems involved in supporting both the Arab states and Israel were illustrated in November 1966, when the United States supported a U.N. resolution condemning a large-scale Israeli reprisal against the Jordanian village of Samu. The raid was probably intended to deter Hussein from joining the new Syrian-Egyptian alliance, but it also inspired the United States to offer additional military equipment to Jordan and to loan Hussein several F–104 aircraft until the planes he had ordered were delivered. See Stookey, *America and the Arab States*, pp. 210–12; Stephens, *Nasser*, p. 463; *MER 1967*, pp. 53, 166; and Brecher, *Decisions in Israel's Foreign Policy*, pp. 356–57.

Table 4. Superpower alliances, 1962-1966

Alliance	Interpretation
Soviet Union-Egypt (1962-1974)	The Soviet Union renews strong support for Egypt to counter the "American approach" to the Arab world. Egypt uses Soviet aid to expand its army and support its campaign in Yemen.
U.S.-Israel (1962-present)	Kennedy commits the United States to protection of Israel's security and offers military equipment to balance Soviet aid to Arabs, in order to keep domestic support for U.S. aid to Arabs and to encourage the peace process.
U.S.-Saudi Arabia/Jordan (1962, 1965)	The United States makes a verbal commitment of support for the kingdom of Saudi Arabia, Saudi Arabia begins a military modernization program with U.S. assistance in 1965. Aid to Jordan is increased as well.
Soviet Union-Yemen Republic (1964-1969)	The Soviets sign a friendship treaty with Yemen to show support for republican forces and Egypt.
Soviet Union-Syria (1966-present)	To promote an anti-imperialist front in the Middle East, the Soviets increase their commitment to Syria after the neo-Ba'th regime comes to power. The Syrians seek to balance Israeli military power. Significant ideological compatibility exists.

summarized in Table 4. The rivalries between and within the coalitions would provide the catalyst for the Six Day War.

THE SIX DAY WAR

Origins

The history of the Six Day War is well known, so I will concentrate on the alliance dimensions of the war.[168] Alliance relations played a major role in the conflict, which would transform the international politics of the Middle East.

The Six Day War was in many ways the product of the interaction between the Arab-Israeli conflict and the continuing rivalry within the

168. Basic accounts of the Six Day War can be found in Brecher, *Decisions in Israel's Foreign Policy*, chap. 7; Safran, *From War to War*, chaps. 6 and 7; Trevor N. Dupuy, *Elusive Victory: The Arab-Israeli Wars* (New York, 1980), bk. 3; Chaim Herzog, *The Arab-Israeli Wars: War and Peace in the Middle East* (New York, 1982), bk. 3, chaps. 1–3. For an Arab view, see *The Arab-Israeli Confrontation of June 1967: An Arab Perspective*, ed. Ibrahim Abu-Lughod (Evanston, Ill., 1969).

Arab world. As already described, by 1966 Nasser's reluctance to confront Israel directly was being attacked by the neo-Ba'th radicals in Syria. Nasser's conservative opponents echoed Syria's criticism, accusing Nasser of "hiding behind the skirts" of the U.N. peace-keeping force in the Sinai. This criticism was a serious challenge to Nasser's status as leader of the Arab world. Among other things, the charges led Egypt to sign a formal defense treaty with the neo-Ba'th regime in November 1966, explicitly aimed at Israel but motivated primarily by inter-Arab concerns. By allying with the Syrians—now the most enthusiastic (and foolhardy) supporters of the Palestinian cause—Nasser sought both to retain his leading role in the Arab world and to restrain dangerous Syrian provocations.[169]

Unfortunately, Nasser's attempt to restrain Syria merely encouraged Damascus to support even greater levels of fedayeen activity against Israel. In response, Israel begin a series of extensive reprisals against Syria in April 1967. Up to this point, however, Nasser still maintained that the defense treaty with Syria called for Egyptian intervention only in the event of a full-scale Israeli assault; individual reprisals were still the sole responsibility of the state attacked.[170]

This policy of restraint began to erode in early April, when Israeli jets shot down six Syrian aircraft and then buzzed Damascus. Egypt's inability or unwillingness to help its Syrian ally was thus dramatically revealed.[171] By early May, reports from a number of sources apparently convinced Nasser that an Israeli attack on Syria was imminent.[172] With his prestige now fully engaged, Nasser ordered his troops into the Sinai on May 16, simultaneously requesting that the U.N. forces stationed

169. See Kerr, *Arab Cold War*, pp. 126–28.

170. This policy had been elaborated after the signing of the Egyptian-Syrian defense treaty in November 1966, and Nasser was careful not to overcommit himself at first. According to an article by Mohamed Heikal at that time, "The Joint Defense Agreement does not mean the immediate intervention of the Egyptian Army in any raid against Syrian positions. These raids must remain the responsibility of the various fronts." See Safran, *From War to War*, p. 273 and passim.

171. See Kerr, *Arab Cold War*, p. 127; Stephens, *Nasser*, p. 466; and Khouri, *Arab-Israeli Dilemma*, p. 245.

172. Nasser's belief that Israel intended to attack Syria was apparently based on (1) Israeli and Lebanese press statements, some of which may have been intended by Israel to deter the Syrians; (2) Syrian intelligence reports; and (3) Soviet intelligence reports confirming the Syrian warnings. The Soviet warnings were clearly provocative and were probably intended to persuade Nasser to take actions that might reduce Israeli pressure on Syria. On these issues, see Brecher, *Decisions in Israel's Foreign Policy*, pp. 321, 357–62; Walter Z. Laqueur, *The Road to Jerusalem* (New York, 1968), p. 73; Khouri, *Arab-Israeli Dilemma*, pp. 242–44; Charles W. Yost, "The Arab-Israeli War: How It Began," *Foreign Affairs*, 46, no. 2 (1968): 307–11; Heikal, *Cairo Documents*, p. 240; *Sphinx and Commissar*, pp. 174–75; Anwar el-Sadat, *In Search of Identity* (New York, 1977), pp. 171–72; Safran, *From War to War*, pp. 275–77; and Michel Tatu, *Power in the Kremlin* (New York, 1970), pp. 532–37.

thre withdraw.[173] In a final fateful step, Nasser ordered a blockade of the Straits of Tiran on May 22. Nasser was improvising as usual, and his success up to this point left him little option of backing down in a direct confrontation with the "Zionist aggressor."[174]

Egypt's sudden belligerence was encouraged by several other factors. First, the Soviet Union offered strong diplomatic support throughout, and the Egyptians may have believed that the Soviets would provide military backing if it were needed.[175] Second, the United States failed to fulfill its earlier promise to Israel that it would keep the Straits of Tiran open.[176] Third, Nasser's bold confrontation with Israel forced his Arab opponents to leap suddenly to his side; King Hussein signed a mutual defense treaty with Nasser on May 30, Iraq joined the growing coalition on June 3, and the other Arab states sent small contingents to Israel's borders to demonstrate their own solidarity. This sudden reconciliation was based on the following calculations: If no war broke out, Nasser's Arab enemies at least were demonstrating their essential Arab solidarity. If war did occur and Egypt were defeated, Nasser's power would be reduced. But if Egypt and Syria won, failure to participate would be politically disastrous. Thus, in a direct conflict with Israel, inter-Arab rivalries were temporarily ignored.[177]

Outcome

The formation of the Arab coalition on June 3 provided the final push for war.[178] On June 5, 1967, Israel staged a stunning surprise attack that destroyed the Egyptian air force and routed the three principal Arab

173. Nasser may have been seeking to duplicate a previous success. In February 1960 a border clash between Israeli and Syrian forces near the abandoned town of Tawafiq led Nasser (who may have believed exaggerated reports of Arab successes) to mobilize troops in the Sinai to deter an Israeli attack on Syria. No such attack occurred (or was planned), which the UAR predictably saw as an Arab victory. See *MER 1960*, pp. 197–204.

174. See the analysis in Safran, *From War to War*, pp. 271–92; and Safran, *Israel*, pp. 390–404.

175. The Soviets deployed the largest fleet of naval vessels they had ever sent to the Mediterranean and adopted an unmistakable deterrent posture against the U.S. Sixth Fleet there. Egyptian beliefs that the Soviets would back them up apparently arose from a misunderstanding between the Egyptian defense minister and Soviet premier Alexei Kosygin. On these points, see Anthony Wells, "The June War of 1967," in Dismukes and McConnell, *Soviet Naval Diplomacy*, pp. 159–65; and Dawisha, *Soviet Foreign Policy towards Egypt*, p. 41.

176. See Quandt, *Decade of Decisions*, pp. 41–43; Spiegel, *Other Arab-Israeli Conflict*, pp. 136–50; and Brecher, *Decisions in Israel's Foreign Policy*, pp. 373–75, 381, 387, 390–92.

177. See Sachar, *History of Israel*, p. 633; "Chronology," *MEJ*, 21, no. 4 (1967): 503; and Hussein, King of Jordan, *My "War" with Israel* (New York, 1969), pp. 37–48.

178. See Brecher, *Decisions in Israel's Foreign Policy*, pp. 412–13; Raymond Tanter and Janice Gross Stein, *Rational Decisionmaking: Israel's Security Choices, 1967* (Columbus, Ohio, 1980), pp. 218–19.

armies. Hussein joined the fighting in response to exaggerated reports of Egyptian successes and because low-level actions by his own forces and by Egyptian units stationed in Jordan triggered a full-scale Israeli attack on the West Bank and East Jerusalem.[179] The other Arab states sent token contingents to the various fronts, and Saudi Arabia led a largely symbolic oil boycott against the United States.[180] After six days of fighting, Israel had occupied the Sinai Peninsula, the West Bank, and the Golan Heights.

Despite their close ties with the warring powers, the United States and the Soviet Union took little direct action. Both superpowers deployed large naval forces in the Eastern Mediterranean, and the Soviets threatened to intervene late in the war when Israel's conquest of the Golan Heights posed a threat to Damascus. The United States moved the Sixth Fleet closer to Syria to deter a Soviet move, and the final acceptance of a U.N. ceasefire resolution on June 11 rendered the Soviet threat largely irrelevant.[181] The Soviet Union broke diplomatic relations with Israel, and Egypt, Syria, and Iraq broke relations with the United States. For the most part, however, the superpowers remained intensely interested bystanders throughout the brief conflict.

The alliance commitments of the Six Day War are summarized in Table 5.

CONCLUSION

The end of the war marked the end of an era. As suggested at the beginning of this chapter, three main developments had dominated the

---

179. The available evidence is unclear regarding why (and how seriously) Hussein sought to enter the war. He did order artillery fire against Israeli positions after receiving false reports of Egyptian successes, but ground operations were probably begun by Egyptian commando battalions stationed in Jordan from the beginning of June (and under Egyptian command). Moreover, Jordanian artillery fire apparently reached the important Israeli air base of Ramat David, thereby posing a major threat to Israel's defense capabilities. Although the Israelis no doubt welcomed the opportunity to extend their control to the West Bank and especially to East Jerusalem, this case may be an example of inadvertant escalation, where one party takes military actions that unwittingly threaten major military assets of the enemy and thus triggers unwanted escalation. In short, the evidence on Jordan's motives is ambiguous; although Hussein bandwagoned with Egypt in signing the defense treaty on May 30, his wartime intentions may have been more circumspect. On these points, see Hussein, *My "War" with Israel*, pp. 57, 60–61, 65–66; Dupuy, *Elusive Victory*, pp. 285–87; Herzog, *Arab-Israeli Wars*, pp. 169–70; Sachar, *History of Israel*, pp. 633, 643–44; and Safran, *From War to War*, p. 360.

180. Dupuy, *Elusive Victory*, pp. 318–26; and Safran, *From War to War*, pp. 379–80.

181. Wells, "The June 1967 War," p. 165; Quandt, *Decade of Decisions*, p. 62; Lyndon B. Johnson, *The Vantage Point: Perspectives of the Presidency, 1963–1969* (New York, 1971), pp. 301–3; and Francis Fukuyama, "Soviet Threats to Intervene in the Middle East," *Research Note N–1577–FF* (Santa Monica, Calif., 1980).

Table 5. The Six Day War

Alliance	Interpretation
The Arab Coalition (May–June 1967)	Amid growing Syrian-Israeli clashes and inter-Arab feuds, Egypt supports its Syrian ally by blockading the Straits of Tiran. Jordan bandwagons with Egypt, and Iraq and Saudi Arabia send token forces to show solidarity. The Soviets support Egypt and Syria during the crisis and rebuild their armed forces after the war.
U.S.-Israel (1962–present)	The United States gives diplomatic backing to Israel but offers no military support until the Soviets threaten to intervene late in the war. The United States warns the Soviet Union, arranges a ceasefire, and declares a temporary embargo on arms shipments.

international politics of the Middle East between 1954 and 1967. The first was Nasser's repeated efforts to establish and sustain Egypt's primacy within the Arab world, relying upon his own charisma, Egypt's size and stature, and the ideology of pan-Arabism. Each of these efforts was defeated by the ability of his enemies to form countervailing coalitions when pressed and by the fact that even ideologically similar allies found Egypt's leadership uncomfortable.

The second development was the evolution of the Arab-Israeli conflict. Israel's existence remained a potent issue to exploit in inter-Arab rivalries as well as a source of repeated low-level violence. Opposition to the Jewish state was the one issue upon which all the Arab states agreed (at least publicly), even if they quarreled violently over how to put that opposition into practice. Moreover, because the conflict could explode into war with little warning—as the Six Day War showed—it remained a powerful motive for the various regional powers to seek external support.

Third, external support was increasingly available. Both superpowers had expanded their alliance commitments in the Middle East substantially prior to the Six Day War. Although there were no formal treaties, by 1967 the general pattern of superpower–client state alignments was clear. As the Six Day War revealed, however, superpower support was confined primarily to arms assistance and diplomatic backing, except when a client was in imminent danger of collapse.

These three features of Middle East politics would be altered significantly by the Six Day War. The evolution of alliances after 1967 is the subject of the next chapter.

[4]

From the Six Day War to
the Camp David Accords

This chapter continues the historical account by describing the alliances that formed in the Middle East from 1967 to 1979. The story
begins in the aftermath of the Six Day War and ends following the
Egyptian-Israeli peace treaty.

MAIN THEMES

This period in Middle East diplomacy can be summarized in terms of
two main themes. The first is the gradual rise and dramatic decline in
Arab collaboration against Israel, both the result of Egypt's abandoning
its quest for hegemony in the Arab world. Egypt's new-found moderation was predictable; the Six Day War had left Nasser dependent on
subsidies from his former rivals, and the ideological conflicts that characterized inter-Arab politics before the war were trivial in light of Israel's
occupation of the Sinai, West Bank, and Golan Heights. As Malcolm
Kerr put it, "There could hardly be a competition for prestige when
there was no prestige remaining."[1] Incapable of pursuing their earlier
ambitions, Egypt's leaders were forced to focus on a far more pressing
set of problems.

This change—begun under Nasser and reinforced by Sadat—made an
effective Arab alliance against Israel both necessary and feasible. It was
necessary because only substantial pressure could regain the territories

1. Kerr, *Arab Cold War*, p. 129 and passim; Dawisha, *Egypt in the Arab World*, pp. 50–54;
and Daniel Dishon, "Interarab Relations," in *From June to October*, ed. Itamar Rabinovich
and Haim Shaked (New Brunswick, N.J., 1978), pp. 159–65. For a thorough analysis of the
effects of the war on Arab political thought, see Fouad Ajami, *The Arab Predicament: Arab
Political Thought and Practice since 1967* (Cambridge, England, 1981), chap. 1.

on terms the Arabs would accept. It was feasible because Egypt was no longer the main threat to the other Arabs. The alliance that fought the October War was one result. Even more important, Egypt's new policy also made possible Sadat's decision to seek a separate peace with Israel while simultaneously realigning Egypt with the United States. Although abandoning Arab solidarity was costly, it was a viable option once Egypt was no longer concerned with maximizing its prestige in the Arab world. Paradoxically, therefore, Egypt's reduced ambitions made both war and peace possible. And once Egypt moved toward a settlement on its own, sharp divisions reemerged in the Arab world.

The second theme characterizing alliance relations in this period is the increasingly active role played by the superpowers, especially the United States. Because the campaign to regain the occupied territories involved large-scale military action (beginning with the War of Attrition in 1969 and culminating in the October War in 1973), both superpowers gave even more support to their clients than ever before. This support continued during the peace process as well, and it enabled the regional states to bargain more effectively with one another. Although Egypt's realignment allowed the United States to seize the diplomatic initiative for several years, Soviet ties with its remaining Middle Eastern clients also increased. To show how these themes affected alliance formation during these years, the chapter will begin by exploring the events that followed Israel's victory in June 1967. Given the extent of the Arab defeat, it is not surprising that Egypt and Syria quickly turned to Moscow for assistance.

SUPERPOWER COMMITMENTS AND THE WAR OF ATTRITION

Although Soviet brinkmanship had helped cause the Six Day War, the crushing defeat that Egypt and Syria had suffered forced them to rely even more heavily on Soviet support. The Soviets responded quickly. President Nikolai Podgorny arrived in Cairo on June 21, 1967, and the Soviet Union had replaced 130 aircraft by July 15. Soviet vessels were moored in Egyptian ports to deter Israeli air raids, and the Soviets dispatched several thousand military advisers to Egypt at Nasser's request. For a leader who had once struggled to rid Egypt of any foreign military presence, the Soviet presence was a humiliating symbol of Egypt's plight. Nasser now granted the Soviets base rights in Egypt as well, and Soviet naval and air units began operating from Egyptian facilities.[2]

2. See Glassman, *Arms for the Arabs*, pp. 66–68; "Chronology," *MEJ*, 22, no. 1 (1968): 60; Alvin Z. Rubinstein, *Red Star on the Nile: The Soviet-Egyptian Influence Relationship since the June War* (Princeton, N.J., 1977), pp. 46–53; McLane, *Soviet–Middle East Relations*, p. 32; and Remnek, "The Politics of Soviet Access," pp. 369–72.

Soviet support for Syria and Iraq increased as well. Podgorny and Soviet Defense Minister Grechko visited Damascus and Baghdad in July 1967 and March 1968 respectively, and both countries received new arms shipments to replace their wartime losses.[3] The Soviets were initially suspicious when the Aref regime was overthrown by the resurgent Iraqi wing of the Ba'th Party in March 1968, because of their difficulties with the Iraqi Ba'th in the early 1960s. The new regime's openly leftist policies gradually overcame Soviet reservations, however, and several important agreements for oil development were signed in July 1969.[4]

Despite these favorable signs, several significant disagreements marred Soviet relations with the two Ba'th states. In Syria, the Soviets favored Ba'th Party leader Salah Jadid in his struggle for power with Defense Minister Hafez el-Assad, which led Assad to question Syria's exclusive military relationship with the Soviet Union. Even more important, the two countries favored very different approaches to the Arab-Israeli conflict.[5] This issue hurt Iraq's relations with the Soviet Union as well, as the new Ba'th regime adopted an extreme anti-Israel policy at variance with the Soviet preference for a political solution. Indeed, Iraqi criticism of Nasser's acceptance of the ceasefire ending the War of Attrition reportedly produced a Soviet threat to cut off all aid if Iraq did not moderate its opposition.[6]

On the Arabian Peninsula, the Soviets both gained and lost an ally after the Six Day War. In Aden, the predominately Marxist National Liberation Front assumed power following the British withdrawal in 1967. A delegation from the PDRY visited Moscow in November 1967, and Soviet military advisers had arrived in Aden by the beginning of 1968. By 1970, Soviet advisers were widely involved in South Yemen's military affairs, and Soviet pilots were reportedly flying combat missions in the low-level border war with Saudi Arabia.[7]

In North Yemen, by contrast, the Soviet position was rapidly eroding. Soviet military assistance increased after Egypt's withdrawal from the

---

3. On relations with Syria, see Laqueur, *Struggle for the Middle East*, pp. 93–94; Petran, *Syria*, p. 202; and Lenczowski, *Soviet Advances in the Middle East*, p. 117.

4. On relations with Iraq, see Khadduri, *Socialist Iraq*, pp. 79–86, 124; Yodfat, *Arab Politics in the Soviet Mirror*, pp. 290–91; Francis Fukuyama, "The Soviet Union and Iraq," *Research Note 1524–AF* (Santa Monica, Calif., 1980); "Chronology," *MEJ*, 23, no. 4 (1969): 513; and Penrose and Penrose, *Iraq*, pp. 427–28.

5. Soviet support for Jadid was based on his radical socialist beliefs and his support for a policy of close ties with Moscow. Assad criticized the quality of Soviet military aid in March and began exploring the possibility of obtaining arms from France. Soviet support apparently helped Jadid preserve his position until Assad ousted him for good in 1970. Soviet-Syrian differences on the Arab-Israeli conflict focused on U.N. Resolution 242, which the Soviets supported and the Syrians rejected. See *MER 1969–1970*, pp. 427–29.

6. *MER 1969–1970*, pp. 435–36.

7. On the establishment of Soviet military relations with South Yemen, see McLane, *Soviet–Middle East Relations*, p. 97; and Katz, *Russia and Arabia*, pp. 83–85 and passim.

Yemen civil war in September 1967 (and after a group of Yemeni military officers ousted the original revolutionary leadership). Soviet and Syrian pilots flew combat missions during a royalist siege of the capital in January 1968, and arms shipments from the Soviet Union played a major role in defeating this final effort by the royalist forces. Despite these efforts, however, a new mediation effort by Saudi Arabia (combined with generous financial subsidies) brought the lengthy civil war to an end in 1970 and supplanted Soviet influence in Sana. By 1970, Soviet priorities on the Arabian Peninsula had shifted decisively toward the radical regime in the south.[8]

In sum, if their clients' failure in June 1967 had damaged Soviet prestige, it had also forced several of the clients (especially Egypt) to rely more heavily on Soviet support. At the same time, however, this new dependence did not erase a variety of substantive disagreements, especially on how best to proceed against Israel.[9]

Interestingly, the United States reacted to Israel's demonstrated superiority by providing even greater support. Not only did the June War increase Israel's strategic value in the eyes of U.S. leaders, but France's decision to cease arms supplies to Israel and the Johnson administration's decision to encourage Israel's withdrawal only if the Arabs agreed to a peace settlement made closer cooperation necessary and feasible.[10] The wartime embargo of weapons ended with the delivery of Skyhawk jets in December, and Johnson increased the original order during Israeli prime minister Eshkol's visit to Washington in January 1968. An informal agreement for the sale of Phantom jets was reached at this time, and Johnson agreed to sell additional HAWK anti-aircraft missiles in July 1968. Thus, in both the military and diplomatic realms, the United States and Israel were working in parallel.[11]

---

8. *MER 1969–1970*, pp. 447–50; Bruce D. Porter, *The USSR and Third World Conflicts: Soviet Arms and Diplomacy in Local Wars, 1945–80* (Cambridge, England, 1984), pp. 79–85; Katz, *Russia and Arabia*, pp. 29–32; and Safran, *Saudi Arabia*, pp. 130–31.

9. Statements by the Soviets described their talks with Arab officials in 1967 and 1968 as "strong" and "frank," but their efforts to weaken the Arab policy of no concessions failed completely. The Syrians were even more recalcitrant than the Egyptians and refused to grant the Soviets base rights in Syria. They also put more stringent limits on the Soviet military advisers assigned to Syria. See George W. Breslauer, "Soviet Policy in the Middle East: 1967–72," in *Managing U.S.-Soviet Rivalry: Problems of Crisis Prevention*, ed. Alexander L. George (Boulder, Colo., 1982), pp. 71–72; Laqueur, *Struggle for the Middle East*, pp. 93–94; Petran, *Syria*, p. 202; and Lenczowski, *Soviet Advances in the Middle East*, p. 117.

10. See Spiegel, *Other Arab-Israeli Conflict*, pp. 158–64; and Quandt, *Decade of Decisions*, pp. 63–67.

11. The United States supported Israel's diplomatic position that withdrawal would require the Arabs both to recognize Israel's right to exist and to sign a formal peace treaty. Johnson's preoccupation with Vietnam, however, prevented a major U.S. campaign for a peace settlement at this time. A partial exception was U.S. sponsorship of U.N. Security Council Resolution 242, which passed in November 1967. On these points, see Quandt,

U.S. ties with Jordan and Saudi Arabia were not significantly affected by the war. The arms embargo to Jordan was lifted in February 1968 (after Hussein made a much-publicized visit to the Soviet Union), and military training and construction in Saudi Arabia continued without interruption.[12] Hussein's dissatisfaction with U.S. support for Israel and with U.S. reluctance to supply him with adequate levels of military aid produced a brief cooling in Jordanian-American relations, though not a real rift.[13] Predictably, U.S. relations with Egypt, Syria, and Iraq were worse than ever and South Yemen broke diplomatic relations in October 1969, before ambassadors were even exchanged. Thus the Six Day War reinforced the division of the Middle East between the two superpowers.

The War of Attrition

This trend continued as the confrontation between Egypt and Israel escalated once again, in the War of Attrition. Arising from the continued diplomatic stalemate and Nasser's need—for both internal and external reasons—to take some form of positive action, the first phase began with a series of artillery exchanges along the Suez Canal in October 1968.[14] The war began in earnest in March 1969. It was intended, in Nasser's words, to be "one long battle to exhaust the enemy." By inflicting a steady stream of casualties on Israel, the Egyptians hoped to exploit their far greater manpower to persuade Israel to withdraw from the Sinai on acceptable terms. At the same time, by creating the risk of further escalation, Nasser hoped to give the superpowers added incentive to compel an Israeli withdrawal, as the United States had done in

---

Decade of Decisions, p. 64; "Chronology," *MEJ*, 22, no. 4 (1968): 483–84; and Spiegel, *Other Arab-Israeli Conflict*, pp. 153–58.

12. See "Chronology," *MEJ*, 22, no. 1 (1968): 65; and SIPRI, *Arms Trade with the Third World*, pp. 541–42.

13. Hussein hinted in early 1970 that if the United States were not more forthcoming, he might turn to "other sources" (i.e., the Soviet Union) to obtain additional weaponry. In addition, riots in Amman forced Undersecretary of State Joseph Sisco to cancel a planned visit to Jordan in April 1970. See *MER 1969–1970*, pp. 475–78; and SIPRI, *Arms Trade with the Third World*, pp. 543–44.

14. Nasser faced student riots in November 1968, a failing economy, and the humiliation of his army sitting idle while the PLO gained growing attention and support for its terrorist exploits. On the domestic and international pressures that encouraged the resumption of fighting, see Stephens, *Nasser*, pp. 517–18, 532–38; and Rubinstein, *Red Star on the Nile*, pp. 71–73. For discussions of the diplomatic efforts preceding the War of Attrition, see Lawrence Whetten, *The Canal War* (Cambridge, Mass., 1974), pp. 55–59, 64–65, and chap. 4; Breslauer, "Soviet Policy in the Middle East," pp. 73–75; and Saadia Touval, *The Peace Brokers: Mediators in the Arab-Israeli Conflict, 1948–1979* (Princeton, N.J., 1982), chap. 6.

1957.[15] Initial Israeli losses were severe, leading both the Soviet Union and Egypt to adopt a hard-line position in the continuing negotiations.[16]

Israel responded with intense and effective aerial attacks against Egyptian positions across the canal, which forced Egypt to rely even more heavily on the Soviet Union. In the fall of 1969, the Soviets made a decision in principle to supply combat personnel, in addition to the three thousand Soviet advisers already present in Egypt.[17] When Israel increased the pressure by beginning deep penetration raids against Cairo in January 1970, Nasser made a secret visit to Moscow to plead for even greater assistance.[18] By threatening to resign in favor of a pro-Western leader if they refused, Nasser persuaded his reluctant Soviet patrons to provide Egypt with a complete air defense system, to be manned by Soviet air defense troops and pilots. By the end of 1970, fifteen to twenty thousand Soviet troops were stationed in Egypt; they were accompanied by unprecedented levels of military equipment.[19]

Soviet intervention caused the Israelis to cease their attacks on Cairo in order to avoid confronting Soviet forces directly. When the air defense system was expanded toward the Canal Zone, however, the Israelis began attacking the missile sites and later ambushed four Soviet-piloted MIGs in July 1970.[20] Facing heavy Egyptian losses and apparently unlimited U.S. support for Israel, and recognizing that a pause in the fighting could be used to improve Egypt's military position, Nasser accepted a U.S. ceasefire proposal on August 7.[21] Egypt and the Soviet Union then seized this opportunity to (illegally) extend the air defense umbrella over the Canal Zone, which brought the War of Attrition to a close.

It is important to recognize both the magnitude and the limitations of

---

15. On Egypt's strategy, see Ya'acov Bar-Siman-Tov, *The Israeli-Egyptian War of Attrition 1969–1970* (New York, 1980), chap. 3, especially pp. 47–59. See also Ahmed S. Khalidi, "The War of Attrition," *Journal of Palestine Studies*, 3, no. 1 (1973): 61–63; and the thorough and insightful analysis in Shimshoni, "Conventional Deterrence," chap. 4.

16. Bar-Siman-Tov, *War of Attrition*, pp. 77–78; and Whetten, *Canal War*, pp. 73–74.

17. Breslauer, "Soviet Policy in the Middle East," p. 76; Rubinstein, *Red Star on the Nile*, pp. 100, 103, and passim; and Arnold Horelick, "Soviet Policy in the Middle East: Policy from 1955 to 1969," in Hammond and Alexander, *Political Dynamics in the Middle East*, p. 596.

18. Israel's objective in these raids seems to have been to pressure Egypt into halting the War of Attrition, to discredit Nasser politically, and to provoke Nasser's ouster if possible. See Bar-Siman-Tov, *War of Attrition*, pp. 121–25.

19. See Bradford Dismukes, "Large Scale Intervention Ashore: Soviet Air Defense Forces in Egypt," in Dismukes and McConnell, *Soviet Naval Diplomacy*, chap. 6; Glassman, *Arms for the Arabs*, pp. 77–79; Mohamed Heikal, *The Road to Ramadan* (New York, 1975), pp. 83–90; Rubinstein, *Red Star on the Nile*, pp. 107–10; and Whetten, *Canal War*, p. 90.

20. Dismukes, "Large Scale Intervention Ashore," p. 233.

21. For an analysis of Nasser's motives for accepting the ceasefire, see Bar-Siman-Tov, *War of Attrition*, pp. 179–81.

the Soviet-Egyptian relationship at this time. Although Egypt's precarious external situation forced Nasser to lean heavily on his Soviet patron, the alliance was still marred by serious policy disagreements.[22] In particular, the Soviets consistently favored a political solution, and Nasser had launched the War of Attrition on his own. The Soviets reportedly begged him to end the war in May 1969, and Egyptian requests for advanced Soviet aircraft (to compete with Israel's Phantoms) were denied. Nasser's decision to end the War of Attrition, although made in consultation with Moscow, no doubt reflected his own perception that he had gained all he could by the summer of 1970. In short, despite the tremendous growth of the Soviet-Egyptian relationship after 1967, Egypt's dependence on the Soviet Union hardly made Nasser a reliable tool.[23]

Similar tensions affected U.S. relations with Israel during the fighting. The Nixon administration—and especially the State Department— sought to end the fighting and begin movement toward an overall settlement, which in its view required an evenhanded approach and concessions by both sides. The Israelis, by contrast, sought to maintain their military edge (which required additional U.S. arms to counter Soviet arms shipments) while refusing any concessions that might prove dangerous in the long run. Thus, despite the growing level of U.S. aid, U.S.-Israeli relations were marred by a series of bitter disputes over the level of U.S. military support and Israel's reluctance to accept any of the peace proposals offered by the various mediators.[24] Efforts to force Israeli concessions by restricting arms generally failed; concessions (such as Israel's grudging acceptance of the July 1970 ceasefire) were usually won through pledges of additional support.[25] Like the Soviet Union, the

22. The relationship between Egypt's external situation and its ties with the Soviet Union was candidly revealed by Nasser in an interview with a U.S. journalist: "We cannot dispense with the Russian experts as long as we are at war with Israel and as long as there is no peace." Quoted in Rubinstein, *Red Star on the Nile*, p. 117.

23. See the analysis in Breslauer, "Soviet Policy in the Middle East," pp. 77–78; Rubinstein, *Red Star on the Nile*, pp. 44–46, 60–63, 75–77, 79, 88; and Shimshoni, "Conventional Deterrence," pp. 318–19.

24. The post-1967 negotiations took place in a bewildering array of forums, including Two-Power (United States–Soviet Union) and Four-Power (the superpowers plus Britain and France) talks, U.N. mediation by Gunnar Jarring, and several independent initiatives by U.S. secretary of state William Rogers. For discussions of these various efforts, see Quandt, *Decade of Decisions*, chap. 3; Spiegel, *Other Arab-Israeli Conflict*, pp. 181–96; Whetten, *Canal War*, chaps. 4–5; Brecher, *Decisions in Israel's Foreign Policy*, chap. 8; and Touval, *Peace Brokers*, chaps. 6 and 7.

25. A deliberate delay in responding to an Israeli request for more advanced aircraft in March 1970 produced at most a modest change in Israel's position. The Israeli cabinet publicly accepted Resolution 242 (previously accepted only by Israel's U.N. ambassador), in part because Nixon offered private assurances that Israel would get the planes. Israel's acceptance of the July 1970 ceasefire was encouraged by U.S. pledges to "maintain the balance of power," to provide advanced electronic countermeasures, and to accelerate

United States was discovering that a client's dependence did not ensure its patron's control.

COOPERATION AND CONFLICT IN THE ARAB WORLD

The disaster of June 1967 also began a process of reconciliation in the Arab world, although it would require several years (and several other events) to develop completely. The first phase featured a gradual rapprochement between Egypt and the Arab monarchies that had long been the targets of Nasser's attacks. A summit meeting in Khartoum produced a near-unanimous statement of Arab policy toward Israel (only Syria failed to attend), and Libya, Saudi Arabia, and Kuwait agreed to provide Egypt and Jordan with a substantial subsidy to compensate for their war losses.[26] United by a common desire to recover their lost territory and to prevent the PLO from becoming too powerful, Egypt and Jordan were now especially close, with Hussein reporting that there was "no difference" between his position and Nasser's.[27]

Saudi-Egyptian relations improved considerably as well. With Egypt now dependent on Saudi subsidies, Nasser was forced to halt the war in Yemen that had long poisoned relations with Riyadh. Feisal and Nasser signed an agreement on Yemen in October 1967, and Egyptian forces withdrew the following month.[28] Thus the rivalry between Egypt and Saudi Arabia was now muted. Their relationship was at most a détente, however, as the Saudis remained suspicious of Egypt's close ties with the Soviet Union, which the Saudis accused (with some validity) of supporting subversive activities on the Arabian Peninsula. Nor were the Saudis likely to forget their long rivalry with Nasser just because Egypt was vulnerable now.[29]

---

aircraft deliveries. On these points, see Quandt, *Decade of Decisions*, pp. 97–98, 100–102; David Pollock, *The Politics of Pressure: American Arms and Israeli Policy since the Six Day War* (Westport, Conn., 1982), pp. 74–77; Brecher, *Decisions in Israel's Foreign Policy*, pp. 487–88, 493–96; and Spiegel, *Other Arab-Israeli Conflict*, pp. 190–91.

26. For accounts of the Khartoum summit, see Lenczowski, *Middle East in World Affairs*, p. 754; Khouri, *Arab-Israeli Dilemma*, p. 310 and passim; and *MER 1967*, pp. 139–40, 262–66. The total subsidy amounted to almost $400 million annually. See Kerr, *Arab Cold War*, p. 139; *MER 1968*, p. 165.

27. See "Chronology," *MEJ*, 22, no. 1 (1968): 61; and the analysis in Kerr, *Arab Cold War*, pp. 129–33.

28. See *MER 1967*, pp. 140–41, 146; and Stookey, *Yemen*, pp. 248–53. For an Egyptian view of these events, see Rahmy, *Egyptian Policy in the Arab World*, pp. 228–40.

29. For a summary of Saudi security perceptions after the Six Day War, see Safran, *Saudi Arabia*, pp. 122–27 and passim. The growing Soviet role in South Yemen was especially worrisome to the Saudis, who were now engaged in a low-level (and ultimately unsuccessful) border war with the Marxist regime in the PDRY. Saudi fears of radical forces inspired a deliberate campaign to reduce Soviet influence in the Middle East. Indeed, Feisal report-

After 1967, Nasser's diplomatic efforts in the Arab world centered on establishing an Eastern Command of Jordan, Syria, and Iraq to increase the pressure on Israel. But this attempt to create an effective Arab alliance against Israel foundered on the rocks of Ba'th radicalism. Despite the Arabs' apparent interest in joining forces to confront Israel more effectively, the bitter ideological rivalry between the Syrian and Iraqi branches of the Ba'th precluded close cooperation, and Syria's refusal to deal directly with "reactionary" Jordan merely compounded this problem.[30] Syria's preference for revolutionary posturing while others fought its battles did not help, and the Jadid regime continued to attack the Arab monarchies even after Nasser had made his peace with them.

After a secret meeting in January 1969, however, a modest level of cooperation within the Eastern Command began to take shape. A contingent of six thousand Iraqi troops was moved to Syria in March, and a defense agreement between the two countries was ratified in July. Small contingents of Syrian troops were also reported in Jordan.[31] Yet Syria refused to commit its air force to the command, and Iraq claimed that the threat from Iran and a continued insurgency among its Kurdish minority prevented greater effort on its part. For all practical purposes, the command collapsed when a group of Syrian sympathizers was arrested in Baghdad, and the two countries renewed their mutual recriminations later in the year. Formal dissolution, however, did not occur until September 1970.[32]

The impotence of the Eastern Command is revealing. Although an effort was made to form a balancing alliance against Israel (largely by Egypt, which had the most to gain from Arab support during the War of Attrition), it failed to produce an effective coalition. This failure is easy to explain: Nasser's potential allies feared an Egyptian recovery as much as they feared Israel; the states of the Eastern Command had a lengthy history of enmity among themselves; and the weaker states of Syria, Jordan, and Iraq were all naturally inclined to pass the buck to Egypt rather than risk another round with Israel.

This combination of obstacles led Nasser to abandon his search for Arab cooperation, beginning at the Rabat summit in December 1969. When the other Arab leaders refused to provide additional support for Egypt in the War of Attrition, Nasser walked out of the meeting, claim-

edly warned Nasser about the dangers of close ties with Moscow. See "'Abd-al-Nasir's Secret Papers," in U.S. Joint Publications Research Service, *Translations on Near East and North Africa*, no. 1865, report 72223 (Washington, D.C., 1978), pp. 128–29. The secret papers are a series of articles by 'Abd-al-Majid Farad, published in the Arabic newspaper *al-Dustur* (London) in 1978. On the Saudi-PDRY conflict, see *MER 1969–1970*, pp. 616–19; Safran, *Saudi Arabia*, pp. 127–30; and Katz, *Russia and Arabia*, pp. 76–77.

30. *MER 1968*, pp. 162–65.
31. *MER 1969–1970*, p. 563–64.
32. See Dawisha, *Egypt in the Arab World*, pp. 55–56; and *MER 1969–1970*, pp. 569–71.

ing (correctly) that "the Conference has not accomplished anything at all."[33] Having demonstrated that the other Arabs were unwilling to make sacrifices, Nasser had cleared the way for Egypt to consider a political settlement, beginning with his acceptance of the Rogers ceasefire the following summer.[34]

The Jordan Crisis

Ironically, the end of the War of Attrition provided the spark for a brief but bloody confrontation between King Hussein and the PLO. The PLO had been increasingly active in Jordan since 1967, and clashes between Jordanian troops and PLO militia continued despite Nasser's periodic attempts to mediate between Hussein and PLO chairman Yassar Arafat.[35] Fearing that the end of the War of Attrition heralded an Egyptian deal with Israel that would exclude the PLO, a radical PLO faction hijacked three airliners to Jordan and blew them up. This action was too much for Hussein, and his army began a thorough crackdown against the Palestinian forces in Jordan.

During the week of fighting that followed, Syrian armored units invaded Jordan while a hastily convened summit met in Cairo to fashion a settlement. Drawing upon U.S. and Israeli support—both the United States and Israel vastly preferred Hussein to either Syria or the PLO— the Jordanians defeated the Syrian forces on September 23.[36] Significantly, Soviet behavior was quite circumspect; the Soviets assured U.S. officials that they were trying to restrain the Syrians, and Soviet advisers did not accompany the Syrian units in Jordan. Given Nasser's support for Hussein and the obvious risks of escalation, Soviet caution is not surprising.[37]

33. Walid Khalidi, ed., *International Documents on Palestine 1969* (Beirut, 1972), pp. 830–31.

34. This interpretation follows that of Kerr, *Arab Cold War,* pp. 145–46.

35. By the beginning of 1970, pressure from the PLO had forced Hussein to remove several cabinet ministers, and a number of truces between the government and the PLO had broken down. Hussein's options were limited by the fact that any action he took to control the PLO in Jordan exposed him to the charge that he was betraying the sacred cause of the Palestinian Arabs. See Dawisha, *Egypt in the Arab World,* p. 55; Sinai and Pollock, *Hashemite Kingdom of Jordan,* pp. 56–57; and Kerr, *Arab Cold War,* pp. 140–45.

36. For accounts of the Jordan crisis, see Quandt, *Decade of Decisions,* chap. 4; Rabin, *Memoirs,* pp. 186–89; Kissinger, *White House Years,* pp. 600–631; Spiegel, *Other Arab-Israeli Conflict,* pp. 196–203; and Safran, *Israel,* pp. 451–56. According to most accounts, Israel agreed to a U.S. request to aid Hussein should the Syrian forces defeat his troops. This pledge encouraged Hussein to commit his entire air force against the Syrian forces in Jordan (while Hafez el-Assad kept the Syrian air force on the ground).

37. On Soviet behavior, see Abram N. Shulsky, "The Jordan Crisis of September 1970," in Dismukes and McConnell, *Soviet Naval Diplomacy,* pp. 168–75; Heikal, *Sphinx and Commissar,* p. 215; and William B. Quandt, "Lebanon, 1958, and Jordan, 1970," in Barry M. Blechman and Stephen S. Kaplan, *Force without War: U.S. Armed Forces as a Political Instrument* (Washington, D.C., 1978), pp. 279–81.

The Jordan crisis was significant for several other reasons. First, Israel's willingness to support Hussein transcended the usual divisions between Arabs and Israelis and greatly enhanced Israel's image as a valuable ally in the eyes of the United States.[38] Second, the crisis brought a renewed U.S. commitment to Hussein, whose struggle with the PLO left him isolated in the Arab world and thus in need of greater outside support.[39] Third, the Syrian defeat led to the ouster of Salah Jadid by Hafez el-Assad, a relatively pragmatic figure who favored cooperation with the other Arab states in the confrontation with Israel.[40] Finally, the Jordan crisis removed Gamal Abdel Nasser from the stage, the victim of a fatal heart attack the day after the Arab summit ended. Although his successor, Anwar Sadat, possessed abilities that few suspected at the time, his assets did not include the charisma that had made Nasser the preeminent pan-Arab figure.[41] These changes would alter alliance relations in the Middle East substantially and would play a major role in causing the October War.

THE DIPLOMACY OF THE OCTOBER WAR

The October War of 1973 can be traced to three main developments: (1) the failure to reach a political solution to the Arab-Israeli dispute, (2) the ability of key Middle East states (especially Egypt and Israel) to obtain increased military support from their superpower patrons, and (3) the formation of the first effective anti-Israeli alliance by the Arab states. The result was a combined Arab attack against Israel's positions in the Sinai and the Golan Heights, which broke the negotiating deadlock and led to a new round of realignments.

The Diplomatic Stalemate

After 1970, several attempts were made to break the diplomatic deadlock between Israel and the Arabs. U.N. envoy Gunnar Jarring resumed his mediation efforts after the Jordan crisis, and President Sadat an-

---

38. See Quandt, *Decade of Decisions*, pp. 122, 131; and Spiegel, *Other Arab-Israeli Conflict*, pp. 201–2. Spiegel notes that the White House was far more appreciative of Israel's response than was the State Department.

39. See SIPRI, *Arms Trade with the Third World*, p. 545; and Quandt, *Decade of Decisions*, pp. 122–23.

40. See Itamar Rabinovich, "Continuity and Change in the Ba'th Regime in Syria," in Rabinovich and Shaked, *From June to October*, p. 226; Bar-Siman-Tov, *Linkage Politics in the Middle East*, pp. 164–65; and Van Dam, *Struggle for Power in Syria*, pp. 89–91.

41. On Sadat's undistinguished reputation, see Rubinstein, *Red Star on the Nile*, p. 131; and Baker, *Egypt's Uncertain Revolution*, pp. 122–24.

nounced that he would be willing to sign a formal peace treaty if Israel withdrew from all of the territory occupied in 1967. This effort collapsed when the Israeli cabinet refused to consider the new proposals.[42] Sadat then revived an earlier proposal for a limited withdrawal along the Canal Zone, and Secretary of State Rogers undertook a lengthy campaign to promote this idea. Despite considerable U.S. pressure, the negotiations eventually foundered over the size of the proposed disengagement and the relationship between an interim agreement and an overall peace settlement.[43] Not only did this failure usher in a period of diplomatic stagnation (caused in part by the U.S. presidential campaign) but it left Sadat increasingly disillusioned about the willingness of the United States to force Israeli concessions.[44]

A Growing Superpower Role

The pattern of expanding military cooperation and intensifying policy disputes between the superpowers and their regional allies continued between 1971 and 1973. Generous material support apparently afforded no guarantee of tranquil relations. If anything, the reverse seemed to be true.

Following the Jordan crisis, Soviet military aid to Egypt increased significantly. The air defense system was expanded, and Sadat was promised additional military supplies during his talks with Soviet officials in May, July, and October.[45] Even more interesting, in May 1971 Sadat signed a Treaty of Friendship and Cooperation with the Soviet Union, which appeared to reinforce the Soviet-Egyptian alliance.[46]

42. Israel's rejection of the Jarring mission was due to (1) domestic splits within the cabinet, (2) the belief that Egypt had violated earlier agreements with impunity, and (3) Israel's insistence that the 1967 boundaries be modified to provide it with "defensible borders." See Whetten, *Canal War*, pp. 144–49; Safran, *Israel*, pp. 457–59; and Quandt, *Decade of Decisions*, pp. 130–36.

43. Israel sought to avoid any linkage between an interim agreement and a final settlement in order to avoid committing itself to future withdrawals under unspecified circumstances. Egypt wanted the interim withdrawal firmly tied to a later agreement in order to avoid any implication that Israeli forces might remain on Egyptian territory permanently. For details, see Quandt, *Decade of Decisions*, pp. 140–43; Safran, *Israel*, p. 459; Whetten, *Canal War*, pp. 171–83, 190–92, 196–99; and Touval, *Peace Brokers*, pp. 177–94.

44. According to Egyptian chief of staff Saad el-Shazly, Sadat told U.S. representative Donald Bergus in November 1971 that "my experiences with you Americans makes it impossible for me to have any confidence in you." See Saad el-Shazly, *The Crossing of the Canal* (San Francisco, 1980), p. 115. See also Whetten, *Canal War*, p. 199. Sadat had repeatedly called 1971 the "Year of Decision," which made the continued stalemate a threat to his own position in Egypt. See Quandt, *Decade of Decisions*, p. 143.

45. The analysis in this section is based on Breslauer, "Soviet Policy in the Middle East," pp. 89–90. See also Glassman, *Arms for the Arabs*, pp. 83–87, 90; and Whetten, *Canal War*, pp. 162–66, 188.

46. See Whetten, *Canal War*, pp. 188–90; and Rubinstein, *Red Star on the Nile*, pp. 146–53.

These developments, however, obscured serious differences on several issues.

First, the Soviets were undoubtedly worried by Sadat's willingness to rely on U.S. mediation for his interim settlement proposal (though they were no doubt relieved when the talks broke down).[47] Second, they were alarmed by Sadat's ouster of the pro-Soviet "Ali Sabry group" in May and by his moves to relax Egypt's socialist economic policies.[48] Third, Sadat was annoyed by Soviet reluctance to provide the weapons he believed were necessary to retake the Sinai, a policy clearly designed to prevent Egypt from taking actions of which the Soviets disapproved. Additional requests in February and April 1972 brought no major change in Soviet support, adding to Sadat's growing frustration.[49] Fourth, Sadat was alarmed and incensed by the conduct of Soviet personnel in Egypt itself. Egyptian officials were prohibited entry to Soviet bases, Soviet intelligence officials reportedly assisted Sadat's domestic rivals, and the Soviet Union used Egyptian facilities to ferry arms to India during the Indo-Pakistani War, thereby using Egyptian territory to help defeat a Moslem country.[50]

Finally, an unsuccessful Communist coup in the Sudan—and the enthusiasm with which Moscow greeted the attempt—apparently affected Sadat's views significantly. Sadat dispatched Egyptian troops to help defeat the rebellion, and he reports in his memoirs that these events "caused the gap between me and the Soviet leaders to widen."[51] Thus the Soviet-Egyptian treaty should be seen as a Soviet attempt to preserve its endangered position in Cairo, not as a sign of enhanced commitment between Egypt and the Soviet Union.

The last straw was the Soviet-U.S. summit meeting in May 1972. Although Sadat had made several conciliatory gestures toward the Soviet Union earlier in the year, the final communiqué from Moscow referred to a "peaceful settlement" in the Middle East and spoke of the need for "military relaxation." This statement convinced Sadat that the

47. Soviet concerns were reflected in two articles in *Pravda* and *Izvestia* on June 2 that accused the United States of trying to "drive a wedge" between the Soviet Union and Egypt. See "Chronology," *MEJ*, 25, no. 4 (1971): 506.

48. Rubinstein, *Red Star on the Nile*, pp. 145–46; Whetten, *Canal War*, pp. 186–88; el-Sadat, *In Search of Identity*, pp. 218, 222–26.

49. On the question of Soviet military support, see Breslauer, "Soviet Policy in the Middle East," pp. 90–91; Heikal, *Road to Ramadan*, pp. 112, 117; Whetten, *Canal War*, p. 154; Glassman, *Arms for the Arabs*, pp. 87–88, 92–94; Robert O. Freedman, *Soviet Policy in the Middle East since 1970* (New York, 1975), pp. 49, 68, 74–79; Rubinstein, *Red Star on the Nile*, pp. 170–80; el-Sadat, *In Search of Identity*, pp. 228–29 and app. A; and Oded Eran, "Soviet Policy between the 1967 and 1973 Wars," in Rabinovich and Shaked, *From June to October*, p. 40.

50. Remnek, "Politics of Soviet Access," p. 373: Whetten, *Canal War*, pp. 186–88; el-Sadat, *In Search of Identity*, pp. 218, 222–26; and Rubinstein, *Red Star on the Nile*, pp. 145–46.

51. el-Sadat, *In Search of Identity*, p. 228.

Soviet Union would never provide the military equipment he sought voluntarily. To jar his patron into providing what he wanted, Sadat abruptly informed the Soviet ambassador that Egypt's Soviet advisers would no longer be needed. By the end of August, only a thousand of the more than fifteen thousand advisers once assigned to Egypt were left.[52]

Sadat's sudden expulsion of his Soviet advisers apparently did the trick. After Sadat made additional conciliatory gestures later in the year (e.g., he renewed the agreement giving the Soviets access to Egyptian military facilities), Soviet military supplies to Egypt began to increase. In April 1973, Sadat announced that he was "completely satisfied" with the quantity and quality of Soviet support.[53]

The turbulent state of Soviet-Egyptian relations encouraged Moscow to hedge its bets by improving ties with its other Arab allies. Both Syria and Iraq responded favorably. Despite earlier Soviet support for his domestic opponents, Assad reaffirmed a policy of close cooperation with the Soviet Union. Two new arms deals were reached in 1971 and 1972; the Soviets now received limited access to the Syrian port of Latakia, and additional Soviet air defense troops, pilots, and other military advisers were dispatched to Syria in late 1972. By the October War, the total number of Soviet personnel in Syria had reached approximately six thousand.[54]

Soviet-Iraqi ties improved even more dramatically. Facing isolation in the Arab world, renewed conflicts with its Kurdish insurgency, and a growing threat from Iran, the Ba'th regime in Baghdad was in dire need of great power support. A Soviet loan worth $224 million was negotiated in April 1971, and Iraqi Vice-President Saddam Hussein reportedly sought a formal Soviet-Iraqi alliance during a visit to Moscow in December.[55] The request was granted in April 1972, military aid was

52. See Breslauer, "Soviet Policy in the Middle East," pp. 95–96; Whetten, *Canal War*, p. 228; Heikal, *Sphinx and Commissar*, pp. 241–45; Rubinstein, *Red Star on the Nile*, pp. 188–91, 202–11; and el-Sadāt, *In Search of Identity*, pp. 228–31.

53. Glassman, *Arms for the Arabs*, p. 96; Freedman, *Soviet Policy in the Middle East*, p. 102; Rubinstein, *Red Star on the Nile*, pp. 215–16, 228–29, and passim.

54. See Roger Pajak, "Soviet Arms Relations with Syria and Iraq," *Strategic Review*, 4, no. 1 (1976): 55–56; and "Soviet Arms Aid in the Middle East since the October War," in U.S. Joint Economic Committee, *The Political Economy of the Middle East: A Compendium of Papers*, 96th Cong., 2d sess., 1980, pp. 476–77; *Strategic Survey 1972*, p. 27. See also Glassman, *Arms for the Arabs*, pp. 96–97; and Galia Golan, *Yom Kippur and After: The Soviet Union and the Middle East Crisis* (Cambridge, England, 1977), pp. 29–30. Significantly, the Syrians apparently declined a Soviet offer for a treaty of friendship and cooperation similar to Egypt's at this time.

55. See Jaan Pennar, *The USSR and the Arabs: The Ideological Dimension* (New York, 1973), pp. 123–25; Robert O. Freedman, *Soviet Policy in the Middle East since 1970*, rev. ed. (New York, 1981), pp. 51, 76–77; Khadduri, *Socialist Iraq*, p. 145. The Soviets turned down the offer of alliance at this time, but Hussein's visit was quite successful in all other respects.

increased substantially, and the two countries signed an agreement to develop Iraq's Rumelia oil field, thereby facilitating Iraq's subsequent nationalization of the Iraqi Petroleum Company. President al-Bakr visited Moscow in September 1972, and the Ba'th agreed to form a Popular National Front, granting the Iraqi Communist Party a modest political role. Motivated by Moscow's troubles with Egypt and Iraq's internal and external difficulties, Soviet-Iraqi ties had thus reached their most significant level since 1959.[56]

Finally, Soviet ties with South Yemen continued to flourish, although the Soviets carefully refrained from taking sides in the brief border war that broke out between the PDRY and the Yemen Arab Republic (YAR) in February and July 1972. Various PDRY officials visited the Soviet Union during the early 1970s, and President Rubay 'Ali signed a major economic and technical agreement during his own trip to Moscow in November 1972. Although Soviet economic assistance was paltry, military aid grew from less than $20 million between 1968 and 1970 to more than $150 million between 1970 and 1974. Soviet naval vessels transported a contingent of PDRY troops sent to aid the Dhofar rebellion in Oman, and both Soviet and Cuban military advisers were present in increasing numbers.[57] With relations with Egypt undergoing obvious difficulties, Soviet ties elsewhere continued to expand.

Interestingly, the relations of the United States with its own regional allies mirrored the Soviet experience. Just as the Soviets clashed with their own allies over the merits of a political solution, the U.S. effort to promote a peace settlement led to another series of tense exchanges with Israel. In particular, Israel's sharp rejection of both the Jarring mission in February 1971 and Sadat's proposal for an interim settlement produced

---

56. Freedman, *Soviet Policy in the Middle East*, rev. ed., pp. 79–81; Khadduri, *Socialist Iraq*, pp. 145–47; and Robert O. Freedman, "Soviet Policy towards Ba'athist Iraq, 1968–1979," in *The Soviet Union in The Third World: Successes and Failures*, ed. Robert H. Donaldson (Boulder, Colo., 1981), pp. 169–72. The Popular Front was a purely symbolic organization, but its formation apparently helped convince the Soviets that the Ba'th was now worthy of greater support.

57. The 1972 border war was caused by the efforts both Yemens made to subvert each other, relying upon disaffected exiles, hostile tribal groups, and (in the case of the YAR) support from Saudi Arabia. Border clashes took place intermittently from February to May 1972 and escalated considerably in September. A ceasefire was then arranged under the auspices of the Arab League, and the two countries unexpectedly announced a decision to unite. This outcome reflected a tension that would persist throughout the 1970s; both governments publicly favored unification of the Yemeni peoples within a single state, but neither trusted the other or was willing to give up power. Although the Soviet Union provided military aid to South Yemen during the fighting, the Soviets consistently called for negotiations and publicly supported the ceasefire agreement. For details, see Katz, *Russia and Arabia*, pp. 32–35, 80–81, 84–85; Safran, *Saudi Arabia*, pp. 131–32; and M. S. El Azhary, "Aspects of North Yemen's Relations with Saudi Arabia," in Pridham, *Contemporary Yemen*, pp. 196–97.

considerable resentment in both Jerusalem and Washington.[58] At the same time, however, Israel was now receiving unprecedented levels of military and economic assistance, including additional F-4 aircraft and a $500 million loan. Indeed, total U.S. aid for 1971 reached $631.8 million, more than six times the previous high. Aid levels increased still further after Sadat's proposal for an interim settlement was rejected; a long-term supply of Phantoms was guaranteed, the United States agreed to supply engines for Israel's Kfir fighter, and Israel was promised additional Phantoms and Skyhawks in February 1972. Finally, the United States agreed to obtain Israel's approval before making any more peace initiatives. As one participant recalled, "In 1972, U.S. Middle East policy consisted of little more than open support for Israel."[59]

This policy was the brainchild of Henry Kissinger, who had become increasingly involved in U.S. Middle East diplomacy. Kissinger was told to "prevent an explosion in the Middle East" that might threaten Nixon's chances for reelection in 1972. Moreover, Kissinger believed that Israel would make concessions only if it had complete confidence in U.S. support. And because he saw support for Israel as a way to "expel the Russians" (by demonstrating that Moscow could not provide its allies with the wherewithal necessary to reconquer the occupied territories), Kissinger sought to increase U.S. aid for Israel and to move slowly on negotiations.[60]

While providing ever greater support to Israel, the United States continued to enjoy good relations with its traditional Arab allies. Jordan received a substantial increase in U.S. aid following the 1970 crisis as a reward for Hussein's moderation and to support his policy of controlling the PLO.[61] Although King Feisal of Saudi Arabia was increasingly upset by U.S. support for Israel, this concern did not prevent the United States and Saudi Arabia from beginning negotiations for a major military mod-

58. On U.S.-Israeli relations during this period, see Quandt, *Decade of Decisions*, pp. 132–33; Pollock, *Politics of Pressure*, pp. 104–10, 121–24; and Spiegel, *Other Arab-Israeli Conflict*, pp. 203–9.

59. Quandt, *Decade of Decisions*, p. 147. Israeli Foreign Minister Abba Eban called this period the Golden Age of U.S. arms supplies. See Pollock, *Politics of Pressure*, pp. 112–14, 124, 126–27; Rabin, *Memoirs*, pp. 193–209; and Safran, *Israel*, pp. 462–66.

60. For discussions of Kissinger's strategy, see his *White House Years*, pp. 1279, 1285, 1289, 1291, and chap. 10; and *Years of Upheaval* (Boston, 1981), pp. 196–202, 204–5. See also Quandt, *Decade of Decisions*, pp. 144–45, 153–54; and Spiegel, *Other Arab-Israeli Conflict*, pp. 172–73, 175–76, 183–84, 211–12, 216. One defect of Kissinger's strategy was the fact that it ignored Sadat's repeated signals (e.g., the interim settlement proposal and the expulsion of the Soviet advisers) that he was willing to make a deal and that he was willing to reduce Egypt's ties with Moscow to get one.

61. U.S. assistance increased to $115.6 million in 1972, and the United States agreed to supply twenty-four F-5 aircraft to modernize the Jordanian air force. See AID, *Overseas Loans and Grants*; Stookey, *America and the Arab States*, p. 233; Quandt, *Decade of Decisions*, pp. 122–23; "Chronology," *MEJ*, 26, no. 3 (1972): 297–98.

ernization program. As a result, Saudi imports of U.S. military equipment rose to $100 million in 1972. Of even greater significance, of course, was the growing importance of Saudi Arabian oil in the world market. Although Feisal had been reluctant to use the "oil weapon" in the past, this policy was about to change.[62]

The Arab Coalition Forms

The final factor leading to the October War was a continued process of reconciliation within the Arab world, which brought Egypt, Saudi Arabia, and Syria into an effective strategic partnership. With Nasser's death and Assad's ascendance in Syria, the last obstacles to effective alignment were removed. Assad and Sadat began a series of consultations in early 1971, Syria accepted U.N. Resolution 242 in March 1972 (with qualifications), and the two countries announced plans for a Joint Action Program linking Egypt's Arab Socialist Union with the Syrian Ba'th.[63] In October 1972 Sadat told his General Staff that "Syria will play their part in the battle; and they agree that action on the two fronts should be coordinated from Cairo."[64]

Cooperation with Saudi Arabia increased as well. Nasser's death considerably reduced Saudi suspicions about Egypt, a trend enhanced by Sadat's overt gestures of Islamic piety and his displays of respect for King Feisal.[65] The two leaders held several summit meetings in 1971 and 1972, and the Saudis apparently pressed Sadat to reduce Egypt's dependence on the Soviet Union. To encourage this step (and to provide Egypt with the forces needed to challenge Israel), the Saudis agreed to finance additional Egyptian arms purchases.[66] For his part, Sadat encouraged

---

62. See Safran, *Saudi Arabia*, pp. 204–5; Holden and Johns, *House of Saud*, pp. 290–96, 360; "Chronology," *MEJ*, 25, no. 4 (1971): 517; ACDA, *World Military Expenditures and Arms Transfers, 1971–1980* (Washington, D.C., n.d.), p. 107.

63. Assad's first cooperative gesture was the announcement in November 1970 that Syria would join the Federation of Arab Republics, the symbolic union of Egypt, Libya, and Sudan that had been established in 1970. Although the federation was a meaningless institution, this gesture demonstrated that Syria now sought to play a cooperative role in inter-Arab affairs. See "Chronology," *MEJ*, 25, no. 3 (1971): 384; 26, no. 1 (1972): 40; Itamar Rabinovich, "Continuity and Change in the Ba'th Regime in Syria, 1967–1973," and Barda Ben-Zvi, "The Federation of Arab Republics," in Rabinovich and Shaked, *From June to October*, pp. 179–80, 226–27.

64. See el-Shazly, *Crossing of the Canal*, p. 177.

65. On Sadat's relations with Feisal, see Holden and Johns, *House of Saud*, p. 289; Rubinstein, *Red Star on the Nile*, p. 241; and Lacey, *The Kingdom*, pp. 392–93.

66. According to Adeed Dawisha, Saudi Arabia provided $2.6 billion to Egypt between 1967 and 1973. Alvin Rubinstein reports that the Arab oil states gave between $300 million and $500 million for arms purchases at the beginning of 1973, plus an additional $400 million to $500 million in balance of payments support, above and beyond the annual subsidy they had provided since the 1967 Khartoum summit. See Dawisha, *Egypt in the Arab World*, p. 186; and Rubinstein, *Red Star on the Nile*, pp. 241–42.

Feisal to trust Assad, a step Assad facilitated by repairing the pipeline carrying Saudi crude oil across Syria to the Mediterranean. In response, the Saudis reportedly gave Syria a $200 million grant in 1972, and the Syrian-Saudi rapprochement was solidified by an exchange of visits by the countries' foreign and defense ministers.[67]

Relations among the other Arab states also improved slightly. Jordan had been ostracized following its campaign against the PLO, but Hussein did meet with Feisal and Sadat on several occasions during 1971. By the beginning of 1973 Syria and Jordan had reopened their border (closed since 1970) to "permit Jordan to participate in a new Eastern Front against Israel." Although Iraq remained isolated throughout this period, Saddam Hussein did visit Cairo and Damascus in 1972, and the Iraqis gave Egypt $12 million for military preparations.[68]

The final steps toward war began with Sadat's decision—apparently taken between November 1972 and January 1973—to prepare for military action as soon as possible.[69] When talks between Kissinger and Egyptian national security adviser Hafiz Ismail in February 1973 brought no progress and the United States announced that Israel would receive forty-eight more Phantoms, Sadat became convinced that a satisfactory settlement would first require a successful war. With an effective alliance now forged, with Soviet support available in sufficient quantities, and with the diplomatic front deadlocked, war was now Sadat's only real option.[70]

The Arab alliance completed its preparations over the summer, concluding with a summit meeting between Assad, Sadat, and Hussein on September 10. Egypt and Syria chose a strategy of limited aims, and Hussein pledged to enter the war only if the Arabs were winning; specifically, he would attack Israel once Syria had regained the Golan

---

67. On Saudi-Egyptian-Syrian relations between 1970 and 1972, see Holden and Johns, *House of Saud*, pp. 294–96, 298–99, 305–7; Heikal, *Road to Ramadan*, pp. 157–58; el-Shazly, *Crossing of the Canal*, pp. 147–49, 168–69; Dawisha, *Egypt in the Arab World*, p. 186; "Chronology," *MEJ*, 26, no. 1 (1972): 50; no. 2 (1972): 178; Lackner, *House Built on Sand*, pp. 118–19; and Safran, *Saudi Arabia*, pp. 144–48.

68. See "Chronology," *MEJ*, 26, no. 3 (1972): 295–96; 27, no. 3 (1973): 361. For an account of Jordan's turbulent relations with the other Arab states between 1971 and 1973, see Whetten, *Canal War*, pp. 219–21.

69. See el-Sadat, *In Search of Identity*, pp. 236–37; and el-Shazly, *Crossing of the Canal*, pp. 31–32.

70. Whetten, *Canal War*, pp. 234–35; *New York Times*, March 13, 1973; el-Shazly, *Crossing of the Canal*, pp. 173–77; and Sunday Times Insight Team, *Insight on the Middle East War* (London, 1974), pp. 34–35. For Kissinger's account of his talks in February 1973 with Egyptian national security adviser Hafiz Ismail, see *Years of Upheaval*, pp. 210–16, 223–27. Not surprisingly, Kissinger denies any connection between these abortive talks and Sadat's decision, claiming that Sadat was already implacably resolved on war. For a different version, see Matti Golan, *The Secret Conversations of Henry Kissinger* (New York, 1976), pp. 144–46.

Heights.[71] In addition to providing financial support to the Arab coalition, the Saudis had begun to hint that their alliance with the United States would not prevent them from using the oil weapon if necessary.[72] For the first time, the Arabs would confront Israel in a coordinated attack that marshaled their full military, economic, and diplomatic resources.

The Conduct of the War

A detailed account of the October War is not necessary here, so this part of the chapter will concentrate on the alliance aspects of the conflict.[73] The fighting can be divided into three general phases.

In the first phase (October 6–10) the Arabs enjoyed both strategic and tactical surprise. The Egyptian army gained a substantial foothold across the Suez Canal while Syrian forces placed enormous pressure on the outnumbered Israeli units on the Golan Heights. Soviet efforts to obtain a ceasefire in place were rejected by the Soviet clients, and the United States rejected the Soviet request in the expectation that Israel would easily defeat its attackers once its mobilization was complete.[74]

In the second phase (October 11–18) the superpowers took an increasingly active role as Israel gradually gained the upper hand. Both the United States and the Soviet Union began massive resupply operations to their respective allies, one indication of the extraordinary intensity of the fighting.[75] When a major Egyptian armored assault in the Sinai was decisively defeated on October 14, pressure for a ceasefire

71. On the concept of a limited aims strategy and the Arab decision, see John J. Mearsheimer, *Conventional Deterrence* (Ithaca, 1982), pp. 53–56, 155–62. See also Sunday Times Insight Team, *Insight on the Middle East War*, pp. 39–40; Whetten, *Canal War*, pp. 235–38; el-Shazly, *Crossing of the Canal*, pp. 39, 203, 205; el-Sadat, *In Search of Identity*, p. 242; and Chaim Herzog, *The War of Atonement* (Boston, 1975), pp. 25–31.

72. In the months preceding the war, King Feisal commented that "America's complete support for Zionism . . . makes it extremely difficult for us to supply the United States's petroleum needs"; Oil Minister Yamani hinted that the Saudis might be unwilling to expand production to meet demand if the United States continued its pro-Israeli policies; and Defense Minister Sultan stated that the Saudis would not buy arms with "strings attached." Sultan added that defense of the Arab countries was self-defense for Saudi Arabia, emphasizing the Saudi commitment to regaining the occupied territories. See Holden and Johns, *House of Saud*, pp. 328, 331–32; "Chronology," *MEJ*, 28, no. 1 (1974): 49; and Spiegel, *Other Arab-Israeli Conflict*, pp. 242–45.

73. For accounts of the fighting, see Herzog, *War of Atonement*; Dupuy, *Elusive Victory*, bk. 5; Quandt, *Decade of Decisions*, chap. 6; Golan, *Yom Kippur and After*, chap. 3; and Sunday Times Insight Team, *Insight on the Middle East War*.

74. Kissinger, *Years of Upheaval*, pp. 471–73; and Quandt, *Decade of Decisions*, p. 172.

75. See Glassman, *Arms for the Arabs*, p. 130; Whetten, *Canal War*, pp. 285–86, 291; William Durch et al., "Other Soviet Interventionary Forces: Military Transport Aviation and Airborne Troops"; and Stephen S. Roberts, "Superpower Naval Confrontations," in Dismukes and McConnell, *Soviet Naval Diplomacy*, pp. 200, 340; William B. Quandt, "Soviet Policy in the October 1973 War," *Research Report R–1864–ISA* (Santa Monica, Calif., 1976), pp. 23–25; and Quandt, *Decade of Decisions*, pp. 185–86, especially note 46.

increased still further. Soviet premier Kosygin arrived in Cairo for talks with Sadat while discreet negotiations between Egypt and the United States continued as well. Indeed, by October 15, Kissinger had been invited to visit Cairo "in appreciation for his efforts."[76] Here was the first clear indication of Sadat's political strategy: even while absorbing massive Soviet assistance, he was turning to the United States for diplomatic support.

In the third phase (October 19–27) the superpowers succeeded in imposing a ceasefire on their warring clients, albeit not without difficulty. By October 19 Israeli forces had routed the Syrians and were threatening to encircle the Egyptian Third Army on the west bank of the canal. Kissinger flew to Moscow and then Jerusalem to negotiate a ceasefire, but the resulting agreement broke down almost immediately. Brezhnev then sent Nixon a curt note threatening unilateral Soviet intervention if Israel did not halt its operations against the trapped Third Army. Nixon responded by ordering a worldwide military alert, and the United States pressured Israel into accepting a second ceasefire on the 27th, which brought the October War to a close.[77]

Although Egypt and Syria bore the brunt of the fighting, their Arab allies contributed as well. Iraq sent two armored divisions and an armored brigade to Syria and reportedly sent five squadrons of aircraft to Syria and Egypt. The Saudis sent an infantry brigade to Syria, and King Hussein limited his own participation to a single armored brigade on the Syrian front.[78] Despite strong Soviet and Arab pressure to open a third front on the West Bank, Hussein did the absolute minimum necessary to show solidarity with the Arab cause. This decision was undoubtedly based on his respect for Israel's military power, as well as the fact that the United States encouraged him to stay out of the war and told Israel not to attack Jordan as long as he did.[79]

Of far greater significance was the Saudi role in organizing and implementing an oil boycott and production decrease on October 20. Imposed in response to the U.S. decision to provide Israel with $2.2 billion worth of emergency foreign assistance, the oil boycott was intended to remind Western consumers of their interest in a more active and impartial role in achieving a Middle East settlement.[80] The war and the embargo

76. Kissinger, *Years of Upheaval*, p. 527.
77. Kissinger, *Years of Upheaval*, pp. 554, 568–91, 597–611; Whetten, *Canal War*, pp. 282–93; and Quandt, *Decade of Decisions*, pp. 191–200.
78. Dupuy, *Elusive Victory*, pp. 467–68; Edward Luttwak and Daniel Horowitz, *The Israeli Army* (New York, 1975), pp. 390–91; Herzog, *War of Atonement*, pp. 137–38, 141–43; and Whetten, *Canal War*, pp. 271–72.
79. Kissinger, *Years of Upheaval*, pp. 490, 494, 500, 506; Quandt, *Decade of Decisions*, p. 177; and Dupuy, *Elusive Victory*, pp. 536–37.
80. On the implementation and effects of the oil weapon, see Quandt, *Decade of Deci-*

Table 6. Middle East alliances, 1968-1973

Alliance	Interpretation
Egypt-Jordan (1968-1970)	Nasser and Hussein coordinate diplomatic positions to maximize pressure on Israel and to prevent the PLO from dominating the diplomatic agenda.
Soviet Union-PDRY (1968-present)	The Soviet Union and the PDRY establish close security ties to weaken imperialism, and the PDRY obtains aid in its border war with Saudi Arabia.
Eastern Command (1969)	After heavy prodding by Nasser, Syria, Iraq, and Jordan join forces to aid Egypt during the War of Attrition. Some Iraqi troops are stationed in Jordan, but the overall level of cooperation is extremely limited.
Jordan-Israel (1970)	Syria invades Jordan during Hussein's campaign against the PLO. Israel agrees to provide air support for Jordan, but the Syrians are defeated by Jordan alone.
Soviet Union-Iraq (1971-1978)	Threatened by the rising power of Iran, the Ba'th regime actively seeks support from the Soviet Union. The Treaty of Friendship is signed in 1972, and security ties expand rapidly.
October War Coalition (1971-1974)	After Nasser's death, Egypt, Syria, and Saudi Arabia establish close security and diplomatic ties to plan a successful war against Israel.

NOTE: Throughout this period, both superpowers provide increasing military aid to their clients (United States: Israel, Saudi Arabia, Jordan; Soviet Union: Egypt, Syria, Iraq, and PDRY). Soviet-Egyptian ties are strained by the Soviet Union's reluctance to provide adequate military equipment and by its interference in Egyptian domestic politics.

served essentially the same purpose: to break the diplomatic stalemate that had arisen since 1967. Egypt and Syria had suffered a military defeat to gain a political victory; both the United States and Israel were now actively interested in making a deal.

The principal alliances between 1967 and 1973 are shown in Table 6.

STEP-BY-STEP DIPLOMACY AND REGIONAL REALIGNMENT

Once attention shifted from preparing for war to moving toward peace, a new set of alignments began to emerge. The coalition that

sions, p. 188; Quandt, *Saudi Arabia in the 1980s*, pp. 128–29; Holden and Johns, *House of Saud*; "Chronology," *MEJ*, 28, no. 1 (1974): 39; and Kissinger, *Years of Upheaval*, pp. 523–24, 528–29, 534–35, 538, 872–74. For a report that the boycott was actually made for technical reasons related to production conditions, see Steven Emerson, *The American House of Saud: The Secret Petrodollar Connection* (New York, 1985), pp. 131–32.

fought the October War began to dissolve, as each member pursued its own interests. At the same time, Egypt gradually abandoned the Soviet Union for an alignment with the United States, which led the Soviet Union and its remaining clients to draw even closer together to preserve their own positions. The history of alliance formation in the Middle East from 1974 to 1979 is primarily the story of these two trends.

U.S. Ascendancy in the Middle East

The most signifiant development was Egypt's dramatic realignment toward the United States, an event closely tied to the dominant role of the United States in the postwar peace process. Kissinger visited Cairo immediately after the war, and he and Sadat agreed to separate the Egyptian and Israeli forces and restore diplomatic relations between the United States and Egypt. By January 1974, Sadat could state publicly that "the U.S. is following a new policy."[81]

Progress was steady after this initial step. Diplomatic relations were restored in February 1974, Sadat snubbed his Soviet patrons by accepting a U.S. offer to clear the Suez Canal, and in June 1974 Richard Nixon became the first U.S. president to visit Egypt. Sadat's "Open Door" economic policy began to attract Western investors, and U.S. aid for FY1975 climbed to $408 million. Sadat and President Ford met for talks in Salzburg in June 1975, Sadat visited the United States in October, and the administration authorized the sale of C–130 aircraft to Egypt, ending the long-standing ban on weapons sales to Egypt.[82] U.S. economic and military assistance to Egypt would grow to almost $2 billion by 1977, effectively signaling Egypt's realignment from the Soviet Union to the United States.[83]

---

81. For Kissinger's account of his first meeting with Sadat, see *Years of Upheaval*, pp. 635–45. See also Quandt, *Decade of Decisions*, pp. 216–17; Whetten, *Canal War*, p. 296; and Safran, *Israel*, pp. 511–13. For Sadat's statement regarding the change in U.S. policy, see Raphael Israeli, ed., *The Public Diary of President Sadat* (Leiden, The Netherlands, 1978), 2: 448.

82. On these events, see Charles C. Peterson, "Soviet Mineclearing Operations in the Gulf of Suez," in *Soviet Naval Influence*, ed. Michael MccGwire and John McDonnell (New York, 1977), pp. 540–45; Quandt, *Decade of Decisions*, pp. 246, 271, 280; Kissinger, *Years of Upheaval*, pp. 1125–1130; "Chronology," *MEJ*, 28, no. 3 (1974): 289; no. 4 (1974): 426–27; AID, *Overseas Loans and Grants*; Freedman, *Soviet Policy in the Middle East*, rev. ed., p. 149; "U.S. Economic and Business Relations with the Middle East and North Africa," *Department of State Bulletin*, 74, no. 1429 (June 14, 1976); Edward R. F. Sheehan, *The Arabs, Israelis and Kissinger* (Pleasantville, N.Y., 1976), p. 17; and Aronson, *Conflict and Bargaining*, p. 296.

83. See Quandt, *Decade of Decisions*, p. 280; AID, *Overseas Loans and Grants*; Shimon Shamir, "Egypt's Reorientation towards the U.S.—Factors and Conditions of Decision-making"; and John Waterbury, "The Implications of Infitah for U.S.-Egyptian Relations," in *The Middle East and the United States: Perceptions and Policies*, ed. Haim Shaked and Itamar Rabinovich (New Brunswick, N.J., 1980), pp. 285–86, 358–61, and passim.

Egypt's realignment brought diplomatic benefits as well. The October War had shown that the Arabs could not hope to defeat Israel militarily—they had had every advantage in 1973 and had still lost—but the costs and risks of another war now led the United States to take a more active role. Sadat was convinced that the United States held the key to Israeli concessions, and most important of all, that Kissinger was willing to use its leverage to get them.[84]

Kissinger's step-by-step diplomacy revealed that Sadat's assessment was correct. With both sides dependent on U.S. mediation, Kissinger was able to fashion three major agreements in 1974 and 1975. The first was a disengagement between the Egyptian and Israeli forces still frozen in the October 1973 ceasefire lines. A second, more difficult round of talks produced a similar disengagement between Syrian and Israeli forces in May 1974. The final step was the Sinai II agreement in September 1975, which combined a partial Israeli withdrawal from Sinai with an agreement for demilitarized zones and a multinational force to supervise the various provisions.[85]

All three agreements required Kissinger to exert considerable pressure on Egypt, Syria, and especially Israel. Because Kissinger's tactics involved a combination of carrots and sticks (i.e., threats to withhold U.S. support matched by subsequent increases), U.S.-Israeli relations were marred by intense disputes throughout the negotiating process.[86] At the same time, U.S. aid to Israel rose even higher than in the years before the October War. Israeli attendance at the Geneva Peace Conference in December 1973 was compelled by a letter from Nixon to Meir hinting that continued U.S. support was contingent on Israel's compliance, and the disengagement agreement in January 1974 was facilitated by a U.S. pledge to waive $1 billion of existing Israeli debts. An additional $500 million was waived following the disengagement with Syria, and a major arms package was approved in November.[87]

The failure to reach agreement for a second disengagement between Egypt and Israel created a similar rift. When the talks broke down in April 1975, Ford and Kissinger announced a reassessment of U.S. Mid-

84. As Sadat recounted his first meeting with Kissinger in his memoirs: "The first hour made me feel I was dealing with an entirely new mentality, a new political method." See el-Sadat, *In Search of Identity*, p. 291.

85. For accounts of the step-by-step process, see Quandt, *Decade of Decisions*, pp. 224–29, 238–45; Aronson, *Conflict and Bargaining in the Middle East*, pp. 227–32, 239–43; Sheehan, *Arabs, Israelis, and Kissinger*, pp. 109–12, 116–28; Safran, *Israel*, pp. 521–34; Touval, *Peace Brokers*, chap. 9; and Spiegel, *Other Arab-Israeli Conflict*, pp. 268–305. For Kissinger's own version, see Kissinger, *Years of Upheaval*, chaps. 18, 23.

86. See Kissinger, *Years of Upheaval*, pp. 619–23; Quandt, *Decade of Decisions*, pp. 215–16; Golan, *Secret Conversations*, pp. 105–11, 242, 246, 251; and especially Pollock, *Politics of Pressure*, pp. 167–70, 179–96.

87. Pollock, *Politics of Pressure*, pp. 180–82.

dle East policy. The key element of this reassessment was a brief suspension of U.S. aid to Israel. Pressured by Congress to lift the ban, Kissinger was able to obtain a second disengagement by pledging to increase aid to Israel still further. The United States also promised (1) to be fully responsive to Israel's defense requirements, (2) to guarantee Israel an adequate oil supply, (3) to provide Israel with the new F–16 fighter, and (4) to coordinate diplomatic positions—including a ban on negotiations with the PLO—regarding any future settlement. The step-by-step process did bring results, but they were bought with a price.[88]

The ascendancy of the United States after the 1973 war was also signaled by the continued growth of its military relations with its traditional Arab allies. Saudi Arabia lifted its oil embargo in March 1974 (after the first Sinai disengagement agreement) and announced a 1 million barrel per day production increase intended for the U.S. market. A $335 million military modernization program was announced the following month, and Nixon and Crown Prince Fahd exchanged visits in June. The U.S. Department of Defense began a long-range survey of Saudi military requirements at this time, and by the end of 1975 more than six thousand Americans were engaged in military-related activities in Saudi Arabia. Saudi arms purchases for the period 1974–1975 totaled over $3.8 billion, and a bewildering array of training missions and construction projects worth over $10 billion were now underway.[89] The Ford administration overcome congressional opposition to the sale of several advanced missile systems in 1976, and the Saudis were promised both F–15 and F–16 aircraft in the future.[90]

As for Jordan, Hussein's restraint in the October War was also rewarded. The FY1975 aid package featured a 72 percent increase over the 1974 total, and additional military shipments were authorized as well. Efforts to bring Jordan into the peace process foundered, however, on

88. On the negotiations for Sinai II, see Pollock, *Politics of Pressure*, pp. 187–88; Sheehan, *Arabs, Israelis, and Kissinger*, pp. 164–67; and Quandt, *Decade of Decisions*, pp. 264–76. For an Israeli perspective, see Aronson, *Conflict and Bargaining in the Middle East*, pp. 292–300. For the full text of the Sinai II agreement (including the secret annexes) see U.S. Senate Committee on Foreign Relations, *Hearings on Memoranda of Agreements between the Governments of Israel and the United States*, 94th Cong., 2d sess., 1975, pp. 249–53.

89. In the words of the director of the U.S. Defense Security Assistance Agency, these developments showed that the United States "viewed Saudi Arabia as a trusted friend." On these developments, see *New York Times*, March 18, 1974; Kissinger, *Years of Upheaval*, pp. 656–66, 774–77; Holden and Johns, *House of Saud*, p. 359; U.S. House Committee on International Relations, *United States Arms Policies in the Persian Gulf and Red Sea Areas: Past, Present, and Future*, 95th Cong., 1st sess., 1976, pp. 5, 12, 27, and passim; "Chronology," *MEJ*, 28, no. 3 (1974): 296; Quandt, *Saudi Arabia in the 1980s*, app. B; and U.S. House Committee on International Relations, *Military Sales to Saudi Arabia, 1975*, p. 2.

90. See Quandt, *Saudi Arabia in the 1980s*, p. 118; U.S. House Committee on International Relations, *Military Sales to Saudi Arabia, 1975*; and Spiegel, *Other Arab-Israeli Conflict*, pp. 308–10.

the unwillingness of either Israel or Jordan to make significant concessions regarding the West Bank. Moreover, the Arab decision to designate the PLO as the "sole legitimate representative of the Palestinians" at the 1974 Rabat summit effectively stripped Hussein of the authority to negotiate for this territory at all, because any agreement he might reach would have defied the Arab consensus. Under the circumstances, prospects for extending the step-by-step process to the West Bank were nil.[91] U.S.-Jordanian relations were also disrupted by a dispute over Jordan's request to purchase I-HAWK anti-aircraft missiles. Although Ford approved the purchase in 1975, Congress repeatedly delayed or altered the terms of sale. The delay led Hussein to adopt his familiar tactic of threatening to obtain a similar system from the Soviet Union. This threat overcame congressional opposition, and the deal was completed in the summer of 1976. Thus Jordan's pro-Western posture was preserved throughout the disengagement process, despite the fact that step-by-step diplomacy brought Hussein no real benefits.[92]

Finally, U.S. stewardship of the disengagement process led to a brief détente with Syria. The United States provided Damascus $104 million in economic aid in 1975—the first U.S. aid offering since the early 1960s—and Nixon became the first U.S. president to visit Syria, in 1974. U.S. motives were hardly subtle; the aid was intended "as an incentive for Syria to adopt a moderate approach to the Arab-Israeli conflict."[93] Unfortunately, the Sinai II agreement—which Syrian President Assad called a "separate peace" between Egypt and Israel that threatened Syrian interests—brought this brief easing of tensions to a close.[94] Nonetheless, by the end of 1976, U.S. diplomacy had established or reinforced close security ties with Egypt, Saudi Arabia, Israel, and Jordan.

On the Outside Looking In: The Soviet Union after the October War

The dominant role of the United States in the peace process forced the Soviet Union to commit increasing resources to its remaining Middle

91. See Spiegel, *Other Arab-Israeli Conflict*, pp. 283–89.

92. On these points, see "Chronology," *MEJ*, 28, no. 2 (1974): 165; 29, no. 4 (1975): 443; 30, no. 1 (1976): 70; no. 4 (1976): 527–28; 31, no. 1 (1977): 54; Sinai and Pollock, *Hashemite Kingdom of Jordan*, p. 150; William Griffiths, "Soviet Influence in the Middle East," *Survival*, 18, no. 1 (1976): 5. For the aid figures, see AID, *Overseas Loans and Grants*.

93. See "Chronology," *MEJ*, 29, no. 2 (1975): 184; AID, *Overseas Loans and Grants*; and Galia Golan and Itamar Rabinovich, "The Soviet Union and Syria: The Limits of Cooperation," in *The Limits to Power: Soviet Policy in the Middle East*, ed. Ya'acov Roi (London, 1979), p. 220.

94. Assad's statement is noted in Spiegel, *Other Arab-Israeli Conflict*, p. 303. See also "Chronology," *MEJ*, 30, no. 1 (1976): 64.

East allies. Although its enormous prior investment in Egypt had come to nought, ties with its other allies were enhanced.

By 1975, the Soviet-Egyptian alliance was moribund. Sadat had abandoned the Soviet Union very gradually, as insurance should his pro-Western policy fail to bear fruit and as a further incentive for the United States to deliver Israeli concessions. Thus, even as he criticized past Soviet support, Sadat called for the Soviets "to remain active in the peace process," and he described the Soviet Union as "a mainstay for peace loving people" in May 1974. But when Sadat continued his flirtation with the United States and attacked Soviet attempts to use arms supplies "as an instrument of leverage," the Soviets canceled two scheduled visits by Brezhnev and began to limit their arms shipments even more. Sadat restricted Soviet access to Egyptian military facilities in May 1975, sharply criticized a Soviet refusal to extend Egypt's loans, announced that he would seek military equipment from alternative sources, and refused to sign a new Soviet-Egyptian trade agreement.[95] The end was not long in coming; Sadat used the Soviet refusal to supply spare parts for Egyptian aircraft as the pretext for abrogating the Treaty of Friendship and Cooperation in March 1976.[96]

The collapse of the Soviet alliance with Egypt was balanced by a growing Soviet relationship with Syria. As Soviet arms shipments to Egypt declined, "arms shipments to Syria . . . reached staggering proportions."[97] The Soviet Union had replaced most of the military equipment Syria had lost in the October War by August 1974, extended Syria's war debts for an additional twelve years, and assigned Cuban and North Korean pilots to fly air defense missions in Syrian MIG–23s while Syrian pilots were being trained.[98] Soviet foreign minister Andrei Gromyko visited Damascus repeatedly in 1974 and 1975—in effect imitating Kissinger's frequent Middle East visits—and Brezhnev denounced the step-by-step process as "ersatz diplomacy." The Syrians welcomed their heightened status, especially after the United States failed to bring them additional diplomatic benefits. Assad's visit to the Soviet Union in October 1975—immediately following the Sinai II agreement between Egypt and Israel—produced another major arms deal,

95. See "Chronology," *MEJ*, 28, no. 3 (1974): 289; no. 4 (1974): 426–27; 29, no. 1 (1975): 71; no. 2 (1975): 187–88; Dawisha, *Soviet Foreign Policy towards Egypt*, pp. 73–74; Rubinstein, *Red Star on the Nile*, pp. 307–11; Amnon Sella, *Soviet Political and Military Conduct in the Middle East* (New York, 1981), pp. 132–36; and Remnek, "Politics of Soviet Access," pp. 376–77.
96. See Rubinstein, *Red Star on the Nile*, pp. 322–24. It is noteworthy that Sadat announced the abrogation of the treaty while on a U.S.-sponsored trip intended to attract economic assistance from Europe.
97. Sella, *Soviet Political and Military Conduct*, p. 138.
98. Pajak, "Soviet Arms Aid," p. 478; and Golan, *Yom Kippur and After*, p. 213.

and the Syrians now agreed to permit the Soviets to operate out of Syrian airfields on a regular basis. By the beginning of 1976 Syria had emerged as the Soviet Union's main ally in the Middle East.[99] This alliance, however, did not provide the Soviet Union with much control over Syrian behavior.

The effects of Egypt's realignment were also felt in Soviet relations with Iraq. The combination of external threats and internal challenges that had led Iraq to seek Soviet support in the early 1970s had declined, and the erosion of Soviet ties with Egypt made the Soviets especially eager to preserve their positions elsewhere. As a result, Iraq gradually acquired the upper hand in its dealings with Moscow. The Soviets continued to provide Iraq's armed forces with advanced equipment—including, for the first time, SCUD surface-to-surface missiles and MIG–23 aircraft—and they reversed their traditional pro-Kurdish policy by aiding the Iraqi government in a renewal of its intermittent war against the insurgents. Indeed, Soviet pilots reportedly flew combat missions in the government's latest campaign against the Kurds.[100] Iraq's increasingly independent stance was facilitated by the settlement of a border dispute with Iran in 1975 and the growing oil revenues that enabled Baghdad to expand its economic and military ties with the West.[101] And when Soviet relations with Syria deteriorated briefly during Syria's intervention in Lebanon, the Soviets countered by leaning toward Iraq; an arms deal reportedly worth $1 billion was arranged during Kosygin's visit in May 1976.[102] Given the improvement in Iraq's regional position and the difficulties now confronting the Soviet Union, the shift in leverage from Moscow to Baghdad is not surprising.

Finally, the Soviets sought to counter the various U.S. initiatives by increasing their support for other radical forces in the region. Soviet ties

99. On these events, see Golan, *Yom Kippur and After*, pp. 183–85, 213–31; Freedman, *Soviet Policy in the Middle East*, rev. ed., pp. 163–67, 210–11; Golan and Rabinovich, "Soviet Union and Syria," pp. 216–19; "Chronology," *MEJ*, 30, no. 1 (1976): 65–66; and Pajak, "Soviet Arms Aid," p. 478.

100. See Pajak, "Soviet Arms Aid," p. 470; John C. Campbell, "The Soviet Union and the Middle East," in U.S. Congress, Joint Economic Committee, *Political Economy of the Middle East*, p. 361; Golan, *Yom Kippur and After*, pp. 242–43; Freedman, *Soviet Policy in the Middle East*, rev. ed., pp. 161–63; and Avigdor Haselkorn, *The Evolution of Soviet Security Strategy, 1965–1975* (New York, 1978), p. 79.

101. Iraq purchased approximately $70 million worth of French arms in 1974, and Vice-President Hussein stated that "Iraq had a free hand in such matters." The Soviet share of Iraq's foreign trade dropped from 22 percent in 1973 to roughly 12 percent over the next two years. Trade with the United States, by contrast, rose from $20 million in 1973 to over $200 million in 1974 and 1975. See Pajak, "Soviet Arms Aid," pp. 47–71; and Orah Cooper, "Soviet–East European Economic Relations with the Middle East," in U.S. Congress, Joint Economic Committee, *Political Economy of the Middle East*, p. 284. For the details of the settlement between Iran and Iraq, see Khadduri, *Socialist Iraq*, pp. 245–60.

102. See Pajak, "Soviet Arms Aid," pp. 471–72.

with Libya expanded steadily after the October War, inspired by the two countries' joint opposition to Sadat's moves toward peace.[103] The Soviet Union's earlier policy of restraint toward the PLO was abandoned as well, and military aid to South Yemen increased to nearly $160 million between 1974 and 1977.[104] Indeed, the Soviet Union's concerns over its position in the Middle East now led it to court King Hussein of Jordan; a Supreme Soviet delegation visited Jordan in 1975, Hussein made a much-publicized visit to Moscow in 1976, and the Soviets offered to provide the air defense systems that Hussein had been seeking from the United States.[105] Thus the Soviet Union sought to balance Egypt's defection by acquiring new allies or increasing its support for old ones.

Step-by-Step Diplomacy and Inter-Arab Relations

The need to confront Israel effectively had brought Egypt, Syria, and Saudi Arabia together between 1970 and 1973, but the pressures of peace-making now drove them apart. The process was gradual because maintaining a common front increased their bargaining leverage and preserved the material benefits of Arab solidarity (e.g., financial assistance from the wealthy oil states). Nonetheless, the years following the October War witnessed the return of inter-Arab competition and a complicated series of maneuvers and realignments.

The problem was how to preserve Arab solidarity while Syria, Jordan, and especially Egypt independently sought the best deal with Israel. As early as January 1974, Syria's insistence that disengagement be simultaneous and linked to a "total Israeli withdrawal" revealed Assad's fear that Egypt would try to sign a separate peace.[106] This tension was an inevitable result of the step-by-step approach; it forced Syria, Egypt, and Jordan to pursue separate negotiations with Israel and the United States.

These inevitable conflicts of interest led the different Arab states to make several diplomatic adjustments. After the first disengagement agreements in 1974, efforts to bring Jordan into the peace process and to promote a further disengagement with Egypt met with strong opposition from Syria and the PLO. Sadat then broke his earlier pledge that Jordan would be next and voted to designate the PLO (not Hussein) as

---

103. See Freedman, *Soviet Policy towards the Middle East*, rev. ed., pp. 159–61, 200–201.

104. On Soviet support for the PLO, see Galia Golan, "The Soviet Union and the PLO," in *The Palestinians and the Middle East Conflict*, ed. Gabriel Ben-Dor (Ramat Gan, Israel, 1979), pp. 230–33 and passim. On relations with the PDRY, see Katz, *Russia and Arabia*, pp. 84–85; "Chronology," *MEJ*, 29, no. 1 (1975): 67; and U.S. House Committee on International Relations, *U.S. Arms Policies in the Persian Gulf*, p. 75.

105. Golan, "Soviet Union and the PLO," p. 241.

106. "Chronology," *MEJ*, 28, no. 2 (1974): 160–61.

the "sole legitimate representative of the Palestinians" at Rabat in November.[107] Sadat's reversal sprang as much from Egypt's own interests as from any commitment to the PLO or to Arab solidarity. By thwarting Hussein's efforts to join the peace process, the Rabat decision inevitably forced the negotiations back toward a second Egyptian-Israeli disengagement agreement. Given Syrian-Israeli animosity and the strategic value of the Golan Heights, a second agreement on the Sinai would be far easier to achieve than further progress along the Syrian-Israeli border.

The Sinai II agreement brought this latent conflict out into the open. Syrian officials denounced the agreement as "strange and shameful" and vowed to reverse it "even if we have to shed blood for it." Open polemics erupted between Damascus and Cairo in 1976, and both countries withdrew their diplomatic personnel after their embassies were attacked by demonstrators in June. The result was an unexpected rapprochement between Syria and Jordan, belying the fact that they had fought each other just five years earlier. The two countries had already begun to coordinate their diplomatic positions while Sadat was negotiating over Sinai, and they agreed to establish joint military and economic commissions in June 1975. Syria, Saudi Arabia, and Jordan conducted a series of joint military exercises shortly thereafter, and Jordan consistently backed Syria's policies during the Lebanese Civil War.[108]

With no territory at stake and enjoying the luxury of distance, Iraq, Libya, and South Yemen took a consistently hard-line view. They refused to attend the Algiers summit in November 1973 and condemned the Rabat decisions for implying the possibility of negotiations with Israel. Together with several radical PLO factions, Iraq established the so-called Rejection Front in October 1974, based on uncompromising

---

107. Itamar Rabinovich, "The Challenge of Diversity: American Policy and the System of Inter-Arab Relations, 1973–1977," in Shaked and Rabinovich, *The Middle East and the United States*, pp. 186–88; Quandt, *Decade of Decisions*, pp. 233–35.

108. See Lenczowski, *Middle East in World Affairs*, p. 497; U.S. House Committee on International Relations, *Military Sales to Saudi Arabia, 1975*, pp. 18–19; "Chronology," *MEJ*, 30, no. 1 (1976): 64; no. 2 (1976): 201; no. 4 (1976): 525; Rabinovich, "Challenge of Diversity," pp. 188–89; Paul Juriedini and Ronald P. McLaurin, "The Hashemite Kingdom of Jordan," in *Lebanon in Crisis: Participants and Issues*, ed. P. Edward Haley and Lewis Snider (Syracuse, N.Y., 1979); and *MECS 1976–1977*, pp. 154–55. Syrian and Jordanian opposition to Sinai II can be explained in two ways. The more common explanation is that a separate Egyptian-Israeli peace was viewed as a betrayal of the Arab cause that allowed Israel to refuse concessions elsewhere with impunity. An alternative is that Assad and Hussein secretly viewed Egypt's moves favorably—Assad because they left Egypt isolated and enhanced his position as the only significant confrontation state (given that other hard-line states such as Iraq and Libya could do little more than adopt bellicose resolutions) and Hussein because a successful Egyptian peace with Israel would legitimate his own efforts to reach an agreement and reduce the ability of the PLO to make any deals in his stead.

opposition to the step-by-step process in general and to Sinai II in particular.[109] This loose coalition (later joined by Libya and South Yemen and renamed the Steadfastness Front) sought to discredit its various Arab opponents by demonstrating greater fidelity to the Palestinian cause while simultaneously working to diminish the now-dominant role of the United States in Middle East diplomacy.[110]

At the same time, however, Iraqi relations with the moderate Arabs began to improve slightly. Sadat visited Baghdad in May 1976, and Saudi Crown Prince Fahd's own trip to Iraq in June marked the first visit by a member of the Saudi royal family in over fifteen years. These developments are not difficult to fathom either. Facing a flare-up in its traditional rivalry with Syria, Iraq now sought allies to counter the new alliance of Syria and Jordan. For Egypt and Saudi Arabia, in turn, a détente with Iraq prevented Sadat's moves toward peace (which the Saudis discreetly favored) from leading to complete isolation.[111]

But just when two new coalitions seemed ready to divide the Arab world again, the Lebanese civil war produced a brief reconciliation between Egypt, Saudi Arabia, and Syria. After the Lebanese government collapsed under pressure from the PLO and the various factions within Lebanon, Syria reversed its previous policy and sent twenty-five thousand of its own troops to suppress the PLO and support the beleaguered Lebanese government.[112] Significantly, Syria chose to intervene despite strong Soviet objections, which Assad termed "merely an expression of a point of view."[113] Although Egypt and Iraq both opposed Syria's

109. See Alan R. Taylor, *The Arab Balance of Power* (Syracuse, N.Y., 1982), p. 55; "Chronology," *MEJ*, 29, no. 1 (1975): 67.

110. Libya was at odds with Egypt after Sadat abandoned a 1971 unity agreement, South Yemen and Saudi Arabia were still extremely suspicious, and Syria and Iraq had been bitter rivals since the early 1960s. Thus the Rejection Front reflected all its members' separate interests.

111. The intermittent feud between Syria and Iraq was intensified over (1) disputes over the division of water from the Euphrates River, (2) an attack on a Syrian official in Iraq, and (3) Syria's expulsion of several Iraqi diplomats. See "Chronology," *MEJ*, 29, no. 3 (1975): 336–37; no. 4 (1975): 441–42, 448.

112. Syria's intervention against the PLO resulted from (1) Syria's desire to keep control over the Palestinian national movement, (2) its fear that the fighting might provide a pretext for Israeli intervention, and (3) its own aim of reinforcing its claims to a Greater Syria, including large parts of Lebanon. On these events, see Khalidi, *Conflict and Violence in Lebanon*, pp. 84–85, 167; Adeed Dawisha, *Syria and the Lebanese Crisis* (London, 1981), pp. 37–38, 72–74; Adeed Dawisha, "Syria in Lebanon—Assad's Vietnam?" *Foreign Policy*, no. 33 (1978–1979): 136–40; and Itamar Rabinovich, "The Limits of Military Power: Syria's Role," in Haley and Snider, *Lebanon in Crisis*, pp. 59–64.

113. On the Soviet reaction to Syria's intervention, see Dawisha, *Syria and the Lebanese Crisis*, pp. 169–70; Pajak, "Soviet Arms Aid," pp. 479–81; and Freedman, *Soviet Policy*, rev. ed., pp. 242–52, 255–60. The Soviets briefly suspended arms shipments, and Assad reportedly expelled a number of Soviet advisers and reduced Soviet access to naval and air facilities in Syria.

action initially (indeed, Egypt sent supplies to several PLO factions and Iraq mobilized troops on the Syrian border), King Khaled of Saudi Arabia eventually persuaded Sadat and Assad to attend a summit meeting in Riyadh in October 1976. Khaled's efforts were aided by Syrian and Egyptian dependence on Saudi financial support and by the Saudis' unusual willingness to use this leverage to gain their compliance. The Riyadh summit produced an agreement to create a multilateral (albeit predominately Syrian) Arab Deterrent Force in Lebanon, thus implicitly endorsing Syria's action.[114]

Thus, by the end of 1976, the earlier alignment of Egypt, Syria, and Saudi Arabia had been temporarily restored. By accepting the Riyadh agreement, Egypt had acknowledged Syrian predominance in Lebanon, and Syria had tacitly accepted Sinai II.[115] Jordan now enjoyed good relations with the three leading Arab states, and Iraq was isolated once again (save for its rather inconsequential allies in the Rejection Front). Although the first steps toward peace had been divisive, a decisive rift had been avoided thus far. However, the reconciliation fashioned in Riyadh proved to be extremely short-lived. The next moves toward peace would bring renewed rivalry and further realignments.

To Camp David and Beyond

The final phase examined in this study began with Anwar Sadat's unprecedented peace initiative in the fall of 1977 and the subsequent signing of the Egyptian-Israeli peace treaty in March 1979. Although Sadat had already shown his willingness to take independent action by signing the 1975 Sinai II agreement, his explicit defiance of the Arab consensus regarding a separate peace with Israel brought about Egypt's near-total isolation in the Arab world.

Sadat's initiative emerged from his reservations about the Carter administration's campaign to convene a multilateral peace conference in Geneva.[116] Rather than participate in a process he saw as doomed to

114. See Safran, *Saudi Arabia*, pp. 245–50; *Strategic Survey 1976*, pp. 84–88; Lenczowski, *Middle East in World Affairs*, pp. 381–86; *MECS 1976–1977*, pp. 147–50; Taylor, *Arab Balance of Power*, pp. 68–69; and Dawisha, *Syria and the Lebanese Crisis*, pp. 112–13.

115. This analysis follows that of Safran, *Saudi Arabia*, p. 251.

116. The administration's efforts were stymied by the formidable difficulties of getting all the necessary parties to agree on an appropriate forum and on the states that should be included. Sadat apparently believed that such a conference would accomplish little. In addition, he feared that this approach would allow the Soviets to regain a position of influence in the region while permitting Syria to exercise a veto on promising proposals. See Touval, *Peace Brokers*, pp. 288–89; Safran, *Israel*, p. 604 and passim; and especially William B. Quandt, *Camp David: Peacemaking and Politics* (Washington, D.C., 1986), chaps. 4–6.

fail, Sadat decided that a dramatic gesture was needed to "break the psychological and political barriers to peace." After a series of covert contacts with Israel (including a warning from Israeli intelligence that enabled Sadat to thwart a Libya-sponsored coup), Sadat announced that "he was ready . . . to go to the Knesset itself" in search of peace. Israeli Prime Minister Menachem Begin soon issued an invitation, and Sadat arrived in Jerusalem on November 19, 1977, after trying unsuccessfully to obtain Assad's approval for his mission.[117]

Despite the excitement Sadat's visit produced, a series of Egyptian-Israeli meetings made little progress. Carter then invited Sadat and Begin to a joint summit at Camp David in September 1978. Through Carter's active mediation, the outlines of a peace agreement and a broader Framework for Peace in the Middle East were signed by the three leaders on September 18, 1978.[118] After another six months of difficult negotiations, a formal peace treaty based on the Camp David Accords was signed. The treaty restored full diplomatic and economic relations between Egypt and Israel, established a timetable for Israel's withdrawal from the Sinai, and outlined a general framework for dealing with the West Bank and Palestinian Arabs. U.S. mediation and financial pledges played a key role in bridging the obstacles to agreement; Egypt was promised some $2 billion in additional economic and military assistance, and Israel stood to receive over $3 billion in additional aid. With this step Egypt's journey to a separate peace with Israel was completed.[119]

Arab Responses to the Egyptian-Israeli Treaty

Although Sadat tried to show Egypt's solidarity with the Palestinians by linking the peace treaty with Israel to a future agreement on the West

117. See Howard M. Sachar, *Egypt and Israel* (New York, 1981), pp. 260–61; Michael Handel, *The Diplomacy of Surprise: Hitler, Nixon, Sadat* (Cambridge, Mass., 1981), pp. 303–5, especially note 19, 328–29, 337–38; Moshe Dayan, *Breakthrough: A Personal Account of the Egypt-Israel Peace Negotiations* (New York, 1981), pp. 38–52; and el-Sadat, *In Search of Identity*, pp. 308–9.

118. For accounts or analyses of the Camp David negotiations, see Quandt, *Camp David;* Sachar, *Egypt and Israel*, pp. 278–86; Jimmy Carter, *Keeping Faith: Memoirs of a President* (New York, 1982), pp. 319–403; Zbigniew Brzezinski, *Power and Principle: Memoirs of the National Security Advisor, 1977–1981* (New York, 1983), chap. 7; Safran, *Israel*, pp. 609–12; *MECS 1977–1978*, pp. 123–29; Spiegel, *Other Arab-Israeli Conflict*, pp. 353–61; and Touval, *Peace Brokers*, pp. 298–303 and passim. The Camp David Accords called for restoration of the Sinai to Egypt and a complete peace with full diplomatic relations between the two countries and stated several general principles for the establishment of a "self-governing authority" for the West Bank, with its final status to be determined in five years. The text of the Camp David Accords can be found in *MECS 1977–1978*, pp. 149–54.

119. The most complete account of the negotiations for the peace treaty is Quandt, *Camp David*, chaps. 10–11; on the aid figures, see pp. 302, 313–14. According to William Burns, Sadat hoped to obtain even more. See his *Economic Aid and American Policy*, pp. 192–93.

Bank and Gaza Strip, Arab responses to the Camp David Accords were almost entirely hostile. Syria denounced the trip to Jerusalem as treason, and the Syrian ambassador to the United Nations claimed that Sadat "had stabbed the Arabs in the back."[120] In response, Syria, Libya, South Yemen, Algeria, and the PLO established a Front of Steadfastness and Resistance at a conference in Tripoli in December 1977, united primarily by their opposition to Sadat's initiative. Iraq was equally opposed to Egypt's policies, but the Iraqis chose not to join the front because of their continuing hostility toward Syria. Accordingly, they condemned the Tripoli summit for not going far enough in its condemnation of Egypt.[121] Criticism from Saudi Arabia and Jordan was more muted; both chided Sadat for not obtaining a "final acceptable formula for peace," but the Saudis continued to provide subsidies to Egypt until the signing of the formal peace treaty.[122] Jordan's response was understandably ambivalent. Hussein could not endorse the peace process openly without strong Arab support, but he did not wish to reject Sadat's initiative prematurely in case it suddenly bore fruit for Jordan. Hussein's refusal to condemn Sadat outright and to join the Steadfastness Front had the immediate effect of undermining the close alignment between Syria and Jordan that had begun after Sinai II.[123]

A more dramatic reversal was the sudden and short-lived rapprochement between Syria and Iraq, beginning in the fall of 1978. United by their opposition to Egypt's actions, alarmed by Israel's invasion of southern Lebanon in March 1978, and concerned by the rise of Shi'ite fundamentalism during the Iranian revolution, the two Ba'th states momentarily suspended their long-standing differences. Talks between Assad and President al-Bakr of Iraq led to the signing of a Charter of National Action in October, and the two leaders committed their countries—once again—to "seek arduously for the closest form of unity ties." A Joint Higher Political Committee met in December, and various subcommittees met periodically through January 1979. Although it was clear by then that the unity scheme was experiencing serious difficulties, it was a striking departure from the decade of hostility that preceded it.[124]

Of equal importance (and far greater duration) was the emergence of a

120. Quoted in *MECS 1977–1978*, p. 217.
121. *MECS 1977–1978*, pp. 225–26.
122. Sadat reportedly refused a joint Arab offer of $5 billion to abandon his peace initiative after Camp David. See *MECS 1977–1978*, pp. 228–29 and passim; and *MECS 1978–1979*, pp. 215–16. On the Saudis' ambivalent attitude toward the entire Camp David process, see Safran, *Saudi Arabia*, pp. 260–63. The Saudis had hoped that Sadat would obtain a deal that the rest of the Arabs would accept. This he clearly failed to do.
123. *MECS 1977–1978*, pp. 232–33.
124. See *MECS 1978–1979*, pp. 236–38.

tacit alliance between Iraq and Saudi Arabia, despite the traditional hostility and radically different domestic systems of the two states. For Iraq, the move provided insurance against revolutionary Iran, additional pressure on Sadat, and furtherance of its aim of supplanting Egypt as the leading Arab state. The Saudis responded favorably, in part to counter Iran and in part because they wanted to temper Arab condemnation of Sadat in the hope of leading Egypt back into the Arab fold. They were at least temporarily successful; an Arab summit in Baghdad in November 1978 called upon Egypt to abandon the Camp David Accords but did not impose sanctions at that time.[125]

Moderation was abandoned, however, with the signing of the peace treaty between Egypt and Israel in March 1979. At a second Baghdad summit, Egypt was formally suspended from the Arab League. The participants (including Jordan and Saudi Arabia) broke diplomatic relations or withdrew their ambassadors, imposed a trade boycott, and cut off all economic aid to Egypt.[126] Thus Sadat's initiative—in essence the culmination of the policy he had followed at least since the October War—had left Egypt isolated in the Arab world.

For Iraq, Egypt's expulsion appeared to be a golden opportunity. Enriched by rising oil exports, strengthened by Soviet arms, and encouraged by the turmoil now consuming its traditional rival in Iran, Baghdad enjoyed a new ascendancy. The Iraqis took the lead in orchestrating the campaign against Sadat, and relations with both Saudi Arabia and Jordan continued to improve in 1979 and 1980. The Saudis agreed to coordinate internal security planning in February 1979 (a move inspired by the growing danger of subversion from revolutionary Iran), and the rapprochement with Baghdad was furthered by an exchange of high-level visits over the next two years.[127] United by their opposition to Iran and their concern over the Soviet invasion of Afghanistan in December 1979, these unlikely allies formed a surprisingly solid alignment by 1980.[128]

125. Taylor, *Arab Balance of Power*, pp. 77–80; *MECS 1978–1979*, pp. 214–17, 235–36, and passim; and Safran, *Saudi Arabia*, pp. 262–64, 275–76, and 279–81.

126. For the resolutions of the Second Baghdad Conference, see Foreign Broadcast Information Service, "Daily Report for Middle East and North Africa," April 2, 1979, pp. A1–A5. See also Quandt, *Saudi Arabia in the 1980s*, pp. 20–21.

127. See Taylor, *Arab Balance of Power*, p. 79; *MECS 1978–1979*, pp. 240–41; and Safran, *Saudi Arabia*, chap. 14.

128. As Safran makes clear, the Saudis had been engaged in a delicate balancing act between Iran and Iraq. They sought initially to appease Iran while reinforcing ties with Iraq, notwithstanding the contradictory nature of this policy. Despite Baghdad's newfound moderation, the Saudis were understandably worried about Iraq's long-term ambitions as well as the threat from Iran, and they therefore sought to exclude Baghdad from direct security arrangements with the smaller Gulf states. When Iran proved impossible to appease, however, the Saudis embraced the lesser of two threats and moved to overt support for Baghdad. See Safran, *Saudi Arabia*, pp. 361–62. See also Ispahani, "Alone Together," pp. 158–60.

Indeed, Iraqi President Saddam Hussein (who succeeded al-Bakr in July 1979) announced in March 1980 that despite Iraq's "friendly ties" with the Soviet Union, should the Soviets invade the Persian Gulf, "the Iraqi Army would fight them even before the Saudi Army did."[129]

Jordan followed a similar path. As noted, King Hussein's ambivalent response to Camp David had weakened his link with Syria without winning him new allies elsewhere.[130] But with Syria opting for a more radical stance, with revolutionary Iran posing as an obvious threat to any pro-U.S. regime, and with Iraq moving to a more moderate position in concert with Saudi Arabia, Jordan's course was clear. After several preliminary exchanges, the two Husseins met in Baghdad in May 1980. Saddam Hussein declared that Iraq's relations with Jordan transcended "temporary, circumstantial factors," and the Jordanian monarch pledged that Jordan was "at Iraq's side with all its strength and all its resources." As he put it, Iraqi-Jordanian relations were now "a living model of what inter-Arab relations should be." Hussein then acknowledged the serious differences that had arisen between Jordan and Syria, an admission he had heretofore avoided.[131] Thus, by 1980, Jordan had shifted completely from alignment with Syria to membership in the Saudi-Iraqi coalition.

Ironically, by the end of 1979, Syria was almost as isolated as Egypt. The unity agreement with Iraq collapsed completely by the summer of 1979, undermined by the burden of past hostility and each side's refusal to subordinate itself to the other. Indeed, by the end of the year, the familiar invective of inter-Ba'th rivalry filled the Syrian and Iraqi media, along with the usual accusations (probably true) that each was trying to subvert the other.[132] Assad's troops were mired in the Lebanese quagmire, his regime faced serious domestic disturbances, and he was the only Arab leader still actively threatened by Israeli military power. Accordingly, Assad now took whatever allies he could get. The Steadfastness Front (largely moribund in 1979) reconvened at Syria's initiative in January 1980, and the foreign ministers of the front met again in Tripoli in April.[133] The reconvening of the front was small compensa-

129. *MECS 1979–1980*, pp. 196–97.
130. Ever seeking to remain within the prevailing Arab consensus, Hussein had called for joint military planning by Syria, Saudi Arabia, Iraq, and Jordan following the Baghdad II summit, in order to avoid having to choose between rival Arab camps should a rift widen. See Taylor, *Arab Balance of Power*, pp. 86–87; and *MECS 1977–1978*, pp. 232–33.
131. *MECS 1979–1980*, p. 198.
132. On the collapse of the Syrian-Iraqi unity agreement, see *MECS 1978–1979*, pp. 238–40.
133. The Steadfastness Front had languished in 1979 because Syria had opted to pursue unity with Iraq and cooperation with the moderate Arab states at the Baghdad summits in order to isolate Egypt. Once these arrangements deteriorated, Syria sought refuge with the

tion, however; symbolic support from Libya and South Yemen hardly equaled opposition from Iraq, Saudi Arabia, and Jordan. Syria's vulnerability during this period also led the country to deepen its ties with the Soviet Union. Thus the Arab world was once again divided into a radical and a moderate camp, although ideology had little to do with it. Indeed, the novelty within this familiar pattern lay in the fact that Iraq was now among the moderates and Egypt was entirely excluded.

Superpower Commitments after Camp David

Soviet and U.S. responses to the Camp David process were predictable. The United States focused its attention on gaining additional support for the peace agreements—an effort that failed completely—while defending its traditional commitments in the face of several new challenges. The Soviet Union, in turn, opposed any developments that excluded it from the peace process. As a result, it welcomed the Arab effort to ostracize Egypt. In pursuing these basic objectives, both superpowers experienced successes and failures. The net result was to preserve the basic division of the Middle East alignments between the two superpowers.

For the United States, stewardship of the peace process created significant tensions with virtually all of its regional allies, even as U.S. involvement in their security planning grew. Following Sadat's initial trip to Jerusalem, the Carter administration announced that the United States would meet a Saudi request for F–15 aircraft and other advanced equipment, together with a major weapons package for Egypt and Israel. Aid to Jordan continued as well, with these various commitments justified as necessary to attract moderate Arab support for the peace process.[134]

Despite heavy pressure, however, neither Jordan nor Saudi Arabia decided to support the Camp David process. Indeed, the U.S. assumption that their support would be easy to obtain exacerbated the resentment that both sides felt.[135] Furthermore, although the peace treaty was completed under U.S. auspices, both the drafting of the formal agree-

---

radical Arabs and Iran, in part to emphasize its status of the principal confrontation state sustaining the Palestinian cause against Israel. On these events, see *MECS 1979–1980*, pp. 178–86.

134. Jordan received over $200 million annually in economic and military aid during these years. On the events described in this paragraph, see Holden and Johns, *House of Saud*, pp. 485–87; Seth P. Tillman, *The United States in the Middle East* (Bloomington, Ind., 1982), pp. 98–106, *MECS 1977–1978*, pp. 686–88; Spiegel, *Other Arab-Israeli Conflict*, pp. 346–50; and Safran, *Saudi Arabia*, pp. 305–6.

135. On this point, see Spiegel, *Other Arab-Israeli Conflict*, pp. 363; and Safran, *Saudi Arabia*, pp. 304–5.

ment and the subsequent negotiations over Palestinian autonomy revealed that the United States, Egypt, and Israel had very different conceptions of what the Camp David Accords implied for the West Bank and Gaza. As a result, relations with both allies were often marred by significant discord during this period.[136]

U.S. regional commitments were also affected by the Iranian revolution and the Soviet invasion of Afghanistan, the two events that dominated the U.S. foreign policy agenda in 1979. Although U.S. fears may have been exaggerated, both Saudi Arabia and Jordan were worried by the rise in Soviet activity in the Horn of Africa and the Arabian Peninsula, by the collapse of the Shah's regime in Iran, and by what they saw as weak or vacillating U.S. responses.[137] To allay these concerns (and to enhance its own capabilities in the area), the United States reinforced its commitments to its remaining regional allies. A squadron of F–15 aircraft visited Riyadh in January 1979 (following the Shah's departure from Iran), although the gesture was weakened by the subsequent admission that the planes had in fact been unarmed. The United States also sent two AWACS early warning aircraft to Saudi Arabia in March and responded quickly to Saudi requests that military aid be sent to North Yemen during its brief war with its Marxist neighbor to the south.[138] Following the Soviet invasion of Afghanistan, Carter announced the formation of a Rapid Deployment Joint Task Force (RDJTF) intended to enhance U.S. intervention capability in the Persian Gulf and Middle East areas, and he stated that "an attempt by any outside force . . . to gain control of the Persian Gulf . . . will be repelled by any means necessary."[139] Egypt and Israel quickly indicated their willingness to provide facilities for the RDJTF, but Saudi Arabia preferred an enhanced U.S. commitment that did not require active Saudi participation.[140] In short, the setbacks the United States endured in 1978 and 1979 once again inspired a renewed commitment to its various regional clients, even though its clients' responses were qualified in several important ways.

As for the Soviet Union and its regional allies, despite their obvious

---

136. See Spiegel, *Other Arab-Israeli Conflict*, pp. 373–77.

137. See Holden and Johns, *House of Saud*, pp. 499–500.

138. On these measures, see *MECS 1978–1979*, p. 22; and Safran, *Saudi Arabia*, pp. 301–4.

139. See *New York Times*, January 24, 1980. On the roles and missions of the RDJTF, see Thomas L. McNaugher, *Arms and Oil* (Washington, D.C., 1985).

140. The Saudis clearly wanted U.S. backing against the Soviet and Iranian threats, but active participation in U.S. military arrangements would have left them vulnerable to accusations (by radical Arab states or Iran) that they were merely tools of "imperialist" forces allied with the "Zionist aggressor." On this point, see Quandt, *Saudi Arabia in the 1980s*, pp. 55–57.

common interest in opposing the U.S.-sponsored peace agreements, relations were strained throughout 1978 and 1979. Soviet-Iraqi relations deteriorated steadily as Baghdad sought closer ties with Saudi Arabia and expanded its military and economic links with the West.[141] A further source of tension was Hussein's discovery that members of the Iraqi Communist Party were forming cells in the armed forces, which led to the well-publicized execution of several dozen Iraqi Communists in 1978.[142] Hussein told a Western interviewer that "the Soviet Union won't be satisfied until the whole world becomes Communist," and the Iraqis refused to permit Soviet planes to overfly Iraqi territory during Moscow's intervention in the Horn of Africa in 1978. The invasion of Afghanistan merely added to Iraqi suspicions and encouraged the non-aligned policy that Iraq was adopting by 1980.[143]

Soviet relations with Syria had been somewhat tense since 1976, when Assad had defied Soviet pressure during the Syrian intervention in Lebanon. Although amity was restored in the months after Sadat's initiative—Assad paid a successful visit to the Soviet Union and Syria received new infusions of Soviet arms—differences persisted between Moscow and Damascus. Indeed, Assad's dissatisfaction with the level of Soviet arms aid and the conditions under which it was provided led him to recall the Syrian ambassador in December 1978 and to cancel his own plans to visit the Soviet Union at this time.[144]

When the unity scheme with Iraq collapsed and the Saudi-Iraqi rapprochement took shape in 1979, however, Syria moved quickly to revive its ties with Moscow. By resurrecting the Steadfastness Front—which brought Moscow's main Arab clients together in one group—the Syrians managed to limit Arab criticism of the Soviet invasion of Moslem Afghanistan. Given Syria's isolation from the other Arab states and Egypt's decision to sign a separate peace, the Syrians were also convinced that Soviet support was essential to any future effort to challenge Israel over the remaining occupied territories (e.g., the Golan Heights).

141. Indeed, in 1980, Iraq purchased more arms from France than from the Soviet Union (measured in terms of dollar value of purchases). See *MECS 1979–1980*, p. 62.

142. See Fukuyama, "Soviet Union and Iraq," pp. 56–61.

143. Iraq did not become pro-Western or pro-United States. The Iraqis continued to purchase Soviet arms (no doubt because their troops were familiar with them and because they were relatively cheap) and remained hostile to the United States. Nonetheless, their policy was a striking change for a regime that had sought a formal treaty with Moscow in 1971.

144. During his visit in April, Assad stated publicly that there were still "differences in views" between the Soviet Union and Syria, but the overall tone of the visit was one of mutual support. On these various events, see Pajak, "Soviet Arms Aid," pp. 481–84; Morris Rothenberg, "Recent Soviet Relations with Syria," *Middle East Review*, 10, no. 4 (1978); and Rashid Khalidi, "Soviet Middle East Policy in the Wake of Camp David," *Institute for Palestine Studies Papers*, no. 3 (Beirut, 1979), pp. 23–25, 31–33.

This conviction overcame Assad's long-standing reluctance to sign a formal treaty with the Soviet Union, and the agreement was completed in May 1980. According to Brezhnev, the treaty raised Soviet relations with Syria "to a new, higher level."[145] All things considered, it was an understandable response to the setbacks both parties had endured over the previous several years.

From the Soviet perspective, events on the Arabian Peninsula were somewhat more encouraging, although there were disquieting elements there as well. In South Yemen, President Rubay 'Ali had begun a process of détente with Saudi Arabia and North Yemen in 1976, encouraged by Saudi offers of extensive economic assistance. Indeed, 'Ali indicated that restoring diplomatic relations with the United States was also a possibility, a development that would have threatened Moscow's position in the only Marxist country in the Arab world.[146] This restoration was not to be, however; the emerging détente was frozen during the Soviet intervention in the 1977 Somali-Ethiopian war, which the PDRY supported. The effort collapsed completely in 1978, when 'Ali was ousted and killed by a hard-line, pro-Soviet faction led by Abdel Fatah Ismail, then secretary-general of the South Yemeni National Liberation Front. Indeed, several accounts suggest that Warsaw Pact and Cuban advisers gave active support to Ismail during the coup.[147] Whether or not the Soviets helped arrange the coup, it did lead to a further expansion in the Soviet relationship with the PDRY; a fifteen-year agreement for naval access was soon announced, and a twenty-five-year Treaty of Friendship and Cooperation was signed in October 1979. The durability of the Soviet-PDRY alliance was highlighted further in 1980, when Ismail was removed from power by his former ally, 'Ali Nasser Muhammed. Ismail went into exile in the Soviet Union, but Soviet relations with the new rulers were unaffected.[148]

To the north, the Yemen Arab Republic continued the policy of nonalignment it had followed since the early 1970s while remaining dependent on Saudi financial assistance.[149] The United States began a modest military aid program in 1976 (financed by Saudi Arabia), and the YAR

145. See *MECS 1979–1980*, pp. 65–66.
146. See *MECS 1977–1978*, p. 667; Katz, *Russia and Arabia*, pp. 91–92; and Safran, *Saudi Arabia*, pp. 285–88.
147. See J. B. Kelly, *Arabia, the Gulf, and the West* (New York, 1980), pp. 470–73; and *MECS 1977–1978*, pp. 655–66. Mark N. Katz concludes that the evidence regarding a possible Warsaw Pact role in the coup is insufficient. See his *Russia and Arabia*, p. 92.
148. See Katz, *Russia and Arabia*, pp. 93–94.
149. According to Christopher Van Hollen, the Saudis were providing North Yemen with roughly $400 million annually in direct budgetary support, plus a variety of other funds for economic development and arms purchases. See his "North Yemen: A Dangerous Pentagonal Game," *Washington Quarterly*, 5, no. 3 (1982): 139.

continued to balance uneasily between the two superpowers, the PDRY, and Saudi Arabia itself. The situation deteriorated rapidly in 1978; the assassination of President al-Ghashmi by a South Yemeni envoy in 1978 (a plot apparently linked to the struggle for power between 'Ali and Ismail in the PDRY) led to a renewal of fighting between the YAR, the PDRY, and the PDRY-backed National Democratic Front.

Eager to restore its credibility in the region, the United States responded to Saudi requests by sending an aircraft carrier to the Gulf of Aden and by agreeing to supply roughly $350 million worth of arms to Sana via Saudi Arabia. The Saudis backpedaled at this point, partly because a ceasefire was negotiated quickly and partly because they feared that large U.S. arms shipments to North Yemen would reduce their own leverage over the government of the YAR. Thus the promised arms arrived either slowly or not at all, forcing North Yemen to turn back to Moscow for military aid. A deal worth several hundred million dollars was reached at the end of 1979, and deliveries were reportedly completed early in 1980. Despite this predictable response to their inability to obtain U.S. arms, the YAR continued to proclaim a policy of nonalignment. According to President Ghashmi's successor, 'Ali Abdallah Salih, North Yemen would "be a tool in neither U.S. hands nor in those of the Soviet Union."[150]

Summary

Sadat's decision to sign a separate peace with Israel triggered a series of events that left the Arab world polarized once again, amid the usual calls for Arab solidarity. In contrast to the 1960s, however, the issue was primarily one of conflicting interests, not ideology. For the moderate camp (now including Iraq) the Arab-Israeli conflict had become a relatively minor issue, either because the moderates had no tangible interests at stake (e.g., Iraq) or because Egypt's defection had made direct action even more impractical than before (e.g., Jordan). Moreover, the perception of a growing threat from the Soviet Union and Iran gave the moderates a powerful incentive to cooperate together while preserving discreet ties with the West. Given the close relationship of the United States and Israel, the moderate Arab states had an additional reason to downplay the Palestinian question. Condemnation of Egypt was still necessary, but it was largely pro forma. Indeed, both Saudi Arabia and

---

150. Quoted in *MECS 1978–1979*, p. 63. See also Katz, *Russia and Arabia*, pp. 46–47; U.S. House Committee on International Relations, *U.S. Arms Policies in the Persian Gulf*, pp. 73–82; and Yodfat, *Soviet Union and the Arabian Peninsula*, pp. 105–8:

Iraq may have welcomed the opportunity to keep Egypt somewhat isolated.[151]

For Syria and the radical states of the Steadfastness Front, the Palestinian question remained the dominant issue, at least in their public posturing. First, Syria had a material interest in the conflict (e.g., the Golan Heights). Second, the Palestinian question remained the best way for the entire Steadfastness Front to demonstrate its commitment to defend the Arab national cause against the forces of "imperialism and Zionism." Neither the Soviet Union nor Iran seemed especially threatening; indeed, both were obvious allies given the radicals' overall objectives. Thus it was not surprising that the Arab world remained divided; each group's objectives tended to undermine those of the other, even in the absence of any specific bilateral antagonisms. And there was no shortage of those either.

The positions of the superpowers, by contrast, were surprisingly unaffected by the peace treaty. Although Iraq moved away from the Soviet Union after 1977, this decision had little to do with Egypt's decision to make peace. The Soviet Union continued its military, economic, and diplomatic support for Syria, South Yemen, the PLO, and Libya, and the United States reinforced its long-standing commitments to Israel, Saudi Arabia, and Jordan. Egypt was now as dependent on the United States as it had once been on the Soviet Union. Iraq and North Yemen were following policies of nonalignment, although both maintained more extensive contacts with the Soviet Union than with the United States.

The final set of alignments, occurring between 1974 and 1979, is summarized in Table 7.

CONCLUSION

Three general observations can be made from this overview. First, throughout the period 1955–1979, the emergence of a dominant regional actor has led others to seek both regional and great power allies to defend their interests. Before 1967, this process centered on thwarting Nasser's aspirations in the Arab world, on preventing attempts by the West to enhance its influence at the expense of nationalist forces and the Soviet Union, and on preserving Western interests against a perceived

---

151. The ostracism of Egypt had cleared the way for Iraq's bid for dominance in the Arab world and had reduced the danger a resurgent Egypt could pose to Saudi Arabia. It should not be forgotten that Egypt had threatened the Saudis and stifled Iraq's ambitions on numerous occasions in the past and that Egypt's size, military strength, and intellectual prominence in the Arab world made it an important latent power in the region, despite its liabilities.

Table 7. Middle East alliances, 1974–1979

Alliance	Interpretation
United States-Egypt (1975–present)	Convinced that the United States holds "95 percent of the cards," Sadat abandons reliance on the Soviet Union and bandwagons with the United States to gain peace and economic aid. The United States continues to oversee the peace process.
Syria-Jordan (1975–1978)	Syria and Jordan overcome mutual hostility to isolate Egypt, as Egypt moves toward a separate peace by signing the Sinai II agreement.
Steadfastness Front (1978–1979)	Syria, South Yemen, Algeria, and Libya ally to pressure Sadat to abandon the Camp David process. Saudi Arabia and Jordan go along reluctantly after the peace treaty with Israel.
Saudi Arabia-Jordan-Iraq (1979–present)	Saudi Arabia, Jordan, and Iraq join forces to balance Syria and the growing threat from Khomeini's Iran.

Soviet challenge. The focus shifted after the Six Day War: Israel's military superiority forced the Arabs to join forces more effectively than ever before while relying even more heavily on Soviet support.

After 1974, the Arabs shifted from cooperating in war to quarreling over peace. Moreover, no single state seemed to attract the same concerns that Egypt and Israel had inspired in earlier periods. The result was a series of ad hoc adjustments as the different regional powers responded to these new circumstances without being sure which states posed the greatest danger or could deliver the largest rewards.[152]

Second, the period 1955–1979 witnessed a steady increase in superpower involvement in the Middle East. As mutual rivals, each sought to enhance its position vis-à-vis the other by exploiting regional conflicts. Setbacks inspired renewed commitments and were usually temporary. This situation is not surprising; as long as regional rivalries persist, it would be unlikely that either superpower could be entirely excluded as long as it was willing to support one side or the other.

Third, the role of ideology declined significantly over time, and especially after 1967. After the Six Day War, attention shifted from preventing Nasser's pan-Arab aspirations to denying Israel permanent con-

152. For example, the Saudis vacillated between support for and opposition to both Yemens, first appeased and then opposed Iran, and gave financial aid to Syria while forming a close alignment with its archenemy, Iraq. The Syrians, in turn, switched from cooperation with Egypt to alignment with the Steadfastness Front, to a unity agreement with Iraq, and back into the Front again.

trol of Arab territory. With pan-Arabism in decline, inter-Arab politics after 1967 were driven more by material interests (e.g., regaining the occupied territories) than by the endless wrangling over which regime had the best plan for reuniting the "one Arab nation with its historic mission." Although the question of Palestine remained a touchstone of Arab nationalist ideology, increased cooperation among some otherwise unlikely partners (e.g., Syria and Jordan, Iraq and Saudi Arabia) was the most important result of the gradual decline in pan-Arab ideology.

[5]

Balancing and Bandwagoning

Chapters 5 through 7 evaluate the propositions developed in chapter 2 in light of the events described in chapters 3 and 4. Specifically, chapter 5 examines the competing hypotheses on balancing and bandwagoning, chapter 6 explores the relationship between ideology and alignment, and chapter 7 assesses the impact of foreign aid and penetration.

This chapter considers first the overwhelming tendency for states to prefer balancing and then the rare cases of bandwagoning that do occur. The analysis addresses four broad questions. First, which of the two—balancing or bandwagoning—is more common? Second, do the responses of the superpowers differ from those of the regional states? Third, if balancing is the prevalent response, what is the relative importance of the different sources of threat (aggregate power, geographic proximity, offensive power, and aggressive intentions) in producing balancing behavior? Finally, are the relatively rare examples of bandwagoning adequately explained by the hypotheses outlined earlier? In answering these questions, I am in effect testing the propositions on balancing and bandwagoning advanced in chapter 2. Before I undertake these tasks, however, I will briefly discuss hypothesis testing.

Three strategies are available to test the different hypotheses developed in chapter 2. The first strategy is to measure covariance. Does the dependent variable (in this case, international alignments) co-vary with the independent variables (level of threat, ideological agreement, etc.) specified in each hypothesis? We can also test the hypotheses indirectly by deducing other predictions (for which evidence may be more readily available) and testing them. The second strategy is to rely on direct evidence (such as the memoirs of a knowledgeable participant) for testimony as to why a particular alliance choice was made. The third strategy is to ask the experts—to compare the judgments of regional specialists with the predictions of each hypothesis, using the expertise of others to substitute for a lack of direct evidence on the perceptions of the relevant actors.[1]

Each of these strategies has been employed in the evaluation of the various hypotheses on alliance formation.[2] None is uniformly feasible or reliable, but together they provide a satisfactory set of tests. A rough measure of the relative validity of the competing propositions is gained by comparing the number of alliances in the sample that fit the predictions of each general hypothesis with the number that do not. Direct evidence on elite perceptions, when available, is also examined. Throughout, expert testimony from secondary sources is used to make specific analytic judgments.

BALANCING BEHAVIOR AND ALLIANCE FORMATION

What does the historical record in the Middle East reveal about the origins of alliances? Four things, primarily. First, and most obviously, external threats are the most frequent cause of international alliances. Second, balancing is far more common than bandwagoning. Third, states do not balance solely against power; as predicted, they balance against threats. Although the superpowers choose alliance partners primarily to balance against each other, regional powers are largely indifferent to the global balance of power. Instead, states in the Middle East most often form alliances in response to threats from other regional actors. Fourth, offensive capabilities and intentions increase the likelihood of others joining forces in opposition, although the precise impact of these factors is difficult to measure. Let us first consider the evidence for these conclusions and then explore why such behavior occurs.

1. I have found the following works on social science methodology helpful: Alexander L. George, "Case Studies and Theory Development," paper presented to the 2d Annual Symposium on Information Processing, Carnegie-Mellon University, October 15–16, 1982; Arthur L. Stinchcombe, *Constructing Social Theories* (New York, 1968); Donald Campbell and Julian Stanley, *Experimental and Quasi-Experimental Designs for Research* (Chicago, 1963); Hubert Blalock, *Basic Dilemmas in the Social Sciences* (Beverly Hills, Calif., 1984); and Paul Diesing, *Patterns of Discovery in the Social Sciences* (Chicago, 1971), especially chaps. 11, 13, 18, and 19.

2. The correlational approach is limited when several independent variables are all contributing to the outcome. With quantitative data, this limitation can be dealt with by controlling for each variable; but there is no simple way to do so with largely qualitative data. Elite testimony can be revealing but must be used with caution, as memoirs and other statements may be heavily influenced by the speaker's instrumental motives. In the same way, expert accounts can reflect the analyst's biases or other errors and therefore should be used with care.

The Dominance of Balancing Behavior

Alliances formed to balance against threats may take several distinct forms. In the most typical form, states seek to counter threats by adding the power of another state to their own. Thus the superpowers have sought allies to counter threats from each other (e.g., by acquiring bases or other useful military assets) or to prevent the other from expanding its influence. The regional states, in turn, have sought external assistance, most often from one of the superpowers but occasionally from other local actors, when they have been engaged in an intense rivalry or an active military conflict.[3]

A different form of balancing has occurred in inter-Arab relations. In the Arab world, the most important source of power has been the ability to manipulate one's own image and the image of one's rivals in the minds of other Arab elites. Regimes have gained power and legitimacy if they have been seen as loyal to accepted Arab goals, and they have lost these assets if they have appeared to stray outside the Arab consensus. As a result, an effective means of countering one's rivals has been to attract as many allies as possible in order to portray oneself as leading (or at least conforming to) the norms of Arab solidarity. In effect, the Arab states have balanced one another not by adding up armies but by adding up votes. Thus militarily insignificant alliances between the various Arab states often have had profound political effects.

We are therefore dealing with two broad types of balancing: balancing conducted by military means for specific military ends and balancing conducted by political means directed at an opponent's image and legitimacy. Common to both types, however, is the desire to acquire support from others in response to an external threat.

Chapters 3 and 4 identified thirty-six distinct international alliances among the states in the sample. (See appendix 1 for the complete list.) Each of these alliances required a decision by two or more states. The thirty-six alliances are thus the result of eighty-six separate alliance choices. As shown in Table 8, at least 93 percent (eighty out of eighty-six) of these decisions were made at least partly in response to a direct external threat and 87.5 percent (seventy out of eighty) were directed against the states that appeared most dangerous. By contrast, the states examined here chose to bandwagon with the principal sources of threat *at most* 12.5 percent (ten out of eighty) of the time. Not only were external threats the most frequent cause of the overwhelming majority of alliances examined in this study, but such threats almost always led

---

3. The most obvious examples are the patron-client relationships that enable the Arabs and Israelis to sustain their rivalry, the support given to the warring sides in the Yemen civil war, and the Arab coalition that fought the October War in 1973.

[149]

Table 8. Alliances formed in response to external threats

Alliance	Duration	Main threats	Balance or bandwagon?		Level of commitment[a]
Baghdad Pact[b]	1955–1958	Soviet Union/Egypt	3	0	Moderate
Arab Solidarity Pact[c]	1955–1956	Iraq/Egypt	4 (2)	1 (3)	Moderate/low
Soviet Union-Egypt	1955–1974	United States/Great Britain/Israel	2	0	High
Soviet Union-Syria (1)	1955–1958	Baghdad Pact/Israel	2	0	Moderate
Soviet Union-YAR (1)	1955–1962	Great Britain	2	0	Low
Suez War Coalition[d]	1956	Egypt	3	0	High
Kings' Alliance[e]	1957–1958	Egypt	3	0	Moderate/low
United States-Saudi Arabia	1957–present	Egypt/Soviet Union	2	0	High
United States-Lebanon	1957–1958	Egypt/Soviet Union	2	0	High
United States-Jordan	1957–present	Egypt/Soviet Union	2	0	High
Iraq-Jordan	1958	Egypt/Syria	2	0	Moderate
Egypt-Saudi Arabia	1958–1961	Iraq/Egypt	1	1	Low
Soviet Union-Iraq (1)	1958–1960	United States/Great Britain/Egypt	2	0	Moderate
Kuwait Intervention[f]	1961	Iraq	3	0	Moderate
United States-Israel	1962–present	Egypt/Soviet Union	2	0	High
Egypt-YAR	1962–1967	Royalists/Saudi Arabia	2	0	High
Saudi Arabia-Jordan	1962–1964	Egypt	2	0	Moderate/high
Tripartite Union[g]	1963	Egypt	0	1	Low
Syria-Iraq	1963	Egypt	2	0	High
Cairo Summit[h]	1964–1965	Syria/Egypt	1	2	Low/moderate
Soviet Union-YAR	1964–1969	United States/Royalists	2	0	High
Soviet Union-Syria (2)	1966–present	United States/Israel	2	0	High
Six Day War Coalition[i]	1967	Israel/Egypt	2	1	High

Alliance	Dates				Involvement[a]
Egypt-Jordan	1967	Israel/PLO	2	0	Moderate
Soviet Union-PDRY	1968–present	United States/Saudi Arabia	2	0	High
Eastern Command[j]	1969–1970	Israel	3	0	Low
Israel-Jordan	1970	Syria/PLO	2	0	Low
October War Alliance[k]	1971–1973	Israel	3	1	High
Soviet Union-Iran (2)	1971–1978	United States/Iran	2	0	High
Egypt-United States	1975–present	Soviet Union/United States	1	1	High
Syria-Jordan	1975–1979	United States/Iraq	2	0	Moderate
Steadfastness Front[l]	1978–1981	Israel/Egypt	2	0	Moderate
Saudi Arabia-Jordan-Iraq	1979–present	Iran/Syria	3	0	High
Total alliances: 33		Total decisions:	70 (68)	8 (10)	

a *High* means that the alliance involves extensive security cooperation or active military involvement. *Moderate* means that the alliance involves diplomatic coordination and significant risk of military involvement. *Low* means that the alliance involves symbolic commitment only.

b Only the United States, Great Britain, and Iraq are counted here. Full membership of the pact was Iraq, Turkey, Great Britain, Iran, and Pakistan. The United States was not an official member but supported the pact via defense treaties with several members.

c Egypt, Syria, Yemen, Saudi Arabia, and Jordan. Saudi Arabia and Yemen joined the alliance to balance against Iraq and Great Britain but remained partly to appease (i.e., bandwagon with) Egypt. Hussein joined reluctantly under Egyptian and Syrian pressure.

d Britain, France, and Israel.

e Iraq, Saudi Arabia, and Jordan.

f Jordan, Saudi Arabia, and Egypt.

g Egypt, Syria, and Iraq. Only Egypt is balancing.

h Rapprochement of Egypt, Saudi Arabia, and Jordan—all seeking to isolate Syria (i.e., to balance), but Saudi Arabia and Jordan also using Arab summits as a means of appeasing Nasser.

i Egypt, Syria, and Jordan (bandwagoning with Egypt), with other Arabs showing solidarity through token military actions.

j Iraq, Jordan, and Syria. Very low level of cooperation.

k Egypt, Saudi Arabia, and Syria; Jordan bandwagoning with Israel by limiting its participation to a token force.

l Only Syria and PDRY counted here, but Libya, Algeria, and, later, Iran also associated with this coalition.

the endangered parties to seek allies to counter the principal sources of danger.

These results are even more striking when the importance of the alliances is considered. Some alliances involve much more extensive commitments than others, and we are, of course, most interested in those that involve the largest exchange of support. Table 8 classifies each of the alliances according to level of commitment and duration. We can distinguish among three levels of commitment. At the highest level, allies sacrificed tangible assets (e.g., territory, money, and people) to fulfill their commitments. At the moderate level, allies risked tangible losses or made important diplomatic sacrifices to support their partners. In other words, these alliances involved significant but largely intangible costs. The lowest level refers to largely symbolic alliances, where the members proved unwilling to make any significant military or diplomatic sacrifices.

These somewhat arbitrary judgments take account of the duration of the alliance as well. Alliances lasting several years reflect repeated calculations of interest and provide a clearer indication of how the members have weighed their options. Other things being equal, therefore, alliances of shorter duration are assumed to be relatively less important.

If alliances that either involved a very low commitment or were of very short duration (or both) are excluded, we see an even more marked preponderance of balancing behavior. Indeed, every alliance that featured a high level of commitment lasting more than three years reflected a decision to balance against a threatening power. By contrast, seven of the ten possible cases of bandwagoning lasted less than a year, and only one (Jordan in 1967) involved a high level of commitment. In other words, decisions to bandwagon show a low level of commitment and are relatively fragile. Indeed, one might say they are hardly alliances at all—just temporary responses to particular situations. The limited scope of most bandwagoning alliances reinforces the conclusion that they play a minor role in international politics.

The results are especially striking when one considers that many of these states were relatively weak and that they were led by relatively inexperienced regimes. Despite the fact that the Middle East lacks an established tradition of balance of power statecraft (in contrast to the European state system, e.g.), the advantages of seeking allies in order to balance against threats have obviously been apparent to the various actors in the Middle East. As described in chapters 3 and 4, the ascendancy of ambitious regional powers (such as Iraq under Nuri al-Said and Egypt under Nasser) consistently led other regional actors to join forces with one another or with one of the superpowers in order to resist the attempt. In short, the record of alliance formation in the Middle East presents strong evidence in favor of the general proposition that states form alliances to balance against external threats and casts grave doubt on the validity of the bandwagoning hypothesis.

The Effects of Power and Proximity

The importance of considering different sources of threat is equally clear. Whereas the superpowers tend to balance primarily against aggregate power alone (i.e., forming alliances to contain the other superpower), states in the Middle East tend to balance against threats from other regional powers. Thus the alliances examined here support the proposition that geographic proximity is an important factor in determining which threats will prompt states to seek allies. A brief comparison of the alliance policies of the superpowers and the Middle East states will demonstrate this proposition.

Balancing Behavior by the Superpowers

If the balancing hypothesis is correct, what behavior should we expect from the two superpowers? Like everyone else, each superpower should seek allies to counter significant threats. Threats from the other superpower will be among the most worrisome. We should therefore expect each superpower to balance more energetically (i.e., to seek additional allies or support the ones it already has more vigorously) whenever its position vis-à-vis the other superpower deteriorates. We would also expect cooperation between the two superpowers to be extremely rare. If this hypothesis is false, however, we would expect significant superpower collusion and indifference on the part of each superpower to gains by the other. Setbacks should lead the loser to abandon the field instead of inspiring renewed efforts at restoring its position.

The history of superpower alliances in the Middle East strongly supports the proposition that these states act primarily to balance one another. As Table 9 indicates, all but two of the superpower commitments examined here were formed primarily to counter the opposing superpower. The remaining cases, moreover, were completely consistent with the general objective of weakening the other superpower's regional position. Thus the Western effort to contain the Soviet Union through the Baghdad Pact led the Soviets to seek closer ties with Egypt and Syria.[4] When this policy bore fruit, the United States proclaimed the Eisenhower Doctrine, began overt and covert pressure on Syria (widely received as a Soviet satellite), encouraged the formation of the Kings'

4. See Hurewitz, *Middle East Politics*, p. 79; Roi, *From Encroachment to Involvement*, pp. 214–16; and Dawisha, *Soviet Foreign Policy towards Egypt*, p. 11.

Table 9. Superpower alliances in the Middle East

Alignment	Duration	Superpower's motive	Client's motive
Baghdad Pact	1955–1958	Contain Soviet Union	Balance Soviet Union/Egypt
Soviet Union-Egypt	1955–1974	Balance United States/Great Britain	Balance Israel/Iraq
Soviet Union-Syria (1)	1955–1958	Balance United States/Great Britain	Balance Israel/Iraq
Soviet Union-Yemen (1)	1955–1962	Balance Great Britain	Balance Great Britain (Aden)
United States-Saudi Arabia	1957–present	Balance Soviet Union	Balance Egypt
United States-Lebanon	1957	Balance Soviet Union	Balance Egypt
United States-Jordan	1957–present	Balance Soviet Union	Balance Egypt
Soviet Union-Iraq (1)	1958–1959	Weaken Baghdad Pact, Support Iraqi Communist Party	Balance Egypt
United States-Israel	1962–present	Balance Soviet Union	Balance Arab states
Soviet Union-YAR (2)	1964–1969	Support Egypt	Defeat Royalists
Soviet Union-Syria (2)	1966–present	Balance United States	Balance Israel
Soviet Union-PDRY	1968–present	Anti-imperialism	Balance Saudi Arabia
Soviet Union-Iraq (2)	1971–1978	Balance United States/Iran	Balance Iran
United States-Egypt	1975–present	Balance Soviet Union	Gain peace, economic aid

Alliance against Nasser (also widely regarded as a Soviet pawn), and offered economic and military support to Jordan, Saudi Arabia, and Lebanon. As Eisenhower put it, "When we give military assistance, it is for the common purpose of opposing communism."[5] In much the same way, Soviet support for Egypt, Yemen, Syria, and the revolutionary regime in Iraq was primarily intended to challenge Western (and especially U.S.) influence in the region.[6]

5. Quoted in Spiegel, *Other Arab-Israeli Conflict*, p. 54 and passim. On the dominance of anti-Communist thinking in U.S. calculations, see George and Smoke, *Deterrence in American Foreign Policy*, chap. 11; Quandt, "United States Policy in the Middle East," pp. 508–12; and Seale, *Struggle for Syria*, chap. 21. The Eisenhower Doctrine, for example, was justified on the ground that "the existing vacuum must be filled by the U.S. before it is filled by Russia." See Eisenhower, *Waging Peace*, p. 178. John Foster Dulles was of like mind, saying that "the leaders of International Communism will take every risk that they dare in order to win the Middle East." Quoted in Seale, *Struggle for Syria*, p. 285.

6. The Soviets criticized the Eisenhower Doctrine as "a means to turn the territories of the Middle East into a military-strategic *place d'armes* directed against the Soviet Union," repeatedly called for the liquidation of all foreign military bases in the region, and consistently supported states adopting anti-imperialist or anti-Western positions. See Roi, *From Encroachment to Involvement*, pp. 214–16, 226; Arnold L. Horelick, "Soviet Policy in the Middle East," in Hammond and Alexander, *Political Dynamics in the Middle East*, pp. 566–73; and Khrushchev, *Khrushchev Remembers*, chap. 16.

In the 1960s, the United States sought a rapprochement with Egypt and Syria—through increased economic aid, sympathetic diplomacy, and recognition of the republican regime in Yemen—in order to entice them away from the Soviet Union.[7] The Soviet threat also inspired increasing support for existing U.S. allies in Jordan, Israel, and Saudi Arabia.[8] The Soviet Union responded by increasing its own military and economic aid to Egypt, republican Yemen, and, later, Syria and by encouraging Algeria, Syria, Egypt, and Iraq to form a "united front of progressive forces" against "imperialism."[9]

During the Six Day War, both superpowers provided diplomatic support to their clients and conducted large-scale military deployments to signal their interests and commitment.[10] After the war, the support of the Soviet Union for its Arab allies grew to unprecedented levels as the Soviets sought to preserve their earlier investments while enjoying important strategic benefits (e.g., access to bases).[11] In response, the United States now sought, as Kissinger admitted, to "expel the Russians." This objective encouraged U.S. support for Jordan in the 1970 crisis, the growing military relationship with Israel, and the diplomatic and military support provided to Israel during the October 1973 war. As Kissinger told the Egyptians after the war: "Do not deceive yourselves, the United States could not—either today or tomorrow—allow Soviet arms to win a big victory . . . against American arms. This has nothing

7. On the motivations behind the U.S. approach to the Arabs, see Gaddis, *Strategies of Containment*, pp. 223–25; Badeau, *American Approach to the Arab World*, pp. 10–13, 17–19, 137; Safran, *From War to War*, pp. 132–33; and Spiegel, *Other Arab-Israeli Conflict*, pp. 97–98.

8. See Spiegel, *Other Arab-Israeli Conflict*, pp. 103–5, 122; Aronson, *Conflict and Bargaining in the Middle East*, p. 44; and Reich, *Quest for Peace*, pp. 39–41. Lyndon Johnson's memoirs support this interpretation of U.S. motives. As Johnson described the situation in the months before the Six Day War, "the danger implicit in every border incident in the Middle East was . . . an ultimate confrontation between the Soviet Union and the U.S." See Johnson, *Vantage Point*, p. 288.

9. According to Nadav Safran, increased support for the radical Arab states "offered precisely the best chance of embroiling these countries with the U.S. and undoing the rapprochement that had begun to take place." See *From War to War*, p. 121. On the aims of Soviet Middle East policy prior to the Six Day War, see Heikal, *Sphinx and Commissar*, pp. 167–68; Dawisha, *Soviet Foreign Policy towards Egypt*, pp. 35–38; Horelick, "Soviet Policy in the Middle East," pp. 580–86; and Oded Eran and Jerome E. Singer, "Soviet Policy towards the Arab World 1955–71," *Survey*, 17, no. 4 (1971): 20–23.

10. See Wells, "The June 1967 Arab-Israeli War," in Dismukes and McConnell, *Soviet Naval Diplomacy*, pp. 158–68. Wells characterizes Soviet behavior in the Six Day War as "the first occasion in which the Soviets utilized significant naval power in Third World coercive diplomacy."

11. According to Heikal, Soviet reluctance to supply air defense troops and pilots to defend Egypt was overcome when Nasser threatened to resign in favor of a pro-United States president. See Heikal, *Road to Ramadan*, p. 82. On the strategic benefits of Soviet access to Egyptian facilities, see Robert G. Weinland, "Land Support for Naval Forces: Egypt and the Soviet Escadra, 1962–1976," *Survival*, 20, no. 2 (1979); and Malcolm Kerr, "Soviet Influence in Egypt 1967–73," in *Soviet and Chinese Influence in the Third World*, ed. Alvin Z. Rubinstein (New York, 1975).

to do with Israel or with you.''[12] Most important of all, Kissinger exploited the Soviet-U.S. détente and the opportunities inherent in the process of step-by-step diplomacy to encourage Egypt to abandon its Soviet patron, a step that cost the Soviets their most important Middle Eastern ally.[13]

After this diplomatic defeat, the Soviets moved to acquire new regional clients (e.g., Libya) and reinforced their commitments to their remaining regional allies (Syria, Iraq, and South Yemen).[14] Although the Carter administration initially sought Soviet cooperation in fashioning a comprehensive peace settlement, the speed with which it abandoned this approach following Sadat's visit to Jerusalem reveals the enduring incentives of a bipolar competition. Faced with the choice of cooperating with the Soviet Union or negotiating a separate peace under U.S. auspices, Carter chose a course that excluded the Soviet Union entirely. At the same time, increasing Soviet activity in South Yemen and the Horn of Africa led the United States to provide additional support to Saudi Arabia and North Yemen.[15] Thus the Carter administration, like its predecessors, eventually made opposition to Soviet influence the cardinal principle of its own Middle East policy.

The eagerness with which each superpower has sought allies in order to balance against the other is revealed in several other ways as well. First, because each seeks to acquire allies at the other's expense, weaker regional powers have profited by encouraging the competition. Thus Egypt received over $1 billion in economic aid from both the United States and the Soviet Union between 1954 and 1965, ranking third among less developed countries in total superpower assistance.[16] In the

12. On the general characteristics of U.S. Middle East policy under Nixon and Kissinger, see Quandt, *Decade of Decisions*, pp. 76–77, 79–80, 121–27; Kissinger, *White House Years*, chap. 10, especially pp. 347, 354, 368, 373–79; and Spiegel, *Other Arab-Israeli Conflict*, pp. 171–73, 216–17, 224–25. Kissinger's remarks are found in *New York Times*, July 3, 1970, p. 1; and *New York Times*, December 5, 1973, p. 18.

13. For a discussion of how Kissinger exploited the détente relationship to undermine the Soviet position in Egypt, see Breslauer, "Soviet Policy in the Middle East"; and Kissinger, *White House Years*, pp. 1246–48. A preoccupation with Soviet actions is apparent throughout Kissinger's account of the October War. See Kissinger, *Years of Upheaval*, p. 468 and passim; and Spiegel, *Other Arab-Israeli Conflict*, pp. 250–52, 255–56.

14. For a survey of Soviet policy after the October War that elaborates Soviet attitudes toward the peace process, see Golan, *Yom Kippur and After*, especially chap. 4.

15. During the 1979 war between North and South Yemen, the United States dispatched two AWACS aircraft to Saudi Arabia as a gesture of support and offered additional military aid to the regime in Sana. For accounts, see *MECS 1978–1979*, p. 63; Katz, *Russia and Arabia*, pp. 35–38; and Holden and Johns, *House of Saud*, pp. 501–2.

16. See Leo Tansky, *U.S. and USSR Aid to Developing Countries: A Comparative Study of India, Turkey, and the UAR* (New York, 1967), pp. 18–19. Nasser apparently viewed the U.S.-Soviet competition as very much to Egypt's advantage and explicitly wanted the superpowers to compete for Egypt's allegiance. See Baker, *Egypt's Uncertain Revolution*, pp. 45–46.

same way, threats to realign have been an effective means of persuading a reluctant patron to provide additional support, as Jordan and Egypt have shown on several occasions.[17] Even the Ba'th regime in Syria managed to receive substantial U.S. assistance during the era of step-by-step diplomacy while remaining the Soviet Union's major regional client. Because the superpowers are so ready to balance against each other, lesser powers can reap ample rewards by threatening to shift their allegiance.

Second, the absence of significant superpower collaboration in Middle East diplomacy (save during intense crises) illustrates the tendency for each superpower to act primarily to limit possible gains by the other. Soviet proposals to neutralize the region in the 1950s were ignored in the West, and the occasional efforts of the superpowers to negotiate a workable solution to the Arab-Israeli conflict (e.g., the Two Power and Four Power talks that followed the Six Day War and the abortive Geneva Conference in 1973–1974) foundered largely because both superpowers placed a higher value on maintaining their existing commitments than on reaching a workable solution.[18]

This summary reveals an important point. The efforts of each superpower to counter the other may take two forms, both of which are consistent with the predictions of the balancing hypothesis. One form is to counter the other superpower by opposing its regional clients, either directly or by supporting other regional states. Soviet and U.S. support for their clients during the various Arab-Israeli wars illustrates this type of behavior. The second form is to try to entice the opponent's clients into realigning (either by offering more or by subverting them), as the United States sought to do with Egypt and Syria on several occasions. Although these forms are quite different, both are intended to serve the larger aim of countering the principal rival by containing or coopting its allies.

The tendency for the United States and the Soviet Union to ally with regional powers primarily to counter each other is hardly surprising. As Kenneth Waltz and others have argued, the dominant powers in a bipolar world are strongly disposed to focus most of their attention on the

---

17. In 1963, hints that Jordan might turn to Moscow for arms led the United States to sell M–48 tanks and advanced aircraft to Jordan. In 1968, Hussein visited Moscow and established diplomatic relations with the Soviet Union, leading the United States to resume weapons shipments to Jordan. In 1976, an announcement that Jordan was negotiating with the Soviet Union for an air defense system overcame congressional opposition to the sale of I-HAWK missiles. The courtship of Nasser by the United States in the early 1960s, Nasser's threats to resign in 1970, and Sadat's expulsion of his Soviet advisers in 1972 all encouraged the Soviet Union to increase its support for Egypt.

18. On this point, see Breslauer, "Soviet Policy in the Middle East"; and Hurewitz, *Middle East Politics*, pp. 94–95.

other superpower, because they are each other's greatest potential threat.[19] Regional powers in the Middle East, however, have been motivated by other concerns.

Balancing Behavior by Regional Powers

I suggested in chapter 2 that regional states are more sensitive to threats from other regional powers, because of the effects of geographic proximity. If this suggestion is correct, then most of the alliances formed by these states will be to counter a threat from another local actor, not to balance one or the other superpower. If it is incorrect, then the opposite result should occur: Middle East states should form defensive alliances against whichever superpower appears strongest. The evidence supports the former view; concern for the global balance of power has played little or no role in the alliance choices of the regional states examined here. As Table 10 summarizes, when regional states choose to enter an alliance (either with another regional state or with one of the superpowers), it is almost always in response to a threat from another regional power.

In short, Middle East states have been far more sensitive to threats from proximate power than from aggregate power: threats from states nearby are of greater concern than are threats from the strongest powers in the international system. And these threats almost always provoke balancing rather than bandwagoning behavior.

Several examples illustrate this tendency. The Arab-Israeli conflict is the most obvious, because it is driven by competing claims to the same territory. As a result, both Israel and its Arab adversaries have sought great power support or forged regional coalitions to improve their positions.[20] Similarly, Iraq's joining the Baghdad Pact encouraged Syria and Saudi Arabia to align with Egypt. But when Nasser's growing prestige made him the more dangerous threat, Iraq, Saudi Arabia, and Jordan formed the Kings' Alliance and embraced the Eisenhower Doctrine. Egypt's intervention in Yemen triggered a countervailing alliance between Amman and Riyadh, and Saudi Arabia's long-standing alignment with the United States has provided a guarantee against hostile neighbors such as Egypt, South Yemen, and, more recently, Ethiopia and Iran. Iraq's 1972 alliance with the Soviet Union and the Saudi-Iraqi alignment in 1979, both the result of threats from neighboring Iran, fit the same pattern.

19. See Waltz, "Stability of a Bipolar World"; Snyder and Diesing, *Conflict among Nations*, pp. 419–29; and Dinerstein, "Transformation of Alliance Systems."

20. Specific examples are Soviet arms support for Egypt and Syria, including the provision of air defense troops during the War of Attrition; Israel's tacit alliance with France in the 1950s and extensive partnership with the United States since the mid-1960s; the abortive Eastern Command of Syria, Iraq, and Jordan in 1969–1970; and the Egyptian-Saudi-Syrian coalition formed to wage the October War in 1973.

Table 10. Middle East alliances against regional threats

Alignment	Duration	Motives of regional states
Iraq-Baghdad Pact	1955–1958	Balance Soviet Union/Egypt
Arab Solidarity Pact	1955–1956	Isolate Iraq
Egypt-Soviet Union	1955–1974	Balance Israel/Iraq/United States
Syria-Soviet Union (1)	1955–1958	Balance Israel/Iraq/Turkey
Yemen-Soviet Union (1)	1955–1962	Pressure Britain re Aden
Suez War Coalition[a]	1956	Weaken Egypt, overthrow Nasser
Kings' Alliance	1957–1958	Balance Egypt
Saudi Arabia-United States	1957–present	Balance Egypt, other regional threats
Lebanon-United States	1957–1958	Balance Egypt/Syria
Jordan-United States	1957–present	Balance Egypt, other regional threats
Iraq-Jordan Union	1957–1958	Balance Egypt
Iraq-Soviet Union	1958–1959	Prevent British intervention, balance Egypt
Kuwait Intervention	1961	Deter Iraqi annexation of Kuwait
Israel-United States	1962–present	Balance Egypt/Syria
Egypt-YAR	1962–1967	Overthrow conservative Arabs
Saudi Arabia-Jordan	1962–1964	Balance Egypt
Syria-Iraq	1963	Balance Egypt
YAR-Soviet Union (2)	1964–1974	Defeat Royalists in civil war
Cairo summits	1964–1965	Isolate Syria, balance Israel, and appease Egypt
Syria-Soviet Union	1966–present	Balance Israel/United States
Egypt-Syria	1966–1967	Balance Israel, pressure conservative Arabs
Egypt-Jordan	1967–1970	Balance Israel, control PLO
Eastern Command	1969–1970	Balance Israel
PDRY-Soviet Union	1969–present	Balance Saudi Arabia, oppose U.S. imperialism
Jordan-Israel	1970	Defeat Syrian invasion of Jordan
October War Coalition	1971–1973	Balance Israel
Iraq-Soviet Union (2)	1971–1978	Balance Iran, Kurdish insurgency
Syria-Jordan	1975–1978	Oppose step-by-step diplomacy
Steadfastness Front	1978–1982	Balance Israel, isolate Egypt
Saudi Arabia-Iraq-Jordan	1979–present	Balance Iran and Syria

[a]France and Israel can both be considered regional powers, as Algeria was still officially part of France at this time and Nasser's alleged support for the Algerian rebels formed the basis for French hostility to Egypt.

By contrast, regional powers have been relatively unconcerned about the global balance of power. This indifference can be seen in several ways. First, if the regional powers were especially concerned about the global balance of power, we would expect all or most of them to ally against the superpower that was currently ahead. But that is precisely what has not occurred. Instead, each superpower has attracted a roughly equal number of regional allies, with each client seeking superpower support in order to deal with other regional states.[21]

21. The Soviet Union gradually established close relations with Egypt, Syria, Yemen, South Yemen, and Iraq; the United States formed an alliance network with Saudi Arabia, Jordan, Iraq (until 1958), Israel and Egypt (under Sadat).

Second, were the global balance an important factor in the calculations of Middle East states, then significant changes in that balance should lead them to realign. Yet the considerable shift in the military balance between the United States and the Soviet Union since the 1950s has failed to alter the alliance policies of the regional states in any discernible way. In the 1950s, the Soviet Union was incapable of significant military activity outside its own border areas, as several Arab leaders learned to their dismay.[22] By the mid-1970s, however, the Soviets had dispatched thousands of troops and advisers to Egypt and Syria, had made credible threats to intervene in both the 1967 and 1973 wars, had acquired an impressive, if still inferior, navy, and had achieved rough parity with the United States in strategic nuclear weapons.[23] At the very least, the United States no longer possessed the overwhelming advantage it had enjoyed two decades earlier.

Yet this significant increase in Soviet capabilities neither won the Soviets new friends nor brought them new enemies, although it did enable them to provide greater support to the allies they already had. Between 1955 and 1979, fourteen alliances were formed between one of the superpowers and one or more regional states, and they have proven remarkably stable. There have been three defections (Iraq in 1958, North Yemen in 1969–1970, and Egypt in 1975), but these shifts had nothing to do with changes in the balance of power between the United States and the Soviet Union.[24] Although the Soviet Union has steadily increased its capabilities vis-à-vis the United States, this effort has not led the regional

22. Mohamed Heikel relates two amusing incidents. During the Suez War in 1956, Syrian President Quwatli, visiting in Moscow, requested Soviet intervention in support of Egypt. According to Heikal, Soviet Minister of Defense Zhukov pulled out a map and asked Quwatli: "How can we go to the aid of Egypt? Tell me! Are we supposed to send our armies through Turkey, Iran, and then into Syria and Iraq and on into Israel and so eventually attack the British and French forces?" See Heikal, *Sphinx and Commissar*, pp. 70–71. Two years later, Nasser requested Soviet support for the Iraqi revolution in the event of Western pressure on the new regime in Baghdad. Warning Nasser that the Soviet Union "was not ready for World War III," Khrushchev said he would order military exercises near the Turkish frontier, but he explicitly cautioned the Egyptian leader that they were "nothing more than maneuvers." See Heikal, *Cairo Documents*, pp. 134–35.

23. One should be cautious in drawing conclusions about the impact of changing military capabilities, because behavior is influenced by perceptions and because many Middle East elites may have accepted the exaggerated claims made by both Soviet and U.S. spokesmen during the 1950s. Because Soviet capabilities were wildly overestimated in the public literature throughout this period, the impressive real growth in Soviet military power may not have been very noticeable.

24. Iraq's shift toward the Soviet Union in 1958 followed the revolution that overthrew Nuri al-Said; Yemen's movement both toward and away from the Soviet Union was the result of the 1962 revolution and the later settlement of the civil war in 1969; and Egypt's realignment was based on Sadat's desire to exploit U.S. influence on Israel, his need for Western investment, and especially the threat that the large Soviet presence in Egypt posed to his freedom of action. The balance of power between the United States and the Soviet Union was unrelated to any of these events.

powers to alter their international position in response. In sum, the distribution of capabilities between the superpowers is not an important factor in the alliance choices of regional states.

This is not to say that Middle East states do not perceive threats from either superpower. Their perception of this type of threat usually occurs, however, when the United States or the Soviet Union is acting in support of a particular regional power. For example, it was Western support for Iraq and Israel—not U.S., British, and French capabilities themselves—that led Egypt to seek Soviet arms in 1955. Similarly, Israel welcomed U.S. military aid in the early 1960s not because it feared the direct use of Soviet power but because Soviet arms shipments were increasing the capabilities of Israel's Arab neighbors.

Furthermore, even when Middle East states have sought allies against a threat from one of the superpowers, their goal has not been to correct an imbalance in the distribution of capabilities between the United States and the Soviet Union. In other words, although regional powers are occasionally threatened by what they fear one of the superpowers might do (either alone or by supporting another local actor), I have not uncovered evidence that a concern for the condition of the global balance of power has any effect on the alliance decisions of the regional powers.

Why Different States Respond to Different Threats

The analysis to this point can be summarized as follows. Balancing behavior is far more common than bandwagoning behavior. Yet states do not simply balance against power, (i.e., the most powerful state or coalition in the world). Although the superpowers seek allies in order to balance against those with the largest capabilities, less capable states within a given region, such as the Middle East, seek allies primarily to balance against those who are close by.

Although this point is fairly obvious (and one that several other authors have emphasized), it is worth exploring it a bit further.[25] The differing perspectives of regional states and the superpowers helps explain why each superpower's efforts to enlist regional allies in a crusade against the other superpower have been undermined by persistent regional conflicts.[26] This evidence also refutes the common assertion that

25. For a general formulation, see Rothstein, *Alliances and Small Powers*, p. 62. For similar observations about the Middle East itself, see Brown, *International Politics and the Middle East*, pp. 198–214.

26. For example, the United States sought to create a Middle East Command in 1951, to establish a solid Northern Tier/Baghdad Pact alignment in 1954–1955, to erect an anti-Communist coalition through the Eisenhower Doctrine in 1957, to wean Egypt from the

a shift in the balance of power between the United States and the Soviet Union will lead regional powers to alter their behavior significantly. Instead, the record of alliance formation in the postwar Middle East suggests that shifts in the global balance of power, however important they may seem to the United States and the Soviet Union, simply do not matter much to other countries.[27]

What explains the differing responses of the superpowers and the various regional powers? Three explanations can be given. First, regional states are indifferent to the global balance because they are much weaker than either of the superpowers and can therefore do little to change the global balance.[28] As the theory of collective goods predicts, those who cannot affect outcomes by their own actions have little incentive to try. Thus regional powers will not align in response to shifts in the distribution of power between the United States and the Soviet Union but instead will ally with the superpower that is most willing to support their own political objectives. For regional powers, the question is not "which superpower is stronger?" but rather "which is most willing to help?"

Second, the regional powers in the Middle East are unlikely to view either superpower as posing an imminent and direct threat. Because states in close proximity tend to experience more frequent conflicts of interest, and because the ability to harm others declines with distance, the superior capabilities of either superpower may seem less threatening simply because the superpowers are further away.

The difference in Egyptian and Iraqi perceptions of the Soviet Union in the 1950s illustrates this tendency nicely. Premier Nuri al-Said of Iraq justified signing the Baghdad Pact by saying, "[Iraq's] borders are very close to the [Soviet] Caucasus, . . . only some 300 or 400 miles

---

Soviet Union in the early 1960s and early 1970s, and to establish a strategic consensus against the Soviet Union in the 1980s. Only the realignment of Egypt can be called a success. The Soviets have behaved similarly; they have repeatedly tried to promote fronts of progressive forces, bemoaned the repeated divisions among these same "progressive" regimes, and hurt their position with one set of Middle East states whenever they helped the others.

27. It is possible, of course, that the magnitude of the changes in the global balance has not been large enough to warrant a response from the regional states. Given the considerable changes that have occurred, it is safe to conclude that extraordinary shifts in either superpower's capabilities would be necessary before they would affect the alliance preferences of lesser powers.

28. In 1975, for example, Soviet GNP was more than 800 times that of Jordan, 63 times that of Iraq, and 150 times that of Syria. Soviet defense spending was more than 400 times that of Jordan, more than 500 times that of Iraq, and almost 42 times that of Israel (the regional state that devoted the largest sums to defense). Of course, similar disparities in capability exist between the United States and these regional actors, to say nothing of the asymmetry created by the nuclear arsenals of each superpower. These calculations are based on data on ACDA, *World Military Expenditures and Arms Transfers 1978*.

[away]."[29] By contrast, Nasser belittled the Soviet threat by pointing out that "the Soviet Union is more than 1000 miles away and we've never had any trouble from them."[30]

Finally, because each superpower will oppose expansion by the other, regional states can be less worried about either one. Thus Nasser once claimed that "Egypt's great strength lay in the rival interests of America and Russia, . . . and that each of the superpowers would protect her from the other."[31] And because the slim but ominous possibility of nuclear escalation increases the risks of superpower intervention, regional powers may believe that neither superpower will risk a direct invasion. Thus Nasser rejected Western requests for an alliance against the Soviet Union by informing Dulles that "there would be no aggression from outside [the Middle East] for the simple reason that . . . nuclear weapons have changed the whole art of war, and rendered any foreign aggression a remote possibility."[32]

For all of these reasons, regional powers are unlikely to seek allies out of fear that one superpower is becoming too powerful. The situation is precisely the opposite, however, in relations among the regional powers themselves. Regional powers seek allies against one another both because their neighbors are more dangerous and because their responses can make a difference.

First of all, imbalances of power within a particular region are more significant and are subject to more frequent changes. Thus Israeli decision-makers saw the Soviet-Egyptian arms deal of 1955 as a major change in the regional balance of power. Yet they also saw this balance as swinging sharply back in their favor when France began to supply them with greater quantities of modern arms. Ben-Gurion was reportedly alarmed by the Tripartite Pact of 1963 (despite its speedy collapse), and Israel's leaders saw both the Egyptian-Syrian defense treaty of November 1966 and Hussein's decision to join forces with Egypt in May 1967 as developments ominous enough to trigger the decision to launch a preemptive attack on June 5.[33]

Regional states are more sensitive to local threats, because how they

29. Quoted in Seale, *Struggle for Syria*, p. 201.

30. Quoted in Heikal, *Cairo Documents*, p. 40. In a subsequent article, Heikal reported that this view was widespread: "While admittedly the Soviet Union did represent a threat, it was felt that there was no immediate or direct danger from that source. Many people, including Nasser, held that the lack of common borders between the Arab nation and the Soviet Union would deter the Soviets from undertaking any military act against it." See Mohamed Heikal, "Egyptian Foreign Policy," *Foreign Affairs*, 56, no. 4 (1978): 720.

31. See Nutting, *Nasser*, p. 271.

32. Quoted in Seale, *Struggle for Syria*, p. 188.

33. See Gazit, *President Kennedy's Policy*, p. 49; David Ben-Gurion, *Israel: A Personal History* (New York, 1971), pp. 688–89; Brecher, *Decisions in Israel's Foreign Policy*, pp. 247–48, 412–13; and Tanter and Stein, *Rational Decisionmaking*, pp. 218–19.

choose to ally can make a significant difference. The impact of these decisions has been especially great in inter-Arab politics, where attracting allies in order to isolate rivals has been an effective means of challenging their legitimacy. For example, Syria's decision to ally with Egypt in 1955 left Iraq isolated and effectively doomed the Baghdad Pact.[34] But realignment could swing momentum back overnight. The formation of the Kings' Alliance checked Nasser's first bid to lead the Arab world, and the Iraqi revolution and the formation of the UAR restored Egypt's predominance once again. Similarly, although Jordan is hardly a great power (even within the Middle East), its strategic location and small but effective military capabilities have increased the importance of obtaining Jordan's cooperation in any Arab-Israeli war. Thus Nasser pressured Hussein to enter the war of 1967 (to Hussein's later regret), and both the United States and Israel worked to keep Jordan on the sidelines in 1973.[35] In the same way, although Saudi Arabia's impressive financial resources are still far too small to alter the global balance of power, the Saudi decision to fund Egyptian purchases of Soviet arms made it possible for Egypt to acquire the capabilities necessary to fight the October War.[36] Although none of these countries can alter the global balance of power, the impact of each one on the regional balance can be potent.

Moreover, regional powers clearly have good reason to fear their neighbors. Five Arab-Israeli wars occurred between 1948 and 1979; and there have been recurrent episodes of low-level violence between Israel and her Arab neighbors, a prolonged Egyptian intervention in Yemen, and occasional skirmishes between Syria, Jordan, and Iraq. Thus a final reason that Middle East states seek allies primarily to counter local threats is the fact that they have rightly perceived that the most imminent threats come from their neighbors, not from either superpower.

In sum, although balancing is the characteristic response to threats, the types of threats to which different states respond vary considerably. Because the superpowers appear roughly equal in overall capabilities, because regional powers can do little to affect the global balance, and because other regional actors present much more immediate dangers, the regional states form alliances primarily in response to threats from proximate powers. As Nasser told a U.S. journalist in 1955: "We look at things a lot differently from you Americans. We don't spend our time

34. See Seale, *Struggle for Syria*, pp. 217, 224, 226.
35. On U.S. pressure on Jordan in 1973, see Kissinger, *Years of Upheaval*, pp. 494–500.
36. In 1979, Saudi Arabian GNP was approximately $76 billion, and the U.S. defense budget was approximately $150 billion. U.S. defense spending, in short, was roughly twice as large as the entire Saudi economy. Saudi defense expenditures totaled $20 billion in 1979–1980, about 13 percent of the U.S. total. Within the Middle East itself, however, Saudi financial assets can make a substantial impact, especially with those who have less disposable revenue.

worrying about a world war, or Russian aggression, or the struggle between East and West. We are interested in Egypt's security, and Egypt's security today means protection against Israel." Some fifteen years later, Anwar Sadat described the difference between Egyptian and Soviet interests in strikingly similar terms: "[The USSR is] a big power with commitments, conditions, responsibilities, and so on. . . . Perhaps to them the Middle East problem is not the most important problem. But to me, . . . the Middle East problem is not only the most important problem, but it is also sleep, life, food, waking hours, and water. It is my problem. It is the problem of my occupied territory."[37]

Offensive Power and Balancing Behavior

The proposition that increases in a state's offensive power will encourage other states to balance is also supported by this study. I make this statement cautiously, however, for several reasons. As defined in chapter 2, offensive power is a state's capacity to threaten the vital interests or the sovereignty of others. This capacity may take many forms, however, depending on both the context and the target.[38] As a result, offensive power is difficult to measure precisely and the hypothesis is difficult to test. Moreover, because offensive power is closely related to other sources of threat (e.g., aggregate power and geographic proximity), assessing the independent impact of changes in a state's offensive power is difficult. The solution is to examine situations where a state's offensive capabilities changed but the other factors remained constant.

Several cases examined here support the hypothesis that increases in offensive power tend to provoke states to balance more vigorously. For example, both the British withdrawal from Suez in 1954 (which removed the buffer of British troops between Egypt and Israel) and the Soviet-Egyptian arms deal of 1955 increased Egypt's ability to threaten Israel. The arms deal also heightened French fears that Nasser would provide

---

37. Nasser's statement is quoted in Meyer, *Egypt and the United States*, p. 123. Sadat's statement is quoted in Aronson, *Conflict and Bargaining*, p. 407. For similar statements by Sadat, see Israeli, *Public Diary of Sadat*, 1: 238, 378. Nasser also indicated his awareness of the difference between the perspectives of the superpowers and their clients in his statement: "When the Americans and the Soviets, as superpowers, get together around a . . . table, they use a language different from that used between a major power and a small country, especially on the issue of a political settlement." See "'Abd-al-Nasir's Secret Papers," p. 70.

38. On the difficulties in conceptualizing and testing hypotheses about offensive and defensive capabilities, see Levy, "The Offense/Defense Balance in Military Technology." Offensive power can result from superior numbers, more effective exploitation of existing capabilities, technological developments, political propaganda and subversion, and so on. Important contextual factors include proximity, geography, and the political cohesion of the states being attacked.

military aid to the rebels in French North Africa. This increase in Egypt's ability to threaten important Israeli and French interests strongly encouraged the formation of close military ties between France and Israel.[39]

Egypt's relations with the rest of the Arab world exhibit the same effects in a different guise. When Nasser's prestige soared following the Suez Crisis, his ability to mobilize popular support in other Arab countries (and thereby undermine their stability) gave Egypt a potent ability to threaten other Arab states. Although Jordan (and, to a lesser extent, Saudi Arabia) initially sought to appease Nasser by bandwagoning, they shifted to a balancing alignment with Iraq and the United States when appeasement proved unsuccessful.[40] By forming their own regional alliance, Nasser's opponents could claim (albeit less persuasively) to be pursuing the same ideals of Arab unity personified by Nasser.

Until the Six Day War, Nasser's ability to exploit his personal prestige on Egypt's behalf made Egypt's relations with the other Arab states at best problematic.[41] But as his prestige declined, cooperation with the other Arab states actually increased. Israel's stunning victory in June 1967—as dramatic a demonstration of Egyptian weakness as one can imagine—brought an immediate improvement in Egypt's relations with the rest of the Arab world. With his army in disarray and his economy dependent on foreign subsidies, Nasser posed little threat to anyone. Egypt's aggregate power was reduced by its defeat, but Nasser's offensive power had declined even more. Nasser recognized that "with no army or air force to defend his own country, he could hardly aspire to the leadership of any other."[42] Moreover, Israel's emergence as the dominant threat to the security of the Arab states provided a positive incentive for greater cooperation among them.[43] The Egyptian-Jordanian alignment, the Khartoum resolutions, Egypt's withdrawal from

---

39. On the effects of these events, see Brecher, *Decisions in Israel's Foreign Policy*, pp. 228–29, 254–55, 258, 262–63; Crosbie, *Tacit Alliance*, pp. 14–15 and passim; Love, *Suez*, pp. 71, 75, 137; Seale, *Struggle for Syria*, p. 247; and Shimon Peres, *David's Sling* (New York, 1970), chap. 3.

40. On the effects of the Suez crisis on Nasser's prestige, see Nutting, *Nasser*, pp. 86–89, 193–96; Stephens, *Nasser*, pp. 251–54; Steven R. David, "The Realignment of Third World Regimes from One Superpower to the Other: Ethiopia's Mengistu, Somalia's Siad, and Egypt's Sadat" (diss., Harvard University, 1980), pp. 201–2; and Nadav Safran, "Arab Politics: Peace and War," *Orbis*, 18, no. 2 (1974): 380.

41. See chapter 6 for a more complete analysis of the turbulent relations among the Arab regimes in this period.

42. Quoted in Nutting, *Nasser*, p. 433.

43. Israel was now the major threat because its military power was now clearly superior and because the humiliating defeat inflicted in June 1967 had weakened the legitimacy of the various Arab powers. Even Nasser faced serious domestic protests in the aftermath of the war.

Yemen, and Nasser's efforts to organize the Eastern Command all illustrate the effects of this trend.

Nasser's death in 1970 removed the final obstacle to significant inter-Arab collaboration. Ironically, because his successor, Anwar el-Sadat, lacked the prestige and charisma that had enabled Nasser to threaten the other Arab states, Sadat's goal of forging effective Arab alliances was easier. The Arab alliance that fought the October War—the high-water mark of Arab cooperation—was the result. Thus a key factor affecting Egypt's relations with other Arab states was the waxing and waning of its offensive power to threaten the other Arab regimes.

The impact of offensive power is revealed by several other examples. Although the Soviet-Egyptian arms deal encouraged Israel and France to join forces against Egypt, the deal was partly the result of an unexpectedly harsh Israeli raid on the Egyptian village of Gaza. By demonstrating Israel's ability to attack Egyptian forces with impunity, the raid increased Nasser's perceived need for great power support.[44] The arms race that developed between Egypt and Israel in the 1960s was the product of similar concerns, and the extensive support that each superpower provided its regional clients after 1967 suggests that acquisition of offensive capabilities (e.g., advanced aircraft and armored forces) will lead—via the familiar logic of balancing—to a quest for new allies or for increased support from old ones.[45] Thus the War of Attrition triggered a renewed Israeli campaign for U.S. arms, and when Israel's offensive power was demonstrated anew during the deep penetration raids on Cairo in January 1970, Nasser was forced to beg for more Soviet aid. The Soviet Union responded by sending thousands of troops to Egypt.

These cases are especially important because they show how increases in offensive power increase the likelihood that other states will ally together, even when other factors are unchanged. Although a state's offensive power is closely related to several other sources of threat, it remains an important incentive for others to form a defensive alliance.

Aggressive Intentions and Balancing Behavior

If the hypothesis that aggressive intentions encourage balancing behavior is correct, then states that are perceived as seeking to overthrow

44. See Stephens, *Nasser*, pp. 157–59; Brecher, *Decisions in Israel's Foreign Policy*, pp. 255–57; and Glassman, *Arms for the Arabs*, p. 9. The Gaza raid probably affected Egypt's perception of Israel's intentions as well.

45. On the Arab-Israeli arms race, see Safran, *From War to War*, chaps. 4 and 5; Hurewitz, *Middle East Politics*, chaps. 24 and 25; Colin S. Gray, "Arms Races and Their Influence on International Stability," and Yair Evron, "Arms Races in the Middle East and Some Arms Control Measures Related to Them," both in *Dynamics of a Conflict: A Reexamination of the Arab-Israeli Conflict*, ed. Gabriel Sheffer (Atlantic Highlands, N.J., 1975).

or dominate others should provoke widespread opposition. As perceptions of intent change, either the direction or the intensity of balancing behavior should change as well. If the hypothesis is incorrect, however, then a state's being seen as aggressive will have little effect or will convince others to support it more strongly, however reluctantly.

Once again, the alliances examined in this study support the former view. Although this conclusion should be viewed with some caution, both superpower commitments and purely regional alliances confirm that states that are seen as especially hostile usually provoke other states to balance against them.

Superpower Alliances with Regional States

In almost all the alliances between a superpower and a regional actor considered here, the regional state perceived one superpower as favorably inclined and the other as hostile. The fact that the Soviet Union had never been an imperial power in the Middle East, the vocal support the Soviets offered for the revolutionary ideals popular in many Arab states, and the Soviet willingness to provide extensive material assistance all encouraged the progressive Arab regimes to align with Moscow, beginning with Syria and Egypt in 1955. By contrast, U.S. support for the conservative monarchies in Saudi Arabia and Jordan, combined with Saudi and Jordanian aversion to Soviet Communism, produced precisely the opposite result.[46] Although Israel's preference for the United States is based in part on unique cultural connections between the two states, growing hostility from the Soviet Union no doubt reinforced Israel's preference for alignment with the United States.[47]

Once again, Egypt's relations with the United States and the Soviet Union nicely illustrate the impact of intentions. In the 1950s, the reluctance of the United States to provide Egypt with modern armaments, the deliberate cancellation of the Aswan Dam offer, and U.S. support for the Baghdad Pact and (through the Eisenhower Doctrine) Nasser's opponents in the Arab world all left Nasser deeply suspicious of the United States. By contrast, Soviet political and military support conveyed a far more favorable attitude. The situation was partly reversed in 1959, when a series of ideological disputes divided the Soviet Union and Egypt. The United States began a deliberate campaign to improve relations with Nasser; and it produced a noticeable thaw until 1962, when Egyptian and U.S. interests diverged over Nasser's intervention in Yemen. After

46. See Seale, *Struggle for Syria*, p. 301; Dawisha, *Egypt in the Arab World*, pp. 125–26; Aruri, *Jordan*, pp. 138–46; and Safran, *Saudi Arabia*, p. 66 and passim.

47. See Safran, *Israel*, pp. 338–40; Brecher, *Decisions in Israel's Foreign Policy*, pp. 115–22; Roi, *Soviet Decisionmaking in Practice*, pp. 417–23; and Karen B. Konigsberg, *Red Star and Star of David: Soviet Relations with Israel* (senior thesis, Princeton University, 1986).

the United States cut off food aid and increased its arms supplies to Egypt's various regional adversaries, Nasser began to see Egypt as the object of an overt imperialist conspiracy. Indeed, Nasser reportedly saw himself as the potential target of the CIA, which he blamed for the ouster of several other nationalist leaders.[48] After the Six Day War, Nasser apparently viewed the United States as unremittingly hostile, although he was reluctantly willing to seek U.S. diplomatic assistance in his campaign to regain the occupied territories.[49] As he told Soviet president Podgorny: "Our enemies will always be the Americans. They are also your enemies. Therefore we have to organize our cooperation, because it is unreasonable for me to stand neutral between he who strikes me and he who helps me."[50]

These images of the two superpowers faded after Nasser's death, and this change played a central role in Sadat's decision to realign.[51] Sadat was alarmed and annoyed by Soviet interference in Egyptian domestic politics, Soviet support for an abortive Communist coup in Sudan, the condescending attitude of Soviet military personnel in Egypt, and the Soviet reluctance to supply him with the weapons he wanted. At the same time, private talks between Kissinger and Egyptian officials led Sadat to conclude that U.S. policy was malleable; U.S. intentions could be changed if Egypt was willing to alter its own position. Although Sadat overestimated U.S. flexibility in 1971 and 1972, Kissinger's even-handed diplomacy after the October War and Egypt's subsequent realignment illustrate how important favorable perceptions of others' intentions can be.[52]

Why are intentions so important in determining which superpower to choose? Because the other components of threat are not. As argued

48. See Stookey, *America and the Arab States*, p. 196; Nutting, *Nasser*, pp. 374–82; Stephens, *Nasser*, pp. 457–65; and Burns, *Economic Aid and U.S. Policy*, p. 168.

49. See Safran, *From War to War*, pp. 279–81. One source reports Nasser as telling a meeting of Egyptian leaders in November 1968: "There will be no coexistence [with America]. . . . As long as Nasir is in power, the Americans will not reach agreement with him." For this and similar statements, see "'Abd-al-Nasir's Secret Papers," pp. 40, 68–69, 87–88.

50. See "'Abd-al-Nasir's Secret Papers," pp. 4–5; and Rubinstein, *Red Star on the Nile*, pp. 63–65, 98–103. Of course, Nasser's favorable statements regarding the Soviet Union may have been due to Egypt's dependence on Soviet aid during this period.

51. Nasser did attempt a brief détente just before his death by imploring the United States to commence a "new, serious, and definite beginning" in April 1970 and by accepting the Rogers ceasefire in July. This effort suggests some softening of Nasser's attitude (and a recognition that the War of Attrition was becoming too costly), but the tensions that reemerged when Egypt extended its air defenses (in violation of the Rogers agreement) suggest that no great breakthrough would have been reached had Nasser lived. On this point, see Shamir, "Egypt's Pro-U.S. Orientation," p. 280.

52. On these points, see Quandt, *Decade of Decisions*, pp. 151–52; el-Sadat, *In Search of Identity*, pp. 230–33; Heikal, *Road to Ramadan*, p. 183; and David, "Realignment of Third World Regimes," pp. 320–24.

[169]

earlier, both the United States and the Soviet Union are economic and military superpowers, both have large military capabilities, and both are outside the Middle East region. Because they are difficult to distinguish on these dimensions, the principal critierion on which to base the choice of one superpower over the other will be how a given regional power perceives U.S. or Soviet intentions. The obvious preference is to ally with the superpower that seems least aggressive.[53]

Alliances between Regional States

The belief that certain regimes harbor aggressive intentions has clearly influenced regional alliance choices as well. For example, the power of Nasser's prestige was dangerous because he was so willing to use it to threaten his opponents. Nasserist subversion undermined the Tripartite Unity Agreement of 1963, and Nasser's repeated attacks against "reactionary" Arab monarchies such as those of Saudi Arabia and Jordan inspired the Kings' Alliance in 1957 and the Saudi-Jordanian axis in 1962. Although tensions between Saudi Arabia and Egypt eased on several occasions (e.g., when Syrian bellicosity seemed even more dangerous) the Saudis remained extremely wary of Egypt until after Nasser's death.[54]

As already noted, Egypt's diplomatic position improved considerably under Sadat. Not only did Sadat lack Nasser's prestige and subversive power, but he was widely viewed as having modest ambitions in the Arab world. In particular, Sadat's carefully cultivated image of moderation and Islamic piety, his open displays of respect for King Feisal, and his decision to rename the United Arab Republic the Arab Republic of Egypt paved the way for the Saudi-Egyptian alliance that lasted until Camp David.[55] The ascendance of Hafez el-Assad—a moderate by Syrian standards—had similar effects. With Egypt and Syria ruled by less bellicose leaders, Saudi Arabia found cooperation with both far more attractive.[56]

53. This conclusion extends the analysis presented by Snyder and Diesing in *Conflict among Nations*, pp. 421–29. They recognize that in a bipolar system, the decision of which side to ally with must be based on other considerations, such as geography or ideology. When geography and offensive power are indeterminate, however, ideology or perceived intentions—which are closely related in any case—will become even more crucial. The impact of ideology will be examined separately in chapter 6.
54. On this point, see "'Abd-al-Nasir's Secret Papers," pp. 125–29; and Safran, *Saudi Arabia*, pp. 124, 126, 139–42, 145–49.
55. See Dawisha, *Egypt in the Arab World*, p. 195; Baker, *Egypt's Uncertain Revolution*, pp. 141–42; and Holden and Johns, *House of Saud*, pp. 288–89, 295–97.
56. After taking power in November 1970, Assad called for a "broad Arab front" and "all-Arab participation" against Israel. In contrast to his predecessors, he also offered a qualified acceptance of U.N. Resolution 242 in 1972, thereby removing another obstacle between Damascus and its new allies in Cairo and Riyadh. See Rabinovich, "Continuity and Change in the Ba'th Regime in Syria," pp. 226–27.

Several other examples reinforce this conclusion. The Arab coalitions against Israel and Israel's continued search for external support reflect the fact that each side views the other as having extremely aggressive intentions.[57] Neither side has become more willing to appease the other as the other's hostility has grown; rather, the search for support has widened as the conflict has grown more intense. On a much smaller scale, the Arab League's collective defense of Kuwait in 1961 was triggered by Iraqi President Qassem's open declaration that he intended to annex the sheikdom. Iran's seizure of three islands in the Persian Gulf and its abrogation of the agreement dividing the Shatt al-Arab waterway prompted Iraq to seek a formal alliance with the Soviet Union, a goal it abandoned when its conflicts with Iran were temporarily resolved. Other regional conflicts—such as the border clashes between Saudi Arabia and South Yemen and the internecine quarrels between the Ba'th regimes in Syria and Iraq—exhibit the same pattern.

The strong relationship between offensive intentions and balancing behavior is to be expected. Although large and powerful states can be either valuable allies or dangerous adversaries, it makes little sense to ally with a state that is known to be hostile, regardless of its other traits. As a result, extremely aggressive states are especially likely to trigger the formation of balancing coalitions.

Summary: Levels of Threat and Balancing Behavior

Taken together, these different sources of threat help explain several characteristic patterns of alliance formation in the Middle East. First, they explain why Soviet and U.S. capabilities do not cause balancing alliances among the regional states, despite the fact that both nations are far more powerful than any of the local actors. Instead, the superpowers are sought as allies against the more imminent threats that arise from other states within the region. Because the superpowers are both more powerful and less threatening to most states in the Middle East, they are ideal allies for a regional power that faces a direct military threat from one of its neighbors. Focusing solely on aggregate capabilities—as traditional balance of power theory does—would ignore the important effects of proximity, offensive capabilities, and intentions.

Second, the impact of the different sources of threat helps explain

---

57. For evidence on Arab and Israeli perceptions, see Yehoshofat Harkabi, *Arab Attitudes to Israel* (Jerusalem, 1972); John Edward Mroz, *Beyond Security: Private Perceptions among Arabs and Israelis* (New York, 1980); Ralph K. White, "Misperception in the Arab-Israeli Conflict," *Journal of Social Issues*, 33, no. 1 (1977); and Daniel Heradstveit, *The Arab-Israeli Conflict: Psychological Obstacles to Peace* (Oslo, 1979); and Heradstveit, *Arab and Israeli Elite Perceptions* (Oslo, 1974).

why Egypt and Israel have been the target of balancing alliances with such frequency. They have long been the most powerful regional actors; they have received extensive great power support, they have possessed considerable offensive capabilities, and they have been perceived as seeking to expand at the expense of others. As a result, Israel faced a host of Arab coalitions between 1948 and 1979 and never formed a durable alliance with any Arab state.[58] In the same way, Egypt's combination of size, offensive capabilities, geographic proximity, and aggressive regional ambitions triggered at least six opposing coalitions between 1955 and 1970.[59] By contrast, weaker states with negligible offensive capabilities and few, if any, aggressive designs (e.g., Lebanon, North Yemen, Saudi Arabia, and Jordan) have rarely, if ever, inspired others to ally against them.

The main point should be obvious: balance of threat theory is superior to balance of power theory. Examining the impact of several related but distinct sources of threat can provide a more persuasive account of alliance formation than can focusing solely on the distribution of aggregate capabilities. Of course, the precise importance of each of these factors (aggregate power, proximity, offensive capabilities, and intentions) is impossible to predict in any given case. For example, states may be forced to choose among potential partners of equal capability, where one appears more aggressive but is also further away. Thus how statesmen will respond to the infinite range of combinations is uncertain. Other things being equal, however, an increase in any of these factors should make balancing behavior more likely.

BANDWAGONING BEHAVIOR AND ALLIANCE FORMATION

Although states almost always choose allies to balance against threats, such behavior is not universal. Under certain conditions, the generally low tendency for states to join forces with the dominant power may increase somewhat.

58. The exception to this observation, which does not undermine the basic point, was Israel's support for King Hussein during the Syrian intervention in the Jordanian civil war. The explanation for this action is straightforward: Israel and Jordan feared a PLO/Syrian victory in Jordan more than they feared each other.

59. The alliances referred to here are (1) the Suez War coalition of Great Britain, France, and Israel; (2) The Kings' Alliance of Jordan, Saudi Arabia, and Iraq; (3) the alignment of Jordan and Saudi Arabia with the United States under the aegis of the Eisenhower Doctrine; (4) the Saudi-Jordanian defense treaty of 1962; (5) the brief Syrian-Iraqi security agreement in 1963; and (6) the Islamic Pact created by Feisal of Saudi Arabia in 1965–1966.

Table 11. Bandwagoning behavior

Alliance	Date
Saudi Arabia allies with Egypt and Syria	1955
Yemen allies with Egypt and Syria	1956
Jordan joins the Arab Solidarity Pact	1956–1957
Assassination plot fails; Saudi Arabia appeases Egypt	1958–1961
Syria joins Tripartite Pact with Egypt and Iraq	1963
Saudi Arabia agrees to détente with Egypt at Cairo summit	1964
Jordan agrees to détente with Egypt at Cairo summit	1964
Jordan signs defense treaty with Egypt	1967
Jordan stays out of October War (tacit bandwagoning with Israel)	1973
Egypt realigns from Soviet Union to United States	1975

Conditions Favoring Bandwagoning Behavior

Chapter 2 suggested that weak states were more likely to bandwagon than strong states, that an absence of potential allies made bandwagoning more likely, and that incentives for bandwagoning increased if the most threatening power was believed to be appeasable. If we adopt a rather broad definition of bandwagoning (i.e., if we include several questionable cases in order to obtain more than a token sample), we can say that states in the Middle East chose to bandwagon on perhaps ten occasions in the period under study (see Table 11). All three hypotheses receive support from these cases.

Weak and Strong States

Weak states are more likely to bandwagon than strong ones—for two reasons: they are more vulnerable to pressure, and they can do little to determine their own fates. The cases of bandwagoning listed in Table 11 support this proposition, as all save Egypt were weak states that faced a significant threat from the ally they reluctantly embraced.

For example, the Arab monarchies of Saudi Arabia, Jordan, and, to a lesser degree, Yemen were especially vulnerable to Nasser's charismatic appeal and political propaganda. Moreover, they could do little damage to Egypt in response. Although they initially sought to balance Great Britain and Iraq, a series of internal disturbances in 1954 and 1955 also encouraged the Saudis to side with Egypt as a means of defusing domestic dissent through association with the leading progressive figure in the Arab world. In much the same way, the deliberate effort to appease Nasser after Saud's ill-conceived assassination plot came during a period of serious fiscal troubles and internal divisions, which weakened the kingdom's ability to resist Egyptian pressure.[60] Similar motives under-

60. See Holden and Johns, *House of Saud*, pp. 187–88 and chap. 14; and Safran, *Saudi Arabia*, pp. 87–90.

lay the alliance of Imam Ahmed of Yemen with Nasser in this period. The alliance with Egypt both enhanced Ahmed's position in the conflict with Britain over Aden and defused Nasser's incentives to criticize Ahmed's rule. Nasser's attitude was hardly a trivial concern, as Ahmed had narrowly defeated a revolt by revolutionary officers in 1955. And Hussein's decision to reject the Baghdad Pact and join the Arab Solidarity Pact instead followed a series of riots in Amman inspired by Egyptian propaganda. As Hussein described his own position: "Jordan is a very special kind of country that depends on good neighbors for its existence. . . . And what would happen to Jordan if she remained friendless while those around her quarreled?"[61]

Hussein also reports that many of his officers believed that "Jordan was too small to stand alone" at that time.[62] By contrast, Iraq adopted an anti-Egyptian policy under both Feisal II and Qassem, because it was strong enough to do so with some hope of success.

Other examples reveal similar tendencies. Syria's vulnerability to Egyptian pressure contributed to the Ba'th Party's decision to seek an alliance with Egypt in 1963. Continued domestic turbulence and repeated efforts by Nasserist forces to gain power convinced the Syrians that they could achieve internal stability only if they were able to gain Nasser's support. Syrian vulnerability to Egyptian pressure thus made them strongly inclined to bandwagon.

Jordan's weakness (in part the result of Hussein's precarious domestic position) dictated Hussein's responses in 1967 and 1973 as well. Apparently convinced that the Arabs were stronger (and fearing the effects of an Arab victory in which he did not participate), Hussein signed a formal defense treaty with Nasser just before the Six Day War. His decision to enter the fighting on June 5 may also have been based in part on false reports of Arab victories in the early stages of the war.[63]

Hussein's behavior in 1973 is equally revealing. Now convinced that Israel was invincible, Hussein stated before the war that Jordan would stay out "unless there was a 50 percent chance of an Arab victory."[64] The odds were nowhere near that good, and Hussein limited his involvement to a single brigade sent north to fight in Syria. This token effort was tantamount to adopting a neutral position, and had Arab solidarity allowed it, Hussein might well have done even less. In short,

61. Hussein, *Uneasy Lies the Head*, p. 104.
62. Hussein, *Uneasy Lies the Head*, p. 157.
63. See Hussein, *My "War" with Israel*, pp. 57, 60–61, 65–66; Dupuy, *Elusive Victory*, pp. 285–87; and Herzog, *Arab-Israeli Wars*, pp. 169–70.
64. Quoted in Whetten, *Canal War*, p. 238. According to one report, Hussein agreed to attack Israel only if the Syrian assault on the Golan Heights was successful. See Herzog, *War of Atonement*, p. 30.

in both 1967 and 1973 Hussein tried to stay on good terms with the likely winners. Although his calculations left much to be desired (especially in 1967), Jordan's overall weakness and vulnerability made this policy a prudent one to follow.

Availability of Allies

States are more likely to bandwagon when useful allies are unavailable, for they will face the threat alone if they choose to resist. A dearth of effective allies is also apparent in most of the cases of bandwagoning already discussed. The Arab monarchs' decisions to bandwagon with Egypt in 1955–1956 were due partly to the lack of alternatives. Britain was an unlikely ally given the disputes over Aden and the Buraimi oasis, and its support was of questionable value. As Arab reaction to the Baghdad Pact showed, close ties with a colonial power merely made Nasser's attacks about imperialist influence all the more potent. The United States had yet to make a clear commitment, and the Soviet Union was already aligned with Nasser (and was anathema to the Saudis and Hussein in any case). By the end of 1956, bandwagoning with Egypt was the best of a set of bad choices.

The unraveling of this coalition is especially revealing. When the Eisenhower Doctrine created the possibility of external support (and Nasser's ambitions continued to grow), Saudi Arabia and Jordan quickly abandoned their alliance with Egypt and joined forces with Iraq and the United States. When the Iraqi revolution removed Iraq from the Kings' Alliance, Jordan continued to rely on Western support while the Saudis—who were especially vulnerable after Saud's bungled plot to assassinate Nasser—once again chose to swing toward Egypt and to downplay their ties with the West.

Syria also lacked effective allies in 1963. After all, Nasser was the only figure who could influence his Syrian supporters, and to seek an alliance elsewhere would have done little to increase Syria's internal stability. Because the civilian members of the Syrian government were reluctant to rely solely on brute force to stay in power (as later Ba'th regimes would do), enlisting Nasser's support by seeking another union with Egypt was the only alternative they could imagine.

A lack of alternatives may have affected Jordan's decision in 1967 as well. In a confrontation with Israel, Hussein could hardly count on Arab support should he reject Nasser's call to close ranks in May. An overt alliance with Israel was unthinkable, and Hussein probably recognized that the United States and Britain could do little to preserve his throne if he failed to participate in an Arab victory. In 1973, Hussein's belief that the Arabs would be no more successful than they had been in 1967 encouraged the token response that he ultimately made. Although the evidence is skimpy, the record does indicate that a lack of effective allies increases a state's propensity to bandwagon with threatening powers.

The Impact of Intentions

The decision to bandwagon with a threatening power is based ultimately on the hope that such a step will moderate its aggressive intentions. Not surprisingly, the belief that a powerful state can be appeased has been present in most cases of bandwagoning.

For example, Jordan and Saudi Arabia joined with Nasser in 1955–1956 both to exploit his popularity and to persuade him to cease his efforts to subvert their regimes. When these attacks continued (indicating that Nasser's aims were still hostile), the two states shifted to a policy of alignment with the United States and Iraq. Significantly, the Saudi-Egyptian rapprochement between 1958 and 1961 led Nasser to halt his criticisms of the Saudis (in part because he was by now more concerned about his quarrel with Qassem of Iraq). When Egypt's reaction to the break-up of the UAR (including a renewed propaganda offensive and military intervention in Yemen) revealed that Nasser still harbored aggressive aims, the Saudi-Jordanian axis was resurrected once again.

The same hopes probably animated the Syrians in 1963, and the Tripartite Unity Agreement did bring a brief period of apparent amity between Egypt, Syria, and Iraq. But when the Nasserist forces in Syria attempted yet another coup, the Ba'th reacted by executing the plotters and denouncing their efforts. Nasser then abrogated the agreement, ushering in three more years of Syrian-Egyptian hostility.

This dispute eventually led Nasser to seek a rapprochement with the conservative Arab states, beginning at the Cairo summit in 1964. The willingness of the conservative states to mend fences with Nasser whenever he halted his propaganda war is instructive. Cooperation with Egypt was attractive to them because it reduced the immediate threat they faced. At the same time, it did not increase Nasser's ability to threaten them later. Because Nasser relied primarily on propaganda and subversion, his willingness to cooperate with the "forces of reaction" reinforced their positions by showing that they were still loyal members of the larger Arab nation. And Nasser's subsequent criticisms were weakened by the fact that he had been willing to cooperate with them earlier. The lesson is extremely important: states are more likely to bandwagon when it will not increase the threat they will face in the future should their more powerful ally decide to turn on them.

Thus Jordan's decision to ally with Nasser in June 1967 followed from Hussein's (unfortunate) calculation that such a course minimized his future risks. If Hussein joined with Egypt and the Arabs won, his position would be no worse and might even be better. If he joined and the

Arabs lost (as they did), he had at least shown solidarity with the Arab cause. But if he stayed on the sidelines while the Arabs won, he would be more vulnerable than ever to Egyptian and Syrian attacks. Joining the Arab coalition thus prevented his Arab opponents from increasing their power to threaten his always fragile legitimacy. As Malcolm Kerr noted after the war, "the Israeli victory [in June 1967] cost Hussein the West Bank, but it may have saved him his throne."[65]

The belief that favoring the stronger side would prove beneficial also played a role in Hussein's decision to sit out the October War. Although Israeli assurances had no effect in 1967, Kissinger's repeated requests that Hussein remain neutral probably reinforced Hussein's own desire to keep the Jordan front quiet.[66] With these assurances, Hussein could tacitly align with the more powerful side, Israel, without fearing that Israel would exploit his forbearance.

The three conditions associated with bandwagoning are present in most of the (rare) examples identified in this study. Taken together, they provide a convincing account of the most significant example: Egypt's dramatic realignment from the Soviet Union to the United States.

Egypt's realignment qualifies as an example of bandwagoning for several reasons. Not only was Egypt choosing to align with the superpower it perceived as more powerful, but this step also involved beginning an unprecedented effort toward peace with Israel. In effect, Sadat was abandoning the effort to balance against Israel and the United States that Egypt had pursued since the mid-1950s. Sadat now sought to ally with the United States in exchange for economic benefits and political concessions. Rather than continuing to oppose Israel through armed resistance via Soviet assistance, Egypt now chose to negate the threat through cooperative diplomacy. Convinced he couldn't beat them, Sadat decided to join them.

The three conditions associated with bandwagoning were all crucial to his decision. First, Egypt was growing steadily weaker, as a host of economic troubles posed a growing threat to Sadat's regime. Egypt's economic difficulties also undermined its capacity to compete militarily, as long as Israel enjoyed generous U.S. support. Moreover, as Egypt's relative power declined, the benefits of gaining economic aid from the West, reopening the Suez Canal, and decreasing Egypt's military burdens by making peace with Israel became increasingly appealing.[67]

---

65. Kerr, *Arab Cold War*, p. 128.

66. On this point, see Kissinger, *Years of Upheaval*, pp. 490, 494, 500, 508; Quandt, *Decade of Decisions*, p. 177; and Dupuy, *Elusive Victory*, pp. 536–37.

67. For descriptions of Egypt's economic plight in the 1970s, see Ajami, *Arab Predicament*, pp. 90–100; Baker, *Egypt's Uncertain Revolution*, pp. 135–37; Yusif A. Sayegh, *The Economies of the Arab World* (London, 1978), pp. 358–59, 363–64; and Dawisha, *Egypt in the Arab World*, p. 186.

Second, Egypt lacked allies that could correct its most pressing problems. Soviet aid to Egypt could not outweigh U.S. support for Israel, and the Soviets were hardly enthusiastic about pouring more resources into Egypt. The October War merely reinforced this point. In spite of strategic and tactical surprise, unprecedented Arab cooperation, a U.S. administration hamstrung by Watergate, and active Soviet support, Egypt and its allies were soundly defeated. Although allies were available prior to Egypt's realignment, they were no longer capable of meeting Egypt's growing needs.

Third, and probably most important, Egyptian perceptions of U.S. intentions changed dramatically after Nasser's death. As noted earlier, Sadat was apparently convinced that U.S. policies could be radically changed if Egypt were more forthcoming. Although his early hints went unrecognized, the October War succeeded in persuading the United States to take his offers seriously. Convinced by January 1974 that "the U.S. is pursuing a new policy," Sadat gradually maneuvered Egypt away from the Soviet Union and into a close alliance with the United States.[68]

Egypt's realignment was thus a decision to bandwagon in response to (1) the vulnerabilities arising from Egypt's economic problems, its military weakness, and the prolonged diplomatic stalemate; (2) the fact that Egypt's other potential allies (e.g., the Soviet Union) could not correct these problems; and (3) Sadat's belief (in contrast to Nasser's) that U.S. opposition could be reversed. It was thus an especially important example of bandwagoning behavior, both in its implications for Middle East politics and as an illustration of the conditions that make such behavior more likely.[69]

CONCLUSION

The record of alliance formation in the Middle East provides strong evidence for many of the propositions advanced in chapter 2. First, states prefer balancing to bandwagoning, even when confronted by significant threats. The rare cases of bandwagoning that one can find are the result of an unusual set of circumstances. And because bandwagon-

68. On these points, see Israeli, *Public Diary of Sadat*, 2: 448; Safran, *Israel*, p. 468; el-Sadat, *In Search of Identity*, pp. 230–31; Golan, *Secret Conversations of Henry Kissinger*, pp. 145–46; and Kissinger, *Years of Upheaval*, pp. 223–27, 460, 637–38.

69. Steven David provides a complete historical account of Sadat's realignment in his "Realignment of Third World Regimes," pp. 418–45. Although he addresses a wider range of factors (focusing especially on the domestic politics of Sadat's decision), his version is consistent with the more theoretical interpretation offered here.

ing is more often the response of weak states, it is most unlikely to alter the global balance of power in any significant way.

Second, these results show that it is more appropriate to focus on how states respond to threats, instead of conceiving of alliances solely as responses to shifts in the balance of power. In addition to economic and military capabilities, threats from subversion or other forms of political pressure can be equally powerful determinants of alignment. Moreover, although the distribution of capabilities is extremely important to the superpowers, it plays little role in the alliance choices of regional actors. As expected, they are far more sensitive to the capabilities and intentions of their neighbors, for the reasons already discussed.

Although geographic proximity is clearly important, the evidence did not reveal a linear relationship between distance and level of threat. This lack of linearity is perhaps due to the fact that many rivalries in the Middle East were conducted primarily through political channels (e.g., propaganda and subversion) in which military power (and thus geography) played a minor role.

Viewed as a whole, these results mean that marginal changes in the balance of power between the United States and the Soviet Union are unlikely to make much difference and that only an enormous shift in this balance will lead regional powers to alter their international commitments significantly. Indeed, even if either superpower were to forge ahead dramatically, the ultimate effects would probably be less significant than one might suppose. Given the overwhelming tendency for states to balance, a state whose power and ambitions are growing can expect to face ever-increasing resistance should it attempt to exploit its superior position. And because regional rivalries are usually more important, efforts to exclude the other superpower by enlisting all the regional powers under one banner are virtually certain to fail.

Third, the importance of intentions has been apparent throughout this analysis. Because power can be used either to threaten or to support other states, how states perceive the ways that others will use their power becomes paramount. In particular, a state's willingness to bandwagon is heavily influenced by whether or not it believes that the threatening power can be appeased by an alliance with it.

This insight helps explain the tendency for states to prefer balancing. Balancing against a powerful state will be viewed as the more prudent response if one's assumptions about intentions are incorrect. Joining a defensive alliance to oppose a potential threat will protect you if the state in question is in fact aggressive. Such an alliance will be superfluous—but probably not dangerous—if the state in question turns out to be benign. By contrast, bandwagoning may fail catastrophically if one chooses to ally with a powerful state and subsequently discovers that its

[179]

intentions are in fact hostile. Balancing will thus be viewed as the safer response when intentions cannot be reliably determined.

Determining intentions is not easy. Accordingly, statesmen often seek shortcuts to identify friends and foes. One approach is to focus on the domestic characteristics of potential partners in order to ally with those whose beliefs or principles resemble one's own. The next chapter assesses the impact of ideological solidarity on alliance formation.

[6]

Ideology and Alliance Formation

In this chapter I analyze the impact of ideological solidarity on alliance formation. I define *ideological solidarity* as a tendency for states with similar internal traits to prefer alignment with one another to alignment with states whose domestic characteristics are different. I consider three questions. First, how powerful is this tendency? Second, does its impact vary as predicted in chapter 2? Third, do certain ideologies exert divisive effects by provoking conflict among adherents rather than encouraging cooperation?

I reach three main conclusions. First, there is a modest association between ideology and alignment. As expected, this association is more pronounced in relations between the superpowers and their regional allies, particularly in the case of the Soviet Union. Second, the observed association probably exaggerates the true impact of ideology. In particular, the extent of ideological agreement between the superpowers and their allies is fairly limited, and the correlation between ideology and alignment may be partly spurious. Third, as proposed in chapter 2, the nature of the ideology is itself a crucial factor. Certain ideologies are more a source of division than of unity, even though the ideology explicitly prescribes close cooperation among the adherents.

I begin the chapter with a broad overview of the relationship between ideology and alliances in the Middle East. Next, I examine this relationship in more detail, beginning with alliances between the superpowers and the Middle East states. Finally, I address the role of ideology in inter-Arab politics, focusing on (1) the ethnic solidarity of the Arab states against Israel, (2) the divisive ideology of pan-Arabism, and (3) the monarchical solidarity among the conservative Arab states.

Ideology and Alliance Formation in
the Middle East: An Overview

The importance of ideology as a cause of alignment is difficult to measure precisely.[1] If ideology does play a major role in alliance choices, however, then states whose domestic system or governing ideology has changed should seek different allies and alliances between states sharing important domestic traits should be more common than alliances between states that are different, even when an alliance entails significant costs.

Are these predictions confirmed by the alliances examined in this study? Only in part. The record does show that when a new regime with a different ideology takes power, it tends to acquire new alliance partners. Thus Iraq withdrew from the Baghdad Pact and its alliance with Jordan after the 1958 revolution; the leftist rebels who overthrew the Imam of Yemen in 1962 quickly turned to Egypt and the Soviet Union; the neo-Ba'th ascendance in Syria and the Marxist revolution in South Yemen led to new links with the Soviet Union; the Iraqi Ba'th's seizure of power in both 1963 and 1968 produced important shifts in Iraq's international position;[2] and Sadat's shift to the West coincided with a simultaneous move to liberalize Egypt's quasi-socialist economy.

The evidence that states with similar domestic systems are more inclined to ally is more ambiguous. Within the Middle East itself, for example, ideology has generally not been a reliable determinant of alliance choices. And when ideology has played a role, the resulting alliances have not been very durable. Although it is true that relations between conservative and progressive Arab states are often hostile and always guarded, hostility among the progressive Arab states is also quite common, as the recurring conflicts between Egypt, Iraq, and Syria have revealed. Indeed, as Malcolm Kerr has shown, "Nasser's relations with his fellow revolutionaries tended to be more difficult than those with the 'reactionaries.'"[3] Furthermore, alliances between radical and

1. The difficulty occurs because (1) common ideological designations (e.g., socialism) can mean different things to different people (thereby creating an erroneous impression of agreement); (2) statesmen may deliberately exaggerate the extent of ideological agreement for instrumental purposes (e.g., to gain greater support from an ally); and (3) alliances between similar states may be produced by other causes (e.g., an external threat), creating a misleading impression that ideology is at work.

2. In 1963, the Iraqi Ba'th first sought alignment with Syria and Egypt in the Tripartite Unity Agreement. When this agreement collapsed, it formed a bilateral alliance with Syria. The Ba'th's ouster by Aref brought Egypt and Iraq back together. After seizing power again in 1968, the Iraqi Ba'th actively courted the Soviet Union; it signed a Treaty of Friendship with Moscow in 1972.

3. Kerr, *Arab Cold War*, p. vi. See also Paul C. Noble, "The Arab System: Opportunities Constraints, and Pressures," in *The Foreign Policies of Arab States*, ed. Bahgat Korany and Ali E. Hillal Dessouki (Boulder, Colo., 1984), pp. 67–68.

conservative Arab states have occurred on several occasions, which suggests that ideological differences are not an insurmountable barrier.

Even more important, the historical record reveals that regional powers have usually ignored their ideological preferences when fidelity to them would entail significant costs. When threatened by the Baghdad Pact, for example, Nasser responded by allying with Syria (at that time a mildly left-wing parliamentary democracy) and the Saudi, Jordanian, and Yemeni monarchies. Revolutionary Egypt and revolutionary Iraq were bitter rivals from 1958 to 1963, and Nasser joined forces with Saudi Arabia and Jordan in 1961 to deter Iraqi annexation of Kuwait. After an intense campaign against Arab reaction in the early 1960s, Nasser suddenly began a détente with Saudi Arabia and Jordan in 1964 to isolate the revolutionary regime in Syria. Both progressive and conservative Arab states closed ranks prior to the Six Day War, and Israel's conquest of the West Bank and Sinai made revolutionary Egypt and monarchical Jordan partners until 1970. Indeed, Nasser abandoned his ideological concerns entirely at this point and sought an all-Arab consensus against Israel instead.[4]

For the same reasons, Syria, Saudi Arabia, and Egypt ignored their own ideological differences to prepare for the October War. Even more remarkably, Hussein ignored the principles of Arab solidarity to accept Israeli support during his confrontation with the PLO and Syria in 1970. Four years later, however, the Ba'th regime in Syria and the Hashemite monarchy in Jordan joined forces to oppose Egypt's separate peace with Israel. Finally, the growing threat from Iran helped cement an alliance between Ba'thist Iraq and the Saudi and Jordanian monarchies in 1979. In short, ideological consistency has been readily abandoned when threats to other interests emerged. In particular, ideological preferences have been less important than more immediate issues of security.

Alliances between the superpowers and the Middle East states, however, suggest the opposite conclusion. The Soviet Union has allied almost exclusively with "progressive states" governed by one-party authoritarian regimes committed to some form of leftist or socialist domestic policy. Moreover, Soviet relations with Middle East democracies (Lebanon, Israel) and the Arab monarchies have generally been poor. The United States, by contrast, has usually opposed the "progressive" Arab states and consistently supported monarchies and democracies. In short, ideological considerations seem to have played a

4. As Mohamed Heikal wrote in July 1967: "Social differences should be relegated to the past or future. Right now, there is a persistent need for a broad national and patriotic [inter-Arab] front." He also stated that "the defense of Arab territory is the joint responsibility of all the Arabs, regardless of their social and political differences." According to Nasser himself: "We do not want to change the social system in any Arab country. . . . [W]e want every Arab country to be truly Arab. . . . The battle calls for the mobilization of every Arab rifle, every Arab piastre, every Arab individual." Quoted in *MER 1967*, p. 135.

major role in determining alliance relations between the superpowers and their various Middle East clients.[5]

This association supports the hypothesis that, in a bipolar world, states will ally with the superpower with which they are most compatible ideologically.[6] From a practical standpoint, the apparent affinity between the Soviet Union and the various leftist dictatorships in the region suggests that the ideology is a powerful force binding the Soviet Union to its various clients. Before these conclusions are embraced, however, some important caveats should be noted.

Caveats

For several reasons, any observed association between domestic character and international alignment probably overstates the true extent of the relationship. First, as noted in chapter 2, if states base their foreign policy on the belief that ideology determines how others will act, they may cause others to behave in ways that appear to confirm this belief. Similar states will become one's allies because one offers them friendship and support, reflecting the expectation that they will reciprocate. States that are different are more likely to become one's enemies if one acts on the belief that they already are. Thus the belief that ideology determines foreign policy will often be a self-fulfilling prophecy.[7]

The same process may also force similar states to form an alliance when they otherwise would not. If one state is hostile to those that are

---

5. A rough measure of this association can be calculated as follows. In the period 1954–1979, there have been five left-wing dictatorships in the Middle East: Egypt 1954–1973, Syria 1963–1979, Yemen 1962–1970, Iraq from 1958 on, and the PDRY. There also have been nine other regimes (either democracies, monarchies, or moderate/right-wing authoritarian governments: Egypt 1974–1979, Syria 1954–1958, Iraq 1954–1958, North Yemen 1954–1961 and 1971–1979, Jordan, Saudi Arabia, Lebanon, and Israel. If ideology had no effect on superpower alliances, then we would expect each superpower to ally with a leftist dictatorship 35 percent (5/14) of the time and to ally with the other regimes 65 percent (9/14) of the time. Instead, six of the eight Soviet alliances in the Middle East were with leftist dictatorships and two were with other states (Syria 1954–1958 and Yemen 1955–1961). (Moreover, Syria during these years was an avowedly leftist state with a large Communist Party.) The United States never allied with a leftist authoritarian regime in the region. Thus the Soviet Union allied with leftist dictatorships more than twice as often as would be expected if ideology had no effect (75 percent instead of 35 percent) and the United States allied with right-wing or democratic regimes almost 50 percent more often than a random expectation would predict.

6. On this point, see Snyder and Diesing, *Conflict among Nations*, pp. 420–21; Dinerstein, "Transformation of Alliance Systems," p. 593 and passim; and Waltz, "Stability of a Bipolar World."

7. As George Kennan once wrote: "It is an undeniable privilege of every man to prove himself in the right in the thesis that the world is his enemy; for if he reiterates it frequently enough and makes it the background of his conduct, he is bound eventually to be right." George F. Kennan (Mr. X), "The Sources of Soviet Conduct," *Foreign Affairs*, 25, no. 4 (July 1947).

different, this hostility will encourage the latter to ally even if they would not ordinarily do so. The situation further magnifies the apparent effect of ideology; similar states end up together because a third party believes they are both hostile and possibly in cahoots, not because they are independently inclined to ally.

In both cases, in short, what appears to be ideologically motivated behavior is really a form of balancing. When it occurs, the observed association between ideological or internal similarities and alliance commitments will exaggerate the true impact of the former.

The evidence suggests that these biases are at work in the events considered here. In the mid-1950s, for example, the United States became alarmed by the emergence of a leftist government in Syria. As a result, it began a campaign to coerce or subvert the Syrian regime, which encouraged the Syrians to move closer to Egypt and the Soviet Union. The United States' own actions helped confirm the belief that a leftist regime in Syria would be hostile and pro-Soviet and increased the degree of cohesion among the leftist governments in Syria, Egypt, and the Soviet Union.[8] In the same way, Nasser's repeated attacks against the Arab reactionaries encouraged Saudi Arabia, Jordan, and Iraq to ally together against Egypt, despite their traditional dynastic rivalries. These alliances were more the result of Nasser's actions than of the independent power of monarchical solidarity.

Finally, there is the possibility of spuriousness. If a third variable affects both domestic ideology and the propensity for certain alliances, then the observed association will exaggerate the relationship between ideology and alignment. Thus the apparently strong effect of ideology on superpower alliance choices could be due to a third variable that has affected both the type of regime (democracy, monarchy, etc.) and the propensity for alignment with one superpower over the other. If this hypothesis is correct (and I will show later that it does appear to be), then the true impact of ideology is smaller than the observed association.

This overview suggests that the relationship between ideology and alignment is complicated. Let us turn, therefore, to a more detailed analysis of the alliances, beginning with the role of ideology on relations between the superpowers and their regional clients.

IDEOLOGY AND SUPERPOWER ALLIANCES IN THE MIDDLE EAST

In describing the ideological affinities between the superpowers and their clients, this section will focus on three questions: (1) Exactly what

8. This is not to say that ideology played no role in Syria's alliance choices, only that any tendency to ally with other leftist states was undoubtedly encouraged by U.S. policy.

beliefs or traits do they share? (2) To what extent do these traits encourage or discourage alignment? (3) What conditions affect these tendencies? The analysis will reveal that ideological agreement between the superpowers and states in the Middle East is confined primarily to the realm of foreign policy. In other words, the alliances are based on common foreign policy aims rather than on shared domestic characteristics. Ideological solidarity therefore is essentially a form of balancing behavior and the apparent relationship between domestic characteristics and alliance preferences is partly spurious. Let us first consider the Soviet case.

The Soviet Experience

Soviet analysts allege that Marxism-Leninism provides a scientific basis for analyzing world events. Because this ideology posits that foreign policy is the product of a state's class content, the Soviet Union should be especially sensitive to domestic and ideological factors when choosing allies.[9] If ideology is an important factor in these alliances, then we would expect the Soviet Union to be allied with states that are (1) ruled by a Marxist-Leninist vanguard party, (2) following socialist economic policies, or (3) ideologically committed to opposing imperialism. If ideology is not that important, however, Soviet allies should include states whose domestic characteristics or ideological traits are different. What does the record show?

Domestic Ideology: Marxism-Leninism versus Arab Socialism

Several noticeable similarities exist between the domestic political systems of the Soviet Union and its principal Middle East allies. With the exceptions of Syria and Yemen in the mid-1950s, all of its allies have been authoritarian systems dominated by a single political movement (e.g., the Ba'th). All have proclaimed some form of revolutionary socialism as their official ideology. All have been relatively intolerant of internal dissent. In this broad sense, therefore, the Soviet Union has allied with states having similar domestic characteristics.

At the same time, however, significant differences exist. Both Syria

9. I found the following works especially helpful for understanding the role of ideology in Soviet foreign policy: Karen Dawisha, "The Roles of Ideology in the Decisionmaking of the Soviet Union," *International Relations*, 4, no. 2 (1972); R. N. Carew-Hunt, Samuel L. Sharp, and Richard Lowenthal, "Ideology and Power Politics: A Symposium," in *The Conduct of Soviet Foreign Policy*, ed. Erik P. Hoffman and Frederic J. Fleron, Jr. (New York, 1980), pp. 101–36; and Vernon V. Asparturian, "Ideology and National Interest in Soviet Foreign Policy," in *Process and Power in Soviet Foreign Policy*, ed. Vernon V. Asparturian (Boston, 1971).

and Iraq allowed rival political parties for much of the period under consideration here, something quite unknown in the Soviet Union. The military has played a much larger political role in both these countries (and in Egypt and Yemen as well) than it has in the Soviet Union. Most important of all, the Soviet Union's Middle East allies—with the exception of the PDRY and (briefly) the neo-Ba'th in Syria—have explicitly rejected Marxism-Leninism. Indeed, Communists within these states were often systematically repressed, just as happened elsewhere in the Arab world.

The historical record shows that an acceptance of Marxist ideas and a tolerant attitude toward local Communists are not prerequisites for alignment with the Soviet Union. Yet the evidence also suggests that these factors are not completely irrelevant either. Tolerance toward local Communists is usually rewarded, and brutality is occasionally penalized. Although ideological agreement is clearly limited and other factors are much more important, it would be a mistake to conclude that domestic political factors exert no effect at all.

In the case of Egypt, Nasser saw the local Communist movement as a disloyal faction that posed a significant threat to his regime.[10] This view was no secret to his Soviet patrons. As Khrushchev revealed in 1956: "Is Nasser a Communist? Certainly not. But nevertheless we support Nasser. We do not want to turn him into a Communist and he does not want to turn us into nationalists."[11] Although this statement suggests a tolerant attitude toward ideological differences, Nasser's attacks on Communism in Egypt and Syria led to serious polemics between Cairo and Moscow in 1959 and 1961. Nasser described Communists in Egypt and Syria as "stooges" and accused them of "carrying out orders to place our country inside the zone of Communist influence."[12] Khrushchev responded by calling Nasser "a hotheaded young man" and described his opposition to Communism as "a reactionary undertaking."[13]

In 1961 Khrushchev told a visiting Egyptian delegation: "Some of those present here will become communists in the future, because life imposes itself on man."[14] The Egyptian reply was straightforward: "We do not believe that the historical development of mankind runs along the blind alley, of which capitalism is the beginning and communism is

10. See Heikal, *Cairo Documents*, p. 41; and Nutting, *Nasser*, pp. 50, 85.

11. Quoted in Karen Dawisha, "The Soviet Union in the Middle East: Great Power in Search of a Leading Role," in *The Soviet Union and the Third World*, ed. E. J. Feuchtwanger and Peter Nailor (New York, 1981), p. 119.

12. Quoted in Laqueur, *Struggle for the Middle East*, p. 65.

13. Quoted in McLane, *Soviet–Middle East Relations*, p. 30; and Roi, *From Encroachment to Involvement*, pp. 275–78.

14. Quoted in Heikal, *Cairo Documents*, p. 152.

the imperative end. We believe that the field of ideological thinking is open to all peoples."[15] To reinforce the point, Nasser's semi-official spokesman, Mohamed Heikal, then published a series of articles outlining in detail the differences between Egypt's Arab socialism and Soviet Communism.[16]

The expansion of Soviet-Egyptian ties in 1964 was encouraged by a partial compromise on these issues. Nasser agreed to release a number of Egyptian Communists from prison, provided that they joined the official party, the Arab Socialist Union. The compromise suggests that the issue was of some importance to both parties but not important enough to prevent their extensive collaboration in other areas.[17]

Thus Egypt continued to reject Marxism while welcoming Soviet support. Even after the Six Day War, with Egypt now dependent on unprecedented levels of Soviet aid, Heikal argued that Soviet-Egyptian cooperation was due primarily to common interests. In matters of ideology, he wrote, "It was a mistake to look upon everything the Soviet Union says as handed down from on high and beyond dispute."[18] And in 1970, Nasser revealed that his attitude had changed little since the 1950s: "The Soviet Union is a Communist country and we are not. Is this a matter of any consequence? No, it is not. . . Russia has not asked us to adopt Communism and we have not asked Russia to change, or to adopt our political system."[19] In the same spirit, Anwar Sadat told the Soviet ambassador: "We Arabs will never be Marxists. . . . [W]e will not allow a Marxist regime to exist in our region."[20] Yet this conviction did not stop Sadat from maintaining Egypt's ties with the Soviet Union as long as they served Egyptian interests.

Soviet relations with Syria and Iraq have also been affected—but not determined—by elite attitudes toward Marxism in general and toward local Communists in particular. Soviet support for Syria in the mid-1950s was encouraged by the fact that the Syrian Communist Party was the largest in the Arab world.[21] Unfortunately for the Soviet Union, the

15. The Egyptian reply took the form of a letter to Khrushchev from Anwar Sadat, head of the delegation to whom the Soviet leader had addressed his remarks. It is reprinted in Roi, *From Encroachment to Involvement*, p. 343.

16. See Mohamed Heikal, "Communism and Ourselves: Seven Differences between Communism and Arab Socialism: History Does not Unfold on a Closed Path," *al-Ahram*, August 4, 1961; reprinted in *Political and Social Thought in the Contemporary Middle East*, ed. Kamal H. Karpat (New York, 1982), pp. 117–22.

17. See Shamir, "The 'Licensed Infiltration' Doctrine in Practice"; and Horelick, "Soviet Policy in the Middle East," pp. 577, 580.

18. Quoted in Roi, *From Encroachment to Involvement*, p. 468 and passim.

19. Quoted in Pennar, *USSR and the Arabs*, p. 81.

20. Quoted in Schwartz, "Failed Symbiosis," p. 22.

21. Indeed, it was the Ba'th Party's fear of a Communist takeover that led the party to seek union with Egypt in 1958.

party was suppressed during the union with Egypt, and the Ba'th remained hostile to Marxist ideas. According to a co-founder of the Ba'th: "There is no link or relationship between Communism and the history of the Arabs, between Communism and the intellectual traditions of the Arabs and their past and present life. [Marxism] deforms the true socialism that the Arabs need."[22] Soviet commentators were equally critical of Ba'th policy toward the most progressive forces (i.e., the Communists) in Syria, and Soviet support for Syria was modest until the mid-1960s.[23]

As the Syrian Ba'th grew increasingly radical and adopted a number of Marxist tenets, however, Soviet support increased significantly. By 1966 the neo-Ba'th had welcomed several Communists into the cabinet, had allowed Syrian Communist Party leader Khalid Baqdash to return from exile, and had spoken approvingly of the "important lessons" that the Soviet Union could give to countries "on the road to socialism."[24] The Soviets began providing Syria with substantial diplomatic, military, and economic assistance for the first time since 1958 and now viewed Syria as one of the leading progressive regimes in the Middle East.[25]

Subsequent Soviet-Syrian relations also suggest both the relevance and the limitations of these concerns. The Soviet preference for Salah Jadid over Hafez el-Assad during the power struggle between the two in 1969–1970 may have reflected Jadid's greater sympathy for Marxist doctrines. But when these actions and those of the restored Syrian Communist Party led other Ba'thists to question Soviet intentions, the Soviet Union quickly took a neutral position.[26] And though the Communists were later granted a nominal role in Syria's National Front, the Ba'th guarded its dominant position carefully.[27]

22. Quoted in Robin Buss, "Wary Partners: The Soviet Union and Arab Socialism," *Adelphi Papers No. 73* (London, 1970), p. 2. See also Pennar, *USSR and the Arabs*, pp. 101–3.
23. See Smolansky, *Soviet Union and Arab East*, pp. 245–62; Yodfat, *Arab Politics in the Soviet Mirror*, pp. 111–17; and Laqueur, *Struggle for the Middle East*, pp. 84–86.
24. See Roi, *From Encroachment to Involvement*, pp. 419–24, 432–34; and Avigdor Levy, "The Syrian Communists and the Ba'th Power Struggle, 1966–1970," in Confino and Shamir, *USSR and the Middle East*, pp. 396–98.
25. Syria received a $120 million loan in 1966, military aid worth approximately $200 million, and a Soviet pledge to finance and build a long-delayed dam on the Euphrates River. For details, see SIPRI, *Arms Trade with the Third World*, p. 548; Lenczowski, *Soviet Advances in the Middle East*, pp. 113–15; and McLane, *Soviet-Middle East Relations*, pp. 91–92, 96.
26. See Levy, "Syrian Communists and the Ba'th"; and *MER 1969–1970*, pp. 427–29, 431–32.
27. See Pennar, *USSR and the Arabs*, pp. 114–15. As an illustration of Ba'th dominance, in the People's Council elected in August 1977, 125 out of 195 representatives were Ba'thists. In August 1976 the Syrian cabinet included 21 Ba'thists out of 36 (with 2 Communists). The crucial portfolios of prime minister and ministers of foreign affairs, defense, and interior were all in Ba'th hands as well. See *MECS 1976–1977*, pp. 608–10.

The same is true for Iraq as well. Soviet-Iraqi relations have been at their peak when the Iraqi Communist Party (ICP) has enjoyed a position of influence or has at least been tolerated. The height of Soviet support for Qassem coincided with the heyday of the ICP, which Qassem used to defeat his Ba'thist rivals in 1959. Indeed, the Soviets favored Iraq over Egypt during this period for precisely this reason.[28] But when Qassem moved to suppress the ICP, Soviet support declined rapidly.[29] It was not suspended, however, because Qassem's anti-imperialist views were still a considerable improvement over Iraq's earlier membership in the Baghdad Pact.[30]

From a Soviet perspective, Qassem's Ba'thist successors were far worse. Until their ouster by General Aref in 1964, the Iraqi Ba'th waged a bloody campaign against the ICP, which they blamed for their defeat in 1959. The Soviet response illustrates that ideological considerations are not entirely irrelevant; the Ba'th regime was described as fascist, its leaders were accused of "mass reprisals" and "monstrous murders," and Soviet economic and military aid was suspended.[31] Although relations improved under Aref, the ICP was still banned and Soviet support for Iraq was modest compared to the assistance given to Egypt and Syria. Significantly, Iraq was termed a "progressive" regime only with reservations.[32]

When the Ba'th seized power again in 1968, the rapprochement that led to the Treaty of Friendship and Cooperation in 1972 was accompanied by significantly greater Iraqi tolerance toward local Communists. As in Syria, the Communists were welcomed in a National Front, a move intended "to smooth the way towards the Friendship Treaty."[33] The tactical nature of this concession is revealed by its sequel. When several dozen Communists were discovered forming cells in the armed forces in 1978, the Ba'th regime executed them and suppressed the ICP once again. Interestingly, the Soviets did not cut off their support this

28. In a direct challenge to Nasser, Khrushchev stated in 1959 that "a more advanced system is being established in [Iraq] . . . than in neighboring countries of the Arab East." Forced to choose between two anti-imperialist Arab states, the Soviets preferred the one in which the Communist party was playing a leading role.

29. See chapter 3, note 79, of this book.

30. Smolansky, *Soviet Union and Arab East*, chap. 7 and p. 108.

31. See Smolansky, *Soviet Union and Arab East*, pp. 235–36; Roi, *From Encroachment to Involvement*, p. 363; SIPRI, *Arms Trade with the Third World*, p. 557; and Fukuyama, "Soviet Union and Iraq," p. 25.

32. Aref's conservative views and strong religious beliefs contributed to his antipathy toward the Iraqi Communists, but he did not actively suppress or persecute them. See Uriel Dann, "The Communist Movement in Iraq since 1963," in Confino and Shamir, *USSR and the Middle East*, pp. 378–81. For examples of Soviet appraisals of the progressive Arabs, see *MER 1967*, pp. 7, 26–28.

33. See Fukuyama, "Soviet Union and Iraq," pp. 44–45; and Khadduri, *Socialist Iraq*, pp. 81–87, 97–99, 145.

time, although these events may have contributed to the overall decline in Soviet-Iraqi relations in the late 1970s.[34]

Finally, Soviet relations with both Yemens illustrate the limited importance of domestic ideology. The Soviets supported the Imamate in the 1950s—despite its feudal character—and have maintained good relations with Yemen since then, despite the fact that neither the revolutionaries nor the moderate regime that gained power in 1970 showed any Marxist predilections. By contrast, South Yemen remains the only Middle East state with a true Marxist-Leninist ruling party. As its ruling factions have grown increasingly enamored of Soviet-style Marxism, relations with the Soviet Union have grown apace. One result was a formal treaty between the two countries in 1979. The Soviets have supplied arms, economic aid, and advisers to the North as well, but their ties with the less populous but ideologically more compatible regime in the South have been both more extensive and more consistent throughout this period.[35] As with other Soviet clients, in short, acceptance of Marxist ideas encourages alignment, but it is far from a prerequisite.

Domestic Economic Policy

Given the primacy of economic factors on Marxist-Leninist ideology, one would expect the Soviet Union to ally primarily with states whose domestic economic policies resemble its own. The evidence is mixed. The Soviets have encouraged their clients to adopt a variety of socialist economic policies (e.g., nationalization of key sectors and development of heavy industry), and they usually have preferred allies whose economic policies are roughly similar to the Soviet model. However, conformity to Soviet economic practices has been quite limited among Soviet Union's Middle East clients, which suggests that this factor is not very important in determining alliance choices.

In the 1950s, for example, the Soviet Union was more than willing to extend support to Egypt, Syria, Yemen, and Iraq, despite the fact that none of these countries followed economic policies similar to those of the Soviet Union. By the mid-1960s, however, Egypt's avowedly socialist development program (begun in 1959 and featuring the nationalization of banks and industry, state support for the public sector, and an ambitious Five Year Plan for industrial development) had prompted Khrushchev to praise Egypt's efforts to build socialism during

34. See Fukuyama, "Soviet Union and Iraq," pp. 49–52, 56–58, 69; Khadduri, *Socialist Iraq*, pp. 87–91; and Helms, *Iraq*, pp. 77–82.
35. For analyses of the internal politics of the PDRY and the Soviet-PDRY relationship, see Mylroie, "Soviet Presence in the PDRY"; and Francis Fukuyama, "A New Soviet Strategy?" *Commentary*, 68, no. 4 (1979): 55–56. For additional details, see Katz, *Russia and Arabia*.

his visit in 1964. Similarly, Soviet support for Syria increased significantly after the Ba'th began an even more radical socialist program in 1965–1966.[36] Soviet economic assistance made it possible for Iraq to nationalize its oil industry in 1971, and Iraq's own program for socialist economic development may have helped pave the way for the Treaty of Friendship signed in 1972.[37] In short, a mild relationship between Soviet support and the degree to which Soviet clients adopted socialist economic principles can be observed throughout the 1960s and early 1970s. It seems more likely, however, that international conditions (e.g., the Yemen War and the accelerating arms race with Israel) played a greater role in the expanding ties between the Soviet Union and its Middle East clients.

Moreover, there were important differences between Soviet economic practices and those of their allies. For example, although all Soviet client states nationalized certain sectors (e.g., banks and heavy industry), the role of the private sector remained quite important. In the same way, the role of central planning was much more limited in the Arab socialist countries than in the Soviet Union. Furthermore, despite the support the Soviets provided for the development of heavy industry, light industry and consumer goods received far more emphasis in Egypt and Syria than they did in the Soviet Union.[38] And although land reform was a key part of Egyptian and Syrian socialism, these efforts were much less extensive than the large-scale collectivization practiced by the Soviets.[39] In short, the Soviet economic model won few converts in the Middle

36. On Egypt's socialist program, see Waterbury, *Egypt of Nasser and Sadat*, especially chaps. 4 and 5; and Baker, *Egypt's Uncertain Revolution*, pp. 60–69 and passim. On Syria, see Rabinovich, *Syria under the Ba'th*, pp. 139–45, 178–79, 207. On the Soviet reaction to these events, see Yodfat, *Arab Politics in the Soviet Mirror*, pp. 64–75, 124–45.

37. On Iraq's development plans, see Penrose and Penrose, *Iraq*, chap. 18; Khadduri, *Socialist Iraq*, chap. 6; and Peter Mansfield, *The Middle East: A Political and Economic Survey*, 5th ed. (London, 1980), pp. 345–55. On relations with the Soviet Union, see Fukuyama, "Soviet Union and Iraq," pp. 35–36, 49, 54.

38. In Egypt, for example, production of consumer goods expanded over 50 percent during the first Five Year Plan. By contrast, production of intermediate and capital goods actually declined during this period. See Waterbury, *Egypt of Nasser and Sadat*, p. 89. Majid Khadduri reports that Iraqi investment in the private sector increased during the 1970s despite the regime's commitment to public sector development. See his *Socialist Iraq*, p. 130.

39. On Egypt, see Waterbury, *Egypt of Nasser and Sadat*, chap. 12. On Syria, see Mansfield, *Middle East*, pp. 537–38; and Petran, *Syria*, pp. 205–9. One should not make too much of this point, given that the trends in Syria point in the direction of greater collectivization (e.g., via agricultural cooperatives) and that Egypt was forced to limit its land reform program after the Six Day War. Although progress has been slow, Iraq has pursued the most aggressive land reform of all, seeking to eliminate the rural private sector through the establishment of cooperative, collective, and state farms. See Penrose and Penrose, *Iraq*, pp. 454–60; Khadduri, *Socialist Iraq*, pp. 117–23; and Robert Springborg, "New Patterns of Agrarian Reform in the Middle East and North Africa," *MEJ*, 31, no. 2 (1977).

East; there were as many differences between the Soviet Union and its Middle East allies as there were similarities.

Finally, fidelity to Soviet economic practices does not appear to have been very important in determining the level of Soviet support. It has already been noted that it mattered little to the Soviets in the 1950s. In addition, John Waterbury has suggested that the Soviet Union may have encouraged Nasser to moderate Egypt's socialist program in 1966 while refusing to provide the aid Egypt needed to continue its socialist transformation. Even more telling is the fact that Soviet diplomatic and military support for Syria increased after the October War, despite Assad's 1974 decision to reverse a number of the socialist decrees the Ba'th had enacted in 1965. Moreover, the Soviets maintained a close alliance with Iraq during the same period, although the Iraqis were concentrating on improving their economic ties with the West. Finally, the Soviets have supplied large-scale military aid to North Yemen on several occasions, despite the fact that its economy has remained almost entirely in private hands.[40] In short, if the Soviets prefer to ally with states whose economic policies are similar to their own, they have also been more than willing to ignore this criterion when heeding it would be politically costly. In the same way, alignment with the Soviet Union does not mean that the regional powers were attracted to the Soviet model of development.

Two points have emerged thus far. First, the Soviet Union has shown a mild preference for states that accept or are at least tolerant toward Marxist ideas or that are pursuing avowedly socialist economic policies. Similarly, such regimes appear more inclined to favor alignment with the Soviet Union. Second, and much more important, the Soviet Union has been willing to ignore these preferences when the opportunity or need arises. We can therefore conclude that purely domestic factors are of some importance, but not much. Let us now examine the impact of ideology in the realm of foreign policy itself.

Opposition to Imperialism

The principal ideological link between the Soviet Union and its Middle East allies has been mutual opposition to imperialism. Given that the Soviet allies are former colonies or protectorates, whose ruling elites have been understandably sensitive to foreign (i.e., Western) interference, this link is not surprising.

Soviet efforts to exploit these sentiments began in earnest in 1956, when Khrushchev added a new category—a "vast zone of peace"—to

---

40. On these points, see Waterbury, *Egypt of Nasser and Sadat*, pp. 96–97; Mansfield, *Middle East*, pp. 147–48, 354, 535, 541; and Petran, *Syria*, pp. 251–52.

Stalin's "two camps" (the capitalist and the socialist). In particular, Khrushchev praised the former colonies for their refusal "to participate in closed imperialist military alignments."[41] In 1961 the 22nd Party Congress devoted an entire section to the National Liberation Movement, and the so-called national democracies in the Third World were described as "a progressive, revolutionary, and anti-imperialist force."[42] By 1964 Moscow spoke of "revolutionary democrats" who "sincerely advocate non-capitalist methods."[43] According to one Soviet scholar, these elites "were fighting against the oppression of the . . . imperialist bourgeoisie. The anti-imperialist orientation of the national liberation movement makes it a constituent part of the world socialist revolution."[44] Although Soviet commentators were divided on the best way to exploit the alleged affinity, the belief that these states would be useful allies against imperialism was largely unchallenged.[45] This view was supported by the fact that the ruling elites in Egypt, Syria, Iraq, and South Yemen all shared Soviet suspicions of imperialist activity.

In Egypt, opposition to imperialism was a constant theme throughout Nasser's career, as well as an important motive for Soviet-Egyptian cooperation.[46] By 1957 Soviet reservations about the Free Officers in Egypt had given way to the claim that "Egypt's anti-imperialist, anti-feudal program had taken concrete shape."[47] Soviet writers praised Egypt's rejection of "imperialist military alliances," and the joint communiqué issued after Nasser's first visit to the Soviet Union denounced

41. See Laqueur, *Soviet Union and the Middle East*, p. 156; Yodfat, *Arab Politics in the Soviet Mirror*, p. 6; and Roi, *From Encroachment to Involvement*, p. 156.

42. Quoted in Roi, *From Encroachment to Involvement*, pp. 351–52.

43. See the discussion and references in Schwartz, "The Failed Symbiosis," pp. 5–9.

44. V. L. Tyagunenko, *Problems of Contemporary National Liberation Revolutions*, quoted in Schwartz, "The Failed Symbiosis," p. 8.

45. For evidence on this point, see Schwartz, "Failed Symbiosis"; Katz, *Third World in Soviet Military Thought;* and U.S. House Committee on Foreign Affairs, *The Soviet Union and the Third World*, pp. 17–37.

46. The following quotations illustrate the continuity of Nasser's statements on this subject: (1) "In the event of aggression, [the Arabs] undertake to defend this area without any link or partnership with the West. . . . Thus we will be secure from the menace of imperialism." Quoted in Love, *Suez*, p. 88. (2) "Throughout the years, imperialism was working for the division of the Arab World. . . . Not only was imperialism against the unity of the Arabs, but it was against their unity of purpose, because . . . [unity] was a powerful force to confront imperialism." Quoted in Dawisha, *Egypt in the Arab World*, p. 125. (3) "The Arab-Israeli conflict is the result of the contradictions between the Arab nation desiring political and social emancipation, and Imperialism wishing to dominate [the area] and continue its exploitation." *MER 1969–1970*, p. 97. See also Harkabi, *Arab Attitudes*, pp. 142–51; Baker, *Egypt's Uncertain Revolution*, p. 46; Vatikiotis, *Nasser and His Generation*, pp. 230–39, 274, 350–53; and Dawisha, *Egypt in the Arab World*, p. 127 and passim.

47. V. B. Lutskiy, "The Revolution of July 1952 in Egypt," reprinted in *The Middle East in Transition*, ed. Walter Z. Laqueur (New York, 1958), p. 502.

colonialism "in all its manifestations."[48] As Khrushchev stated in 1959, "We and the leaders of the UAR have different views in the ideological field, but in the question of the struggle against imperialism . . . our positions coincide with the positions of these same leaders."[49]

As the Soviet-Egyptian alliance deepened, the public emphasis placed on cooperation against imperialism increased. The communiqué issued during Khrushchev's visit to Egypt in 1964 contained an explicit condemnation of imperialism and foreign military bases, and the Soviets labored to create a "united front of progressive forces against imperialism" during the mid-1960s. By the War of Attrition, Nasser saw a direct link between Soviet support for Egypt and his own anti-imperialist views: "The only means to make the continuation of our struggles possible is to get allied with the Soviet Union. . . . We either succumb to the United States, . . . [and] submit to imperialism, or we fight and struggle. Here we must agree with the Soviet Union. We are struggling against imperialism and we support national liberation."[50] As Karen Dawisha concludes in her own study of Soviet-Egyptian relations, "The anti-imperialist component of Soviet ideology was certainly shared by the Egyptian leaders who throughout the 1950s and 1960s pursued a consistent anti-Western policy."[51]

The same convictions helped bring Syria and the Soviet Union together. Given the anti-imperialist sentiments of groups such as the Ba'th Party, Western attempts to pressure Syria in the mid-1950s merely encouraged closer ties with Moscow.[52] Thus Syrian premier Khalid al-Azm praised (and greatly exaggerated) Soviet support for the Arabs during the Suez crisis, claiming that "this intervention delivered the Arabs from the major catastrophe which imperialism wanted to inflict upon them."[53]

As the Ba'th grew more radical in the 1960s, both the level of ideological affinity and the scope of Soviet-Syrian cooperation increased. In 1963, the Sixth National Congress of the Ba'th declared that "it is pure fantasy to think that the construction of a new society . . . can be achieved without a continuous struggle against imperialism," and it

---

48. "President Nasser's Visit," *New Times*, May 1958; and *Soviet News*, May 16, 1958. Both reprinted in Roi, *From Encroachment to Involvement*, pp. 252–54.

49. Nikita S. Khrushchev, "On the Middle East—Speech to the 21st Congress of the Communist Party of the Soviet Union, January 27, 1959." Reprinted in *The Foreign Policy of the Soviet Union*, ed. Alvin Z. Rubinstein (New York, 1969), p. 401.

50. "'Abd-al Nasir's Secret Papers," p. 5. See also Rubinstein, *Red Star on the Nile*, pp. 59–65.

51. Dawisha, *Soviet Foreign Policy towards Egypt*, p. 118.

52. See Torrey, *Syrian Politics and the Military*, pp. 269–70, 294–96, 303–4; and Devlin, *Ba'th Party*, pp. 31–32.

53. Quoted in Roi, *From Encroachment to Involvement*, p. 232.

concluded further that "the policy of non-alignment must not prevent the strengthening of ties between the people of the socialist world."[54]

The neo-Ba'th faction that gained full power in 1966 placed even greater weight on ideological compatibility. According to the joint communiqué issued during Syrian prime minister Yusuf Zuayyin's visit to Moscow in April 1966: "[The two sides] . . . proclaimed their determined support for the struggle of the Arab people . . . against foreign occupation by imperialist powers. . . . They support the struggle of States, which have gained freedom, against inequitable treaties . . . imposed upon them by the imperialist States, and also support the struggle for the liquidation of foreign bases."[55] Although the neo-Ba'th was ousted in 1970, Syria has continued to maintain a consistent opposition to all forms of imperialism while maintaining close relations with the Soviet Union.[56]

Soviet relations with Iraq showed similar tendencies. Soviet support for the revolutionaries who overthrew Nuri al-Said followed predictably from Soviet opposition to the "imperialist" Baghdad Pact.[57] After Aref ousted the Iraqi Ba'th in 1963, his consistent, if mild, opposition to imperialism led the Soviets to describe Iraq as "among those Arab countries that resist imperialist machinations."[58] When the Ba'th returned to power in 1968, its anti-imperialist ideology encouraged the Soviets to view Iraq's desire for closer ties favorably. According to the Iraqi National Charter of 1971, Iraq's foreign policy stressed "the resolute adherence to the policy of struggle against world imperialism, . . . [and] consolidating relations with the peoples and governments of the so-

---

54. "Resolutions of the Sixth Congress of the Arab Ba'th Socialist Party," *Arab Political Documents 1963*, p. 444. The Congress also declared that strong ties with the socialist camp would "create new and genuine possibilities of demolishing imperialist strategic positions." These resolutions were not embraced by a number of Ba'th leaders, and the stated goal of improving ties with Moscow was not implemented for several years.

55. Representatives from the Syrian Ba'th and the Communist Party of the Soviet Union issued a joint communiqué in January 1967 stating that "Both parties . . . condemn the intrigues of imperialism and reaction in the Arab world. . . . They affirm the need for the further rallying of all the socialist and progressive forces in the world for a complete victory over colonialism, imperialism, and reaction." These statements are quoted in Roi, *From Encroachment to Involvement*, pp. 422–23, 434.

56. For evidence on Syrian beliefs about imperialism, see Dawisha, *Syria and the Lebanese Crisis*, pp. 103, 106, 108, 147, 152, 182, and passim; and Raymond A. Hinnebusch, "Revisionist Dreams, Realist Strategies: The Foreign Policy of Syria," in Korany and Dessouki, *Foreign Policies of Arab States*, pp. 291–92.

57. See Khadduri, *Republican Iraq*, pp. 10–11, 14, 47; Fukuyama, "Soviet Union and Iraq," pp. 23–24; and Smolansky, *Soviet Union and Arab East*, pp. 102–6, 112–16.

58. Quoted in Yodfat, *Arab Politics in the Soviet Mirror*, p. 180. Aref claimed that the Egyptian-Iraqi unified political command "breeds a power that stuns imperialism." See Khadduri, *Republican Iraq*, p. 225. After the Six Day War, Aref told Brezhnev that the Arabs viewed the Soviet Union as "a friendly people that stands with them in the struggle against imperialism." See "'Abd-al-Nasir's Secret Papers," p. 20.

cialist camp in a manner securing mutual interests, and elevating the balance of world struggle to defeat imperialism."[59] Thus the Soviet-Iraqi Friendship Treaty of 1972 committed the two countries "to wage an unrelenting struggle against imperialism and Zionism."[60] According to the Political Report of the Iraqi Ba'th Eighth Regional Congress in January 1974: "Our struggle is directed mainly against certain international forces . . . imperialism, Zionism and their local allies. . . . For these reasons, alliance with other international forces with comparable . . . resources, . . . is a correct move. The Soviet Union and the socialist countries are closest to us of the strong and advanced countries. This is in spite of differences of opinion on many matters. They are closest to us in principles, aims and interests. . . . The alliance of revolutions is natural."[61] As with Syria and Egypt, therefore, opposition to imperialism has been the principal ideological bond between the Soviet Union and Iraq.

Finally, opposition to imperialism also encouraged Soviet ties with both Yemens. Although the Imamate was in no way progressive, Soviet commentators praised Ahmed's hostility toward British imperialism while providing military equipment and training to his armed forces.[62] This case is especially revealing, as it shows that domestic characteristics can be utterly irrelevant if foreign policy goals coincide. The revolutionaries who overthrew the Imamate provided more promising opportunities to undermine imperialist influence on the Arabian Peninsula, and the Soviets gave considerable support to the republican faction until the end of the civil war.[63] As for the PDRY, its consistent hostility to imperialism—a legacy of its lengthy struggle against British rule—provides ample ideological justification for close ties with the Soviet Union.[64]

---

59. Reprinted in Khadduri, *Socialist Iraq*, pp. 228–29. The communiqué issued during Iraqi vice president Saddam Hussein's February 1972 visit to Moscow "condemned the attempts of international imperialism . . . to break the solidarity of the Arab countries and peoples and the cooperation with their friends—in the socialist countries." Quoted in Roi, *From Encroachment to Involvement*, pp. 565–66.

60. Reprinted in Khadduri, *Socialist Iraq*, pp. 241–42. According to Francis Fukuyama, "any sympathy for the Soviet Union on the part of the Iraqi Ba'th has always been on the level of foreign policy, coming as a corollary of Ba'thist anti-imperialism." See his "Soviet Union and Iraq," p. 16.

61. See *Revolutionary Iraq, 1968–1973: The Political Report Adopted by the Eighth Regional Congress of the Arab Ba'th Socialist Party–Iraq* (Baghdad, 1974), pp. 219–21 and passim.

62. See V. Maevski, "In the Interests of Peace and Security in the Near and Middle East," *Pravda*, November 5, 1955, reprinted in Roi, *From Encroachment to Involvement*, pp. 14648; and Wenner, *Modern Yemen*, p. 176, especially note 10.

63. See Dawisha, "Saudi Arabia's Search for Security," pp. 20–21; and Katz, *Russia and Arabia*, pp. 24–32, 44–45.

64. For a sympathetic view of the PDRY by a British Marxist, see Fred Halliday, *Arabia without Sultans* (New York, 1975), pp. 265–71. For representative statements of Soviet and South Yemeni views, see *MER 1969–1970*, 1: 447–48; and *MECS 1976–1977*, pp. 559–60.

Of course, as the only Marxist regime in the Middle East, it has more substantial ideological ties as well. In this sense, South Yemen is more the exception than the rule.

The analysis so far can be summarized as follows. Although there is some relationship between domestic characteristics and alignment with the Soviet Union, it is not strong. Soviet allies have almost always rejected Marxism-Leninism and have often been less tolerant of domestic Communists than many other states (including the United States and Israel). Furthermore, although most Soviet allies have adopted certain socialist economic policies, they do not follow the Soviet model. Yet these differences have neither prevented them from seeking Soviet help nor convinced the Soviet Union to withhold it.

The key is opposition to imperialism. As Nasser put it: "We have one common aim with the Soviet Union—to resist imperialism. . . . Our ideological and national interest is against imperialism, the Soviet Union's ideological interest and strategy are against imperialism."[65] Or in the words of Syrian president Assad: "[The Soviet Union helps us] with its own interest in mind—that is to combat the expansion of American power. But . . . Soviet interest coincides with ours."[66] And the Soviets have apparently agreed. According to a leading Soviet expert: "The important thing is not . . . that 'national democracy' is still a non-Marxist trend [but] its actual fight against imperialism . . . and that the revolutionary democrats make a constructive effort to build a new society. . . . That is what determines the Marxist attitude to revolutionary democratic programs in the developing world."[67]

The fact that ideological agreement is largely confined to foreign policy raises an important question of interpretation, to which we will return in a moment. If the most important element of ideological solidarity is agreement on a key element of foreign policy, opposition to imperialism, it is just another way of saying that states are more likely to ally when their foreign policy interests are similar. And if ideological solidarity is confined primarily to the realm of foreign policy, then ideological solidarity should be seen as merely another form of balancing behavior. In particular, the Soviet Union and its allies are united by their desire to oppose what they perceive as a common threat. The question thus becomes: If it is opposition to imperialism that unites the Soviet Union with its Middle East allies, then why have the leftist regimes in the Middle East viewed imperialism (however they define it) as es-

65. "Speech to the Arab Socialist Union on the 16th Anniversary of the July 23 Revolution," quoted in Roi, *From Encroachment to Involvement*, p. 488.
66. Quoted in Dawisha, *Syria and the Lebanese Crisis*, p. 75.
67. R. Ulyanovsky, quoted in U.S. House Committee on Foreign Affairs, *The Soviet Union and the Third World*, p. 23 and passim.

pecially threatening? Because the answer to this question helps explain the alliances of the United States as well, I will describe the U.S. experience before offering an answer.

Ideology and U.S. Alliances in the Middle East

If ideological solidarity were the most important determinant of alignment, the United States would have few allies in the Middle East. The fact that the United States has been allied with the conservative monarchies of Iraq, Jordan, and Saudi Arabia, the parliamentary democracies of Israel and Lebanon, and (since 1975) the moderate authoritarian government in Egypt suggests that ideological factors have been relatively unimportant.[68] Moreover, the United States sought closer relations with both Syria and Egypt on several occasions (ignoring their avowedly socialist policies) and provided military and economic aid to the authoritarian regime in North Yemen in the late 1970s.[69]

As with the Soviet Union, ideological solidarity between the United States and its Middle East allies is confined largely to issues of foreign policy. Just as Soviet allies proclaim a consistent opposition to imperialism, the United States and its Middle East allies share an aversion to revolutionary change in general and Soviet Communism in particular. For the conservative Arabs, Communism is suspect because it is both atheistic and openly hostile to monarchical rule. Thus both Saudi Arabia and Jordan have favored alignment with the United States because they recognize that the United States is equally hostile to Communism.[70] By

68. Although U.S. support for Israel is frequently justified by the fact that Israel is the only democracy in the Middle East, the relatively minor role of this factor is revealed by the fact that the United States refused to make an explicit security commitment to the Jewish state until 1962. If ideological solidarity had been all that important, one would have expected to see an alliance between the two states much sooner. It is also worth remembering that Israel originally adopted a policy of nonalignment and received military aid from the Soviet bloc, only to shift toward the West when Soviet friendship waned in the early 1950s.

69. As John Badeau, a former U.S. ambassador to Egypt, wrote in 1968: "It would be impossible to conduct a foreign policy in which the fostering of democratic institutions and a free enterprise economy is rated equal in importance with strategic interests. . . . In fact, no country in the Arab world either fits the American prescription for democracy and free enterprise or shows much likelihood of doing so in the next few decades. Rigorously applied, a policy of promoting democracy and free enterprise as basic interests would impede U.S. relations with all Arab states." See Badeau, *American Approach to the Arab World*, p. 116.

70. As William B. Quandt has written: "Throughout the 1950s and 1960s, the Saudis were particularly concerned about the indirect Soviet threat to the region. Radical ideologies—Nasserism, Ba'thist socialism, and Communism—were viewed by the Saudi leadership as disruptive forces that served to advance Soviet interests in the Arab world." See Quandt, *Saudi Arabia in the 1980s*, p. 65. For additional evidence of Saudi and Jordanian hostility toward Communism, see Holden and Johns, *House of Saud*, pp. 248–49, 307, 357, 390; "'Abd-al-Nasir's Secret Papers," p. 129; Hussein, *Uneasy Lies the Head*, pp. 95–96, 210–11; and *MER 1960*, p. 334.

the same logic, the inability (and unwillingness) of the United States to foster good relations with Nasser's Egypt, the Ba'th in Syria, and the PDRY may have been due in part to the commitment of these states to revolutionary goals (such as Egypt's intervention in Yemen) and to their perception of the United States as the world's leading imperialist power.

Ideological solidarity between the United States and its allies is limited in other respects as well. Just as the Soviets did not embrace Arab unity, Arab socialism, or the liquidation of Israel, the United States is neither a welfare-state theocracy such as Israel nor an Islamic monarchy such as Saudi Arabia and (nominally) Jordan. The United States officially rejects both the ideological basis for Israel's claims to the West Bank and the anti-Israeli dogma of the various Arab allies of the United States. Although Saudi Arabia still refuses to establish diplomatic relations with the Soviet Union, ideological differences have not prevented Hussein of Jordan from establishing relations with Moscow or from threatening to go further if U.S. support wavers. In short, the total degree of ideological agreement among both Soviet and U.S. allies in the Middle East is not perfect, even in the area of foreign policy.

Explaining the Impact of Ideology

What does this analysis reveal about the relationship between ideology and superpower alliances in the Middle East? Three things primarily. First, although the Soviet Union has allied with leftist regimes and the United States has not, neither superpower has insisted that its allies follow domestic policies similar to its own. The clients of the two superpowers, in turn, have shown little desire to do so. Having seized power ostensibly to eliminate foreign influence, the nationalist leaders of the progressive Arab states have been understandably reluctant to embrace a foreign ideology. Thus Nasser stressed that "Egypt is determined to have and maintain ideological independence from all foreign ideologies," and Michel Aflaq, co-founder of the Ba'th Party, insisted that "Communism is strange to the Arabs, just as the capitalist system is."[71] As for the conservative Arabs, the spread of any foreign ideology would have undermined their traditional authority and invited political suicide. Thus most Middle East states have rejected both superpowers' domestic ideology.

Second, to the extent that ideological agreement has affected alliance choices, it is confined to foreign policy preferences such as opposition to imperialism. As a result, the observed association between domestic ideology and superpower alignment may be partly spurious. In particu-

71. These statements are found in Torrey, *Syrian Politics and the Military*, p. 371; and Love, *Suez*, p. 645. See also Buss, "Wary Partners," pp. 2–6.

lar, it is due in part to the legacy of British and French imperialism and to the self-fulfilling dynamics described in chapter 2.

The imperialist legacy had several effects. The imperial powers based their rule on close ties with the traditional authorities in the regions under their control (e.g., the Hashemites in Jordan and Iraq and King Farouk in Egypt). Opposition to British and French rule thus tended to be opposed to the conservative political and social order that prevailed in these countries. As a result, wherever the revolutionaries gained power, they adopted domestic and foreign policies at odds with those of their conservative predecessors. Thus the progressive regimes were leftist because their domestic opponents were conservative, and they were anti-imperialist because the regimes they overthrew were products of the imperialist past.

The close collaboration between the imperial powers and the traditional rulers encouraged the revolutionary Arabs to be suspicious of the West. Moreover, the fact that these movements overturned existing Western allies (e.g., the Hashemites in Iraq) meant that their suspicions were usually justified. Predictably, this increased the tendency of the revolutionary states to ally with the Soviet Union. As Mohamed Heikal has described it, "The nationalist leaders . . . needed allies, and the natural direction for them to turn was towards the Soviet Union . . . because the Soviet Union was innocent of a colonial past in the area."[72]

This factor suggests that regime change, not domestic ideology itself, is the common factor linking domestic characteristics with alliance preferences. The pattern is striking: the principal allies of the Soviet Union in the Middle East have been states whose postimperial governments were overthrown by nationalist revolutions: the principal allies of the United States in the Middle East have been the states in which the regimes created by the West remained in power.[73] Indeed, the latter have favored the United States because they owe their positions to Western support and because leftist change poses a direct threat to their own authority. Thus the historical experiences of both leftist and conservative regimes have conditioned their attitudes and policies toward both superpowers.

72. Heikal, *Sphinx and Commissar*, p. 276. See also Hudson, *Arab Politics*, chap. 5; and Kerr, *Arab Cold War*, pp. 2–5.

73. The exceptions do not challenge this interpretation. Israeli democracy is mildly leftist in orientation, but the Western powers ultimately played a constructive role in creating the Jewish state. Accordingly, Israel found it relatively easy to abandon its early policy of nonalignment to favor the West. Similarly, conservative Yemen was a nominal Soviet ally in the 1950s, but primarily to gain Soviet support in its challenge to British rule in Aden. Thus Israel could be leftist and pro-Western because it has had no imperialist past; Yemen could be conservative and pro-Soviet because the Imam had his own quarrel with a Western power.

These historical factors were reinforced by subsequent events. The conflict with Israel—viewed as an imperialist creation by the progressive Arabs—reinforced incentives to align with the Soviet Union. Moreover, because the United States and Great Britain viewed the revolutionary states with suspicion and occasional hostility (in part because they suspected them of pro-Soviet inclinations), the progressive states were forced even closer to Moscow. As described in chapter 3, the Baghdad Pact, the Suez war, the Eisenhower Doctrine, and the U.S. intervention in Lebanon merely confirmed Arab suspicions that the United States had inherited the imperial role abandoned by Britain and France. By contrast, the Soviet Union welcomed the progressive Arabs, not because they shared its domestic ideology but because they were useful allies against the West. Thus the alignment between the progressives and Moscow was reinforced by how each superpower behaved.

The process worked the other way as well. When the progressive states turned to Moscow for support, the conservative Arab preference for alignment with the United States increased. Thus, as suggested earlier, the division of the Middle East between the two superpowers was at least partly the result of self-fulfilling beliefs and predictable responses. In short, what might appear to be ideological alliances also contain important elements of balancing behavior.

If this interpretation is correct, it means that the true impact of ideology on superpower alliances is less than it appears to be. The distinction is important, because it reveals that these alliances were not the product of domestic political affinities. Instead, they were produced by the ways that each superpower's actions reinforced their opponents' fears. The fears, in turn, were based primarily on the different perceptions and preferences derived from the historical experience of colonial rule.[74]

Finally, these alliances offer modest support for the hypothesis that ideology is more important when other threats are low or when defensive advantages exist. Because neither superpower has tried to conquer the region (which would encourage balancing with the other superpower irrespective of ideology), the regional states have been free to indulge their ideological preferences.[75] In other words, because the superpowers deter each other, the regional powers enjoy a diplomatic defensive advantage vis-à-vis both. As a result, they are free to align with the superpower they perceive as most compatible (even if the sim-

74. I am not suggesting that ideology has no effect, as the cases of the Marxist regime in South Yemen and the neo-Ba'th in Syria suggest. Rather, I am suggesting that the impact of ideology is probably exaggerated.
75. See chapter 5 for further discussion on this point.

ilarity is small), because they need not be as worried that either one is preparing to attack.

By contrast, as noted earlier, Middle East states have readily ignored ideological distinctions when major threats have emerged from within the region itself. This tendency reflects the fact that direct threats from other regional powers have been more common. It also implies that an attempt by either the United States or the Soviet Union to seize significant territory in the Middle East would probably lead its present allies to ignore ideology in their rush to obtain support from the other superpower.[76]

Summary

Ideological solidarity has played an important but ultimately limited role in alliances between the superpowers and the various Middle East states. A final lesson is that its impact may be due less to the intrinsic appeal of either superpower's system (i.e., Marxism-Leninism or liberal democracy) than to the overall context in which the alliances occurred. In a bipolar world in which nuclear weapons are present, in a region outside either superpower's sphere of influence, and in the decades immediately following decolonization, it was overwhelmingly likely that regional states would choose their patrons along rough ideological lines. We may question how durable this division would be if bipolarity eroded and the colonial legacy faded, and thus question the lasting importance of ideology as a cause of these alliances. The realignment of Egypt in the 1970s, the nonaligned policies of Iraq and North Yemen, and the recent hints that conservative opposition to the Soviet Union may be moderating all suggest that the impact of ideology on superpower commitments may be gradually declining. Thus what seems to have been an important cause in the past may be of little consequence in the future, should more pressing threats confront the regional states or more promising opportunities beckon the superpowers.

IDEOLOGY AND INTER-ARAB POLITICS: UNITY AND DIVISION

The evolution of inter-Arab alliances from 1955 to 1979 supports the hypothesis that the content of a given ideology determines its effects on

76. Among other things, we would expect that a U.S. attempt to seize Middle East oil fields would probably drive the Arabs closer to Moscow, and a Soviet effort to expand in the region would lead its present allies to move toward the West. One piece of evidence to support this prediction is Iraq's move closer to the West in response to the Soviet invasion of Afghanistan.

alliance formation. As elaborated in chapter 2, when an ideology calls for its followers to form a centralized, hierarchical movement, it is more likely to incite conflict than cooperation among them. Conversely, when the ideology proclaims more modest goals and does not threaten the independence of the various member states, durable alliances are more likely and intense ideological rivalries are discouraged.

This section will examine the three ideological issues that have dominated Arab politics in the postwar period: (1) the ethnic nationalism that has inspired Arab cooperation against Israel; (2) the ideology of pan-Arabism, which has advocated the uniting of the Arab nations into a single state; and (3) the conflict between progressive and conservative regimes within the Arab world. Two questions are salient. First, in what ways did each set of ideological beliefs either encourage or discourage alignment? Second, what explains their varied effects?

Ethnic Solidarity: The Arabs versus Israel

The belief that the Arab peoples form a single nation has been a recurrent theme in contemporary Arab politics. As we have seen, cooperation rarely has been assured—indeed, inter-Arab quarrels often have been extremely vicious—but the power of the idea is still substantial.[77] Indeed, as suggested in chapter 5, balancing behavior in the Arab world usually takes the form of seeking to isolate and weaken one's rivals by portraying them as violating this basic norm, which testifies to its enduring relevance.

The most obvious example of ideologically inspired cooperation among the Arabs is their universal opposition to Israel. This opposition follows from the belief that the inhabitants of the various Arab states form a single nation (including the Palestinians) and that Israel is an illegitimate and alien presence on Arab territory. As a result, all Arab states are obliged to cooperate in the struggle against Israel in order to demonstrate their loyalty to the Arab nation as a whole.[78]

Because of these beliefs, no Arab state has ever openly allied with Israel (Israel's support for Jordan in 1970 is but a partial exception) and only Egypt has been willing to sign a peace treaty and establish diplomatic relations with Israel.[79] In addition, the Arab League imposed an

77. See Hudson, *Arab Politics*, chap. 2, especially pp. 54–55. For a discussion of Arab solidarity with special reference to Egypt, see Dawisha, *Egypt in the Arab World*, chap. 10.

78. Examples of these Arab beliefs are far too numerous to present here. For summaries, see Harkabi, *Arab Attitudes*, especially pp. 362–83; Hudson, *Arab Politics*, chap. 5, especially pp. 115–19, 124; and Dawisha, *Egypt in the Arab World*, p. 128.

79. Jordan did rely upon tacit Israeli support during the civil war in 1970 and on Israeli forbearance during the October War. These examples however, support the argument that Arab states believe overt cooperation with Israel to be illegitimate, as Jordan and Israel did not publicize these actions as such.

economic boycott against Israel; troops from Egypt, Syria, Jordan, Iraq, and Saudi Arabia fought together in the 1967 and 1973 wars; and the Arabs created and financed the PLO, sought to divert the Jordan River to reduce Israel's water supply, and provided economic assistance to the states that bore the greatest military burdens in the conflict. And as the Arab reaction to Camp David showed, any Arab leader who breaks ranks to make peace is certain to be ostracized by the rest of his Arab brethren. These various measures often are ineffective and motivated as much by inter-Arab rivalries as by hostility to Israel itself. But the fact that this issue could be used to discredit opponents or enhance one's own position reveals its political potency: the ideal of Arab solidarity has been a constant force sustaining Arab alignments against Israel, irrespective of Arab conflicts with one another.

The central lesson is that Arab solidarity against Israel has been nearly universal because it usually has not been very demanding. To be a good Arab has required opposing the "Zionist entity" but has not required agreement on how to deal with Israel's continued presence and potent capabilities. In addition, it has not involved great sacrifices on the part of the Arab states, at least prior to 1967. Then, as now, the impact of Arab solidarity was primarily negative; it could impede recognition of or cooperation with Israel, but it provided little positive force for alignment.

The Six Day War marks the key historical division. Before the war, Arab cooperation against Israel was largely symbolic.[80] From 1957 to 1967, Nasser showed that one could demonstrate impeccable Arab credentials by making fiery speeches while simultaneously stressing that the time was not yet ripe for action.[81] In May 1967, however, a combination of overconfidence and misleading information led Egypt and Jordan to take the demands of Arab solidarity too seriously, leading to what Hussein later termed "our historic error." What should be emphasized, however, is that the heavy price the Arabs paid in this war was unin-

80. This symbolism is nicely illustrated by the Arab summits between 1964 and 1966. Pressed by the Syrians to take more direct action but aware that direct action was unwise, Nasser defused the pressure by arranging an Arab summit to endorse rather innocuous actions (such as the establishment of the PLO and the diversion of the Jordan River waters away from Israel's water projects). The diversion was never completed, and the PLO remained firmly under the control of the states providing it with financial support, but Egypt and the conversative Arabs had shown fidelity to the Arab cause.

81. For example, in 1965 Nasser declared: "We shall not enter Palestine with its soil covered in sand. We shall enter it with its soil saturated in blood." Quoted in Harkabi, *Arab Attitudes*, p. 38. Yet despite pressure from his rivals in Syria and elsewhere, Nasser made it clear that he would not "fight at a time when I was unable to do so. I would not lead my country to disaster and would not gamble with its destiny." Accordingly, he called incessantly for strengthening the Arab states for the coming battle but refrained from provoking a conflict until his major miscalculation in May and June 1967. On this point, see Kerr, *Arab Cold War*, pp. 98–100; *MER 1960*, pp. 171–73; *MER 1961*, pp. 181–83; and Harkabi, *Arab Attitudes*, pp. 4–6 and passim.

tended and the war itself was due as much to inter-Arab rivalries as to hostility toward Israel. Because Arab losses in 1967 provided a far more powerful incentive for cooperation, a gradual trend toward more effective Arab action began to emerge, culminating in the Arabs' successful surprise attack in October 1973.

To summarize: The nationalist solidarity of the Arabs has been a constant force for cooperation against Israel, but usually not a very powerful one. The Arab alliance against Israel is large but lacks cohesion, except when more tangible incentives are present. For any Arab leader, failure to support the cause invites criticism, but meeting one's obligations is relatively easy to do. Although this component of Arab ideology encourages a broad Arab alignment against Israel, the coalitions that it creates have been neither especially cohesive nor effective, unless direct material incentives reinforce the general ideological line.

Birds of a Feather Flying Apart: The Effects of Pan-Arabism

According to Fouad Ajami, "Pan-Arabism dominated the political consciousness of modern Arabs."[82] If, as one writer suggests, the "Arab world has been awash with ideology," the prominence of pan-Arab ideas helps explain why it was also awash with conflict.[83] In simple terms, the ideology of pan-Arabism called for the unification of the Arab nation in a single state.[84] Yet the more widely it was accepted and the more intently the goal of unity was pursued, the more conflictive inter-Arab relations became. This conflict is the paradox of pan-Arabism; although the ideology called for close cooperation and was widely accepted, it was in fact a source of intense division among the elites who claimed to embrace it.

There are ample grounds for the concept of Arab unity, including a common language, religion, and culture.[85] Moreover, the widespread

82. See Fouad Ajami, "The End of Pan-Arabism," *Foreign Affairs*, 57, no. 2 (1978–1979): 355.
83. Hudson, *Arab Politics*, p. 20.
84. For representative statements, see Abdullah al-Alayili, "What Is Arab Nationalism?" in Haim, *Arab Nationalism*, pp. 120–27; and "The Background of Arab Nationalism," in Karpat, *Political and Social Thought*, pt. 1, sec. 2. See also Hudson, *Arab Politics*, chap. 2; Devlin, *Ba'th Party*, chap. 3; Sayegh, *Arab Unity*; Gershoni, *Emergence of Pan Arabism in Egypt*; and Binder, *Ideological Revolution in the Middle East*, chap. 7, especially pp. 204–12.
85. To say that there are ample grounds for Arab unity does not mean it is very likely; it means only that unity is a plausible vision for the Arabs to embrace. There are important schisms within both the Islamic and the Arab spheres, including the existence of minority groups such as Lebanese Christians, Egyptian Copts, Syrian Alawites, and Iraqi Kurds. The division between Sunni and Shi'ite Moslems has become increasingly important, to say nothing of the linguistic, tribal, and judicial divisions that exist throughout the Arab world. My point is that although there are important divisions, the existence of equally important common features combined with a popular ideology that stresses the similarities among the Arab peoples and extolls the virtues of Arab nationalism has made the idea of formal political unity plausible.

belief that the division of the Arab world was the result of foreign inter-ference increased the conviction that this artificial situation should be corrected.[86] Thus it is not surprising that pan-Arabism became popular.

For many Arabs (and many others as well), Nasser's rise to power heralded a new Arab resurgence through political unification. As one of his Ba'thist rivals admitted, "Nasser was the first and only Arab leader capable of taking the leadership of an Arab renaissance."[87] For Nasser and Egypt, moreover, invoking pan-Arab ideals provided a potential defense against imperialist interference (through Arab cooperation) while enhancing Nasser's own charismatic authority.[88] According to Adeed Dawisha, by the end of 1955 "Egypt had . . . firmly moved from the periphery to the core of the Middle East international system and as such had become the focus not only of the Arab political situation, but also, and perhaps more importantly, of its major ideological manifesta-tion, the 'Arab nationalist movement.'"[89] And despite the fact that Nasser was a late convert whose true commitment to formal unity was questionable, there is little doubt that he saw himself as the rightful leader of that movement.[90]

Between 1955 and 1979, at least five attempts to implement the goal of Arab unity were made, all of them failures. They reveal how ideologies such as pan-Arabism ultimately can be more divisive than unifying, that birds of a feather can and do fly apart.

The most important example, the union of Egypt and Syria into the UAR, restored the momentum Nasser had lost when the Arab Solidarity Pact unraveled after the Suez War. The decision to unite was based on both ideological and pragmatic motives, as Nasser and his Syrian part-ners each sought to enhance their internal and external positions by exploiting pan-Arab sentiments.[91] The immediate response reveals the

86. In the words of Kemal Karpat, "Nasser's foreign policy . . . can be regarded as born out of protest against the artificial division of Arab lands into several states, and against their backward economic, social, and political systems. . . . The ultimate goal of this view was a Pan-Arabism that would lead eventually to unification and integration in the form of one Arab state." See Karpat, *Political and Social Thought*, p. 159; and Dawisha, *Egypt in the Arab World*, pp. 142–43. The goal of Arab unity was even more explicit in the ideology of the Ba'th. See Devlin, *Ba'th Party*, pp. 23–29.
87. Quoted in Stephens, *Nasser*, p. 343. See also the statements quoted by Malcolm Kerr in *Arab Cold War*, pp. 55–56; and Safran, *From War to War*, chap. 2, especially pp. 68–74.
88. See Dawisha, *Egypt in the Arab World*, pp. 11–12, 135; Hudson, *Arab Politics*, p. 242; and Dekmejian, *Egypt under Nasir*, chap. 4. Interestingly, Nasser's own pan-Arab views emerged rather late in his rise to power. On this point, see Seale, *Struggle for Syria*, pp. 225–26.
89. Dawisha, *Egypt in the Arab World*, p. 14.
90. See Seale, *Struggle for Syria*, pp. 225–26; and Dawisha, *Egypt in the Arab World*, pp. 134–35.
91. Both sides wanted to prevent a Communist takeover in Syria—which Nasser's prestige could quell—and to enhance their standing within the Arab world at large. See Seale, *Struggle for Syria*, chap. 22; Torrey, *Syrian Politics and the Military*, pp. 378–81; Kerr,

power of the pan-Arab ideal: the union was acclaimed throughout the Arab world, and Nasser's rivals in Jordan and Iraq immediately sought to imitate the UAR by forming their own Federal Union.[92] When Nasser was joined by the Imam of Yemen and (briefly) by the Iraqi revolutionaries in 1958, progress toward "one Arab nation with an immortal mission" must have seemed almost inevitable.

These hopes were soon dashed. General Qassem ousted the pan-Arab forces in Iraq and reasserted Iraq's separate national identity. When Nasser called the UAR "the first achievement of Arab nationalism" and pledged that the UAR "would endeavor to realize complete Arab unity," Qassem spoke of "the immortal Iraqi republic" and argued that "every Arab country has its independent political identity which all must recognize."[93] Qassem's explicit rejection of formal unity thus challenged Nasser's position as leader of the pan-Arab movement, and Egypt and Iraq remained rivals until Qassem's assassination in 1963.

In the UAR itself, Nasser refused to share power with his Ba'thist partners and imposed Egyptian institutions on Syria's political system and economy.[94] By 1961 dissatisfaction within Syria led a group of Syrian army officers to stage a coup and secede from the UAR. The postmortem by Ba'th leader Salah Bitar was revealing: "The rupture between Nasser and the Ba'th was caused by a certain Egyptian hegemonic view of the union."[95] Although Nasser and the Ba'th apparently shared similar goals, the first attempt to implement the pan-Arab vision had failed.

The turbulent relations between Egypt, Syria, and Iraq after the Syrian secession illustrate the paradox of pan-Arabism even more fully. After an unsuccessful attempt to mollify pan-Arab sentiment by moving closer to Iraq, the secessionist regime was overthrown by a Ba'thist coup in March 1963. The Iraqi Ba'th had seized power in Baghdad several weeks earlier, and suddenly three openly pan-Arab regimes faced the challenge of fulfilling their stated commitment to unity.

The result was the abortive Tripartite Unity Agreement of April 1963. Both its origins and its failure are revealing. The civilians in the Ba'th were committed to unity, but a union with Egypt was sought primarily

---

Arab Cold War, pp. 7–12; Heikal, *Sphinx and Commissar*, pp. 86–87; and Dawisha, *Egypt in the Arab World*, pp. 19–21.

92. As noted in chapter 5, this alliance was essentially another case of balancing. By enhancing Nasser's prestige and thus his ability to invoke the symbols and power of pan-Arab ideology, the formation of the UAR threatened the legitimacy of Nasser's rivals. Imitation was both a sincere form of flattery and a reflection of sincere concern on the part of King Hussein and Iraqi Premier Nuri al-Said.

93. Qassem also avoided any references to the goal of formal unity. See *MER 1960*, pp. 116–20.

94. See Rabinovich, *Syria under the Ba'th*, pp. 16–18; and Devlin *Ba'th Party*, pp. 135–45, 196.

95. Quoted in Stephens, *Nasser*, p. 343.

to keep their domestic political rivals (and especially the Nasserists) at bay. As Itamar Rabinovich points out: "The [Syrian] government constituted a unionist regime in the sense that its leaders wanted to establish normal, even close relations with Nasser. One important lesson of the previous eighteen months was that this had become a prerequisite for political stability in Syria."[96] Or in the words of Malcolm Kerr, "The weight of Nasser's prestige was the priceless asset that the Syrian and Iraqi delegations had come to [the Tripartite unity talks] to seek."[97] Because pan-Arabism was the dominant ideological vision and Nasser was its leading apostle, his support had become a crucial component of legitimacy for any Arab regime whose popularity rested on support for similar ideals.

Not only did the negotiations themselves reveal little practical basis for cooperation—each party had different ideas regarding how unity might be achieved—but the resulting agreement for union collapsed quickly.[98] When Nasserist forces continued their attempts to overthrow the Syrian government, the Ba'th was forced to repress them violently. (Indeed, the Ba'th military, never enthusiastic about the prospect of another union, welcomed the opportunity.) Nasser then renounced the unity agreement and left Syria and Iraq to their fates. The two Ba'th regimes continued the union on a bilateral basis until November 1963, when yet another coup in Iraq removed the Ba'th from power and brought the alignment to an end.

Over the next three years, Syria and Egypt waged an intense ideological conflict, while the Syrians adopted increasingly extreme positions at home and toward Israel.[99] But because neither Egypt nor the conservative Arabs wanted a war with Israel at this time, and because their extremism made the Arab monarchies even more suspicious of the Ba'th than they were of Nasser, this policy succeeded only in keeping the Ba'th isolated within the Arab world.

These events are extremely revealing. Still claiming allegiance to the

96. Rabinovich, *Syria under the Ba'th*, pp. 52–54.

97. Kerr, *Arab Cold War*, chaps. 3 and 4, especially p. 56. For an Egyptian account of the Tripartite talks, see *Arab Political Documents 1963*, pp. 73–213. I have found Kerr's fascinating analysis of these negotiations extremely helpful in preparing this section.

98. To avoid a repetition of their experience in the UAR, the Syrians sought to limit Nasser's formal powers. Predictably, Nasser insisted on reserving the dominant role for himself or his supporters. Given that the Syrians and Iraqis needed him far more than he needed them, Nasser got his way. See Kerr, *Arab Cold War*, pp. 50, 57, 70, 75–76.

99. As a leading expert on the Ba'th described this trend: "The Ba'th realized that it was politically even more imperative . . . to demonstrate that it did have an ideology distinct from Nasser if not superior [to him]. Since they could neither effectively dispute Nasser's leadership of Arab nationalism nor afford to speak for Iraqi and Syrian particularism, they felt they could legitimize their conflict with him by convincing Arab public opinion that it was an ideological one." See Rabinovich, *Syria under the Ba'th*, p. 84.

ideal of Arab unity, the Ba'th was forced to compromise repeatedly in 1964 and 1965. Whenever Nasser called for an Arab summit, the Syrians faced the unenviable choice of cooperation on Nasser's terms or complete isolation. Until 1966, their lingering commitment to unity and still-precarious internal position effectively prevented an independent Syrian policy.

By contrast, the neo-Ba'th radicals who seized power in February 1966 faced no such problem, and they turned the tables on Nasser with remarkable ease. The neo-Ba'th rejected the traditional goal of Arab unity and maintained its authority through unchallenged control of the Syrian armed forces. As a result, it had little need for Nasser's support. And because it was willing to act alone against Israel—despite the costs and risks—Nasser was unable to call its bluff by threatening to isolate it.[100] Having seized the initiative on the crucial issue of Palestine and having proclaimed a far-reaching socialist program at home, the neo-Ba'th forced Nasser to join forces on its terms in order to preserve his own position as acknowledged leader of the Arab revolution. Ironically, once the Syrians abandoned the ideology of pan-Arabism, their ability to pressure Egypt into supporting them in fact increased.[101]

Significantly, the potential for conflict inherent in highly centralized movements is illustrated by the fate of the Ba'th party itself. Originally the chief advocates of Arab union, the radicals of the Syrian Ba'th Party provoked a quarrel with the Iraqi branch of the party. This quarrel soon led to a complete rift within the avowedly transnational movement. The schism has divided Iraq and Syria ever since, and it has helped discredit the pan-Arab ideal even more. As Nadav Safran points out, "If a small group of leaders from one and the same party could not operate in harmony, how could they bring together the leaders and peoples of the different Arab countries?"[102]

The Arab Unity Pact between Egypt and Iraq in 1964 suggests an answer to this question: formal unity was possible only when it was not taken very seriously. Having ousted the Iraqi Ba'th, President Aref was free to pursue his personal admiration for Nasser and his earlier commitment to unity.[103] But in contrast to the UAR, neither Iraq nor Egypt

100. Nasser's ability (and willingness) to do so was also reduced by the decline in Egypt's relations with Jordan and Saudi Arabia in 1966.
101. See Kerr, *Arab Cold War*, pp. 121–22; and Dawisha, *Egypt in the Arab World*, p. 48.
102. Safran, "Arab Politics: Peace and War," p. 395.
103. Aref had been co-leader (with Qassem) of the Iraqi government that succeeded Nuri al-Said and Feisal II in 1958. He had negotiated a union agreement with Egypt at that time but lost a power struggle with Qassem and was forced into exile. He returned to power in 1963 in partnership with the Ba'th and then ousted the Ba'th several months later. Evidence regarding Aref's pan-Arab convictions can be found in Roi, *From Encroachment to Involvement*, pp. 379–85; and Heikal, *Cairo Documents*, pp. 155–57.

became heavily involved in the other's internal affairs. Although Aref began a number of domestic reforms in order to facilitate the union, they were quickly abandoned when they proved unsuitable for Iraq.[104] Several Nasserist plots against Aref discouraged additional progress, although the Egyptian role in these events is unclear.[105] Egypt and Iraq remained loosely aligned until after the Six Day War, and the modest success of the Unity Agreement lay precisely in the fact that the participants sought very limited objectives throughout. Thus pan-Arab alliances could succeed if and only if the sovereignty of the member states was not seriously challenged.[106]

What explains the failure of pan-Arabism? Why did its most enthusiastic proponents find cooperation so difficult to sustain? The answer lies in the contradictory premises of the ideology itself. Pan-Arabism threatened the security of the separate Arab regimes, because it called for them to merge into a single state. The long-range goal of unity could not be openly abandoned, because it provided an important source of legitimacy for the revolutionary Arab states. But if the goal were ever achieved, all regimes save the one that emerged on top would be replaced. Thus the various attempts to implement an Arab union quickly became struggles for hegemony. As the collapse of the UAR illustrates, even the most serious efforts were highly unstable. Indeed, even the most dedicated advocate of pan-Arabism, the Ba'th, fell victim to bitter factional quarrels once it acquired political power in more than one country. In the politics of pan-Arabism, in short, nothing failed like success.

Finally, because the ideology of pan-Arabism was an important source of legitimacy, setbacks required renewed efforts and a search for scapegoats. For example, Nasser blamed reactionary forces for the break-up of the UAR, and the National Charter that Egypt adopted in 1962 openly proclaimed Egypt's right to intervene against these opponents.[107] Thus pursuit of the pan-Arab ideal undermined relations

104. See Khadduri, *Republican Iraq*, pp. 224–28, 233–36, 247–49, 252–61.

105. For different versions of these events, see Lenczowski, *Middle East in World Affairs*, pp. 303–4; Khadduri, *Republican Iraq*, pp. 245–46, 255; and Penrose and Penrose, *Iraq*, pp. 329–30, 345.

106. Much the same description applies to the Federation of Arab Republics formed among Egypt, Sudan, Syria, and Libya in 1971. Largely the brainchild of Libyan leader Muammar Qadhafi (who was an intense admirer of Nasser), the federation was a rather limited affair that Anwar Sadat probably agreed to join simply to show loyalty to Nasser's ideas. See Peter K. Bechtold, "New Attempts at Arab Cooperation: The Federation of Arab Republics, 1971–?" *MEJ*, 27, no. 2 (1973).

107. As the charter stated: "[Egypt] . . . is bound to spread its mission and put the principles upon which it rests at the disposal of all the Arabs, disregarding the wornout notion that in doing so it is interfering in other people's affairs." Quoted in Dawisha, *Egypt in the Arab World*, p. 35.

between its advocates and its opponents alike. The reason is simple: as an ideology explicitly aimed at all Arab states, its success posed a potential threat to all regimes save the ultimate victor, regardless of whether the regime shared the same goal or not.

This interpretation receives additional support from the evolution of Arab politics after Nasser's death. His successor, Anwar Sadat, possessed neither the charisma nor the desire to pursue pan-Arab ideals. For Sadat, legitimacy could be won only through practical achievements. As he put it, he was more interested in the "essence of Arab unity" than the forms. In other words, effective alliances were more important than leadership over a united Arab world. As we have already seen, this more modest goal proved to be quite feasible.[108]

In short, pan-Arabism is a classic example of how an ideology that calls for its members to form a centralized movement is likely to produce precisely the opposite result.[109] Interestingly, Nasser seems to have drawn the same lesson from his experiences with the UAR and the Tripartite Unity Agreement. The more realistic appraisal that these failures produced is a fitting summary to this analysis: "A natural, legitimate union is assured and inevitable. . . . But nowadays the concept of Union itself is in crisis. . . . This kind of multiplicity of nationalist activities seems to lead us to clashes. . . . While every Arab country boasts a [revolutionary] party, union seems utterly impossible. True political opposition would degenerate into regionalism, with Syria at odds with Egypt, Iraq at odds with Syria, and so forth."[110]

Birds of a Feather Flocking Together: Monarchical Solidarity

In contrast to the conflicts that pan-Arabism produced among the various progressive regimes, the conservative Arab monarchies main-

108. In Sadat's own words: "What are the disputes that have endangered Arab solidarity? First of all, ideological rifts, which we transposed onto our differences of opinion, and used to categorize Arab regimes [into different slots]." There is also evidence that the disaster of June 1967 had led Nasser to similar views. His willingness to cooperate with Jordan and his efforts to promote an all-Arab front against Israel (with no intimations of formal unity) suggest that he too had abandoned pan-Arab ideals under the pressure of external circumstances. Sadat's preferences are revealed both by his statements and by his decision to change Egypt's formal name from the United Arab Republic to the Arab Republic of Egypt. On this aspect of Sadat's policies, see Kerr, *Arab Cold War*, p. 129; Hudson, *Arab Politics*, pp. 248–49; Heikal, "Egyptian Foreign Policy," p. 720; Heikal, *Road to Ramadan*, pp. 133–34; Baker, *Egypt's Uncertain Revolution*, p. 126; and Israeli, *Public Diary of Sadat*, 1: 403, 369, 2: 501.

109. Majid Khadduri puts it well: "As an ideology, Arab socialism was intended to be a unifying rather than a disruptive factor in the movement towards Arab unity. But no sooner had the nucleus of an Arab union been achieved—the United Arab Republic—then several variants began to develop, stemming partly from parochial and partly from personal and procedural differences." See Khadduri, *Political Trends in the Arab World* (Baltimore, 1970), pp. 171–72.

110. Speech on the eleventh anniversary of the July 23 revolution, reprinted in *Arab Political Documents 1963*, p. 333 and passim.

tained generally good relations throughout the period examined here. Not only did they avoid serious rivalries from the early 1950s, but their similar domestic orders provided a strong motive for cooperation, as the Kings' Alliance, the Iraqi-Jordanian Federal Union, and the bilateral defense treaties between Saudi Arabia and Jordan in 1962 reveal.

Two lessons should be drawn from these events. First, these alliances were not the result of any intrinsic affinity between monarchical regimes. Indeed, the Hashemites in Jordan and Iraq and the House of Saud had been dynastic rivals for several decades, and King Saud initially allied with Egypt against the Baghdad Pact. The monarchical solidarity that developed later was based primarily on the common threat posed by the revolutionary Arab nationalism of Nasser and the Ba'th. As a result, the independent power of monarchical solidarity was probably slight.

At the same time, the ease with which the conservative Arabs maintained good relations with one another stands in sharp contrast to the behavior of the progressive states that proclaimed broader pan-Arab goals. Unlike the revolutionary Arabs, the Arab monarchies based their legitimacy on traditional values and allegiances.[111] For them, "Arab unity" meant nothing more than seeking a consensus among the Arabs, beginning with acceptance of one another's sovereignty. As King Hussein summarized his differences with Nasser: "My own concept of Arab nationalism . . . is quite different from . . . Nasser's. . . . He believes that Arab nationalism can only be identified by a particular brand of political unity. . . . I disagree. The seeking of popular support for . . . one form of leadership . . . has fostered factionalism to a dangerous degree. . . . It is nothing more than a new form of imperialism, the domination of one state by another. Arab nationalism can survive only through complete equality."[112] Saudi Arabian views were similar, and the Saudis actively opposed the Arab revolutionaries on several occasions.[113]

Although the threat from revolutionary movements is the principal cause of monarchical solidarity, these alliances were easier to maintain because cooperation did not at the same time pose a threat to the independence of the states involved. Because the basis of monarchical rule is

111. See James Piscatori, "Islamic Values and National Interest: The Foreign Policy of Saudi Arabia," in *Islam and Foreign Policy*, ed. Adeed Dawisha (Cambridge, England, 1983).
112. Hussein, *Uneasy Lies the Head*, p. 92 and passim. See also Hussein's statements in *Arab Political Documents 1963*, pp. 349–50, 362–64.
113. Saudi Arabia supported the royalist forces in the Yemen civil war and fought a border war with South Yemen in the 1970s. See Dawisha, "Saudi Arabia's Search for Security," pp. 7–8, 20–21; and King Feisal's press conference of June 5, 1965, in *Arab Political Documents 1965*, p. 232. The Saudi attitude toward the goals of the Ba'th Party are revealed by Feisal's terse comment to Nasser during a meeting in 1969: "May God destroy the Ba'th Party." See " 'Abd-al-Nasir's Secret Papers," p. 127.

the absolute sovereignty of each monarch over his own realm, inter-ference in the realm of another legitimate sovereign violates the political principles upon which one's own rule was founded. Where pan-Arab-ism called for its advocates to sacrifice their sovereignty in order to unite (and, in Nasser's view, justified interference or subversion to bring uni-ty about), the implicit ideological basis of a monarchical alliance rein-forces the sovereignty of each monarch. Thus relations among the con-servative Arabs have been remarkably stable since 1955. This stability does not mean that dynastic rivalries will not occur; it means only that they will not arise from ideological competition.

CONCLUSION

The history of alliance formation in the Middle East offers only modest support for the hypothesis that states with similar domestic systems are more likely to ally with one another. Not only are alliances among dis-similar states almost as common as those among similar ones, but the degree of ideological conformity within many of the alliances is small. Furthermore, the evidence confirms that states are usually willing to ignore ideological considerations when strict fidelity to them would be costly or dangerous.

As predicted, ideological factors exerted their greatest effect on rela-tions between the superpowers and their regional allies. This associa-tion, however, probably exaggerates the true importance of ideology. Ideological agreement has been confined primarily to the realm of for-eign policy, and these alliances have relatively little to do with shared domestic traits. Instead, they are the result of particular historical experi-ences (e.g., colonialism) and the beliefs that these experiences encour-aged, reinforced by how both superpowers subsequently behaved. In-deed, ideology may be more of a rationalization than a cause.

Although the general proposition that like states attract appears ques-tionable, several other hypotheses receive greater support. First, as just noted, states are more likely to respond to ideological factors when they do not face imminent threats from other sources. Thus ideology does affect how regional powers select superpower patrons, because the di-rect threat that either superpower presents is small. And because both superpowers are usually eager to gain new allies, regional powers can choose whichever is ideologically more compatible, even if the true de-gree of ideological similarity is slight. Moreover, it is surely no accident that ideological rivalries in the Arab world were most influential before the Six Day War. When Israel's victory created a new and vital set of security concerns, the importance of ideology in the Arab world declined precipitously.[114] This result is especially important; it suggests that ideological alliances will be rather fragile if they are subjected to serious conflicts of interest among the members.

Second, the failure of pan-Arabism provides an especially strong test of the hypothesis that ideologies seeking to bring the members into a single unified movement are unlikely to promote effective alliances. Despite widespread popular support, a charismatic leader (Nasser), and a common enemy (Israel), the repeated attempts to translate the pan-Arab dream into practical reality succeeded only in dividing the movement's followers further. Like the Communist International, pan-Arabism led to conflict because it required its members to give up their privileged positions at home and subordinate themselves to a foreign elite. They rejected this choice and gradually abandoned the centralist premises of pan-Arabism in favor of the more modest (and thus more feasible) goal of simple Arab solidarity.

Third, these alliances also indicate that nationalism remains the most common form of ideological solidarity. Despite their other differences, the Arab states have all agreed on the need to support each other (and the Palestinians) in the conflict with Israel. Although this support rarely has required more than symbolic gestures, on several occasions the need to show solidarity against Israel has imposed significant costs. The Six Day War provides the most obvious example, but by no means the only one.

We should also recognize, however, that this type of nationalist solidarity is rather rare in international politics. Inter-Arab relations are unusual in part because the Arab nation is larger than the individual states that compose it. As a result, Arab nationalism encourages alliances against a perceived foreign presence such as Israel.[115] Because the division of one nation or people into many states is unusual, we can conclude that the number of cases where ethnic solidarity will be an important cause of alignment will be small.

Finally, the analysis performed in this chapter reveals that the common distinction between ideological solidarity and external threats is often mistaken. When states lack legitimacy, the ability to manipulate a popular ideology can provide opponents with a potent offensive capability. In the Arab world, the threat of ideological subversion has been

114. This tendency is nowhere better revealed than in Egypt's withdrawal from Yemen and Nasser's calls for an "all-Arab front, regardless of left or right political ideology," against Israel, which began after the Six Day War.

115. The most notable other example of this type of solidarity is the British Commonwealth. In this case, ethnic solidarity helps explain why Australia and Canada fought on Britain's side in both World Wars, even when their own security was not directly threatened.

far more important than the threat of direct conquest. Thus ideological quarrels—between conservatives, progressives, and pan-Arabists alike—are not all that different from the external threats examined in chapter 5. In the same way, the strong association between ideology and superpower alliances is due primarily to the fact that the historical origins of these states left the superpowers and their respective clients with similar views on which states posed the greatest threats. It is also worth noting that these ideological challenges usually led the endangered states to balance against the states that posed them. Thus balance of threat theory in fact subsumes ideological explanations, at least under certain conditions.

In this way, these alliances also illustrate what happens when statesmen exaggerate the unifying effects of ideology. If one statesman believes ideology to be the most critical cause of alignment and conducts his relations with others on that basis (as Nasser did in the early 1960s), then we would expect to see sharp ideological divisions emerge (as indeed they did). As suggested earlier, such divisions occur because similar states will be courted and dissimilar ones attacked (as they were following Syria's secession in 1961). But if ideology is in fact not that powerful, differences among the alleged brethren will rapidly undermine these fragile alliances. The turbulent state of inter-Arab relations prior to 1967 provides several examples of this dynamic: ideological divisions were created because Nasser took ideology seriously, but the alliances of Arab revolutionaries broke down because he greatly exaggerated its unifying effects.

One sees elements of this dynamic in superpower alliances as well. Both superpowers have taken certain ideological criteria very seriously (e.g., both are sensitive to leftist states, albeit in opposite ways), thereby helping create the very divisions they expect. But these affinities may have been exaggerated by both sides; in particular, Moscow's assorted leftist clients have shown remarkable independence, even, as in the case of Egypt, to the extent of defecting to the West. External forces and leaders' personalities may be far more important than ideological solidarity.[116]

In sum, one might say that there is less to ideological solidarity than meets the eye. The tendency for states with similar domestic systems to

---

116. On this point, see Adeed Dawisha, "The Soviet Union in the Arab World: The Limits to Superpower Influence," in *The Soviet Union in the Middle East: Policies and Perspectives*, ed. Adeed Dawisha and Karen Dawisha (London, 1982), pp. 19–21. For evidence that the Soviets are increasingly aware of the limited impact of ideological solidarity, see Elizabeth K. Valkenier, "Revolutionary Change in the Third World: Recent Soviet Reassessments," *World Politics*, 38, no. 3 (1986); and Francis Fukuyama, "Gorbachev and the Third World," *Foreign Affairs*, 64, no. 4 (1986).

form effective alliances is greatest when they are fairly secure, when the ideology does not require that sovereignty be sacrificed, and when a rival movement creates a powerful threat to legitimacy. In other words, ideology is an important cause of alliance formation when states face no significant external threats, when threats are equally distributed, or when ideological factors are part of the threat itself. As the analysis in chapter 5 showed, the characteristic response in such circumstances is to counter the threat by forming an alliance against it.

[7]

The Instruments of Alliance:
Aid and Penetration

In this chapter, I examine a number of hypotheses about the impact of foreign aid and transnational penetration on alliance formation. My analysis supports the predictions made in chapter 2: both aid and penetration play subordinate roles in determining how states choose their allies. To show why this is the case, I first consider the impact of foreign aid and then examine the effects of penetration.

FOREIGN AID AND ALLIANCE FORMATION

As outlined in chapter 2, the hypothesis about foreign aid and alliances predicts that states select alliance partners in order to obtain side payments of material assistance, such as economic or military aid. If the hypothesis is correct, then providing such bribes will enable donors to create effective and cohesive alliances. If aid has a powerful independent impact on alliance choices, then patrons should wield considerable leverage over their clients, because the latter will be reluctant to jeopardize the benefits of assistance.

Foreign aid has obviously been a popular policy instrument in the Middle East. Since 1955, both superpowers have provided extensive economic and military aid to a variety of states in the region, as have wealthy Middle East countries such as Saudi Arabia and Kuwait.[1] More-

---

1. According to the CIA, total Soviet military assistance (grants, sales, and training) to the Middle East between 1953 and 1979 was $18.6 billion. Economic aid agreements were for roughly $7.8 billion, although actual deliveries were less. Total U.S. economic and military aid (loans and grants but not direct cash sales) from 1953 to 1980 was roughly $30 billion. See CIA, *Communist Aid to Non-Communist LDCs, 1979 and 1954–1979;* and AID, *Overseas Loans and Grants.*

Table 12. Superpower foreign aid to the Middle East, 1955–1979 (in millions of current dollars)[a]

Country	Soviet Union			United States		
	Economic aid	Military aid	Total	Economic aid	Military aid	Total
	(1955–1979)	(1955–1974)		(1954–1979)		
Iraq	$ 705	$1,600	$2,305	$ 48	$ 50	$ 98[b]
Syria	770	2,100	2,870	624	0	624[c]
South Yemen	205	80	285	0	0	0
North Yemen	145	80	225	112	2	114
Egypt	1,440	3,450	4,890	5,030	1,500	6,530[d]
Israel	0	0	0	4,691	17,623	22,314
Jordan	25	0	25	1,342	921	2,263
Lebanon	0	3	3	202	104	306
Saudi Arabia	0	0	0	28	296	324

SOURCES: U.S. Department of State, Bureau of Intelligence and Research, *Communist States and Developing Countries: Aid and Trade in 1974* (Washington, D.C., 1975); CIA, *Communist Aid to Non-Communist Less Developed Countries, 1979 and 1954–1979* (Washington, D.C., 1980); and AID, *U.S. Overseas Loans and Grants* (Washington, D.C., various years).

[a]Aid refers to loans and grants, not to cash sales of arms or other contracted military services.

[b]All U.S. aid to Iraq provided prior to 1958 revolution.

[c]All U.S. aid to Syria provided in 1960–1962, 1975–1977.

[d]The United States gave no aid to Egypt in 1957, 1958, and 1968–1973; 78 percent of all U.S. aid to Egypt was delivered after 1974, and 100 percent of all military aid to Egypt was delivered in 1978–1979.

over, as Tables 12 and 13 show, there is a strong association between foreign aid and political alignment. The superpowers rarely provide large amounts of aid to the same states at the same time, and decisions to realign invariably involve a shift in the principal sources of external support.[2]

Despite this evident association, testing the hypothesis that aid causes alignment is not easy. Data on arms transfers and economic aid are often unreliable, and accurate evidence on elite perceptions is scarce. As a result, it is impossible to draw direct inferences about the impact of aid with confidence.[3] Even more important, assessing the precise impact of

2. Iraq in 1958 and Egypt in 1974–1975 are the most obvious examples. Iraq received virtually no U.S. aid after the 1958 revolution, but it obtained a number of Soviet loans and grants. Egypt received no Soviet assistance after 1975, but it became a major recipient of U.S. economic and military aid.

3. Data on arms transfers are often unavailable on an annual basis (especially for the Soviet Union), and existing sources vary widely. For discussions, see Michael Brzoska, "Arms Transfer Data Sources," *Journal of Conflict Resolution*, 26, no. 1 (1982); Gur Ofer, "Soviet Military Aid to the Middle East," in U.S. Congress, Joint Economic Committee, *Soviet Economy in a New Perspective*, 94th Cong., 2d sess., 1976; and Moshe Efrat, "The Economics of Soviet Arms Transfers to the Third World—A Case Study: Egypt," *Soviet Studies*, 35, no. 4 (1983).

Table 13. Superpower arms transfers to the Middle East, 1965–1980 (in millions of current dollars)

Country	1965–1975		1976–1980		Percent from largest supplier	
	United States	Soviet Union	United States	Soviet Union	1965–1974	1975–1980
Iraq	$2	$1,343	$ 0	$5,000	78% (Soviet Union)	64% (Soviet Union)
Syria	3	1,758	0	5,400	92 (Soviet Union)	82 (Soviet Union)
South Yemen	0	114	0	775	90 (Soviet Union)	99 (Soviet Union)
North Yemen	1	27	170	625	42 (Soviet Union)	52 (Soviet Union)
Egypt	0	2,465	430	20	89 (Soviet Union)	32 (France)
Israel	3,856	0	4,300	0	96 (United States)	98 (United States)
Jordan	400	0	725	0	74 (United States)	73 (United States)
Lebanon	21	4	40	0	61 (France)	50 (United States)
Saudi Arabia	473	0	2,000	0	46 (United States)	43 (United States)

SOURCE: ACDA, *World Military Expenditures and Arms Transfers* (Washington, D.C., various years).

foreign aid on alliance choices is difficult because an aid relationship is itself a political response to the specific circumstances facing suppliers and recipients.[4] This point is crucial and merits further discussion.

Foreign Aid and Balancing Behavior

The issue is essentially one of interpretation. Does aid cause alignment, enabling wealthy states to attract reliable allies by offering generous side payments? Or is a large aid relationship primarily the result of alignment? That is, is it merely one way that states with common, or at least compatible, interests can achieve their objectives?

This study supports the latter interpretation. Although the desire to obtain economic and military aid has been a common motive for establishing close relations with a wealthy and powerful ally, the choice of which potential patron to prefer is determined by other factors. This conclusion rests on several considerations.

First, wealthy states prefer to support regimes that are either already friendly or likely to become so, and they are reluctant to provide extensive support to those they believe are irredeemably hostile.[5] For example, the United States withdrew its offer to finance the Aswan Dam in part to punish Egypt for its ties with the Soviet bloc, but it renewed its economic aid in 1959, when Soviet-Egyptian relations cooled.[6] In the same way, U.S. economic and military aid to Egypt in the 1970s was made possible by Sadat's abandonment of his Soviet ally and his willingness to make peace with Israel under U.S. auspices.[7]

The same is true for the Soviet Union. Economic aid for Iraq, for example, began after the 1958 revolution altered Soviet perceptions of Iraq's international orientation. Soviet support for the republican regime in Yemen, the neo-Ba'ath in Syria, and the Marxist regime in South Yemen was the result of similar reappraisals. In all these cases, changing political relations paved the way for economic assistance.

Second, as Table 14 shows, superpower support is usually provided in response to particular external challenges, although other motives are

4. As William J. Burns has written, "The political influence that one country derives from the provision of economic assistance to another is not the neat mathematical product of a simple calculus of economic costs and benefits: it results from the complicated interaction of the needs, perceptions, and ambitions of the donor with those of the recipient." See his *Economic Aid and American Policy*, pp. 211–12.

5. This tendency is a form of selection bias: the apparent impact of aid on alignments is exaggerated by the fact that it is offered only when the donor thinks it will have an effect, and it is never offered when the donor is sure it won't.

6. On these events, see Burns, *Economic Aid and American Policy*, chap. 3, especially pp. 80–83; chap. 4, pp. 112–14, 119–20.

7. See Burns, *Economic Aid and American Policy*, pp. 180–81.

Table 14. Foreign aid and balancing behavior

Alliance/alignment	Year	Activity	Likely cause
Soviet Union–Egypt	1955	Arms deal	Gaza raid
	1957	Arms deal	Resupply after Suez War
	1963	Increased military aid	Yemen civil war
	1967–1970	Increased military aid, air defense troops	Resupply after Six Day War, War of Attrition
	1972–1973	Increased military aid, offensive weapons	Expulsion of Soviet advisers, preparation for October War
Soviet Union–Syria	1955	Arms deal	Threats from Iraq and Israel
	1957	Increased military aid	Syrian crisis, threats from Iraq and Turkey
	1966	Increased military aid	Ideological solidarity, growing conflict with Israel
	1967	Increased military aid	Resupply after Six Day War
	1971–1973	Increased military aid	Preparation for October War
	1975	Increased military aid	Egypt's realignment with United States
	1976	Temporary arms embargo	Dispute over intervention in Lebanon
Soviet Union–Iraq	1958–1959	Arms deal, economic aid	Coup against pro-Western monarchy
	1963	Arms aid suspended	Purge of Iraqi Communist Party
	1964	Arms aid resumed	Truce in Kurdish War
	1972	Friendship treaty and increased military aid	Threat from Iran, ideological solidarity
	1976	Increased military aid	Soviet dispute with Syria over Lebanon
Soviet Union–South Yemen	1969	Economic and military aid	Ideological solidarity
	1972	Increased military aid	Border wars with Saudi Arabia and North Yemen
	1979	Friendship treaty, increased military aid	War with North Yemen, triumph of pro-Soviet faction
Soviet Union–North Yemen	1964	Friendship treaty, arms deal	Civil war
	1967	Increased military aid, combat support	Egyptian withdrawal, Royalist offensive
	1971–1975	Military aid suspended	Saudi influence increasing
	1978	Arms deal	War with South Yemen, Soviet countering of U.S.-Saudi aid package

(continued)

Table 14 (*Continued*)

Alliance/alignment	Year	Activity	Likely cause
United States–Jordan	1957	Economic subsidies	Replacement of British and Arab subsidies
	1964	Military aid increased	Countering of Arab pressure, prevention of acquisition of Soviet arms
	1967	Arms embargo	Six Day War
	1971	Military aid increase	Civil war against PLO
United States–Israel	1962–1964	Security pledge, arms deals	Balancing of Soviet aid to Arabs, discouragement of proliferation
	1967–1972	Increased military aid	War of Attrition, Rogers peace process
	1973	Major military aid package	October War
	1975	Major military aid package	Sinai II agreement
	1978–1979	Major military aid package	Camp David Accords, peace treaty with Egypt
United States–Saudi Arabia	1964	Arms deal (air defense)	Egyptian air raids during Yemen civil war
	1970	Major arms deal	Conflict with South Yemen, threats from radical forces
	1974	Major military modernization	Increased oil wealth, threats from radical forces
United States–Egypt	1975	Economic aid and arms sales	Encouragement of realignment, Sinai II agreement
	1979	Military aid package	Peace treaty with Israel

occasionally involved.[8] In other words, the level of economic or military aid is greater when other incentives for alignment (e.g., the emergence of a common threat or ideological affinities) are present. This type of

8. To mention but a few examples: Nasser sought Soviet arms assistance after the Gaza raid revealed Egypt's vulnerability (which in turn led Israel to acquire more arms from France); the United States agreed to provide Israel with advanced weaponry in 1962 to counter Egypt's growing arsenal of Soviet weapons; Soviet military aid to Egypt and Syria more than doubled after the Six Day War and continued throughout the War of Attrition, matched by expanded U.S. arms shipments to Israel; Soviet aid to Yemen rose briefly after Egypt's withdrawal in 1967 (while Saudi Arabia began extensive arms purchases to modernize its forces); U.S. aid to Jordan more than doubled after the Jordan crisis of 1970, and U.S. arms transfers to Saudi Arabia soared after 1970 as a result of the shared perception that Saudi Arabia faced more imminent external threats than before.

behavior continues once a close relationship is established; patrons and clients adjust the level of support in response to changing circumstances.

Taken together, these observations confirm a proposition advanced in chapter 2: a large aid relationship is often just another form of balancing behavior. To infer that aid causes alignment is too simple; it is more accurate to say that aid is usually a manifestation of political alignment. In short, both the willingness to provide aid and the desire to obtain it are the result of more basic causes—causes examined in the preceding two chapters.

It is not surprising, therefore, that even rather generous levels of foreign aid failed to create effective alliances when important political differences intruded. For example, U.S. efforts to wean Egypt away from the Soviet Union in the early 1960s (by providing food aid) could not overcome the effects of disputes over Egypt's intervention in Yemen, its continued rivalry with Israel, and Nasser's support for revolutionary nationalism in Asia and Africa.[9] Similarly, the United States gave Syria almost $500 million in economic aid in 1974 and 1975 to provide Syria with "an incentive to adopt a moderate approach" in the peace process.[10] But because U.S. support for the Sinai II agreement, the Camp David Accords, and the Egyptian-Israeli peace treaty threatened important Syrian interests, U.S. aid had little or no effect on Syria's foreign policy orientation.[11]

Despite the wealth and largesse of Saudi Arabia, its efforts to create close political ties through economic aid have brought equally meager results in the absence of shared interests. In the mid-1970s, economic aid to South Yemen produced no more than a brief thaw in Saudi-PDRY tensions. Although aid to North Yemen has been somewhat more successful, it has hardly led to a durable alliance between the two countries.[12] Although Saudi aid programs have encouraged moderation and enabled other Arab states to buy arms or balance their budgets, they have generally failed to determine alliance choices or policy preferences when important interests have intervened.

Jordan provides a final example. Utterly dependent on budgetary support, Hussein's (reluctant) decision to reject the Baghdad Pact in 1955–1956 and to join the Arab Solidarity Pact was made possible by an Arab

9. See Burns, *Economic Aid and American Policy*, chaps. 5 and 6.
10. See "Chronology," *MEJ*, 29, no. 2 (1975): 184.
11. It might be argued that the limited impact of U.S. aid was due to the fact that the Soviet Union was providing even greater levels of support (especially military equipment) during the period. This argument overlooks the fact that the U.S. aid program showed Syria that it was possible to obtain significantly greater assistance from the United States provided Syria was willing to make the same political concessions (e.g., expulsion of the Soviets and peace with Israel) that Anwar Sadat had made.
12. On this point, see Safran, *Saudi Arabia*, pp. 284–89, 387, 391–97; and J. E. Petersen, "The Yemen Arab Republic and the Politics of Balance," *Asian Affairs*, 12, no. 3 (1981).

pledge to replace the British subsidy. When the threat from Nasser became overwhelming and the United States proved willing to supply the necessary funds, however, Hussein abandoned alignment with the other Arabs and returned to a pro-West position.[13] His motives were political; money was simply the means needed to make his realignment possible.

These examples reveal that economic and military aid can do little to produce effective alliances in the absence of shared political interests. Should we conclude that aid has no effect at all? Of course not. First, aid can be an effective way to strengthen an ally and thus to protect common or compatible interests. Second, because actions speak louder than words, providing assistance (and especially military aid) is an effective way to convey friendly intentions. Indeed, a refusal to offer support may be viewed as a sign of hostility.[14] As William Burns has noted, foreign aid usually serves to "reinforce an interest in mutual accommodation derived from more basic shared political interests."[15]

Foreign Aid and Political Leverage

In the absence of shared political interests, even generous foreign aid programs do not create effective alliances. This conclusion prompts a further question. When shared interests do exist, does a large aid program enable patrons to wield substantial leverage over their clients? Does aid create loyal satellites, or do recipients retain their independence under most circumstances? The question is crucial for this analysis, because it tells us how much to worry about Soviet economic and military aid and how much to expect from similar U.S. programs.

This study strongly suggests that aid has brought patrons significant leverage only under rare conditions. Before I analyze why this is so, a brief summary of the historical record is in order.

Egypt

From 1955 to 1970, the Soviet Union was Egypt's largest source of economic aid and its only important source of military equipment.[16]

---

13. Saudi Arabia was the only Arab state to actually deliver the promised subsidy to Jordan. See Majduddin Omar Khairy, *Jordan and the World System: Developments in the Middle East* (Frankfurt, Germany, 1984), p. 68.

14. Here again, the U.S. policy of restricting military aid to Egypt and the later cancellation of the U.S. offer to build the Aswan Dam clearly reinforced Nasser's suspicions, whereas the Soviet willingness to fulfill Egypt's requests—even during periods of disagreement—provided tangible evidence of the Soviet Union's favorable inclination toward Egypt. See David, "Realignment of Third World Regimes," pp. 188–93; Hoopes, *Devil and John Foster Dulles*, chap. 21; and Meyer, *Egypt and the United States*, pp. 120–24, 146.

15. See Burns, *Economic Aid and American Policy*, p. 208.

16. For the dates of the major Soviet-Egyptian arms deals, see Glassman, *Arms for the Arabs*, pp. 24–25; McLane, *Soviet–Middle East Relations;* and Lenczowski, *Soviet Advances in the Middle East*, chap. 8. For total Soviet aid to Egypt, see Tables 12 and 13 in this book.

Indeed, Egypt's dependence on Soviet military aid increased steadily from 1955 through 1973.[17]

Yet Soviet leverage on Egypt was slight. The Soviets opposed the union with Syria in 1958, Nasser imprisoned Egyptian Communists despite Moscow's repeated protests, and Egypt's relations with the rest of the Arab world evolved independently of Soviet preferences. Nasser quarreled with Qassem of Iraq (at that time a promising Soviet ally) and either attacked or accommodated the conservative Arab states as it suited his purposes. Although Soviet aid enabled Egypt to intervene in the Yemen civil war, Nasser insisted that Soviet aid be channeled through Egypt in order to preserve his own influence.[18] Finally, Egypt consistently denied Soviet requests for access to Egypt's airfields and naval facilities. In short, the Soviet-Egyptian relationship between 1955 and 1967 was almost entirely one-sided; Egypt took and gave relatively little in return.

Egypt's vulnerability after the Six Day War produced a major concession: the Soviets were permitted regular access to Egyptian military facilities.[19] Yet, despite Egypt's growing dependence on the Soviet Union, Nasser retained his freedom of action on most issues. The Soviets were forced to disavow the Rogers Plan when Nasser rejected it, despite their active role in drafting the proposal.[20] Nasser began the War of Attrition on his own, successfully persuaded the Soviets to provide unprecedented levels of support—including combat troops—during the fighting, and made an independent decision to accept the July 1970 ceasefire as well.[21]

Sadat displayed similar independence. Reliance on Soviet aid did not prevent him from seeking U.S. help for an interim Canal settlement in 1971, and Soviet attempts to control Egypt by limiting arms shipments helped trigger the expulsion of Egypt's Soviet advisers in 1972. The expulsion persuaded the Soviet Union to supply the arms needed to fight the October War, but Sadat went to war on his own and paid little

17. Egypt's growing need for external support resulted from the Yemen war, Nasser's inter-Arab rivalries, and the escalating conflict with Israel. For testimony regarding the importance of Soviet support for Egypt, see Dawisha, *Soviet Foreign Policy towards Egypt*, pp. 56–63; Glassman, *Arms for the Arabs*, pp. 88–89; and el-Shazly, *Crossing of the Canal*, pp. 172–81.

18. See Laqueur, *Struggle for the Middle East*, pp. 105–7; and Yodfat, *Soviet Union and the Arabian Peninsula*, pp. 2–3.

19. For the details of Soviet access arrangements, see Remnek, "The Politics of Soviet Access," pp. 369–72. According to Glassman, the Soviet resupply effort to Egypt after the Six Day War was so extensive that "by mid-1968, Egypt had almost reached its prewar combat aircraft strength." See Glassman, *Arms for the Arabs*, p. 66 and passim.

20. See Whetten, *Canal War*, pp. 79–80; and Rubinstein, *Red Star on the Nile*, pp. 100–101.

21. See Rubinstein, *Red Star on the Nile*, pp. 83–87, 336, and passim; Breslauer, "Soviet Policy in the Middle East," pp. 77–78; and Shimshoni, "Conventional Deterrence," pp. 318–19.

attention to Soviet advice during the fighting itself.[22] He then added insult to injury by inviting the U.S. Secretary of State to Cairo "in appreciation of his efforts" and by abandoning the Soviet Union for the United States.[23]

In short, the enormous Soviet investment in Egypt ultimately bought the Soviets neither leverage nor loyalty, though it did "buy" them bases for seven years. When Egyptian objectives and interests changed, so did Egypt's choice of allies.[24]

It is, of course, true that Egypt's desperate economic condition after the October War constrained Sadat's diplomatic options.[25] Sadat's hope that the United States would provide substantial economic assistance undoubtedly encouraged him to ignore the threats and blandishments the other Arab states made to prevent the peace treaty with Israel. Indeed, Sadat rejected a Saudi offer of $5 billion, saying that "all the gold in the world cannot buy our dignity or our decisions."[26] Thus U.S. economic aid did play an important role in sustaining Egypt's movement toward peace.

Yet U.S. influence was hardly absolute. Sadat's decision to go to Jerusalem took Washington by surprise; indeed, it was partly caused by U.S. efforts to convene a comprehensive peace conference in Geneva.[27] Sadat proved to be a tough negotiator at Camp David, and despite considerable U.S. pressure, both he and his successor, Hosni Mubarak, ultimately refused to grant the United States access to the Egyptian airbase at Ras Banas. Despite its continued dependence on U.S. aid, Egypt increased its public support for the PLO, "froze" the peace with Israel after the Israeli invasion of Lebanon, and hinted on occasion that improved ties with the Soviet Union were not out of the question.[28] It would be un-

---

22. For example, Sadat rejected the Soviet Union's early recommendations for a ceasefire and accepted one only after Egypt's early gains had been erased.

23. See Kissinger, *Years of Upheaval*, p. 527.

24. Alvin Rubinstein concludes his detailed study of Soviet influence in Egypt: "Moscow's leverage on issues of importance to Egyptian leaders has been at best marginal. . . . On no major issue in Soviet-Egyptian relations was Moscow able to make Egypt do something against its will, although it was occasionally able to restrain what Egypt did or wanted to do." See Rubinstein, *Red Star on the Nile*, p. 334 and passim.

25. According to William Burns, "the promise of U.S. economic aid provided Sadat with an important incentive to negotiate a peace treaty in 1977–79." See his *Economic Aid and American Policy*, p. 192.

26. Quoted in *MECS 1977–1978*, pp. 234–35. The Arab summit in Baghdad in March 1979 agreed to halt all further economic subsidies to Egypt. See Safran, *Saudi Arabia*, p. 263. This sanction was hardly trivial; the Arab oil states had given Egypt as much as $7 billion to $8 billion between 1973 and 1978. See Waterbury, *Egypt of Nasser and Sadat*, p. 416 and passim.

27. See Quandt, *Camp David*, pp. 136–48; and Touval, *Peace Brokers*, pp. 288–89.

28. Mubarak withdrew the Egyptian chargé d'affaires from Tel Aviv after the invasion of Lebanon in 1982 and has refused to visit Israel. Diplomatic relations with the Soviet Union were restored in 1984, and ambassadors were exchanged at that time.

wise to conclude, therefore, that economic aid has made Egypt any more loyal to the United States than it was to the Soviet Union, should Egyptian interests dictate actions contrary to U.S. preferences.[29]

Syria

The Soviet Union has given Syria almost $1 billion in economic aid since 1955 and has provided roughly 85 percent of Syria's military equipment.[30] As with Egypt, the Soviets provided ever-larger amounts of modern weaponry and resupplied Syria promptly after each Middle East war.[31]

This generosity did not make Syria an especially reliable client. The Soviets have been powerless to influence Syria's domestic struggles, whether during the suppression of the Syrian Communist Party in the 1950s or at the triumph of Hafez el-Assad over the Soviet favorite, Salah Jadid, in 1970.[32] Nor were the Soviets any more effective in foreign policy. They were unable to halt Syrian provocations prior to the Six Day War, and when the fighting was over, they could not persuade the Syrians to accept U.N. Resolution 242, despite the fact that defeat had left the Syrians more dependent than ever on Soviet aid.[33]

Although Soviet aid to Syria increased significantly after 1970, the Soviet capacity to influence Syrian policies remained minimal at best.

29. Egypt's reaction to the highjacking of the Italian cruise ship *Achille Lauro* in October 1985 illustrates this point nicely. Because support for the PLO enables Egypt to enhance its precarious legitimacy within the Arab world (and insulates Mubarak from accusations of being a U.S. lackey), Egypt sought to obtain release of the ship while permitting the hijackers to go free. This motive also explains why Mubarak reacted so strongly after the Egyptian airliner carrying the hijackers was intercepted by U.S. jets and forced to land in Sicily, where the hijackers were taken into custody and put on trial.

30. According to one authority, by 1970 "Syria was almost totally dependent on the Soviet Union for the sustenance of its military machine." See Pajak, "Soviet Arms Aid," p. 476.

31. The growth of Soviet arms aid is revealed by the fact that almost 50 percent of total Soviet arms transfers to Syria occurred after 1974. See ACDA, *World Military Expenditures and Arms Transfers*; and CIA, *Communist Aid to Non-Communist LDCs, 1979 and 1954–1979*. This figure is somewhat misleading, as it does not allow for the effects of inflation. According to Israeli sources, the Soviet resupply effort to Syria after the October War was so extensive that Syrian forces were actually better equipped by August 1974 than they had been before the war. See Pajak, "Soviet Arms Aid since the October War," p. 477. After Syria's defeat during the 1982 Israeli invasion of Lebanon, the Soviets supplied Damascus with advanced SA–8 surface to air missiles, and—as they had done with Egypt in 1970— began to man and operate the Syrian air defense system themselves. See Robert G. Neumann, "Assad and the Future of the Middle East," *Foreign Affairs*, 62, no. 2 (1983–1984): 242.

32. On this point, see Buss, "Wary Partners," pp. 18–20.

33. See Glassman, *Arms for the Arabs*, pp. 42, 66. Similarly, when the Syrians rejected a joint Soviet-U.S. draft resolution for a negotiated settlement in July 1967, the Soviets let the matter drop. See Whetten, *The Canal War*, pp. 47–48; and Rubinstein, *Red Star on the Nile*, pp. 24–27.

Syria resisted Soviet pressure for a formal treaty of alliance until 1980, when the Iraqi invasion of Iran and the U.S. deployment of AWACS to Saudi Arabia served to underscore Syria's isolation in the region. Syria also rejected Soviet requests for permanent access to Syrian ports and airfields on several occasions, and one source claims that Soviet persistence on this score led Assad to accuse the Soviet Union of acting "like an imperialist power."[34] And when the Soviets refused to provide advanced aircraft in the absence of a formal treaty, Assad countered by restricting the movements of his Soviet advisers. In the words of Soviet ambassador Mukhitdinov, "those damned Syrians will take anything except advice."[35]

Although Syria was Moscow's most important Middle East client after the October War, the Soviets played little role in Kissinger's step-by-step disengagement on the Golan Heights.[36] In 1976 Syria intervened against the PLO in Lebanon in direct defiance of Soviet pressure and a brief (and ineffective) suspension of Soviet arms deliveries. Assad called Brezhnev's request that Syria withdraw "merely an expression of a point of view," and he added that "we have a different point of view which is not subject to compromise."[37] In short, although Syria has received abundant Soviet assistance since 1955, this support rarely, if ever, allowed the Soviet Union to control Syria's actions.

Iraq

Until the 1970s, Soviet military aid to Iraq trailed the amounts provided to Egypt and Syria substantially. Economic aid was considerable, however, reaching a total of $1 billion by 1974. Soviet technical support made possible the nationalization of the Iraqi Petroleum Company in 1972, and Iraq's desire to modernize its armed forces inspired its determined quest for a formal treaty with the Soviet Union in 1971. Growing oil revenues enabled Iraq to purchase large amounts of arms from the Soviet Union and Western Europe after 1973, and the Soviet-Iraqi arms

34. See Safran, *Saudi Arabia*, pp. 322–23; Remnek, "The Politics of Soviet Access," pp. 381–82; and Pajak, "Soviet Arms Aid," pp. 481–82.

35. Quoted in Roger F. Pajak, "The Soviet-Syrian Military Aid Relationship," in *The Syrian Arab Republic: A Handbook*, ed. Anne Sinai and Allen Pollock (New York, 1976), p. 99.

36. The Soviet view of the step-by-step process was summarized in Brezhnev's description of Kissinger's efforts as "ersatz diplomacy." See Golan, *Yom Kippur and After*, pp. 183–85; 213–31; Freedman, *Soviet Policy in the Middle East*, rev. ed., pp. 163–67; and Golan and Rabinovich, "The Soviet Union and Syria," pp. 216–19. Kissinger's account of these negotiations suggests that the Syrians paid little attention to their Soviet allies during this period. See Kissinger, *Years of Upheaval*, pp. 971, 1033–35, 1099–1100, 1104–5.

37. Quoted in Dawisha, *Syria and the Lebanese Crisis*, pp. 169–70. Soviet-Syrian relations remained troubled until the signing of the Egyptian-Israeli peace treaty, although matters improved slightly after Assad visited the Soviet Union in 1977.

deal of 1976 (reportedly worth $1 billion) placed Baghdad first among Soviet Middle East clients in total value of arms received.[38]

Yet, Moscow's support (whether in the form of economic aid or arms sales at bargain prices) gave the Soviet Union little influence over Iraqi policies. When Soviet arms aid strengthened Qassem's position within Iraq in 1958–1959, Qassem quickly turned against his Communist partners. The Ba'th used its Soviet weapons to exterminate the Iraqi Communist Party in 1963, and the resulting Soviet arms embargo had little or no effect. Renewed Soviet aid did not prevent the Aref regime from cultivating closer ties with the West either.[39]

Since the restoration of the Ba'th in 1968, Iraq has clashed with the Soviet Union over the question of peace with Israel (Iraq rejected the joint Soviet-U.S. proposal for peace in July 1967 and consistently refused to accept U.N. Resolution 242).[40] Shortly after the growing threat from Iran led Iraq to seek a formal treaty with the Soviet Union in 1972, Iraq began to diversify its economic and military ties. As a result, the Soviet share of Iraq's arms purchases fell from 96 percent between 1964 and 1973 to roughly 70 percent between 1974 and 1979, and the Soviet share of Iraqi foreign trade dropped from 22 percent in 1973 to 11 percent in 1977.[41] The Iraqis have continued their lengthy and bitter quarrel with Syria (despite repeated Soviet efforts to moderate the dispute), and they have remained deeply suspicious of Communist influence elsewhere in the Arab world. Indeed, Iraq executed two dozen Communists in 1978, refused to permit Soviet planes to use Iraqi airspace during the Soviet intervention in Ethiopia, openly condemned the Soviet invasion of Afghanistan, and formed an alliance with Saudi Arabia (a traditional Soviet enemy) in 1979.[42]

All things considered, Moscow's influence on Iraq has been meager. In the words of Robert O. Freedman: "Soviet influence . . . has been very limited indeed. Only in the period 1972 to 1975, when Iraq was in the greatest need of Soviet help, were the Ba'thists willing to make concessions. . . . Iraq . . . has given relatively little in the way of political obedience in return for a large amount of Soviet economic and military assistance."[43]

38. See Pajak, "Soviet Arms Aid," p. 471.
39. See Khadduri, *Socialist Iraq*, pp. 171–74; and Fukuyama, "Soviet Union and Iraq."
40. See Khadduri, *Socialist Iraq*, pp. 171–72; and Lenczowski, *Middle East in World Affairs*, pp. 305–6.
41. See ACDA, *World Military Expenditures and Arms Transfers;* and Orah Cooper, "Soviet–East European Economic Relations with the Middle East," in U.S. Congress, Joint Economic Committee, *Soviet Economy in a New Perspective.*
42. On these events, see Pajak, "Soviet Arms Aid," pp. 473–74; and Adeed Dawisha, "The Soviet Union in the Arab World," pp. 16–17.
43. Freedman, "Soviet Policy towards Ba'athist Iraq," pp. 186–87.

North Yemen

In the 1950s Soviet aid to the Imam encouraged his opposition to British rule in Aden, but it neither reduced his suspicion of the Soviets nor gave them much voice in his decisions. Although Soviet support for the republican regime from 1962 to 1967 helped prevent its collapse, the Soviets gained little leverage through their efforts. Soviet aid was controlled by Egypt until 1967, and the republican leadership was replaced by a pro-Saudi faction after 1969.[44] Soviet aid has waxed and waned since then—although an arms deal reportedly worth $700 million was signed in 1979—but the Soviets have gained little influence over either the turbulent course of Yemeni internal politics or the corresponding shifts in Yemen's foreign policy.[45]

Saudi Arabian aid programs have been somewhat more effective, though there are still clear limits to their control. Aid to the royalist tribes, for example, helped bring a conservative government to power after the civil war. During the mid 1970s, President Ibrahim al-Hamdi followed the Saudi line fairly closely (e.g., he dismissed several ministers of whom the Saudis disapproved and announced that relations with the Soviet Union were frozen) in exchange for continued economic aid and a freer hand in dealing with the still recalcitrant tribal forces in Yemen.[46] Thus Yemen's dependence on Saudi aid did give Riyadh some influence over Yemeni policy choices.

Yet Saudi leverage was not unlimited. The Saudis delayed but could not prevent North Yemen's two unity agreements with the PDRY (a prospect the Saudis strenuously opposed), and they were unable to persuade North Yemen to sever its aid relationship with the Soviet Union.[47] They also were unable to halt a gradual leftward shift in North Yemeni

44. See Porter, *USSR in Third World Conflicts*, pp. 75–79, 88–89; Safran, *Saudi Arabia*, p. 131; and Peterson, "Yemen and the Politics of Balance," p. 262.

45. Since 1967, North Yemen has endured several sudden changes of government, each one tending to produce shifts in its policy toward Saudi Arabia South Yemen, and the superpowers. The post–civil war regime of Abdel Rahman al-Iryani was ultimately replaced in 1974 by a military government led by Ibrahim al-Hamdi, who was assassinated by unknown assailants in 1977 and replaced by Lieutenant Colonel Ahmad al-Ghashmi. al-Ghashmi was subsequently assassinated by a South Yemeni envoy in 1978 and replaced by yet another military officer, 'Ali Abdullah Salih. In addition to their shifting relations with Saudi Arabia, North and South Yemen fought border wars in 1972 and 1979, yet also agreed to seek formal unity between the two countries. On these events, see Peterson, "Yemen and the Politics of Balance"; "Chronology," *MEJ*, 29, no. 2 (1975): 197; no. 4 (1975): 450; *MECS 1978–1979*, pp. 65–66; Yodfat, *Soviet Union and the Arabian Peninsula*, pp. 5, 44–46, 105–8; and Van Hollen, "North Yemen," p. 140 and passim.

46. See Safran, *Saudi Arabia*, pp. 284–85. Safran points out that although relations with the Soviet Union were allegedly frozen, a military delegation from the YAR visited Moscow shortly after this announcement.

47. And with Communist China. At the height of Saudi-Yemeni relations in 1976, President al-Hamdi visited Peking and signed an agreement for economic and technical cooperation. See Safran, *Saudi Arabia*, p. 286.

internal politics.[48] Indeed, despite the level of support the Saudis have provided over the years (roughly $400 million annually), Yemen has gradually increased its freedom from Saudi influence.[49]

Finally, the modest U.S. effort to aid North Yemen during the 1979 border war with the PDRY proved of little value, save perhaps in reinforcing Yemen's ability to resist its other patrons. Undertaken at Saudi request, the U.S. assistance program was smaller than the corresponding Soviet effort and limited by Saudi ambivalence regarding the merits of making North Yemen strong enough to stand on its own.[50] Accordingly, it was hardly a source of significant political leverage.

South Yemen

Soviet aid to the PDRY has grown steadily since Aden achieved independence in 1967. South Yemen has been a remarkably loyal ally, providing the Soviets with naval facilities and other forms of logistical support while echoing Soviet positions on most international issues.[51] But because there is little evidence of serious policy disagreement between the two countries, it is impossible to say whether this loyalty is the result of ideological agreement or a reflection of South Yemen's near-total dependence on Soviet support.[52]

The PDRY has not been a completely tame client, however. For example, South Yemen has consistently favored a more extreme policy in the Arab-Israeli conflict—rejecting any form of political settlement. More-

48. On these points, see Peterson, "Yemen and the Politics of Balance," pp. 261–63; and Safran, *Saudi Arabia,* pp. 131–33 and chap. 11.

49. The annual aid figure is given by Van Hollen, "North Yemen," p. 139. Safran reports that Yemen received a total of $460 million in 1975 and a pledge of $570 million in December 1977, but he does not say if these amounts are typical. It should also be noted that Saudi Arabia paid for most of the military equipment supplied by the United States, whereas Soviet military assistance consisted primarily of direct arms sales, albeit on very lenient credit terms. See Safran, *Saudi Arabia,* pp. 285–86, 288–90; and Katz, *Russia and Arabia,* p. 47.

50. After urgently requesting U.S. military aid for North Yemen, the Saudis later sought to delay the arms shipments for fear North Yemen might become too strong. As J. E. Peterson put it, "the effect of American military assistance was dampened by the nonarrival of the equipment during the fighting and by the Saudi finger on the pursestrings." See his "Yemen and the Politics of Balance," p. 262. For a summary of the origins and nature of the U.S. aid program to Yemen, see U.S. House Committee on International Relations, *U.S. Arms Policies in the Persian Gulf,* pp. 73–82. See also Safran, *Saudi Arabia,* pp. 286, 290–93; and Yodfat, *Soviet Union and the Arabian Peninsula,* pp. 105–8.

51. Thus the Soviet Union made extensive use of South Yemeni facilities during its intervention in the Horn of Africa in 1978. South Yemen also supported the Soviet invasion of Afghanistan, opposed the U.N. resolution condemning the Soviet action, and refused to participate in a meeting of the Islamic Conference in Pakistan, which condemned the invasion. See Safran, *Saudi Arabia,* pp. 272, 318–19.

52. One suspects it is the former, as South Yemen did have the opportunity to obtain Saudi (and conceivably Western) assistance in 1976–1977, only to reject this option after the ouster of Rubay 'Ali in 1978.

over, PDRY president Rubay 'Ali's attempt to achieve a rapprochement with Saudi Arabia and the United States in 1976–1977 suggests that Soviet aid did not guarantee complete loyalty. However, the outcome of this attempt—the assassination of Rubay 'Ali in 1978 and his replacement by the pro-Soviet leader Ali Nasser Muhammed, reportedly with the help of Soviet and Warsaw Pact advisers—suggests that the Soviets may possess a greater capacity to control events and choices in Aden than anywhere else in the Arab world.

Israel

Israel has been quite dependent on U.S. public and private assistance, especially since the Six Day War. From 1975 to 1980, for example, official U.S. aid was nearly 20 percent of Israel's GNP, and the United States was supplying 98 percent of Israel's arms imports.[53]

As a result, the United States has exercised considerable leverage over Israeli decision making on several occasions. Threats to restrict both public and private aid halted Israel's diversion of the Jordan waters in 1953, helped persuade Israel to withdraw from the Sinai after the Suez war, and may have affected Israel's nuclear research program in the early 1960s.[54] Israeli leaders were reluctant to preempt Egypt and Syria before both the 1967 and 1973 wars for fear of losing U.S. support, and their acceptance of both the Rogers agreement ending the War of Attrition and the ceasefire ending the October War were produced in part by U.S. threats to withhold arms shipments if they did not comply.[55] Finally, Israel's acceptance of the Sinai and Golan disengagements, the Sinai II agreement, the Camp David Accords, and the final peace treaty with Egypt was facilitated in large part by pledges of additional U.S. assistance.[56] More than in any other bilateral relationship examined in this study, U.S. aid to Israel has brought significant leverage on occasion.

---

53. For another indication of Israel's dependence, consider that U.S. aid between 1968 and 1979 composed 66 percent of Israel's total defense expenditures for that period. These calculations are based on data from ACDA, *World Military Expenditures and Arms Transfers;* and AID, *Overseas Loans and Grants.*

54. See Brecher, *Decisions in Israel's Foreign Policy,* pp. 174–75, 296–302, 310; Neff, *Warriors at Suez,* pp. 416–17, 431–34; Aronson, *Conflict and Bargaining in the Middle East,* pp. 50–51; Stock, *Israel on the Road to Sinai,* pp. 62–63; and Earl Berger, *The Covenant and the Sword* (London, 1965), pp. 116–18.

55. See Tanter and Stein, *Rational Decisionmaking,* pp. 162–65; Brecher, *Decisions in Israel's Foreign Policy,* pp. 322, 378–79, 391–93, 398–400, 417, note 1; and Michael Brecher with Benjamin Geist, *Decisions in Crisis: Israel, 1967, 1973* (Berkeley, Calif., 1981), pp. 177–79, 187–88. On acceptance of the ceasefire agreements, see Pollock, *Politics of Pressure,* pp. 72–74, 176–78; and Brecher and Geist, *Decisions in Crisis,* pp. 224–29.

56. See Pollock, *Politics of Pressure,* pp. 179–92; and Quandt, *Camp David,* pp. 302, 313–14.

Yet there are clear limits to U.S. influence. Efforts to promote a comprehensive peace after the Six Day War—through proposals such as the first Rogers Plan—were bluntly rejected by Israel. Although U.S. aid played a major role in making the step-by-step and Camp David negotiations work, the length and difficulty of the process suggests that Israel's dependence on U.S. support hardly made it easy for U.S. policymakers to extract concessions.[57] Even more important, Israel has refused to alter its position on the West Bank and the Golan Heights, and it has proved unwilling to moderate its long-standing policy of reprisal despite occasionally stiff protests from Washington.[58] Although Israel remains vulnerable to U.S. pressure, the record shows that its dependence on material support has not made it a compliant ally.

Saudi Arabia

The United States and Saudi Arabia have enjoyed a long history of economic and military cooperation, dating back to World War II. Dependence is essentially mutual; given the U.S. role in Saudi security planning and the importance of Saudi oil to the United States and its allies, each side has become increasingly dependent on assets that the other controls. U.S. arms deliveries and other military assistance programs averaged almost $1 billion per year from 1971 to 1979, and another $19 million worth of weapons, training, and military construction agreements had been negotiated by 1979.[59] At the same time, however, Saudi Arabia provided 17 percent of U.S. crude oil imports in 1979, and 27 percent and 33 percent of the oil imported by U.S. allies in Europe and Japan respectively.[60] Economic relations remain somewhat skewed in favor of the United States; trade between the two countries composed 17

57. In the most obvious example, the celebrated 1975 reassessment of U.S. policy in the Middle East brought at best a minor change in Israel's position. Further concessions were achieved only by a variety of U.S. pledges, including increased economic and military aid. On this point, see Pollock, *Politics of Pressure*, pp. 192–96; and Abraham Ben-Zvi, *Alliance Politics and the Limits of Influence: The Case of the U.S. and Israel, 1975–1983* (Boulder, Colo., 1984), pp. 12–21.

58. After 1977, Israeli and U.S. policy diverged on a number of occasions, including (1) a 1978 air raid against PLO offices in Beirut, (2) the Israeli invasion of southern Lebanon in 1978, (3) the decision to annex the Golan Heights in 1981, (4) the continued expansion of Israeli settlements in the West Bank, (5) the bombing of the Iraqi nuclear research facility in 1981, (6) Israel's sharp and swift rejection of the 1982 Reagan Plan for a comprehensive peace, and (7) the 1982 invasion of Lebanon and siege of Beirut.

59. See U.S. House Committee on International Relations, *U.S. Arms Policies in the Persian Gulf*, p. 28. For a thorough survey of Saudi defense programs and the U.S. contribution, see Safran, *Saudi Arabia*, chaps. 7 and 17. The U.S. share of Saudi arms imports declined from 64 percent between 1964 and 1973 to 46 percent between 1973 and 1979. See ACDA, *World Military Expenditures and Arms Transfers*.

60. See David Deese and Joseph Nye, eds., *Energy and Security* (Cambridge, Mass., 1981), pp. 436–37.

percent of Saudi GNP in 1977 but a mere 0.5 percent of U.S. GNP for the same year.[61] Moreover, given the size of Saudi investments in the United States and the Saudi reliance on U.S. firms for ambitious development programs, Saudi Arabia's ability or interest in withholding oil must be judged as small.

As a result of these strong mutual interests, neither country has been able to wield much leverage over the other. The role of the United States as the Saudis' chief defender, for example, did not prevent direct (if quite modest) Saudi participation in the various wars against Israel.[62] Indeed, Saudi financial assistance has kept Syria and the PLO solvent, helped Egypt wage the War of Attrition, and paid for much of the equipment that Egypt and Syria used in the October War. The U.S. connection was strained further by the 1973 oil embargo, and the Saudis withstood persistent U.S. pressure to support the Camp David agreements and the Egyptian-Israeli peace treaty. As one Saudi general explained their independence from U.S. pressure: "You are just arms salesmen. And we pay cash."[63] In short, Saudi reliance on U.S. arms and assistance does not give Washington much voice in how Riyadh chooses to handle important regional issues.

Saudi leverage over the United States has been equally slim, the oil weapon notwithstanding. The United States recognized the republican regime in Yemen in 1962, despite open Saudi opposition. Even more important, U.S. aid to Israel has increased steadily since 1967, despite the growing importance of Saudi oil exports. Although the United States has continued to be Saudi Arabia's largest arms supplier, each major deal has generated considerable controversy, much to the Saudis' annoyance.[64] The bottom line is clear; neither country has been able to exert leverage over the other on matters of real importance. Symbiosis rather than dependence remains the essence of the Saudi-U.S. relationship.

Jordan

Finally, Jordan has been especially dependent on foreign assistance throughout the postwar period. As noted earlier, Hussein's alignment

---

61. Calculated from U.S. Bureau of the Census, *Statistical Handbook of the United States: 1977* (Washington, D.C., 1976); and International Monetary Fund, *International Financial Statistics* (Washington, D.C., 1981).

62. Whether this participation has been based on intrinsic hostility to the Jewish state or has been merely a gesture of solidarity intended to defuse potential Arab pressure is irrelevant. The point is that the Saudis clearly see their own interests as best served by adopting a hostile stance toward Israel, despite Israel's special relationship with Saudi Arabia's own superpower patron.

63. Quoted in *New York Times*, February 9, 1982.

64. See Quandt, *Saudi Arabia in the 1980s*, pp. 142–43.

with the Arabs in 1956 was facilitated by their pledge to replace the British subsidy, and his decision to realign with the United States in 1957 was made possible by U.S. economic and military aid.[65] All told, U.S. aid composed more than 10 percent of Jordan's GNP for the period 1959–1979.[66]

Yet U.S. largesse has not made Hussein especially responsive to U.S. wishes. Jordan's ties with the United States did not prevent its entrance into the Six Day War, its more limited participation in 1973, or its reluctant decision to accept the 1974 Rabat agreement naming the PLO as sole representative of the Palestinians.[67] U.S. support could not overcome Hussein's reluctance to join the Camp David process, despite his obvious interest in regaining the West Bank through negotiation. In short, although the United States has been Jordan's principal patron since the mid-1950s, other factors are at least as important in determining how Jordan will act. Because Jordan relies upon aid from other sources (and because Hussein has other options should the United States reduce its support), U.S. leverage has usually been slight.[68]

Why Foreign Aid Does Not Bring Leverage

These summaries reveal that providing foreign aid rarely gives patrons significant political leverage over their clients. Why is this so? In chapter 2 I argued that patrons will wield extensive leverage over their clients when (1) they have a monopoly on the type of aid being sought, (2) they enjoy an asymmetry of motivation regarding the issues involved, and (3) they face few domestic obstacles to manipulating the

65. U.S. aid equaled 84 percent of Jordan's defense expenditure in 1958, and cash subsidies from the United States enabled Hussein to retain the loyalty of his army. Moreover, Hussein apparently received direct cash payments for his personal use as well. See ACDA, *World Military Expenditures and Arms Transfers;* and AID, *Overseas Loans and Grants.* On direct U.S. payments to Hussein, see *Washington Post,* February 18, 1977.

66. After the Jordan crisis in 1970, U.S. aid more than doubled, with over 50 percent going to military assistance. Indeed, the United States provided roughly 83 percent of Jordan's military equipment between 1974 and 1978. By way of contrast, military aid was only 16 percent of total U.S. aid prior to 1967, but made up 52 percent of the total package from 1971 to 1979. See ACDA, *World Military Expenditures and Arms Transfers;* and AID, *Overseas Loans and Grants.*

67. As explained in chapter 5, these decisions were based on Hussein's calculations regarding who was likely to win and on his overriding need to maintain an image of Arab solidarity.

68. According to the 1967 Khartoum summit agreements, Jordan was to receive 43 million pounds annually from Saudi Arabia, Kuwait, and Libya. In 1975 and 1976 Saudi financial support for Jordan was $49.3 million and $165 million respectively. See *MER 1968,* p. 165; and Dawisha, "Saudi Arabia's Search for Security," p. 18. Hussein has threatened to obtain arms from the Soviet Union on at least three occasions—in 1963, 1968, and 1975–1976. These threats have been used to overcome U.S. reluctance to supply various types of advanced weaponry and have generally worked.

level of aid for political purposes. Because these conditions are rarely met, they help explain why economic and military aid are rarely effective instruments of political control.

First, the leverage a patron can wield is reduced by the fact that alternative sources are usually available. The existence of alternatives is one obvious effect of bipolarity: the Soviet-U.S. rivalry enables client states to defy their patrons by threatening to obtain support from the other superpower. Thus, when the United States tried to induce Egypt to make peace with Israel by refusing Nasser's requests for arms in 1954–1955, Egypt turned to Moscow instead.[69] During the War of Attrition, Nasser reportedly persuaded a reluctant Soviet leadership to send air defense troops to Egypt by threatening to resign in favor of a pro-U.S. president.[70] In the same way, Sadat's open flirtation with the United States in 1972 convinced the Soviet Union to supply the arms it had withheld the previous year. Finally, Hussein has repeatedly overcome U.S. reluctance to supply Jordan with advanced weaponry by threatening to obtain weapons from the Soviet Union.[71] Thus leverage is reduced by the fact that alternative sources are usually available.

When alternatives are unavailable or unappealing, however, patrons have wielded greater control. Nasser withdrew from Yemen, accepted subsidies from his conservative enemies, and granted a Soviet request for naval and air facilities in 1967, because Egypt's dire need for immediate support gave him little choice.[72] This situation explains the partial success of U.S. pressure on Israel as well; threats to withhold support have forced Israeli concessions on several occasions (halting the Jordan water project in 1953, withdrawing from the Sinai in 1957, accepting the Rogers ceasefire in 1970, sparing the Egyptian Third Army at the end of the October War, etc.), in part because Israel lacks a ready alternative to U.S. assistance. Finally, because the Soviet Union could not provide the level of economic aid that Egypt needed, Sadat turned toward the United States and made the compromises necessary to preserve its support.

---

69. See Burns, *Economic Aid and American Policy*, pp. 18–19, 22–23. Nasser's motives for seeking Soviet aid went beyond a desire to resist U.S. pressure for a peace settlement; the point is that U.S. leverage was limited by the fact that Egypt had an alternative source of support.

70. See Heikal, *Road to Ramadan*, pp. 83–90.

71. See note 68 of this chapter.

72. See Remnek, "Politics of Soviet Access," pp. 369–72; *MER 1967*, pp. 135, 140–41, 263–64; and "'Abd-al-Nasir's Secret Papers," p. 5. Remnek argues that this decision was not a major Egyptian concession, because granting the Soviets access served Egyptian interests as well. This statement may be true, but the decision was also a complete reversal of Nasser's long-standing opposition to any foreign presence in Egypt. Had circumstances not forced this policy upon him, it is most unlikely that he would ever have moved so close to the Soviet Union.

In short, aid is more likely to yield some leverage for the donor when the recipient is especially needy and when alternatives are unavailable. The key point, however, is that this situation is relatively rare; most states can find acceptable alternatives most of the time.

Second, leverage is reduced because dependence is rarely a one-way street. Thus Soviet leverage on Egypt and U.S. leverage on Saudi Arabia was limited by the fact that the clients have been seen as intrinsically valuable in their own right.[73] Not only are important allies more likely to receive large amounts of support—as Egypt and Israel have done—but their patrons will be much more reluctant to jeopardize an especially valued client by withholding support.

Furthermore, providing aid—especially military aid—usually commits the donor's prestige to the fate of the recipient. As Brezhnev told a group of Arab leaders after the Six Day War: "We were very pained [by the Arab defeat] because we have put our reputation with yours."[74] Or as Henry Kissinger put it, the United States "could not let Soviet clients defeat a traditional American friend."[75] As a result, a patron's willingness to enforce obedience by restricting the flow of aid will be reduced even more, because it will fear a loss of prestige should the client realign or be defeated. Indeed, as Soviet-Egyptian and U.S.-Israeli relations suggest, a large aid relationship may actually be a reflection of the client's ability to extort support from its patron, rather than being a sign of the patron's ability to control its client.

Third, providing aid can be self-defeating, because it strengthens the recipient's position and thus reduces its need to follow the patron's advice. As Kissinger described the bargaining process that accompanied step-by-step diplomacy: "I ask [Israeli prime minister] Rabin to make concessions, and he says he can't make concessions because Israel is weak. So I give him more arms, and he says he doesn't need to make concessions because Israel is strong."[76] Paradoxically, the more aid one provides, the less control it is likely to bring.

Fourth, because recipients of foreign aid are almost always weaker than their patrons, they are likely to bargain harder when disputes arise. Moreover, because relations between the superpowers and their regional allies focus primarily on regional issues, the client will usually have a far greater stake in the outcome. Thus the asymmetry of motivation will usually favor clients, even when they are extremely dependent on external support.

73. Egypt was the leading Arab state and provided superb military facilities for the Soviet Union; Saudi Arabia was and is the world's largest oil exporter.
74. See "'Abd-al-Nasir's Secret Papers," p. 22.
75. Kissinger, *Years of Upheaval*, p. 468.
76. Quoted in Sheehan, *Arabs, Israelis, and Kissinger*, p. 199.

This study supports this proposition. For example, Hafez el-Assad explained Syria's defiance of a Soviet arms cutoff in 1976 by remarking that the action in dispute—the Syrian intervention in Lebanon—was in Syria's "firm national interest."[77] As Anwar Sadat put it, "[The Soviets] believe that this problem [of the occupied territory] can be placed in spot number 3, 4, or 5, but for me it is top priority, it means everything."[78] The same problem reduces U.S. leverage over Israel. According to an unnamed U.S. diplomat, "they can outlast us on almost any issue," because Israel's interest in the outcome is almost always greater than that of the United States.[79]

The importance of relative interests can also be seen in the ability of clients to defy their patrons on most (if not all) domestic issues. Neither superpower has been able to prevent client states from taking independent action in what clients regard as their internal affairs, whether it be the suppression of the local Communist party or the continued settlement of occupied territory such as the West Bank. The reason is simple; such issues are far more important to the client than they are to the patron, especially when they are perceived as vital to the survival of the regime itself.

When a patron's vital interests are fully engaged, however, its ability to extract concessions increases. This point has been most apparent during the various Middle East wars. Not only must clients worry more about external support when war is imminent, but war increases the concern of both superpowers for protecting their clients while avoiding a confrontation with each other. Thus Ben-Gurion refused to go to war in 1956 until Israel had great power protection (Britain and France), and his successors hesitated to launch preemptive strikes in both 1967 and 1973 for fear of losing U.S. support.[80] Similarly, the United States successfully compelled Israel to accept the Rogers ceasefire in 1970, because it was concerned about the dangers of the growing Soviet role in Egypt.

77. Soviet interests were limited to helping preserve the PLO and to avoiding a major conflict between Israel and the Soviet Union's Arab clients. Syrian interests were significantly greater, including the desire to (1) prevent Israeli domination of Lebanon, (2) achieve effective control over the PLO, and (3) assert Syria's traditional claims to portions of Lebanese territory. See Dawisha, *Syria and the Lebanese Crisis*, pp. 169–70.

78. See Israeli, *Public Diary of President Sadat*, 1: 238.

79. Quoted in Jonathan Randal, *Going All the Way: Christian Warlords, Israeli Adventurers, and the War in Lebanon* (New York, 1984), p. 205. Abraham Ben-Zvi makes a similar argument in his study of the U.S.-Israeli relationship in the 1970s. As he notes: "The preconditions for . . . an effective policy of coercive diplomacy never materialized within the framework of American-Israeli relations. A solid base of domestic support . . . never emerged. Nor did there develop an asymmetry of motivation favoring the [United States]." See Ben-Zvi, *Alliance Politics*, p. 58 and pp. 14–16.

80. See Brecher, *Decisions in Israel's Foreign Policy*, pp. 270–74; and Spiegel, *Other Arab-Israeli Conflict*, pp. 137, 141–43, 147.

And when a serious superpower confrontation began to take shape during the October War, the United States did not hesitate to force Israel to spare the trapped Egyptian Third Army.[81] In short, although a superpower's level of motivation will rarely equal that of its clients, the ability to translate dependence into leverage will increase in those rare instances when it does.

Finally, this study also provides some support for the proposition that aid will bring little leverage if domestic constraints prevent the patron from manipulating the level of support the client state receives. In particular, the decentralized nature of the U.S. foreign policy process—especially pronounced in the case of foreign aid—has clearly made it difficult to use this instrument for political purposes. Thus presidential efforts to use aid to Egypt as a tool of influence were undermined by congressional objections in the mid-1950s and early 1960s.[82] Attempts to pressure Israel by restricting military and economic aid—such as Kissinger and Ford's celebrated reassessment in 1975—have also succumbed to congressional opposition.[83] Indeed, as David Pollock has shown, presidential attempts to withhold support have been most effective when the decision-making process has been highly centralized (as it was under Nixon) and when domestic political considerations have been minimized (i.e., when it has not been an election year).[84]

For all these reasons, even large amounts of foreign aid will rarely enable donors to control their clients. This situation does not arise because the superpowers lack diplomatic skill or because the aid they provide is unimportant. Instead, it is the result of several durable features of patron-client relations. The more important the client is to the patron, the more aid it can command. Whether for reasons of strategic value or prestige, its patron will rarely be willing to enforce obedience by

81. The fact that Israel had effectively won the war by this point no doubt reduced its resolve to resist U.S. demands. See Pollock, *Politics of Pressure*, pp. 176–80; and Spiegel, *Other Arab-Israeli Conflict*, pp. 264–65.

82. See Burns, *Economic Aid and American Policy*, pp. 46–50, 68–70, 85–89, 143–48, 155–57.

83. One should be careful here. Threats to restrict economic aid were effective after the Suez war, despite congressional opposition; and presidential pledges to increase assistance have encouraged Israeli concessions on several occasions. The point is that Israel's domestic political support in the United States, combined with the decentralized decision-making process that governs foreign aid, makes it much more difficult for U.S. policymakers to withhold support for political purposes. On the limited effects of the 1975 reassessment, see Ben-Zvi, *Alliance Politics*, pp. 18–20.

84. Thus the U.S. ability to manipulate aid was greatest in 1970, 1973, 1975, when election year considerations were less important. See Pollock, *Politics of Pressure*, pp. 200–202, 305–6. One might also interpret Eisenhower's success in 1957 as the result of (1) his overwhelming domestic popularity (i.e., he had just won reelection easily), (2) the fact that U.S. Jews were a small part of his electoral constituency, and (3) the relative weakness of pro-Israeli forces in U.S. politics at that time, at least in contrast to later periods.

reducing support. And because relations between a superpower and its clients will inevitably tend to focus on issues that are more important for the latter than the former, patrons will usually lack the level of motivation necessary to overcome either their clients' resistance or their own domestic constraints when a dispute emerges.

Paradoxically, therefore, aid is likely to bring reliable political control only over those states that are so weak, isolated, and vulnerable that they have little choice. And this is just another way of saying that aid is most likely to provide leverage over those countries that don't really matter very much. Obtaining the support and cooperation of more consequential states, as always, will require agreement on basic interests and the willingness to tolerate differences when they emerge.

Of course, this analysis neglects the possibility that clients will anticipate their patron's wishes in advance and adapt their behavior accordingly. Thus the only disputes identified here are those where the issue was so important to the client that it was forced to defy its patron. To the extent that clients do alter their conduct on other issues without being asked (a tendency that cannot be easily measured), this analysis may understate the overall impact of aid on the behavior of recipients.

Summary

The hypothesis that aid causes alignment receives little support from this study. Although foreign aid has been a ubiquitous instrument of superpower diplomacy in the Middle East throughout the Cold War, this analysis suggests that, by itself, economic and military assistance has relatively little impact on alliance choices. In particular, efforts to attract allies by offering aid will fail in the absence of compatible political goals.

Even when shared interests do exist, the limited impact of aid is revealed by the ease with which clients have retained their freedom of action, despite often heavy reliance on external support. Thus the common inference that Soviet or U.S. aid programs can create reliable proxies is misleading at best and usually simply wrong. Client states may serve their patron's interests, but only when such programs serve their own interests as well.

This conclusion does not mean that foreign aid is not a useful instrument of foreign policy, but it does tell us what aid can and cannot accomplish. It can strengthen weaker states whose goals complement one's own. It can help persuade other states that a wealthy power is favorably inclined. It can weaken a rival's attempt to gain influence by providing an alternative. What aid cannot do is overcome a recipient's own sense of where its interests lie, unless the recipient is exceptionally weak or vulnerable. In short, foreign aid can make an existing alignment more effective, but it rarely creates reliable allies by itself. Similar conclusions emerge in the case of penetration.

Transnational Penetration and Alliance Formation

The final set of hypotheses addresses the impact of transnational penetration on alliance formation. *Penetration* is defined here as the manipulation of the target state's domestic political system to promote alignment. By altering mass political attitudes or the perceptions of the national elite, a deliberate campaign of penetration may create a basis for alignment even when other motives are lacking.

As with foreign aid, the precise impact of penetration is difficult to measure. Penetration is often hard to detect; those who seek to manipulate other states in this way are unlikely to do so openly, and those who are affected by penetration may be reluctant to admit that foreign interference played a role in their decisions.[85] Moreover, penetration rarely succeeds in the absence of other motives for alignment. As a result, separating the impact of penetration from that of other factors is not easy.

These results should therefore be viewed as tentative. Even so, the evidence supports most of the hypotheses outlined in chapter 2. As predicted, when powerful motives for alignment are lacking, efforts to create allies by manipulating a state's domestic political system are more likely to generate resistance than to encourage alignment. (Paradoxically, when strong motives for alignment—such as a common enemy—are present, then manipulating a prospective ally's domestic political system may not be necessary.) The hypothesis that democratic systems are especially vulnerable to penetration receives support as well, especially when the ends are limited and the means are carefully chosen. A brief examination of the three main examples of penetration identified in this study will show why this is so. The examples are (1) Nasser's use of pan-Arab propaganda; (2) the efforts of both superpowers to attract allies through educational, cultural, and military assistance; and (3) the role of pro-Israeli forces in the United States.

---

85. For example, a great power that uses a military training program to acquire influence is unlikely to emphasize this program for fear of provoking resentment. Similarly, politicians whose loyalties are affected by foreign penetration have little interest in admitting that they are either agents of a foreign power or easily intimidated by domestic political pressure.

The Limits of Nasser's Charisma

The exploitation of Nasser's personal charisma by Egyptian propagandists was a major asset in Egypt's quest for hegemony within the Arab world. At the same time, it was also an important reason that these efforts failed. According to Adeed Dawisha: "The Egyptian propagandists endeavored to create . . . an image of the UAR and its President as the sole custodians of the 'Arab Nationalist Movement,' thus positing Nasser as an alternative leader to the indigenous leadership of the various Arab states."[86] As we have seen, these efforts were at least partially successful. Nassser's ability to manipulate public opinion (through the novel device of Radio Cairo) combined with the rapid emergence of Nasserist sympathizers throughout the Arab world to encourage the formation of the Arab Solidarity Pact in 1955–1956, the unity experiments with Syria in 1958 and 1963, and the Unified Political Command with Iraq from 1964 to 1967.[87] In the most obvious example, the revolutionaries who overthrew the Imamate of Yemen in 1962 were apparently inspired (if not completely coopted) by their exposure to Nasserist ideas in Egypt. Thus Egypt's penetration of the Yemeni elite led to a formal alliance between Egypt and the YAR and ultimately to Egypt's disastrous intervention in the Yemen civil war.[88]

But, as chapters 5 and 6 discussed at length, Nasser's efforts to exploit his prestige ultimately created more enemies than allies, because his use of penetration (e.g., radio propaganda and support for dissident groups) worked by threatening his potential partners. Because the other Arab states were often reluctant to support Egypt, Nasser could gain their compliance only by threatening their domestic stability. Even when he succeeded temporarily (e.g., Jordan in 1956 and Syria in 1958 and 1963), there was no guarantee that the affected regime would remain loyal. Thus the continued threat posed by Nasser's followers led the Ba'th civilians to seek Nasser's blessing for union in 1963, but it also led the Ba'th Military Committee to purge all Nasserist officers and thereby destroy the Tripartite Unity Agreement. These events confirm

86. See Dawisha, *Egypt in the Arab World*, p. 164 and passim; and Campbell, *Defense of the Middle East*, pp. 77–78.

87. Nasser's propaganda triggered riots in Jordan in December 1955, which encouraged Hussein to reject the Baghdad Pact in favor of a brief alignment with Egypt, Syria, and Saudi Arabia. Egypt's union with Syria was partly the result of Nasser's prestige within the Syrian army, whereas the Tripartite Unity Agreement was viewed by the Syrian Ba'th as a way to coopt the pro-Nasser groups that had endanged Syrian domestic stability since the break-up of the UAR in 1961. Finally, the largely symbolic union with Iraq was partly the result of Iraqi President Abdel Salam Aref's own interest in Arab unity and personal admiration for Nasser.

88. See Wenner, *Modern Yemen*, pp. 182–83, 189, 195; Peterson, *Yemen*, pp. 85–88; and Lenczowski, *Middle East in World Affairs*, pp. 626–28.

that when penetration threatens a prospective ally's internal stability, it is more likely to create hostility than to encourage an effective alliance.

Superpower Penetration in the Middle East

A second type of penetration consists of the efforts both superpowers have made to promote close relations with Third World states through educational, cultural, and military exchanges. Although such efforts are of obvious concern to Soviet and U.S. analysts, the historical record suggests that the effectiveness of this instrument is usually exaggerated.[89] In fact, transnational penetration has played a minor role in alliance formation in the Middle East. Indeed, most of the superpowers' efforts to exploit domestic political forces have been counterproductive.

First, if penetration were an effective instrument of alliance formation, we would expect clients to be fairly compliant with the superpower patron's wishes. But as indicated earlier in this chapter, client states in the Middle East in fact retain considerable freedom of action. Neither foreign aid nor extensive personal contact has given the superpowers a significant ability to control their clients. We can conclude that indirect manipulation has had little independent impact on alliance choices or other important foreign policy decisions.

The available data help explain why. As Table 15 reveals, there is a modest association between superpower commitments and the level of elite interactions. The pattern, however, is hardly clear-cut. For example, roughly equal numbers of students from Egypt, Syria, and Iraq have chosen to study in either the United States or the Soviet Union, and the numbers are at best loosely related to the state of political relations between these countries.[90] Predictably, the association is quite strong in

89. According to a former CIA analyst: "In the Middle East, military groups historically have been a major source of authority. The earliest indicator of Western influence was evident in their organization of the military. The effect of present Soviet training on future military leaders may be expected to influence to some degree the political and economic orientation of these countries." See Tansky, *U.S. and USSR Aid to Developing Countries*, pp. 18–19. This concern was voiced more recently in the 1981 edition of the U.S. Department of Defense pamphlet *Soviet Military Power*. It reports on p. 86 that "the Soviets project power and influence through . . . less visible elements including the KGB, diplomats . . . military advisors, . . . cultural, media, and educational diplomacy . . . and propaganda. . . . These tools allow Moscow to develop an 'infrastructure of influence' in a target country . . . allowing the penetration of areas that may be beyond the immediate reach of Soviet military forces." In short, these indirect means are seen as an effective way for the Soviet Union to influence or control distant countries.

90. For example, the number of Egyptians studying in the United States changed little between 1960 and 1974, despite the sharp deterioration in Egyptian-U.S. relations that occurred during this period.

the case of military training. but this strength is due to the obvious fact that military personnel are likely to receive their training from whoever is providing the bulk of their equipment.

Even more important, the number of people involved in these exchanges is quite small. As Karen Dawisha has shown, the number of Arab students receiving educational assistance in the Soviet Union, the United States, and Great Britain is paltry compared to the total student population of these countries.[91] The same is true of military training.[92] Thus, even if penetration does affect attitudes favorably, the effort thus far has been too small to alter foreign policy behavior significantly.

Second, the belief that penetration can create effective alliances rests on the assumption that such contacts will create favorable attitudes. For example, Sadat expelled Egypt's Soviet advisers in part because Egyptian military personnel resented the Soviets' condescending and officious behavior.[93] Similar problems have apparently plagued the Soviet educational exchange program.[94] According to the Central Intelligence Agency: "Returning students . . . have not greatly increased Soviet influence; . . . few seem to have changed their political persuasions after four to five years of residence in the USSR; indeed, some have become intensely anti-Communist. Only a handful . . . have attained Cabinet-level status, mostly because they compete with the better-trained and more numerous professionals who were educated in the West."[95] In short, because there is no guarantee that familiarity will not breed contempt or that sympathetic elites will acquire and retain positions of influence, the impact of such contacts has been erratic at best.

Third, several cases examined here suggest that an ally's efforts to manipulate the internal politics of a regime in order to enhance its own position are quite likely to backfire. Nasser's concerns over possible Communist subversion marred relations with the Soviet Union in 1959 and 1961, and Heikal reports that the Egyptians were upset to learn that

91. In Egypt, for example, no more than a thousand students were sent to the Soviet Union in any given year, out of a total university population of nearly two hundred thousand. Although the percentage is larger in the case of both Syria and Iraq, students receiving training in either the United States or the Soviet Union still compose less than 3 percent of the total university population. See Dawisha, "Soviet Cultural Relations," p. 435.

92. Roughly six thousand Egyptian military officers received training in the Soviet Union between 1955 and 1976. And even if we assume that these officers were especially promising and therefore likely to rise to positions of prominence, their exposure to Soviet training did not prevent Sadat from turning to the United States in 1974, when Egypt's interests lay elsewhere.

93. See Rubinstein, *Red Star on the Nile*, pp. 195–96; el-Sadat, *In Search of Identity*, pp. 230–31; and David, "Realignment of Third World Regimes," pp. 297–99, 319–20, 328–29.

94. See U.S. House Committee on Foreign Affairs, *The Soviet Union and the Third World*, p. 82; *Los Angeles Times*, November 23, 1976, pt. 7, pp. 6, 8–9.

95. CIA, *Communist Aid to Non-Communist LDCs, 1979 and 1954–1979*, p. 9.

Table 15. Indicators of superpower penetration

a. Students studying in the United States and the Soviet Union

Country	1959 United States	1959 Soviet Union	1963 United States	1963 Soviet Union	1965 United States	1965 Soviet Union	1969 United States	1969 Soviet Union	1974 United States	1974 Soviet Union	1978 United States	1978 Soviet Union
Egypt	453	138	1,136	240	1,279	248	1,015	450	980	925	1,500	125
Iraq	732	789	815	1,262	919	840	586	820	376	650	1,190	250
Israel	723	0	1,208	0	1,539	0	2,079	0	2,070	0	2,550	0
Jordan	591	n.a.	663	0	654	0	828	0	977	0	2,120	0
Lebanon	544	n.a.	602	n.a.	700	n.a.	921	n.a.	1,493	480	3,370	450
North Yemen	12	n.a.	17	n.a.	12	n.a.	17	200	25	575	0	455
Saudi Arabia	66	0	271	0	552	0	1,057	0	1,540	0	6,560	0
South Yemen	1[a]	n.a.	6[a]	n.a.	9[a]	n.a.	23	50	21	515	0	660
Syria	312	150	327	146	434	199	461	495	416	1,215	450	2,135

SOURCES: Karen Dawisha, "Soviet Cultural Relations with Iraq, Syria, and Egypt, 1955–1970," *Soviet Studies*, 27, no. 3 (1975); CIA, *Communist Aid to Non-Communist LDCs, 1979 and 1954–1979* (Washington, D.C., 1980); and Institute of International Education, *Open Doors: Report on International Educational Exchange* (New York, various years).

n.a. = Data not available.

[a] South Yemen received independence in 1967; figures for 1959, 1963, and 1965 refer to Aden Crown Colony.

b. Military personnel trained in the United States and the Soviet Union

Country	1950–1976 United States	1950–1976 Soviet Union	1977 United States	1977 Soviet Union	1978 United States	1978 Soviet Union	1979 United States	1979 Soviet Union	Total United States	Total Soviet Union
Egypt	0	5,665	0	0	12	0	24	0	36	5,665
Iraq	406[a]	3,250	0	300	0	100	0	60	0	3,710
Israel	0	0	0	0	0	0	0	0	0	0
Jordan	1,240	0	287	0	277	0	247	0	2,051	0
Lebanon	1,520	0	3	0	57	0	56	0	1,636	0
North Yemen	15	1,100	20	75	35	5	17	180	87	1,360

South Yemen	0	775	0	1,500[b]	0	75	0	225	0	0	1,075
Saudi Arabia	1,425	0		0		0	0	0	n.a.	4,400+	0
Syria	20	3,525		125	0	95	500	0		4,245	

SOURCES: U.S. Department of Defense, *Foreign Military Sales and Foreign Assistance Facts* (Washington, D.C., various years); CIA, *Communist Aid Activities in Non-Communist LDCs, 1979 and 1954–1979* (Washington, D.C., 1980); CIA, *Handbook of Economic Statistics* (Washington, D.C., various years); and U.S. House Committee on International Relations, *United States Arms Policies in the Persian Gulf and Red Sea Areas: Past, Present, and Future*, 95th Cong., 1st sess., 1976.

n.a. = Data not available.

[a]All prior to the 1958 revolution.

[b]Figures are approximate.

c. Superpower military presence in the Middle East

	1971		1973		1974		1976		1978		1979	
	United States	Soviet Union	United States	Soviet Union	United States	Soviet Union	United States	Soviet Union	United States	Soviet Union	United States	Soviet Union
Egypt	0	5,500[a]	0	750	0	750	n.a.	0	35[b]	0	39[b]	0
Iraq	0	500	0	750	0	1,000	0	1,000	0	1,200	0	1,065
Israel	n.a.	0	n.a.	0	21[c]	0	20[c]	0	40[b]	0	45[b]	0
Jordan	n.a.	0	n.a.	0	6	0	n.a.	0	15	0	15	0
Lebanon	n.a.	0	n.a.	0	0	0	n.a.	0	9	0	2	0
North Yemen	0	n.a.	0	25	0	120	5	n.a.	0	155	6	130
South Yemen	0	100	0	200	0	200	0	n.a.	0	550	0	2,100[d]
Saudi Arabia	141	0	131	0	2,250	0	5,000–6,000[c]	0	5,000–6,000[c]	0	5,000–6,000[c]	0
Syria	0	n.a.	0	1,650	0	2,200	0	2,500	0	2,580	0	2,480

SOURCES: CIA, *Communist Aid Activities in Non-Communist LDCs, 1979 annd 1954–1979* (Washington, D.C., 1980); U.S. House Committee on International Relations, *U.S. Arms Policies in the Persian Gulf and Red Sea Areas: Past, Present, and Future*, 95th Cong, 1st sess., 1976; and U.S. Department of Defense, "U.S. Military Strength Outside the U.S.: Fact Sheet" (Washington, D.C., quarterly, various years).

n.a. = Data not available. Figures for United States are under 100.

[a]Omits approximately 10,000 Soviet air defense troups stationed in Egypt during the War of Attrition.

[b]Omits Marine Corps personnel assigned to embassy security.

[c]Includes civilian contract personnel in defense-related activities.

[d]Includes 1,000 Cuban troups stationed in South Yemen. Some sources place this figure at over 4,000.

Egyptian military officers were being given political instruction during training assignments in the Soviet Union.[96] Sadat's expulsion of Egypt's Soviet advisers reflected his conviction that Soviet intelligence officers had supported his domestic opponents, and the exposure of Communist officers within the Iraqi armed forces apparently undermined Soviet relations with Iraq in 1978. As we saw with Nasser's efforts to create alliances through aggressive propaganda, when states perceive superpower penetration to be potentially subversive, it is likely to discourage alignment and may provoke overt hostility.

Fourth, what was true for foreign aid is also true for penetration: extensive personal contacts are a product of alignment, not the reason behind it. In the cases examined here, alignment with one of the superpowers usually preceded widespread elite exchanges.[97] Moreover, because the scope of these contacts has usually been determined by external events (e.g., military advisers and political visits increase in response to the level of threat), they are best viewed as a predictable result of shared interests.

For example, the Soviet presence in Egypt and Syria soared after the Six Day War, at Egypt and Syria's request.[98] Other Soviet contacts with Syria and Iraq have waxed and waned in response to the client's needs and the state of relations with Moscow.[99] In the same way, the number of Jordanians receiving military training in the United States tripled after the Jordan crisis in 1970, and Saudi Arabia's decision to upgrade its defense capabilities in the early 1970s brought roughly 1,500 trainees per year to the United States. (By contrast, the total for the entire period 1950–1975 was only 1,368.)[100] In short, extensive elite exchanges may be

96. Heikal, *Sphinx and Commissar*, p. 166.

97. There are three possible exceptions to this observation. Saudi Arabia's alignment with the United States was forged in part through the influence of the U.S. oil companies, which began operations in the kingdom in the 1930s. See Safran, *Saudi Arabia*, pp. 57–67 and passim; and Irvine Anderson, *Aramco, the United States, and Saudi Arabia: A Study of the Dynamics of Foreign Oil Policy, 1933–1950* (Princeton, N.J., 1981). In addition, North Yemen signed a defense agreement with the Soviet Union in 1956, in part because Crown Prince Badr had been favorably impressed during several previous trips to the Soviet Union. In both cases, however, external threats were also involved. Ibn Saud saw U.S. support as a way to balance threats from Britain and its Hashemite clients in Transjordan and Iraq. Badr's father, the Imam Ahmed, saw Soviet backing as a means of pressuring Great Britain to abandon the Aden crown colony. Finally, U.S. ties with Israel are an obvious exception to this generalization; they will be discussed in detail in the next section.

98. See Nutting, *Nasser*, pp. 431–32; and Heikal, *Road to Ramadan*, pp. 83–90.

99. Iraq withdrew its students from the Soviet Union and expelled a number of Soviet advisers in 1963, and Iraq reportedly reduced the Soviet presence in 1978 after the Soviet invasion of Afghanistan and the exposure of a Communist plot in the Iraqi armed forces. The Syrians asked a number of Soviet advisers to leave in 1976, apparently the result of a quarrel with Moscow over Syria's intervention in the Lebanese civil war. See SIPRI, *Arms Trade with the Third World*, p. 557.

100. See U.S. Department of Defense, *Foreign Military Sales and Foreign Assistance Facts* (Washington, D.C., various years); and U.S. House Committee on International Relations, *United States Arms Policies in the Persian Gulf*, p. 39.

one indicator of good relations, but they are not an especially important cause.[101]

This conclusion is not surprising, because authoritarian regimes will be more comfortable exposing their current or future elites to countries with which they already enjoy favorable relations. Thus the conservative Arab states have sent many students to Western universities (especially those of the United States) but not to any Communist countries.[102] Although the progressive Arab states have been more flexible, the number of students studying in the West has generally declined whenever relations with the United States deteriorated. The point is simply that the development of informal channels of influence is far more likely when favorable political relations already exist.[103]

Fifth, there is little evidence to suggest that the leaders of any of these countries are easy to manipulate, even by allies for whom they do feel strong sympathies. Because impeccable nationalist credentials remain an important qualification for leadership in most developing countries, a potential leader who is seen as a foreign puppet is unlikely to reach a position of power or to remain there for long.[104]

101. Jordan provides an apt example. Jordan's pro-Western position has been reinforced by Britain's original role in establishing the kingdom, which included forming and training the Arab Legion and educating Hussein at Harrow and Sandhurst. The key point is that these factors were themselves the result of the close ties (i.e., British control) between Britain and Jordan established under the U.N. mandate.

102. As a congressional study of Saudi education policy reports: "Saudi Arabia has made a conscious decision to rely heavily on the U.S. for the higher education of its young people. . . . It was [a decision] made by well-informed leaders, fully aware of the risks involved in exposing a generation to customs and values quite different from its own. The Deputy Minister for Economic and Cultural Affairs put it this way: 'By inculcating the American system into Saudi children, you will have a whole generation oriented towards the United States. I recognize the dangers . . . but it is the best alternative I have.'" U.S. House Committee on International Relations, *Notes on Educational and Cultural Exchange between the United States and Countries of the Middle East*, 95th Cong., 1st sess., 1977, p. 24.

103. Thus Karen Dawisha concludes that "the main themes utilized in Soviet cultural relations are those which reinforce existing attitudes or encourage nascent ones." See her "Soviet Cultural Relations," p. 423. According to an extensive congressional study on Soviet relations in the Third World: "The main contribution to date of the Soviet cultural program in the Third World [including educational programs] has been to bolster already existing friendly relations. . . .[I]f the overall state of relations . . . is on the decline, then cultural relations would usually suffer accordingly. . . . [P]olitics is the real determining factor in Soviet-Third World relations." See U.S. House Committee on Foreign Affairs, *Soviet Union and the Third World*, p. 82.

104. This assertion cannot be proven, but it is worth noting that Nasser vowed he would never be a "foreign stooge," Assad criticized the Soviets for "imperialist behavior" when they pressed him for base rights in Syria, and Saddam Hussein is described by one expert on Iraqi politics as a man with a "long-held hatred of all kinds of foreign domination." See Khadduri, *Socialist Iraq*, p. 74. Such views are not confined to the Arab world. Menachem Begin reportedly responded to U.S. suspension of an agreement for strategic cooperation with Israel by complaining: "Are we a vassal state of yours? Are we a banana republic?" Quoted in Spiegel, *Other Arab-Israeli Conflict*, p. 411. These statements suggest that strong nationalist convictions remain a common trait among most, if not all, Middle East leaders.

Taken together, these considerations tell us why penetration has played little role in creating alliances between the superpowers and most Middle East states. Penetration will be a significant cause of alignment if and only if (1) substantial contacts can be established between two states that are not already allied, (2) the exchanges create a favorable impression on a significant number of the relevant elites, (3) these elites gain and hold power, and (4) they continue to view close alignment with the foreign power in question as being in their national or personal interest. There are serious obstacles to each of these conditions, and the probability that all will be satisfied in any given case is low, unless such an alignment is viewed as desirable in its own right. And if that is true, penetration may have little to do with the decision to ally.

The most obvious exception to this argument—the Marxist regime in South Yemen—actually reinforces it. In South Yemen, a combination of ideological solidarity, internal instability, and external threats led to a large Warsaw Pact presence by the mid-1970s. In the recurring struggle for power among various South Yemeni factions, the Warsaw Pact's extensive involvement in South Yemen's internal security apparatus apparently enabled the Soviets to assist the group they preferred on several occasions.[105] This case supports the proposition that penetration may be especially effective when the state in question lacks established government institutions and independent internal security forces. In such circumstances, penetration may provide the foreign power with exceptional influence. (However, recent events in South Yemen suggest that the degree of Soviet influence there is by no means perfect.)[106] In any case, because few states are as lacking in basic institutions of government as the PDRY, this type of penetration will probably remain quite rare. Needless to say, states that are vulnerable to it are seldom, if ever, very important or powerful.

By creating a network of supporters and a climate of favorable perceptions, informal contacts can make established alliances more durable. But when a potential ally does not favor a political commitment, efforts to create one through indirect means are likely to backfire. All things considered, Middle East states have been remarkably impervious to su-

105. See Kelly, *Arabia, the Gulf and the West*, pp. 470–73; Mylroie, "The Soviet Presence in the PDRY"; and *MECS 1977–1978*, pp. 655–66.

106. In January 1986 PDRY President 'Ali Nasser Muhammed attempted to assassinate most of his colleagues on the ruling Politburo. The attack led to a week of fierce fighting between the two factions, in which as many as thirteen thousand South Yemenis may have been killed. The Soviet embassy in Aden was heavily damaged, and Muhammed was eventually defeated and replaced. The new government remains pro-Soviet, but these events indicate that even a large Warsaw Pact presence does not guarantee control over domestic events. For an account of the attempted coup, see *New York Times*, January 30, 1986, p. A4.

perpower penetration, when they view it as contrary to their own calculations of interest.[107]

Transnational Penetration and U.S. Middle East Policy

The final case to consider is the influence of domestic political lobbies
on U.S. policy in the Middle East. The openness of the U.S. political
system should make the United States especially vulnerable to this type
of transnational penetration, and there are several well-documented
cases of such activity in the past.[108]

Even more important, the belief that U.S. foreign policy in the Middle
East is determined more by domestic politics than by calculated appraisals of the national interest is widespread. For some, U.S. Middle
East commitments are assumed to be heavily influenced by a coalition of
pro-Israeli forces in the United States, led by organized Jewish political
groups who coordinate their actions with the Israeli government.[109] For
others, U.S. policy is assumed to be prone to manipulation by well-
funded lobbyists representing Arab oil states or U.S. corporations with
extensive business ties to the Arab world.[110] In both cases, the conduct
of U.S. Middle East policy is attributed primarily to transnational manipulation of U.S. domestic politics.

Unraveling these competing claims is a major undertaking, because
any attempt to assess the relative importance of penetration on U.S.

107. Jordan is the most obvious exception. See note 101 in this chapter.

108. The most obvious example is the China Lobby in the 1950s. See Koen, *The China
Lobby in American Politics;* and Bachrack, *The Committee for One Million.* For more general
discussions of this issue, see Charles McC. Mathias, "Ethnic Groups and Foreign Policy,"
Foreign Affairs, 59, no. 5 (1981); and Lawrence H. Fuchs, "Minority Groups and Foreign
Policy," in *American Ethnic Politics,* ed. Lawrence H. Fuchs (New York, 1968).

109. Examples of this genre include Paul Findley, *They Dare to Speak Out: People and
Institutions Confront Israel's Lobby* (Westport, Conn., 1985); Stephen Green, *Taking Sides:
America's Relations with a Militant Israel* (New York, 1984); Richard H. Curtiss, *A Changing
Image: American Perceptions of the Arab-Israeli Dispute* (Washington, D.C., 1982); and John
Snetsinger, *Truman, the Jewish Vote, and the Creation of Israel* (Stanford, Calif., 1974). Other
works that examine the impact of pro-Israeli forces on U.S. Middle East policy include
Wolf Blitzer, *Between Washington and Jerusalem: A Reporter's Notebook* (New York, 1985);
Congressional Quarterly, *The Middle East,* 5th ed. (Washington, D.C., 1981), pp. 63–65, 68;
I. L. Kenen, *Israel's Defense Line: Her Friends and Foes in Washington* (Buffalo, N.Y., 1981);
Peter Grose, *Israel in the Mind of America* (New York, 1983); M. C. Feuerwerger, *Congress
and Israel,* (Westport, Conn., 1979); Stephen Isaacs, *Jews and American Politics* (New York,
1974); Robert H. Trice, "Domestic Interest Groups and a Behavioral Analysis," in *Ethnicity
and U.S. Foreign Policy,* ed. Abdul Aziz Said (New York, 1981); and Spiegel, *Other Arab-
Israeli Conflict.*

110. The best example of this view is Emerson, *American House of Saud.* See also the
discussions in Curtis, *Changing Image,* chaps. 17 and 18; Kenen, *Israel's Defense Line,* chap.
10; Blitzer, *Between Washington and Jerusalem,* chap. 8; Congressional Quarterly, *Middle East,*
pp. 65–70; and Spiegel, *Other Arab-Israeli Conflict.*

alliances in the Middle East faces several significant barriers. Not only is public testimony regarding lobbying activities often suspect, but lobbying groups operate through a variety of channels that are difficult to identify and assess with precision.[111] Moreover, policy-makers are likely to anticipate the wishes of important domestic constituencies; they may alter their behavior in order to avoid being pressured by domestic groups. Because no overt pressure can be observed in such circumstances, the impact of penetration will be understated.[112] Finally, penetration is difficult to measure when the alliance in question is the product of several different causes. Determining the relative importance of these different factors may be impossible if external circumstances and domestic pressures are reinforcing each other.[113]

This last point reveals an important insight: how one judges the importance of domestic lobbies will be determined by one's view of what U.S. foreign policy should be. To argue that a particular interest group exerts a significant influence on alliance policy assumes that U.S. policy would be significantly different if the group did not exist—that U.S. interests would dictate a different policy in the absence of this domestic pressure. Thus those who argue that pro-Israeli forces determine U.S. Middle East policy generally believe that U.S. interests lie in a more evenhanded position (i.e., less support for Israel and greater sympathy for the Palestinian problem). In the same way, those who downplay the impact of pro-Israeli interest groups claim that strategic interests and ideological factors provide the principal motives for the U.S. commitment to Israel. The same arguments can be made for pro-Arab groups as well. The point is obvious but often overlooked: one cannot easily separate one's vision of what U.S. policy should be from one's assessment of how different factors determine what U.S. policy is.

111. Direct testimony is questionable because lobbyists will either exaggerate their influence to present themselves as a potent political force or deny that they are influential to avoid a backlash, and because political elites who are influenced by penetration are likely to deny that it played a major role in their decisions. The overall impact of penetration is difficult to measure because it can be wielded through direct contacts, lobbying efforts, and various forms of public relations (including the news media and the arts). Focusing solely upon the direct influence of lobbying groups on policy-makers may understate the overall importance of domestic supporters by ignoring the indirect effect such groups exert through their public relations efforts.

112. As Robert Trice has noted regarding the influence of Jewish-Americans: "Over time, Congressmen come to anticipate the reactions of organized Jewry to their position on relevant legislation. . . . Direct pressures by Jewish voters become less necessary, and the support of Congressmen . . . for pro-Israeli legislation becomes more automatic." See his "Congress and the Arab-Israeli Conflict: Support for Israel in the U.S. Senate, 1970–73," *Political Science Quarterly*, 92, no. 3 (1977): 456.

113. As we have seen throughout this analysis, many alliances may be "overdetermined"; that is, the precise impact of any single factor may not be readily separable from the impact of the others.

Overcoming these obstacles completely is beyond the reach of this study. What follows, therefore, is tentative and impressionistic. The question is: has a form of penetration—specifically, the activities of domestic and foreign lobbies with a strong commitment to particular foreign powers—played a major role in U.S. alliance policy in the Middle East? If so, what do their activities tell us about this particular instrument of alliance formation? Most important of all, does this case support the hypotheses presented in chapter 2 regarding the conditions under which penetration will be most effective?

The answer is a qualified yes. Although pro-Israeli forces do not control U.S. policy making in the Middle East, they have had a significant impact on U.S. Middle East policy in general and toward Israel in particular. This case supports the hypothesis that penetration will be especially effective in open political systems. It also supports the hypothesis that penetration will be most effective when such activities are perceived as legitimate and limited in scope and when they are seen as reinforcing larger national interests. The propositions advanced earlier also help explain why pro-Israeli forces have been far more successful than their pro-Arab counterparts. What is the basis for these conclusions?

The impact of pro-Israeli forces on the U.S. commitment to Israel is unquestionable. Every post-war president has been acutely aware of domestic pressure to support Israel, and most presidents have responded to the pressure by adopting policies favorable to the Jewish state. According to numerous accounts, Truman's decision to support the U.N. Partition Plan in 1947 and to recognize the State of Israel in 1948 was heavily influenced by his concern for the Jewish vote and the efforts of pro-Israeli supporters within his administration.[114] Although Eisenhower resisted domestic pressures by maintaining an arms embargo to the Middle East, by forcing Israel to halt diversion of the Jordan

114. On this point, see Snetsinger, *Truman, the Jewish Vote, and the Creation of Israel*, pp. 35–39, 41–42, 53–54, 67–71, 78–81, 102–6, 119–23; Evan Wilson, *Decision on Palestine: How the U.S. Came to Recognize Israel* (Stanford, Calif., 1981), p. 58; and Grose, *Israel in the Mind of America*, pp. 216–17, 231–32, 264–66, 269–71, and passim. This is not to say that Zionist groups in the United States were the sole determinant of Truman's decisions. Steven Spiegel downplays their influence by pointing out that Truman himself was basically sympathetic to the plight of the Jewish refugees, that he was often annoyed by Zionist pressures, and that he had "insisted privately as well as publicly that he would not be influenced by domestic politics." See Spiegel, *Other Arab-Israeli Conflict*, p. 39 and passim. Yet he also points out that Truman's vacillation on this issue reflected his attempt to reconcile competing demands. Truman's annoyance with Zionist pressure suggests that this pressure was not inconsequential, and his statements that he would not be influenced by domestic politics were probably defensive gestures. The question is what he did, not merely what he said. Truman's decisions were the product of many factors. It is clear that pressure from pro-Zionist groups in the United States was one of the most important.

River in 1953, and by pressing Israel to withdraw from Sinai after the 1956 war, both he and Secretary of State Dulles were well aware of the political hazards of such a course.[115] Eisenhower's ability to defy this pressure was no doubt enhanced by his enormous personal popularity and the relative weakness of pro-Israeli forces at that time.[116]

The expansion of U.S.-Israeli security ties after 1960 was the result of several factors. For Kennedy, the decision to extend an informal security guarantee to Israel and to sell it advanced weaponry was partly a response to Soviet arms shipments to Egypt and Iraq, partly a means of enhancing Kennedy's efforts to promote a peace settlement, and partly a way to maintain domestic support while seeking a rapprochement with Nasser.[117] For Johnson and Nixon, a growing commitment to Israel followed logically from the imperatives of domestic politics, the growing Soviet commitment to Israel's adversaries, and the French decision to suspend arms shipments to Israel after 1967.[118] Once the commitment was made, moreover, U.S. support for Israel was self-sustaining; like most overseas commitments, it became necessary for maintaining prestige and credibility.[119]

The creation of an extensive U.S.-Israeli commitment, in short, was partly a response to changing external circumstances and the growing perception that Israel was a valuable regional ally. At the same time, however, pro-Israeli forces now wielded greater political influence.[120]

115. See Neff, *Warriors at Suez*, pp. 386, 432–33; Brecher, *Decisions in Israel's Foreign Policy*, pp. 292–93, 297–98, especially note 2; Finer, *Dulles over Suez*, pp. 470–84 and passim; and Love, *Suez*, pp. 664–68.

116. Members of Jewish political groups have admitted that they were inadequately prepared during the mid-1950s. See Kenen, *Israel's Defense Line*, p. 105; and Blitzer, *Between Washington and Jerusalem*, p. 15.

117. See Spiegel, *Other Arab-Israeli Conflict*, pp. 106–8; and Gazit, *President Kennedy's Policy*, pp. 35–48. Ben-Gurion's biographer, Michael Bar-Zohar, reports that Kennedy told the Israeli prime minister in 1962: "I was elected by the votes of American Jews. I owe them my victory. . . . Is there something I should do?" He also notes that Ben-Gurion was not impressed by this remark. See his *Ben-Gurion* (New York, 1977). As in the Truman administration, pro-Israeli forces enjoyed important avenues of influence in the Kennedy White House. For example, both Shimon Peres (then Israel's defense minister) and I. L. Kenen (founder of the American-Israel Public Affairs Committee) have revealed that Myer Feldman, a Kennedy aide with close ties to the U.S. Jewish community, was a particularly effective liaison between the Kennedy and Johnson administrations, U.S. Jewry, and the Israeli government. See Peres, *David's Sling*, pp. 94–96, 99; Kenen, *Israel's Defense Line*, pp. 160–62, 167, 177, 183; and Spiegel, *Other Arab-Israel Conflict*, pp. 95–96, 100.

118. See Spiegel, *Other Arab-Israeli Conflict*, pp. 169, 180, and passim; Kissinger, *White House Years*, pp. 202–3; and Quandt, *Decade of Decisions*, pp. 79–80.

119. Thus Kissinger justified U.S. support for Israel during the October War by saying that the United States "could not permit Soviet clients to defeat a traditional [U.S.] friend." See his *Years of Upheaval*, p. 468.

120. Of course, the two factors are not unrelated. Israel's supporters in the United States have long argued that Israel is an important and valuable ally, and their case became much more persuasive after the Six Day War and the Jordan crisis, when Israel's military capability was widely perceived as major barrier to the growth of Soviet influence in the

Since the mid-1960s, their growing political clout has set clear limits on the ability of U.S. presidents to adopt policies that could be seen as hostile to Israel.

The chief avenue of influence has been Congress. Although U.S. presidents have repeatedly sought to maintain some distance from Israel in order to promote other regional objectives, Congress has remained overwhelmingly supportive of the Jewish state.[121] Congress has consistently backed increased military and economic aid to Israel, and aid levels have grown steadily since 1970.[122] Indeed, although U.S. foreign assistance worldwide has declined, Congress has usually voted Israel more economic and military aid than requested by Democratic and Republican administrations alike.[123]

Second, prompted by Israel's U.S. supporters, Congress has also placed restrictions on initiatives viewed as harmful to Israel. This is especially true of attempts to provide economic or military aid to Israel's Arab opponents. Congressional opposition contributed to the decision to abandon the Aswan Dam in 1956, undermined the provision of economic aid to Egypt after 1962, and led to significant restrictions on arms sales to Jordan and Saudi Arabia in 1975 and 1978.[124]

Third, pro-Israeli groups such as the American-Israel Public Affairs Committee (AIPAC) have successfully undermined U.S. pressure for Israeli concessions by mobilizing congressional opposition. For example, the Nixon administration's attempt to pressure Israel by delaying a shipment of Phantom aircraft in March 1970 produced a congressional resolution protesting the delay.[125] Even more important, Kissinger's

---

region. For examples of these arguments, see Steven L. Spiegel, "Israel as a Strategic Asset," *Commentary*, 75, no. 6 (1983); and Steven J. Rosen, "The Strategic Value of Israel," *AIPAC Papers on U.S.-Israel Relations* (Washington, D.C., 1982).

121. According to Wolf Blitzer: "Over the years, whether Democrats or Republican controlled the White House, Israel has almost always been able to count on its friends in the Senate and the House of Representatives to come to its defense during periods of friction with the administration. . . . Almost invariably, the administration was left with no choice but to go along with the pro-Israeli congressional initiatives." Blitzer, *Between Washington and Jerusalem*, pp. 98–99. See also Spiegel, *Other Arab-Israeli Conflict*, p. 388 and passim.

122. Aid to Israel was $127 million in 1966, $632 million in 1971, and over $2 billion in 1974 and 1976. By the 1980s, aid to Israel was running approximately $3 billion per year. See AID, *U.S. Overseas Loans and Grants*. As Wolf Blitzer points out: "Before the Yom Kippur War, Israel ranked twenty-fourth among recipients of postwar U.S. foreign aid. . . . By 1979, however, Israel had climbed to number two on the all-time list; only South Vietnam had received more." See Blitzer, *Between Washington and Jerusalem*, p. 99.

123. See Feuerwerger, *Congress and Israel*, pp. 29–40.

124. On these events, see Burns, *Economic Aid and American Policy*, pp. 68, 143–46; Kenen, *Israel's Defense Line*, pp. 170–72, 180–81, 184–85; and Spiegel, *Other Arab-Israeli Conflict*, pp. 303–4, 308–9, 346–49. See also Feuerwerger, *Congress and Israel*, pp. 34–35.

125. The delay was intended to induce Israeli concessions, to show U.S. displeasure over Israel's deep penetration raids against Cairo, and to convince the Soviet Union to

celebrated reassessment of U.S. policy in 1975 was effectively neutralized by an AIPAC-sponsored letter from seventy-six senators urging continued support for Israel. As one senator later admitted: "The pressure was just too great. I caved." Another explained his signature by saying. "It's easier to sign one letter than to answer five thousand."[126]

All things considered, Israel's supporters within the United States have been a major constraint on the freedom of action of U.S. policymakers and an important link between the United States and Israel. This constraint is most evident in the case of Congress—whose members are well aware of the political costs of inadequate support for Israel—but it is also a political factor in the calculations of the executive branch.[127]

Of course, pro-Israeli forces are not all-powerful. As already noted, Eisenhower defied domestic pressures on several occasions, and Kennedy sought a rapprochement with Nasser despite domestic opposition. Johnson's support for Israel in the crisis preceding the Six Day War was lukewarm at best, and Nixon, Ford, and Carter all made policy decisions that clashed with the stated preferences of Israel and its supporters in the United States.[128] Pro-Israeli forces have failed in their efforts to obtain a formal alliance between the United States and Israel, were unable to prevent the 1978 sale of F–15 aircraft to Saudi Arabia, and failed to overturn the 1981 decision to supply Saudi Arabia with AWACS early-warning aircraft and a significant enhancement package for the F–15s. They have also been unable to prevent—at least until recently—military aid and training for Jordan. Although Israel's domestic backers

---

moderate its own support for Egypt at this time. The delay may have moderated Israeli conduct in the War of Attrition but did not bring other positive results. See Spiegel, *Other Arab-Israeli Conflict*, pp. 190–92; and Pollock, *Politics of Pressure*, pp. 67–72.

126. The two senators were John Culver of Iowa and Daniel Inouye of Hawaii, quoted in Tillman, *The United States in the Middle East*, pp. 66–67. See also Ben-Zvi, *Alliance Politics*, pp. 17–20.

127. As William B. Quandt has noted: "Domestic factors do seem to enter into consideration by defining boundaries beyond which it seems imprudent to step. This restriction of the scope of possible initiatives has been the most visible effect of domestic factors over the past few years and generally seems more important than the influence of domestic factors in bringing acceptance of favored policies." See his "Domestic Influence on United States Foreign Policy in the Middle East: The View from Washington," in *The Middle East: Quest for an American Policy*, ed. Willard A. Beling (Albany, N.Y., 1973), pp. 274–75. See also Spiegel, *Other Arab-Israeli Conflict*, pp. 389–90; Nadav Safran, *The United States and Israel* (Cambridge, Mass., 1963), pp. 276–79; and Mathias, "Ethnic Groups and Foreign Policy," pp. 992–93; and Blitzer, *Between Washington and Jerusalem*, chaps. 5–7.

128. For Nixon, the Rogers Plan in 1969, the canal ceasefire in 1970, and the attempt to negotiate a limited settlement along the canal all provoked significant disputes with Israel. Kissinger's step-by-step diplomacy led to several overt quarrels and ultimately produced a brief but intense rift in 1975. Jimmy Carter endured the greatest trials of all, as a result of his efforts (1) to convene a comprehensive peace conference, (2) to bring the Palestinian question to the forefront of the peace process, (3) to sell advanced military equipment to Saudi Arabia, and (4) to serve as "honest broker" in the Camp David negotiations.

play a key role in preserving the special relationship between the United States and Israel and in restricting presidential options in related areas, they fall well short of controlling U.S. Middle East policy.

Nor are they alone. Pro-Arab forces (e.g., Arab-American political groups, corporations with extensive Arab interests, and professional lobbyists) have all sought to influence U.S. policy in the Middle East. Until the 1970s, however, their activities and impact were marginal at best.

Since then, however, Arab efforts to penetrate the U.S. political system have become both more extensive and marginally more successful. Corporations and Arab governments (especially Saudi Arabia) have sought to promote a more favorable public image through several avenues, and professional lobbying efforts have become increasingly more common.[129] These efforts have failed to reduce U.S. support for Israel (either in terms of overall aid or in terms of public opinion), but they have helped persuade Congress to provide increasingly sophisticated military equipment to Arab countries such as Saudi Arabia.[130] It is worth noting, however, that Jordan has also enjoyed U.S. support since the 1950s, despite the fact that it lacks economic clout and significant corporate backing. Thus it would be unwise to attribute too much to the efforts of pro-Arab groups.

To summarize: both pro-Israeli and pro-Arab forces have succeeded in manipulating U.S. Middle East policy on occasion, although pro-Israeli forces have been far more influential. The question becomes: What does the greater impact of pro-Israeli forces—itself an important independent cause of the U.S. commitment to the Jewish state—tell us about the role of transnational penetration in alliance formation?

First, pro-Israeli forces are influential because they possess the essential attributes of a politically potent interest group. Compared with other interest groups in the United States (and especially with Arab-American groups), U.S. Jews are relatively prosperous, well-educated, politically active, and united in their support for a U.S. commitment to Israel.[131] According to Hyman Bookbinder, chairman of the American Jewish Committee, "the essence of the Jewish lobby is an organized, committed, concerned Jewish community in America." He adds: "There is a

129. These efforts include support for academic research, subsidizing of publications, formal lobbying, mass media participation, and so on and are described in Emerson, *American House of Saud;* Kenen, *Israel's Defense Line;* and Congressional Quarterly, *Middle East.*

130. In particular, Senate approval for the sale of sixty F–15s in 1978 and five AWACS in 1981 was the result of extensive lobbying by the incumbent administration and a variety of pro-Arab forces and professional lobbyists within the United States.

131. See Isaacs, *Jews and American Politics,* especially chaps. 1 and 13; and Feuerwerger, *Congress and Israel,* chap. 3, especially pp. 82–86, 90–95.

feeling of guilt as to whether Jews should double-check the Israeli government. . . . [T]hey automatically fall into line for that reason."[132] As a result, the cohesion of U.S. Jews on this issue enhances their political impact significantly.

Pro-Arab forces lack this advantage. There is one Israel, but there are many Arab states. Because the Arab states often differ considerably, identifying a coherent pro-Arab policy would itself be difficult. Moreover, Arab-Americans come from a number of separate Arab states, and many do not have a strong affinity for their native countries.[133] Corporate interest groups (such as oil companies and arms contractors) often oppose particular Arab states if these regimes are at odds with important clients.[134] As a result, pro-Arab forces are neither as willing nor as able to present a united front in the struggle for influence over U.S. Middle East policy.

Second, pro-Israeli groups are effective because their activities are seen as consistent with the interest group traditions of the U.S. political system.[135] According to Morris Amitay, former executive director of AIPAC: "What is important . . . is that none of this is untoward. . . . [Y]ou use the traditional tactics of the democracy: . . . letters, calls."[136] By contrast, pro-Arab forces—especially professional lobbyists and public relations organizations financed by Arab oil money—are weakened by their lack of an indigenous domestic base and by the resulting perception that they are mere agents of a foreign power.[137] Although Jewish leaders such as Hyman Bookbinder have admitted that "we don't go around saying Israel is wrong about its policies," that "unless something is terribly pressing, . . . you parrot Israel's line," the fact that groups such as AIPAC can claim to represent a large indigenous population insulates them from the charges that their actions are illegitimate.[138]

132. Quoted in Congressional Quarterly, *Middle East*, p. 64; and Blitzer, *Between Washington and Jerusalem*, pp. 147–48.

133. See Congressional Quarterly, *Middle East*, pp. 66–67; and Ben Bradlee, Jr., "Lobbying for Israel," *Arizona Republic*, May 27, 1984.

134. For example, U.S. oil companies did not support Kennedy's rapprochement with Nasser, because Egypt was an enemy of Saudi Arabia. See Spiegel, *Other Arab-Israeli Conflict*, pp. 95, 120.

135. See Mathias, "Ethnic Groups and Foreign Policy," pp. 975–77.

136. Amitay described the role of Israel's supporters on Capitol Hill as follows: "There are now a lot of guys at the working level up here . . . who happen to be Jewish, who are willing . . . to look certain issues in terms of their Jewishness. . . . These are all guys who are in a position to make the decision in these areas for these senators. . . .[I]f they're willing to become involved, you can get an awful lot done just at the staff level." Quoted in Isaacs, *Jews and American Politics*, pp. 255–57. In short, as Amitay has said, "The name of the game, if you want to help Israel, is political action." Quoted in Blitzer, *Between Washington and Jerusalem*, p. 122.

137. Predictably, this accusation is a favorite of pro-Israeli groups. For examples, see Congressional Quarterly, *Middle East*, p. 68.

138. Quoted in Blitzer, *Between Washington and Jerusalem*, pp. 147–48.

Third, pro-Israeli forces have objectives that are limited and relatively easy to justify. As one senator put it, "They have a pretty good product to sell."[139] Pro-Israeli groups have focused their attention on a small number of key issues directly related to Israel, but they do not seek to manipulate U.S. policy in other areas. Moreover, they have worked hard to reinforce the belief that support for Israel—consistently described as the "only stable democracy in the Middle East"—is, in the overall interest of the United States, which protects them from accusations of dual loyalty and justifies continued U.S. support.[140] As Morris Amitay put it, "Unless you can always translate this in terms of what's in America's interest, you're lost." Moreover, because Israel's principal enemies have been Soviet clients, making the case for a U.S. commitment has been relatively easy.[141]

In the same way, pro-Arab forces have enjoyed greater success when their recommendations were perceived as consistent with U.S. interests. Thus their success in winning congressional approval for the sale of advanced military equipment to Saudi Arabia was greatly facilitated by the obvious U.S. interest in the oil-rich kingdom and by the claim that this approval would encourage Saudi support for the Camp David agreements. Because the objective was limited (i.e., the F–15 and AWACS sales did not require abandoning U.S. commitments elsewhere in the region) and because support for oil-exporting anti-Communist governments is relatively easy to justify, pro-Arab groups were more successful in this case. Aid to Jordan is justified on similar grounds.

Finally, when foreign countries overstep the bounds of legitimate political activity, even a relatively open political system such as that of the United States is likely to generate at least a modest backlash. Thus Israeli ambassador Yitzhak Rabin was widely criticized for endorsing Richard Nixon's reelection bid in 1972, Menachem Begin's heavy-handed pressure on both Carter and Reagan generated considerable domestic opposition, and the exposure of an Israeli plot to acquire U.S. military secrets in 1985 led to significant recriminations in both countries.[142] Although these events have not jeopardized the basic ties between the

139. Senator Warren Rudman, quoted in Bradlee, "Lobbying for Israel."
140. According to Bookbinder, U.S. Jews "react viscerally to even the remotest suggestion that there's something 'unpatriotic' about their support for Israel." Quoted in Congressional Quarterly, *Middle East*, p. 68.
141. As Marvin C. Feuerwerger puts it: "Pro-Israeli groups ask relatively little of the member [of Congress], only that he reassert his commitment to a position with which he generally agrees." See Feuerwerger, *Congress and Israel*, pp. 95–96. This tendency does not mean that the current level of U.S. support is in fact in the U.S. interest; it means only that the association of Israel with democracy and opposition to Soviet expansion invokes themes that generate reliable support within the U.S. political system.
142. For details on these events, see Rabin, *Memoirs*, pp. 232–33; Spiegel, *Other Arab-Israeli Conflict*, pp. 409–10; and *New York Times*, November 28, 1985, p. B8.

United States and Israel, they illustrate that penetration remains effective only when it is limited in scope and confined to legitimate political channels. Put another way, penetration can create effective alliances when it reinforces existing motives for alignment and does not threaten the political system itself. When interests conflict, efforts to manipulate domestic political forces are more likely to appear subversive and dangerous. As a result, they run the risk of causing more harm than good.

These factors reinforce each other. Because the U.S. political system provides numerous points of access, foreign groups or their sympathizers can adopt very limited objectives and confine their aims to a small number of issues. In other words, it is not necessary to threaten the regime in order to influence decisions. Similarly, when national interests are viewed as compatible, less domestic pressure is needed and the pressure that is exerted will seem less intrusive.

Thus the outcome of what Steven Spiegel has called the "other Arab-Israeli conflict" (i.e., the struggle for influence in Washington) provides modest support for the hypotheses about the impact of penetration on alliance formation. Democracies are more vulnerable to penetration. Penetration is more effective when foreign powers seek to influence policy through a cohesive domestic constituency, thus appearing more legitimate. Finally, penetration works best when its practitioners adopt limited aims, but it can create serious problems if they become too greedy. Although the evidence is not definitive, it suggests that the hypotheses outlined in chapter 2 should be provisionally accepted, pending further study.

Summary

The cases examined in this chapter reveal that the importance of transnational penetration is often exaggerated and that its effect on alliance formation is usually misunderstood. The opportunity to establish informal avenues of influence with another state usually requires cordial or even close relations, which indicates that such ties are largely one result of alignment, not an independent cause. Even more important, these cases suggest that penetration is usually counterproductive when a state tries to alter the target's preferred alignment in an especially significant way. Thus in the cases where penetration might produce the greatest overall effect, the likelihood of a hostile backlash is most likely. By contrast, penetration is most effective when alignment is likely for other reasons, which means that these indirect pressures are somewhat superfluous. In short, penetration is not an especially common or powerful cause of alignment. It may reinforce commitments that are made for other reasons, but it rarely leads to such commitments in the absence of other motives.

This chapter has examined the effects of two popular instruments of alliance formation. The evidence confirms that focusing on foreign aid or penetration alone usually does not explain much about how states choose their allies. Although large assistance programs and extensive transnational contacts may be characteristic symptoms of alignment, they are rarely reliable tools of influence. Aid and penetration can enhance alliances between states with similar interests, but neither is an especially effective instrument by itself.

For these reasons, it is unwise to conclude that either foreign aid or extensive transnational contacts will make client states obedient or reliable allies. These ties reflect the coincidence of interests that have always brought allies together, but client states retain considerable capacity for independent action. And as the prevailing array of threats, opportunities, and affinities changes, past assistance and personal relationships exert a weak grip on recipients.

This argument does not mean that the various policy instruments available to a great power are useless. Economic and military aid, educational assistance, and the like can serve a variety of national security objectives. Indeed, it is the impressive capabilities of superpowers that make it less important for them to obtain obedience from their clients on most issues. The lesson of this chapter is that the lasting effects of these instruments will usually be slight. When other incentives for alignment exist (incentives already examined in chapters 5 and 6), these instruments can help alliance members achieve their various aims efficiently and smoothly. But when interests diverge, neither is likely to overcome the durable constraints that states in an anarchic system inevitably face.

[8]

Conclusion: Alliance Formation and the Balance of World Power

I began this book by arguing that the forces that shape international alliances are among the most important in international politics. In particular, I suggested that many debates over foreign policy and grand strategy are based primarily on conflicting beliefs about the origins of international alliances. These beliefs have been especially important in postwar U.S. foreign policy, but the United States is hardly unique in this regard.[1] By examining existing theory, European diplomatic history, and the contemporary debate on U.S. foreign policy, I identified several popular hypotheses that are often used to explain how states choose their friends. After surveying changing alliance commitments in the Middle East—a region that seemed especially appropriate for testing these different hypotheses—I compared the evolution of Middle East alliances with the predictions offered by each one. Balance of threat and ideological explanations each contributed useful insights; the other hypotheses fared less well.

Three tasks remain. The first is to summarize the analysis in chapters 5 through 7 and compare the explanatory power of these competing hypotheses directly. The second is to extend the analysis beyond the Middle East. Because my aim has been to evaluate a set of propositions applicable to the broader realm of international politics, it is important that I consider whether these propositions can account for other patterns of alliance formation. To show that they can, I will use the ideas developed here to explain the current array of superpower commitments, what one might call the fundamental division of world power. Finally, because alliance theory continues to play a crucial (if largely unrecognized) role in contemporary debates on grand strategy, the third

1. On the role of hidden assumptions about alliances in postwar U.S. grand strategy, see Larson, "The Bandwagon Metaphor."

task is to outline the lessons that policy-makers in the United States should draw from these results.

ANALYZING ALLIANCE FORMATION: AN ASSESSMENT

Balancing and Bandwagoning

Compared with the other hypotheses examined in this book, the general hypothesis that states choose allies in order to balance against the most serious threat was the clear winner. Its merits were shown in two important ways. First, balancing was far more common than bandwagoning, and bandwagoning was almost always confined to especially weak and isolated states. Second, the importance of ideological distinctions declined as the level of threat increased; ideological solidarity was most powerful when security was high or when ideological factors and security considerations reinforced each other.[2]

Balance of Power versus Balance of Threat

The evidence presented in this book demonstrates the value of balance of threat theory, which should be viewed as a refinement of traditional balance of power theory. As discussed in detail in chapter 5, states balance against the states that pose the greatest threat, and the latter need not be the most powerful states in the system. Just as national power is produced by several different components (e.g., military and economic capability, natural resources, and population), the level of threat that a state poses to others is the product of several interrelated components. Whereas balance of power theory predicts that states will react to imbalances of power, balance of threat theory predicts that when there is an imbalance of threat (i.e., when one state or coalition appears especially dangerous), states will form alliances or increase their internal efforts in order to reduce their vulnerability.

The distinction is subtle but important. Balance of threat theory improves on balance of power theory by providing greater explanatory power with equal parsimony.[3] By using balance of threat theory, we can

2. Saudi Arabia, Syria, and Egypt joined forces after 1967; Jordan and Israel(!) collaborated to thwart Syrian intervention in 1970; and Syria and Jordan staged a dramatic rapprochement after Sinai II. One could recite examples ad infinitum, but the point should be clear: the need to balance an external threat was usually more important than the desire to support states espousing similar ideologies.

3. Balance of threat theory may appear to be less parsimonious than traditional balance of power theory, because threats are the product of several different components, including the distribution of aggregate power. In fact, the two theories are equally parsimonious; balance of threat theory, however, is more general and abstract. Whenever one moves to a more general or abstract level of analysis, one inevitably includes more variables. More general theories by definition incorporate a broader range of phenomena. But a more

understand a number of events that we cannot explain by focusing solely on the distribution of aggregate capabilities. For example, balance of threat theory explains why the coalitions that defeated Germany and its allies in World War I and World War II grew to be far more powerful than their opponents, in contrast to the predictions of balance of power theory. The answer is simple: Germany and its allies combined power, proximity, offensive capabilities, and extremely aggressive intentions. As a result, they were more threatening (though weaker) and caused others to form a more powerful coalition in response.[4] In the same way, balance of threat theory helps explain why states in the Middle East form alliances primarily to deal with threats from their neighbors, not in response to shifts in the global balance of power. They do so because their neighbors are usually more dangerous than either superpower, partly because of geographic proximity. Similarly, Nasser's turbulent relations with the other Arabs are explained as much by shifts in Egyptian intentions as by changes in Egypt's relative power. The same is true for Syria; its isolation during much of the 1960s was based in part on the extremism of the Ba'th, not on Syria's rather modest capabilities during this period.

Finally, balance of threat theory can also explain alliance choices when a state's potential allies are roughly equal in power. In such a circumstance, a state will ally with the side it believes is least dangerous. Thus balance of threat theory can also predict how states will choose between the United States and the Soviet Union, something that balance of power theory cannot do.[5]

In short, as shown in Figure 1, balance of threat theory subsumes balance of power theory. Aggregate power is an important component of threat, but not the only one. By conceiving of alliances as responses to imbalances of threat (not just imbalances of power), we gain a more complete and accurate picture of behavior in the international political realm.

---

general theory is not less parsimonious, as long as the principal ideas that organize its relevant variables are as few in number as the principal ideas of the less general theory it replaces. The principal concept that informs balance of power theory is power, which consists of components such as military and economic capability and population. The principal concept that informs balance of threat theory is threat, which consists of aggregate power, proximity, offensive capability, and perceived intentions. Balance of threat theory is a more general explanation of state conduct but not a more complicated one.

4. Moreover, the alliances against Germany remained united until Germany was totally defeated, largely because of the widespread recognition of German bellicosity. Thus the two most important alliances in the twentieth century are inconsistent with balance of power theory but are readily explained by balance of threat theory.

5. As Glenn Snyder has written: "It might be argued that the alignment . . . [of lesser powers in a bipolar world] is not affected by the logic of system structure [i.e., the distribution of power] at all. If left to their own devices, they will align with the superpower that appears least threatening to their own security or that is most congenial ideologically." See Snyder and Diesing, *Conflict among Nations*, p. 421.

Conclusion

BALANCE OF POWER THEORY

Imbalances of power ———————— cause ————————▶ alliances against the strongest state

An imbalance of power occurs when the strongest state or coalition in the system possesses significantly greater power than the second strongest. Power is the product of several different components, including population, economic and military capability, technological skill, and political cohesion.

BALANCE OF THREAT THEORY

Imbalances of threat ———————— cause ————————▶ alliances against the most threatening state

An imbalance of threat occurs when the most threatening state or coalition is significantly more dangerous than the second most threatening state or coalition. The degree to which a state threatens others is the product of its aggregate power, its geographic proximity, its offensive capability, and the aggressiveness of its intentions.

Figure 1. Balance of power versus Balance of threat theory

Focusing on threats rather than power alone also helps account for several apparent anomalies in the evidence. The first is the unwillingness of Arab states to ally with Israel, even when such an alliance would have been an obvious military asset. This failure is readily understood when we recall that such an alliance would have posed a potentially lethal threat to the legitimacy of the Arab states involved because of the importance attached to Arab solidarity.[6]

An even more intriguing anomaly is the difficulty the Arab states have faced when seeking to form alliances together to balance against Israel.[7] Although Israel has grown steadily larger and stronger since 1948, its neighbors have been surprisingly incapable of joining forces effectively in response. Israel's Arab opponents have balanced by allying with either the United States or the Soviet Union, but not with one another. With the exception of the alliances during the October War in 1973, Arab alliances against Israel were largely symbolic, in contrast to what the balancing hypothesis would predict.[8]

This anomaly can be explained in two different ways. First, it illustrates the natural tendency for states to pass the buck, in the hope that

---

6. The exception is Jordan, which relied on implicit Israeli military guarantees during its brief war against the PLO and Syria in 1970.

7. The most obvious example is Nasser's inability to obtain significant support from the Eastern Command during the War of Attrition.

8. As described in chapter 3, the Arab coalition in the Six Day War was as much a product of inter-Arab rivalries as it was a response to a perceived threat to the Arabs from Israel.

other similarly situated states will accept the "honor" of opposing the common enemy.[9] This tendency was apparent during the War of Attrition. Why should Syria, Iraq, and Jordan risk war with Israel when Egypt was willing to do their fighting for them? The tendency was even stronger before 1967, because none of the states had a strong material interest in challenging Israel.

This type of behavior is especially pronounced in multipolar, regional subsystems embedded within a bipolar global system. In this circumstance, the regional states need not cooperate with one another because they can rely upon superpower support instead. Thus balancing behavior predominates, but regional powers prefer the support of a distant superpower to cooperation with another regional actor. The reason is obvious: the superpowers can do more to help, and helping a neighbor may be dangerous if it becomes too strong as a result. This situation is due, of course, to geographic proximity. Thus the Arabs balanced by seeking Soviet or U.S. support rather than by aiding one another.

A second reason the Arab states often failed to balance effectively against Israel is the fact that they posed greater threats to one another than Israel did. As shown in chapter 6, the ideology of pan-Arabism contributed to this problem, by making each Arab state an enemy of Israel and a potential threat to all the other Arab states. Nasser's ambitions and charisma simply made it worse. And as noted, alignment with a superpower was just as effective and far less dangerous than helping an Arab rival challenge Israel successfully. Thus, until the Six Day War made Israel a real enemy (instead of a largely symbolic one), effective balancing behavior among Arab states was confined primarily to thwarting the ambitions of Arab rivals.

In short, these anomalies are readily explained in light of the theory. All things considered, balance of threat theory is strongly endorsed by the evidence examined here. As we will see, evidence from a global perspective is equally compelling.

Ideological Solidarity

This study also showed that ideological solidarity is less important than external threats as a cause of alliances. The states examined here did show a slight preference for alignment with other similar states, but the preference was readily abandoned in the face of significant threats or discredited by the rivalries that emerged between ideologically kindred regimes.

This hypothesis was most useful in explaining alliance decisions when

9. On the concept of buck-passing, see Posen, *Sources of Military Doctrine*, pp. 63, 232.

the prevailing array of threats was either modest or indeterminate. Thus ideology was a more important factor in explaining superpower commitments largely because the two superpowers are roughly equal in terms of their other characteristics. Ideological considerations become crucial by default.

Another important conclusion was that many apparently ideological alliances were a particular form of balancing behavior. Thus balance of threat theory also subsumes the hypotheses about ideological solidarity. For the fragile regimes of the Arab world, a challenge to the ruler's legitimacy could easily be a more potent threat than any enemy army. The various pacts among Jordan, Saudi Arabia, and monarchical Iraq, for example, were alliances among similar regimes, intended to counter the threat from the aggressive revolutionary nationalism espoused by leaders such as Nasser. The failed attempts to unite the Ba'th regimes of Syria and Iraq (and thus isolate Egypt) sprang from essentially the same desire (i.e., to balance an ideological threat).

In the same way, the apparently strong effect of ideology on alliances between the superpowers and the regional states may in part reflect balancing behavior as well, in the form of a self-fulfilling prophecy. Because both superpowers have behaved as if ideology were important, they have reinforced any innate tendency for regional powers to favor one superpower over the other for ideological reasons. We should be cautious, therefore, in interpreting the tendency for superpower-client relations to exhibit ideological solidarity; the role of ideology alone in such alliances is probably less than it would appear.

Finally, the impact of ideological factors was most evident in the case of pan-Arabism, but its effects were almost entirely negative. As long as the goal of Arab unity was a touchstone of Arab legitimacy, each Arab regime posed a potential threat to all the others. But the more fiercely any single state sought the objective professed by all, the more likely it was to experience conflicts with the rest. As noted earlier, the divisive character of pan-Arab ideology was one important reason the Arab world did not balance effectively against Israel. Among other things, this example shows that ideological factors can in some circumstances override other incentives for alignment. To repeat, however, this ideology tended to discourage alignment rather than promote it.

The history of inter-Arab relations reveals a final paradox, one with several important implications. The greater the devotion to Arab solidarity, the greater the conviction that Israel is a foreign invader that all Arab states should oppose. At the same time, however, this belief makes it more difficult to pursue that goal effectively. Paradoxically, therefore, as pan-Arab sentiment declines (and is replaced by a more limited, state-centered nationalism) the need to fight for the "sacred" cause of the Palestinian Arabs declines, but the ideological barriers to coordinated action are reduced. Inter-Arab cooperation becomes easier as it becomes less important, and vice versa.

This paradox has obvious implications for Israeli security, which is threatened by Arab military cooperation. The analysis suggests that the likelihood of a grand Arab coalition is slight, unless it is based on tangible objectives such as recovering the occupied territories. An ideological alliance against the Jewish state will be either extremely unstable (because each member fears its partners) or extremely unlikely (because the power of pan-Arab ideology has evaporated). Among other things, this situation means that territorial concessions are very much in Israel's interest, because they remove the most significant incentives for the formation of an effective Arab alliance. Returning the Sinai to Egypt was an obvious example of this approach, and one that greatly enhanced Israel's security.

Foreign Aid and Penetration

Neither foreign aid nor penetration has proven to be of much use as an explanation of alliance formation. Both hypotheses ignore the prior motives that encourage the provision of foreign assistance or the establishment of extensive elite contacts—and both can be subsumed within the more general hypotheses already considered. Foreign aid is merely one form of balancing behavior, and the establishment of extensive contacts between separate national elites is often an indicator of a close alignment.

Even more important, the modest independent impact of aid and penetration is revealed by the fact that even extremely vulnerable and dependent clients have retained considerable freedom of action. Efforts to use foreign aid to control an ally usually have led to considerable resentment, and attempts to manipulate an ally's foreign or domestic policies through covert penetration usually have backfired badly. In short, both of these instruments have been found to be a predictable result of political alignment, but neither has been a very powerful cause.

The principal exception to both these conclusions is the U.S. relationship with Israel. By manipulating its level of foreign assistance, the United States has been able to extract significant concessions from Israel on a number of occasions. Although U.S. leverage is not absolute, the lack of ready alternatives to U.S. support has made Israel especially vulnerable to this type of pressure.

At the same time, however, the success of pro-Israeli forces in penetrating the U.S. political system in recent years has greatly reduced the impact of Israel's substantial overall dependence. Their success in this

[268]

regard is an obvious exception to the conclusion that penetration is not an effective instrument of alliance diplomacy. However, this success is the result of a unique array of circumstances. The extreme openness of the U.S. political system, the unusual cohesion of U.S. Jewry as a political interest group, and the limited goals that pro-Israeli forces seek have all contributed to the considerable political impact of pro-Israeli forces in the United States.

As a result, although this exception has a significant impact on U.S. foreign policy in the Middle East, its theoretical importance is limited. In most cases, penetration remains at most a minor cause of alliance formation. What this case does suggest is that the usual U.S. concerns about foreign penetration are often misplaced. This study suggests that Soviet penetration of the relatively impermeable regimes of the Third World is not a significant danger, because such efforts almost always fail when other incentives for alignment are lacking. A greater problem may well be the manipulation of U.S. foreign policy by elites whose interests may not always be identical with those of the nation as a whole.[10]

A Regional Update

The conclusions reported here were derived from an analysis of alliances in the Middle East between 1955 and 1979. Before the analysis is extended to the current array of global alliance commitments, it is worth noting that more recent events in the Middle East tend to confirm these results.

The dominant tendency of states to balance has continued. The United States began the 1980s seeking to balance what it perceived as a growing Soviet threat to the Middle East and to counter the effects of the revolution in Iran.[11] Two related steps were implemented. First, U.S. military capabilities in the region were enhanced by the creation of a Rapid Deployment Joint Task Force to deter or defeat a Soviet attack. Second, the United States sought to forge an anti-Soviet strategic consensus among its existing allies. Like every previous attempt (e.g., the Baghdad Pact, the Eisenhower Doctrine, and Soviet sponsorship of a coalition of anti-imperialist, progressive forces during the 1960s), the

10. As noted elsewhere in this book, how one evaluates the impact of pro-Israeli forces (or other ethnic lobbies, for that matter) will be governed by whether or not one feels that the allegiances such groups advocate are harmful or beneficial to the overall national interest. Resolving that question—if it is possible at all—is obviously beyond the scope of this book.

11. Thus President Reagan announced in October 1981 that the United States would not allow Saudi Arabia "to be an Iran," implying that the United States would defend the kingdom against either external attack or internal revolt. See *New York Times*, October 2, 1981.

latter effort illustrated the tendency for the superpowers to view regional problems primarily in terms of their own bipolar rivalry. And like these earlier campaigns, the effort failed because the regional powers were more worried about one another than about the superpowers.[12] As always, the regional powers sought "to use the faraway foreigner as a counterweight to the foreigner nearby."[13] In other words, proximate threats remained more important than the global balance of power.

Balancing behavior has also been evident within the region itself. The divisions between the Saudi-Jordanian-Iraqi grouping (which Egypt supported tacitly) and the radical coalition of Syria, Libya, the PDRY, and (increasingly) Iran have deepened as the Iran-Iraq war has dragged on. Each group has provided increasing levels of assistance to the warring parties, whereas the superpowers have taken neutral positions in public and have given modest support to both sides in private.[14] Furthermore, Saudi Arabia took the lead in establishing a Gulf Cooperation Council among the relatively weak states of the Persian Gulf. The council was designed as a vehicle for enhanced economic and security cooperation, intended to limit potential pressure from both Iran and the Soviet Union.[15]

As always, inter-Arab rivalries have prevented effective balancing behavior against Israel. Israel's bombing of Iraq's nuclear research facility in June 1981 brought widespread verbal condemnation but nothing else, and the limp Arab response to the Israeli invasion of Lebanon in June 1982—an action intended to destroy the PLO and establish a Christian government favorable to Israel—revealed the continued decline of Arab solidarity. Although the invasion failed to destroy the PLO, it did deliver a sharp blow to Syrian military power and eventually led to the PLO's withdrawal from Lebanon under the cover of a U.S.-sponsored ceasefire. The lack of Arab solidarity is not surprising; Assad's Arab neigh-

12. Israel objected strongly to U.S. arms sales to Jordan and Saudi Arabia, whereas these allies preferred to keep their U.S. connections quiet so as not to appear too closely tied to Israel's principal supporter. For discussions of the strategic consensus, see Spiegel, *Other Arab-Israeli Conflict*, pp. 400–401; Barry Rubin, "The Reagan Administration and the Middle East," in *Eagle Defiant: United States Foreign Policy in the 1980s*, ed. Kenneth A. Oye, Robert J. Lieber, and Donald Rothchild (Boston, 1983); and John C. Campbell, "The Middle East: A House of Containment Built on Shifting Sands," *Foreign Affairs*, 60, no. 3 (1981): 596–97, 612.

13. See Dankwart A. Rustow, "Realignments in the Middle East," *Foreign Affairs*, 63, no. 3 (1984): 588 and passim.

14. Egypt and Jordan reportedly sent volunteers to fight with the Iraqi forces, Saudi Arabia provided large amounts of financial assistance, and Egypt sent quantities of Soviet-made military equipment. Syria sent unspecified amounts of military equipment to Iran, and Damascus and Teheran apparently coordinated their support of certain radical factions in Lebanon.

15. On the Gulf Cooperation Council, see Ispahani, "Alone Together."

bors undoubtedly welcomed Syria's defeat, which temporarily reduced the threat that Syria posed to them.

As usual, however, the balance was soon restored. Although Moscow maintained an unheroic detachment during the fighting in Lebanon, the Soviets moved quickly to replace Syria's military losses. They also provided a more sophisticated air defense network.[16] With the PLO gone from Lebanon, Syria aligned with the Lebanese factions that had suffered most from Israel's collusion with the Christian forces. This policy proved quite effective: (1) The government of Amin Gemayel was unable to command popular support or maintain the loyalty of the Lebanese army. (2) The U.S. marines originally deployed to supervise the ceasefire abandoned their neutral role and began to support the government against the Moslem militias backed by Syria. (3) The marine headquarters were destroyed by a Syrian-sponsored terrorist attack in October 1983. (4) The United States withdrew the marines from Lebanon in February 1984. (5) Israel began a painful retreat in the face of continued resistance in Lebanon and a ravaged economy at home.[17]

Thus the final outcome in Lebanon "left Syria as the potentially hegemonic power over Lebanon. Syria, in effect, replaced Israel as the most immediate threat to the region's fragile balance." In response, the moderate Arabs began to welcome Egypt back into the Arab fold and resumed their cautious efforts to promote a peace settlement that would reduce Syria's stature as the leading confrontation state.[18] As of this writing, however, no breakthrough has been reached.[19]

In short, balancing behavior has remained the characteristic response to emerging threats, despite the obvious difficulty of choosing allies when multiple dangers are present. Dankwart Rustow puts it well (in terms that are completely consistent with the main arguments in this book): "While many Middle Eastern countries individually nurse expansionist or hegemonic ambitions, all of them collectively, by their prefer-

16. See Neumann, "Assad and the Future of the Middle East," p. 242.

17. This paragraph obviously does not do justice to the events in Lebanon. For excellent accounts of the Lebanon war and its aftermath, see Ehud Ya'ari and Ze'ev Schiff, *Israel's Lebanon War* (New York, 1984); Rabinovich, *War for Lebanon;* and Randal, *Going All the Way.*

18. See Rustow, "Realignments in the Middle East," p. 588.

19. Aware that the growth of Israeli settlements on the West Bank could soon become irreversible (if they are not already), Jordan, the PLO, and Israel engaged in a variety of formal and informal discussions in 1985. Despite several attempts, Hussein and Arafat failed to reach agreement on a common negotiating position for talks with Israel, and Hussein and Israeli prime minister Shimon Peres apparently failed to find an acceptable formula for Palestinian participation without Arafat. With little support from elsewhere in the Arab world (Syria is staunchly opposed and the Saudis will not shoulder the burden of leadership on an issue that does not concern them directly), Hussein's inability to move on his own has been sustained.

ence for the weaker side and their readiness to shift alignments regardless of ideology, offer strong support for the status quo. . . . [T]he pattern of hostility, interaction, and maneuver thus has its self-balancing features."[20]

As Rustow implies, the role of ideology was even more limited after 1980 than it had been before. The division between the moderate and the radical camp in the Arab world was not and is not an ideological one; these labels describe foreign policy positions rather than domestic political visions.[21] Furthermore, certain ideologies have retained their divisive character, as the continued rivalry between Syria and Iraq reveals. Finally, the superpowers remain willing to overlook ideological matters when necessary; the United States supports regimes as varied as democratic Israel, monarchical Jordan, Saudi Arabia, and Oman, and the military dictatorship in Egypt. The restoration of diplomatic relations with Iraq suggests that U.S. support for a Ba'thist totalitarian state is not out of the question either. On the Soviet side, the widespread campaign against the communist Tudeh Party in Iran has not prevented the Soviet Union from seeking warmer relations with Khomeini's regime. As argued in chapter 6, ideology is not irrelevant, but it is hardly crucial either.

More recent events also reinforce the conclusion that foreign aid brings patrons limited leverage. Israel's enormous dependence on the United States did not stop it from bombing Iraq, annexing the Golan Heights, invading Lebanon and laying siege to Beirut, expanding settlements on the West Bank, and rejecting the so-called Reagan Plan within twenty-four hours, despite the fact that each step was contrary to expressed U.S. preferences. Nor did the United States do much better with its Arab clients. The controversial sale of AWACS aircraft to Saudi Arabia did not lead the Saudis to support the Reagan Plan, they refused to provide military facilities for the RDJTF, and they offered no support for Hussein's efforts to begin peace talks with Israel. Continued U.S. aid to Jordan had equally limited effects, and even Egypt, now receiving over $1 billion in economic and military aid annually, has taken an independent line on several occasions.[22] Foreign aid has made allies stronger but not more obedient.

20. See Rustow, "Realignments in the Middle East," p. 598 and passim.
21. Both Khomeini's Iran and Qadhafi's Libya espouse radical Islamic values (albeit with strong differences), in sharp contrast to the secular approach in Ba'thist Syria or Marxist South Yemen. Jordan and Saudi Arabia are both monarchies, of course, but they have been closely allied with the Ba'thist dictatorship in Iraq.
22. A lengthy negotiation over U.S. plans to expand Egypt's base at Ras Banas for use by the RDF eventually broke down in 1983, when Egypt took an unexpectedly tough position on the terms of the arrangements. In 1985, Egypt's decision to release a group of PLO terrorists who had hijacked the Italian cruise ship *Achille Lauro* and murdered a U.S.

Finally, U.S.-Israeli relations are still affected—but not determined—by transnational penetration. The Reagan administration's ability to pressure Israel was undoubtedly reduced by the well-organized actions of pro-Israeli forces in the United States. Even so, Israel's informal annexation of the Golan Heights in 1981 led to cancellation of an earlier agreement for strategic cooperation, and Israel's U.S. supporters suffered a notable defeat when the Senate approved the AWACS sale to Saudi Arabia in 1981. In addition to showing that pro-Israeli forces were not all-powerful (although the victory did require a major presidential effort), the AWACS sale also showed how exceeding the bounds of legitimate political activity can undermine the effectiveness of penetration. In particular, Israeli prime minister Menachem Begin's attempts to encourage opposition to the sale during a visit to the United States in September 1981 led Reagan to retort angrily that no foreign country would dictate U.S. foreign policy. By helping define the AWACS debate as a vote for Reagan or Begin, the Israeli prime minister in fact undermined opposition to the sale.[23] Penetration remains an important element of U.S.-Israeli relations, but it is hardly a foolproof means of preserving U.S. support on all issues.

This brief summary suggest that the propositions derived from an examination of alliance formation in earlier periods remain valid. The question now becomes: do these same hypotheses account for important and enduring patterns of alliance formation elsewhere? To show that they do, I will now consider the following question: what explains the current balance of power between the Soviet Union and the United States?

Alliance Formation and the Balance of World Power

The propositions developed in this book tell us a great deal about the current balance of world power. I make two claims in particular. First, contrary to the usual pessimism, I believe the present distribution of world power greatly favors the United States and its allies. Second, this favorable *im*balance of power can be explained by the central propositions I have advanced and tested in this book. To support these claims, I offer a rough assessment of the current distribution of capabilities and

---

passenger (and the subsequent U.S. interception of the Egyptian airliner carrying the terrorists to Sicily) caused a serious rift between Cairo and Washington. Once again, even states that are extremely dependent on outside support will follow their own interests at the risk of angering their patrons.

23. See Campbell, "The Middle East," p. 610; and Spiegel, *Other Arab-Israeli Conflict*, pp. 408–11.

then show how this situation is the direct result of the general tendencies identified earlier.

The Fundamental (Im)Balance of World Power

Measuring the effective power of states or coalitions is complicated and difficult. Fortunately, a detailed net assessment is not necessary here. A rough but reliable comparison of the Soviet and U.S. alliance systems can be obtained by considering the following items: population, GNP, size of armed forces, and defense expenditures.[24] Members of the respective alliance networks have been identified either by the existence of a formal security treaty or by the presence of a significant level of security cooperation between the ally and the superpower in question.[25] The Soviet system includes the Warsaw Pact and Moscow's various regional clients; the U.S. alliance network includes NATO, Japan, and the regional powers with substantial security ties to the United States.

The current distribution of capabilities between these two alliances is shown in Table 16. The results are striking. The United States and its allies surpass the Soviet alliance network by a considerable margin in the primary indicators of national power. This statement is true if one looks solely at the core alliances of NATO and the Warsaw Pact, if China and India are included or excluded, and if each superpower's array of allies within the developing world is considered. Significantly, the worst case for the Soviet Union—China tacitly allied with the West and India neutral—is probably the most likely case as well. The Soviet Union faces a gap of more than 3 to 1 in population and GNP, to say nothing of its

24. On the problems of estimating national power, see Knorr, *Power of Nations*, chaps. 3 and 4; Harold Sprout and Margaret Sprout, *Foundations of International Politics* (Princeton, N.J., 1962); Morgenthau, *Politics among Nations*, pt. 3; and Ray S. Cline, *World Power Assessment 1977: A Calculus of Strategic Drift* (Washington, D.C., 1978).

25. In addition to formal treaty relationships, these calculations include states with permanent military training missions from either superpower. States that accept security assistance from both superpowers at the same time are considered neutral and are not included. See the information presented in U.S. Joint Chiefs of Staff, *U.S. Military Posture for FY1987*, overleaf to p. 1; and U.S. Department of Defense, *Soviet Military Power 1986*, pp. 126–27 and passim. Of course, one might argue that many of the states that are included in these calculations are not really allied with either superpower, because the presence of military advisers or the provision of military equipment does not by itself constitute a significant commitment. If so, this problem affects both superpowers. As a result, these figures should not be biased. To minimize any possibility of distortion, however, Table 16 reports results reflecting several different assumptions about each superpower's allies. Moreover, the sources used to identify each superpower's military commitments are more likely to exaggerate Soviet strength than to minimize it. These calculations thus provide a strong test of the proposition that the United States enjoys a considerable advantage.

Table 16. Comparison of capabilities of U.S. and Soviet alliance systems

Coalitions	Population	GNP	Number in armed forces	Defense spending
U.S. + NATO[a] / USSR + WTO[b]	1.95:1	2.93:1	1.06:1	1.14:1
U.S. + NATO + PRC[c] / USSR + WTO	4.61:1	3.08:1	1.77:1	1.25:1
U.S. + NATO + Other[d] / USSR + WTO + Other	2.64:1	3.25:1	1.15:1	1.25:1
U.S. + NATO + Other + PRC / USSR + WTO + Other	4.19:1	3.39:1	1.58:1	1.36:1
U.S. + NATO + Other / USSR + WTO + Other + India	1.25:1	3.04:1	1.03:1	1.23:1

SOURCE: See appendix 2 for the data used to compile this table.
[a]NATO is the North Atlantic Treaty Organization plus Japan.
[b]WTO is the Warsaw Treaty Organization.
[c]PRC is People's Republic of China.
[d]"Other" refers to allies outside of NATO and the WTO.

technological disadvantages.[26] The disparity is smaller in terms of mobilized power (defense spending, size of armed forces), because the Soviets and their allies have sought to compensate for their relative weakness by devoting a larger percentage of their national resources to defense. Despite these efforts, however, the Soviet alliance system still trails that of the United States in these categories as well.

These results highlight the explanatory power of balance of threat theory. If states were concerned solely with balancing power, we would expect to see many of the current allies of the United States align with the Soviet Union instead.[27] This anomaly is even more striking when we recall that the United States was overwhelmingly the world's most powerful country immediately after World War II, yet was able to bring

26. According to the U.S. undersecretary of defense, research and engineering, in 1986 the United States led the Soviet Union in fourteen out of twenty areas of basic technology. The two states were tied in the other six areas (the Soviets led in none). In terms of deployed military systems, U.S. technology was superior in sixteen out of thirty-one, even in nine, and behind in only four. See "The Statement by the Undersecretary of Defense, Research and Engineering to the 99th Congress," in U.S. Department of Defense, *The FY1987 Department of Defense Program for Research and Development* (Washington, D.C., 1986), pp. II–11, II–12.

27. This result contradicts the size principle that William Riker and others have derived from the postulates of *n*-person game theory. Riker predicts that coalitions will be just large enough to win (but no larger) in order to maximize each player's share of the spoils. But as Table 16 shows, the margin of aggregate power amassed by the United States and its allies far exceeds the minimum necessary to oppose the Soviet Union. For Riker's argument, see his *Theory of Political Coalitions*.

most of the other industrial powers into an alliance against the Soviet Union.[28] The explanation of the anomaly lies in the fact that although the United States has been more powerful, the Soviet Union has appeared to be more dangerous.

Explaining the Imbalance

What explains this striking imbalance of power? Why is the Soviet Union at such a disadvantage? Recall the main themes developed in the previous three chapters. First, states tend to balance against threats, and the level of threat is determined by several factors. Second, ideology is usually a less important cause of alignment, and certain ideologies may promote conflict more than they encourage cooperation. Third, attempts to induce alignment through bribery or penetration will face a host of obstacles and are unlikely to succeed in the absence of other incentives for alignment. Taken together, these propositions provide a persuasive explanation of the durable imbalance of power between East and West.

Aggregate Power

In a bipolar world, competition between the two greatest powers is virtually guaranteed. Thus the current rivalry between the United States and the Soviet Union is itself an example of balancing against power. For the Soviets, this prospect is especially daunting. The rigid logic of bipolarity has locked them in competition with history's wealthiest and most technologically advanced society. Even before we consider the allies that each superpower has attracted, therefore, we see that the Soviet Union begins from a relatively weaker position.

Proximity

As the events examined in earlier chapters showed, states are more sensitive to threats that are nearby than to dangers from far away. This tendency contributes directly to Soviet isolation. Because the Soviet Union is the largest and most powerful country on the Eurasian landmass, it poses a significant threat to the numerous countries that lie on or near its borders. Soviet relations with neighbors tend to be either imperial or hostile; the neighbors are either under de facto Soviet control or aligned with the United States.

The United States, by contrast, has only two countries on its borders. Neither is especially powerful. Because U.S. policy toward both has

---

28. In 1950, the United States produced approximately 40 percent of gross world product; the Soviet Union managed only 13.5 percent. U.S. naval and air power were far superior, and the United States had a clear advantage in deliverable atomic weaponry.

been benevolent in recent decades, both have chosen to ally with the United States.[29] Even more important, the United States is separated by two oceans from the other vital centers of world power. For the middle-level powers of Western Europe and Asia, the United States is the perfect ally. Its aggregate power ensures that its voice will be heard and its actions will be felt, and it is driven by its own concern for Soviet expansion to contribute substantially to its allies' defense. At the same time, the United States is far enough away so as not to pose a significant threat to these allies. Thus the United States is geographically isolated but politically popular, whereas the Soviet Union is politically isolated as a consequence of its geographic proximity to other states.[30] The distribution of aggregate power places the Soviet Union against the United States; geography places the Soviet Union against virtually all the other important and powerful countries in the world. If a Soviet strategic planner could be granted one wish, it should be to move his country somewhere else.[31]

Offensive Power

The Soviet response to this unfavorable situation is both predictable and self-defeating. Faced by an encircling coalition of vastly superior latent resources, the Soviet Union devotes a large share of its national income to amassing military power. The Soviet Union leads the world in total defense expenditures, and it spends a far greater percentage of GNP on defense than the United States and its principal allies spend. This response is itself a form of balancing behavior; the Soviets compensate for their lack of powerful allies through greater internal effort.[32]

29. Significantly, the two most anti-U.S. countries in the Western hemisphere—Cuba and Nicaragua—have both been the targets of considerable U.S. interference in recent decades.

30. This observation stands Halford Mackinder's notion of the heartland on its head. He suggested that Russia gained great advantages from its central position, because "who rules Eastern Europe commands the Heartland, who rules the Heartland commands the World Island: who rules the World Island commands the World." By this logic the outcome of World War II should have established Soviet rather than U.S. hegemony. Mackinder's analysis may be true in a purely military sense, but it neglects the implications of balance of threat theory. In particular, occupation of the heartland greatly increases the number of potential enemies one must face. For Mackinder's analysis, see "The Geographical Pivot of History;" *Geographical Journal*, 23, no. 4 (1904): 421–44. For recent analyses, see Robert E. Harkavy, *Great Power Competition for Overseas Bases: The Geopolitics of Access Diplomacy* (New York, 1982), chap. 6; and Paul M. Kennedy, "Mahan vs. Mackinder: Two Views on Naval Strategy," *Strategy and Diplomacy: Collected Essays* (London, 1983).

31. The aim of the U.S. strategy of containment, of course, is to prevent them from doing just that.

32. Thus Soviet emphasis on military power, which is usually attributed either to the political clout of the Soviet military or to the expansionist aims of the CPSU, may in fact be largely the result of the Soviet Union's unfavorable geopolitical position.

At the same time, the Soviet Union spends its rubles primarily on offensive capabilities. Soviet conventional forces are tailored for offensive warfare, and Soviet military doctrine places great emphasis on preemption and the virtues of the offensive.[33] This emphasis may be due in part to its unfavorable geographic position; like Wilhelmine Germany and contemporary Israel, the Soviet Union may view an offensive capability as desirable if it must fight on several fronts.[34] Whatever the motive, this response merely increases Soviet isolation. Because it also increases the potential threat to others, the Soviet Union's large offensive capability reinforces the cohesion of the alliance that is already arrayed against it.[35]

Aggressive Intentions

The final source of threat—perceived intentions—also works against the Soviet Union. Soviet statements suggest that the nation sees bandwagoning as the normal behavior of states, a view consistent with its emphasis on offensive military forces.[36] The result has been a coun-

33. On the offensive character of Soviet military doctrine, see Phillip A. Peterson and John G. Hines, "The Conventional Offensive in Soviet Theater Strategy," *Orbis*, 27, no. 3 (1983); Stephen M. Meyer, "Soviet Theatre Nuclear Forces, Part 1; Development of Doctrine and Objectives," *Adelphi Paper No. 187* (London, 1984); Benjamin Lambeth, "How to Think about Soviet Military Doctrine," *RAND Paper P-5939* (Santa Monica, Calif., 1978); and Jack L. Snyder, "Civil-Military Relations and the Cult of the Offensive," *International Security*, 9, no. 1 (1984).

34. If encircled states have offensive capabilities, they can try to deal with their enemies sequentially, as Germany's Schlieffen Plan attempted in World War I and as Israel accomplished during the Six Day War. As Germany found out, there are serious problems with this approach, in part because the scale of operations and quality of opposition was far greater than that faced by Israel. On this point, see Richard Ned Lebow, "The Soviet Offensive in Europe: The Schlieffen Plan Revisited?" *International Security*, 9, no. 4 (1985); and Snyder, "Civil-Military Relations." The Soviet preference for an offensive doctrine may also reveal a lack of effective civilian influence, given that most modern militaries prefer offensive doctrines. On this point, see Posen, *Sources of Military Doctrine*, pp. 42–51.

35. Recent examples of balancing behavior by the West are the sustained U.S. defense buildup begun by the Carter administration and accelerated under Reagan; the rapprochement with China in the 1970s; the modernization of Norwegian coastal and air defenses and the pre-positioning of equipment for a U.S. marine battalion in Norway itself; NATO's decision to deploy 572 intermediate-range nuclear missiles to balance Soviet deployment of the SS–20; and the 1976 agreement for an annual 3 percent real increase in alliance defense spending. Allied responses still fall short of U.S. preferences, a phenomenon best explained by the theory of collective goods. See Olson and Zeckhauser, "Economic Theory of Alliances."

36. The Soviet concept of the correlation of forces, for example, is reminiscent of bandwagoning logic. Soviet commentators maintain that as the correlation of forces shifts towards socialism, the result is a progressive acceleration of favorable world trends. The idea that countervailing tendencies might balance a temporary advantage is notably absent. On this point, see William Zimmerman, *Soviet Perspectives on International Relations* (Princeton, N.J., 1969), pp. 159–64 and passim; and Simes, "Soviet Policy towards the United States," pp. 310–11.

terproductive reliance on threats and intimidation, ranging from Stalin's pressure on Turkey, Iran, and Norway to the more recent attempts to browbeat NATO into halting deployment of intermediate-range nuclear missiles. The invasion of Afghanistan and the periodic interventions in Eastern Europe, Soviet support for terrorist organizations, and events such as the downing of a Korean airliner in 1983 also reinforce suspicions about Soviet intentions.

Finally, the Soviet leaders have never abandoned their public commitment to promoting world revolution. Although this policy may increase their popularity with radical groups, it reinforces the already strong tendency for the world's most capable and powerful states to ally against them. To make matters worse, the radical allies of the Soviet Union are neither powerful nor popular, especially with their neighbors. Soviet support for world revolution, in short, may cost the Soviet Union more friends than it gains.

So on virtually every dimension of threat, the Soviet Union ends up the loser. Given the general tendency for states to balance, this situation is good news for the United States. Although the United States has failed to play its hand perfectly, it has retained the friendship of the world's most important countries. By comparison, the Soviet Union has succeeded in drawing into its orbit a set of regimes that combine serious internal problems with widespread regional unpopularity. Given the Soviet Union's geographic position, past Soviet policies, and the tendencies analyzed in this book, that is precisely what one would expect.

Further confirmation can be found by comparing each superpower's experience in the Third World. These different sources of threat have been partly reversed in the developing world, which explains why the Soviet Union has done relatively better there. The Soviet Union's ability to project military power on a global scale has been and remains distinctly inferior to that of the United States, and the Soviets have adopted a more sympathetic attitude toward Third World nationalism and the nonaligned movement.[37] By contrast, the United States denounced neutralism as immoral, was hostile to leftist nationalist movements, and repeatedly used its considerable military capabilities against a variety of developing countries.[38] Thus where Soviet power and perceived intentions threatened the developed world but not the former colonies, U.S. power and U.S. actions did just the opposite. The same factors that explain the close ties of the United States with the industrial states of

37. See Andrew Marshall, "Sources of Soviet Power: The Military Potential in the 1980s," in *Prospects of Soviet Power in the 1980s*, ed. Christoph Bertram (Hamden, Conn., 1980), pp. 65–66; and Stephen S. Kaplan, *Diplomacy of Power: Soviet Armed Forces as a Political Instrument* (Washington, D.C., 1981), chap. 5.

38. See Barnet, *Intervention and Revolution;* and Blechman and Kaplan, *Force without War.*

Eurasia therefore also account for its relatively poorer standing through-out much of the rest of the world.

The Impact of Ideology

In light of the analysis presented in chapter 6, the Soviet situation looks even worse. As noted, Marxism-Leninism threatens many of the world's most powerful countries. Less widely recognized is the fact that, like pan-Arabism, Leninism is a divisive ideology that inadvertently promotes conflict among its adherents. Soviet Marxism-Leninism calls for leadership to be wielded by an infallible vanguard party, the CPSU. Any Marxist states that follow their own interests rather than Soviet directives thus pose a direct challenge to the authority of the ruling ideology. Ideological disagreements can escalate quickly into fratricidal quarrels, because the legitimacy of each member's position is at stake.[39] It is hardly an accident that every Communist state that has been phys-ically able to establish a position independent from Moscow has done so and that conflicts between Communist regimes have been among the world's most virulent quarrels. Ideological disagreements are not the only source of intra-Communist conflicts, but they have clearly exacer-bated relations between Communist states. In short, the alleged unity of leftist forces in contemporary international politics is probably more apparent than real.

The U.S. democratic system provides an advantage here as well. Democratic regimes enjoy unusually good relations because they do not engage in intense ideological disputes with one another. And because the world's democracies are wealthy and technologically advanced (whereas most Marxist countries are not), the U.S. alliance system is both impressive in its capabilities and unusually cohesive, by both his-torical and contemporary standards.[40]

Foreign Aid and Penetration

Neither foreign aid nor penetration is likely to help the Soviet Union overcome these serious liabilities. There is little the Soviets can offer the

---

39. See Lowenthal, "Factors of Unity and Factors of Conflict"; and Brzezinski, *Soviet Bloc*, chap. 19, especially pp. 494–96.

40. Despite the perennial predictions of NATO's impending collapse, it is still remark-able that a coalition of fifteen (with the inclusion of Spain, sixteen) nations has endured for more than thirty years. For a pessimistic view, see Eliot A. Cohen, "The Long-Term Crisis in the Alliance," *Foreign Affairs*, 61, no. 2 (1982–1983). For more optimistic assessments, consult Bruce Russett and Donald R. Deluca, "Theatre Nuclear Forces: Public Opinion in Western Europe," *Political Science Quarterly*, 98, no. 2 (1983); and Richard C. Eichenberg, "The Myth of Hollanditis," *International Security*, 8, no. 2 (1983): 143–59. As events in Hungary, Czechoslovakia, and Poland reveal, the Warsaw Pact is hardly a model of cohesion, assuming one is concerned with voluntary adherence to an alliance.

industrial economies of Western Europe and Japan (save for raw materials, whose importance is declining), and they have already demonstrated their inability to provide competitive economic benefits to the Third World.[41] The superiority of the Western economic system helps explain why even Marxist states such as Angola have sought close economic ties with the West.[42] Similarly, Soviet efforts to penetrate the Western alliance via propaganda and subversion have failed completely, and Soviet attempts to foster loyal Third World allies through subversion and educational assistance have yielded few rewards save in a small number of backward and weak countries. In any case, the United States and its allies retain the dominant position in educating most Third World elites.[43]

Finally, as chapter 7 showed, these instruments do not ensure that clients will be either obedient or loyal, and efforts to use them to enforce compliance are more likely to produce suspicion and hostility. In short, the powerful role of nationalism in most countries will limit the impact of these instruments as independent causes of alignment, for the reasons noted earlier.

The global position of the United States is thus doubly reassuring. Not only is the United States the leading member of a coalition possessing superior latent and mobilized capabilities, but this alliance is bound together by a host of powerful and durable forces. And the effects of the controllable causes of alignment place the Soviets in a vicious circle. Surrounded by a powerful coalition led by their principal rival, they respond by devoting a disproportionate effort to amassing military power. But the more they seek to balance this geopolitical dilemma by mobilizing greater resources, the more they reinforce their own encirclement. The current balance of world power, in short, is likely to remain extremely stable.[44] The question thus becomes: What should U.S. policy-makers do to exploit these advantages to the fullest? What does balance of threat theory imply for U.S. grand strategy?

41. For example, less than 1 percent of all global development assistance comes from the Soviet Union. On the limitations of the Soviet Union as a source of economic aid, see Henry Bienen, "Soviet Political Relations with Africa," *International Security*, 6, no. 4 (1982); U.S. House Committee on Foreign Affairs, *The Soviet Union and the Third World*, p. 170 and passim; and CIA, *Communist Aid to Non-Communist LDCs, 1979 and 1954–1979*, p. 8. On the declining importance of raw materials, see Peter Drucker, "A Changed World Economy," *Foreign Affairs*, 64, no. 4 (1986).

42. See Feinberg and Oye, "After the Fall."

43. See CIA, *Communist Aid to Non-Communist LDCs, 1979 and 1954–1979*, p. 9; and U.S. House Committee on Foreign Affairs, *The Soviet Union and the Third World*, p. 82.

44. As it has been throughout the Cold War. The U.S. alliance network has controlled over 60 percent of gross world product since 1950; the Soviets and their allies have controlled about 15 percent. There have been minor fluctuations, and the distribution within the Western alliance has shifted as U.S. allies have recovered from World War II, but the stability of this overall distribution is striking.

Maintaining Containment: Alliance Formation and U.S. Grand Strategy

Since the onset of the Cold War, U.S. grand strategy has sought to prevent any single power from controlling the war-making potential of industrial Eurasia. In practice, this goal means containing Soviet expansion.[45] More recently, the United States has added the goal of preserving Western access to oil from the Middle East. In light of the results derived in this study, what steps will best achieve these objectives?

First, because balancing is the dominant tendency in international politics, the world's most important countries are strongly disposed to ally with the United States. As a result, the United States can afford to take a relaxed view of most international developments. Not only is it relatively immune from most adverse events (especially relative to other countries), but it can count on widespread support from a set of valuable allies when truly serious threats emerge.

Second, the precise level of U.S. power is probably less important than the way in which it is used. Because lesser powers are usually insensitive to the state of the superpower balance, only a truly massive shift in the relative power of the United States and the Soviet Union is likely to alter their alliance preferences. A military buildup will not win the United States new friends, and a marginal decline will not cause its current allies to defect. Indeed, given the propensity for states to balance, U.S. allies would be likely to do more if the United States did not insist on trying to do everything.

Third, the United States should worry far less about its allies defecting and worry more about how it provokes opposition through misplaced belligerence. The fear that U.S. allies will bandwagon if U.S. credibility weakens has been pervasive since World War II, and it is responsible for the most counterproductive excesses in postwar U.S. foreign policy.[46] This fear is exacerbated by the allies themselves, which have an obvious interest in voicing their doubts so as to persuade the United States to do more on their behalf. Their doubts should not be taken too seriously; it will rarely be in their interest to abandon U.S. protection.[47] This book

45. See Gaddis, *Strategies of Containment*, especially chap. 2; Kennan, *Realities of American Foreign Policy*; Lippmann, *The Cold War*; and Nicholas Spykman, *America's Strategy in World Politics* (New York, 1942).

46. See the discussion of bandwagoning in chapter 2; Larson, "The Bandwagon Metaphor"; and Hoffman, "Détente," in Nye, *Making of America's Soviet Policy*, p. 242.

47. Indeed, the United States might well be better off were its credibility slightly less reliable. By allowing incompetent clients to founder on occasion, the United States would provide its other allies with additional incentives to perform well both at home and in relations with the United States. The belated decisions to encourage the ouster of Ferdinand Marcos of the Philippines and Baby Doc Duvalier of Haiti suggest that it is possible to

has suggested, I hope, how fanciful the fear of bandwagoning really is.

Among other things, the predominance of balancing behavior means that intervention in peripheral areas for the sake of credibility can be greatly reduced. Indeed, efforts to demonstrate U.S. credibility through the frequent use of force are more likely to cause others to fear U.S. ambitions or to question U.S. judgment.[48] Because balancing is more common than bandwagoning, the less threatening the United States appears, the more popular it is likely to be.

Fourth, the United States should not overestimate the consensus that unites it with many of its allies in the developing world. Regional powers are far more concerned with local threats than with superpower rivalry. As a result, attempts to enlist them in an anti-Soviet crusade will continue to be counterproductive. Those countries that are directly threatened by Soviet power are natural U.S. allies. To seek a "strategic consensus" against the Soviet Union in other areas, as John Foster Dulles and Alexander Haig sought to do, ignores the regional issues that are of greater importance to these erstwhile partners. And efforts to forge a global alliance against Moscow make it much easier for clients of the United States to exploit its assistance for their own reasons. At best, these grand designs will be stillborn. At worst, they will exacerbate regional rivalries and increase the likelihood of substantial Soviet involvement.[49]

Fifth, knee-jerk opposition to leftist forces in the Third World should be abandoned. Not only is ideology a relatively weak cause of alignment, but the Marxist doctrines that the United States is so fearful of are as likely to lead to intra-Communist conflict as they are to produce unity. The examples of Mao, Tito, Togliatti, Mugabe, Berlinguer, Carillo, and Pol Pot all demolish the myth of Marxist solidarity, a fact that has escaped many of those responsible for postwar U.S. foreign policy.[50] As George Kennan's original formulation of containment pre-

---

abandon corrupt and unpopular allies without endangering commitments elsewhere. Indeed, the effects on similarly situated allies may be salutory.

48. The widespread condemnation the United States received after the bombing of Libya in April 1986 is an obvious example of this problem, as is current U.S. support for the contras in Central America.

49. Secretary of State Alexander Haig's green light for Israel's invasion of Lebanon was undoubtedly part of the U.S. effort to increase strategic cooperation with Israel in 1981–1982 in order to counter the Soviet Union. In retrospect, this decision led to a setback for the United States and a disaster for Israel. On Haig's role in Israel's decision to attack, see Ze'ev Schiff, "Green Light, Lebanon," *Foreign Policy*, no. 50 (1983).

50. To mention but one example, Henry Kissinger repeatedly warned of the dangers that revolutionary Marxist regimes posed to world order. This fear underlay U.S. intervention in Chile and Angola and prolonged the futile search for "peace with honor" in Vietnam. Yet Kissinger's memoirs reveal his awareness that Marxist ideology is ultimately divisive. As he wrote there: "One of the great ironies of relations among Communist

scribed, the United States should seek to exploit these natural divisions, rather than working to reinforce the fragile unity of leftist regimes through its own actions.[51]

Sixth, the United States should also reject the simplistic belief that Soviet arms recipients are reliable agents of the Kremlin. As shown repeatedly in this study, neither superpower has gained much leverage through the use of military or economic assistance in the Middle East. The provision of arms did not give the Soviet Union reliable influence in Yugoslavia, China, Somalia, Indonesia, or Zimbabwe either. At the same time, U.S. statesmen should recognize that U.S. aid programs will rarely enable the United States to control its clients. To cite the most obvious case, Israel is both dependent on U.S. support and independent of U.S. control. By exaggerating the effectiveness of aid programs, the United States exaggerates the size of the Soviet bloc and overlooks the possibility of weaning clients away from Moscow by providing appropriate political incentives. It is also likely to provide its allies with too much, in the mistaken belief that such aid will cement their allegiance and enhance its control.

A final implication is that the domestic situation of the United States may be more important than anything else. External events impinge on U.S. power; internal conditions generate it. Losses abroad will add up slowly (if at all) and will be compensated by balancing behavior by allies and by the United States itself. Thus a final prescription is to avoid policies that jeopardize the overall health of the U.S. economy. It is far more important to maintain a robust and productive economic system than it is to correct minor weaknesses in defense capability or to control the outcome of some insignificant clash in the developing world.

A FINAL WORD

In international politics, no agency or institution guarantees security and prosperity. The United States should find it heartening, however, that its position in the world and the most important causes of security cooperation among states combine to favor it. These conclusions do not

---

countries is that Communist ideology, which always claimed that it would end conflict, has in fact made it intractable. In systems based on infallible truth there can be only one authorized interpretation; a rival claim to represent true orthodoxy is a mortal challenge." See Kissinger, *Years of Upheaval*, p. 47. On Kissinger's suspicion of revolutionary forces, see Gaddis, *Strategies of Containment*, pp. 337–39; Hoffmann, "Détente," pp. 241–42; and especially Henry A. Kissinger, "Domestic Structure and Foreign Policy," in Kissinger, *American Foreign Policy* (New York, 1974), especially pp. 12, 34–43.

51. On this point, see Gaddis, *Strategies of Containment*, pp. 42–48.

mean that U.S. alliances are indestructible, that isolationism is preferable, or that Western defense capabilities could not be improved.[52] What they do mean is that the United States could hardly ask for much more. The principal causes of alliances work to its advantage and isolate the Soviet Union from virtually all of the world's strategically significant states. If this fact is recognized, the task of formulating a grand strategy that would reinforce these advantages should be greatly simplified. In the preceding pages, I have tried to sketch what such a strategy would be.[53]

My argument thus comes full circle. By clarifying and testing a number of hypotheses about the causes of alliances, I have sought to resolve several important debates about U.S. foreign and military policy. This approach is appropriate, because the realm of international politics remains one in which states must base their choices on predictions of how other states will respond. Armed with a better understanding of how states choose their friends, the goal of maximizing international support (and minimizing opposition) should be greatly simplified. These insights do not ensure success, of course, but they certainly improve the odds.

52. For analyses of the security problems facing the United States and its allies, along with various solutions, see Barry R. Posen and Stephen W. Van Evera, "Reagan Administration Defense Policy: Departure from Containment," *International Security*, 8, no. 1 (1983); Carnegie Endowment for International Peace, *Challenges for U.S. National Security: Assessing the Balance: Defense Spending and Conventional Forces* (Washington, D.C., 1981), pt. 2; William W. Kaufmann, "Non-Nuclear Deterrence," in *Alliance Security: NATO and the No-First-Use Question*, ed. John Steinbruner and Leon V. Sigal (Washington, D.C., 1984); Asa Clark et al., *The Defense Reform Debate* (Baltimore, Md., 1984); Report of the European Security Study, *Strengthening Conventional Deterrence in Europe: Proposals for the 1980s* (New York, 1983); Barry R. Posen, "Measuring the European Conventional Balance: Coping with Complexity in Threat Assessment," *International Security*, 9, no. 3 (1984–1985); and Jeffrey Record, *Revising American Military Strategy: Tailoring Means to Ends* (Washington, D.C., 1984).

53. Of course, should the Soviet Union reduce its military forces significantly, or should Mikhail Gorbachev succeed in convincing the West that Soviet intentions are essentially benevolent, then the cohesion of the Western alliance would almost certainly decline. Under these conditions, however, the alliance might also be less necessary.

Alliances and Alignments in the Middle East, 1955–1979

Alliance	Balance/Bandwagon	Ideological Solidarity
Baghdad Pact (1955)[a]	Balance	Low/moderate
Arab Solidarity Pact (1955)[b]	Both	Low/moderate
Soviet Union–Egypt (1955)	Balance	Low/moderate
Soviet Union–Syria (1955)	Balance	Moderate
Soviet Union–Yemen (1955)	Balance	Nil
Suez War Coalition (1956)[c]	Balance	Low
Kings' Alliance (1957)[d]	Balance	High
United States–Saudi Arabia (1957)	Balance	Low
United States–Lebanon (1957)	Balance	Moderate
United States–Jordan (1957)	Balance	Low
United Arab Republic (1958)[e]	n.a.	High
Iraq-Jordan (1958)	Balance	High
Egypt–Saudi Arabia (1958)	Both[f]	Nil
UAR-Iraq (1958)	n.a.	High
Soviet Union–Iraq (1958)	Balance	Moderate
Kuwait Intervention (1961)[g]	Balance	Nil
United States–Israel (1962)	Balance	Moderate
Egypt–Yemen Republic (1962)	Balance	High
Saudi Arabia–Jordan (1962)	Balance	High
Syria-Iraq (1962)	Balance	High

n.a. = Not applicable.

[a]Great Britain, Iraq, and the United States (as observer). Other members were Turkey, Iran, and Pakistan.

[b]Members: Egypt, Saudi Arabia, Syria, Yemen, and Jordan. Egypt was balancing Iraq and Israel, Yemen was balancing Britain, Saudi Arabia switched from balancing Iraq to bandwagoning with Egypt, and Jordan was bandwagoning all the way.

[c]Great Britain, France, and Israel.

[d]Saudi Arabia, Iraq, and Jordan.

[e]Egypt and Syria.

[f]Egypt sought to balance its rivals in Iraq and elsewhere; Saudi Arabia was bandwagoning after the Saudi plot to assassinate Nasser failed.

[g]Participants were Egypt, Saudi Arabia, and Jordan; the goal was to deter Iraqi annexation of Kuwait.

(continued)

Alliance	Balance/Bandwagon	Ideological Solidarity
Tripartite Unity Pact (1963)[h]	Bandwagon (?)	High
Egypt-Iraq (1964)	n.a.	Moderate/high
Cairo Summit (1964)[i]	Both	Low
Soviet Union–Yemen Republic (1964)	Balance	Moderate/high
Soviet Union–Syria (1966)	Balance	High
Six Day War (1966–1967)[j]	Both	Moderate
Egypt-Jordan (1967)	Balance	Low
Soviet Union–PDRY (1968)	Balance	High
Eastern Command (1969)[k]	Balance	Low
Israel-Jordan (1970)	Balance	Nil
Soviet Union–Iraq (1971)	Balance	Moderate
October War Coalition (1973)[l]	Balance	Low
Egypt–United States (1975)	Both	Nil
Syria-Jordan (1975)	Balance	Nil
Steadfastness Front (1978)[m]	Balance	Moderate
Saudi Arabia–Jordan–Iraq (1979)	Balance	Nil
Total number of alliances: 36	Total membership: 86	

[h]Egypt, Syria, and Iraq. Although the Ba'th's pan-Arab ideology played a major role in instigating this agreement, the Syrians were also bandwagoning with Egypt to reduce the threat from Nasserist factions within Syria.

[i]Egypt, Saudi Arabia, Iraq, and Jordan. This summit was the result of Egypt's efforts to isolate Syria, the Saudi and Jordanian interest in appeasing Egypt, and (to a much lesser extent) the shared desire to counter Israel.

[j]Egypt and Syria balance against Israel, Jordan bandwagons with them, and other Arabs offer symbolic participation to show solidarity.

[k]Syria, Iraq, and Jordan. Very modest level of cooperation achieved.

[l]Egypt, Syria, and Saudi Arabia, with symbolic support from other Arabs.

[m]Syria, Libya, PDRY, and Algeria. Only Syria and PDRY included in total.

The Balance of World Power

THE U.S. ALLIANCE NETWORK

Country	Population (in millions)	GNP (in billions of dollars)	Number in armed forces (in thousands)	Defense spending (in millions of dollars)
NATO and Japan				
Belgium	9.9	$ 87.7	109	2,911
Canada	24.9	299.4	81	6,439
Denmark	5.1	58.2	30	1,482
France	54.7	564.2	578	23,793
Greece	9.9	40.9	177	2,526
Italy	56.8	350.7	498	9,609
Japan	119.3	1,137.7	241	11,500
Netherlands	14.4	143.8	104	4,673
Norway	4.1	57.4	41	1,844
Portugal	10.0	23.0	93	814
Spain	38.2	190.1	340	4,070
Turkey	49.2	57.7	824	2,840
United States	234.5	3,297.8	2,222	217,154
United Kingdom	56.0	507.4	333	27,444
West Germany	61.5	698.9	496	23,565
Total	748.5	$7,514.9	6,167	$340,664
Other U.S. Allies				
Argentina	29.7	$ 56.4	175	$ 1,523
Australia	15.3	166.1	73	4,637
Belize	n.a.	n.a.	n.a.	n.a.
Bolivia	5.9	5.1	27	196
Botswana	1.0	0.8	3	26
Brazil	131.3	272.0	460	1,769
Chile	11.5	22.6	126	1,021
China (Taiwan)	18.8	52.1	454	3,925
Colombia	28.3	39.6	70	436
Costa Rica	2.5	2.3	4	17
Dominican Republic	6.2	8.2	23	122

(*continued*)

Country	Population (in millions)	GNP (in billions of dollars)	Number in armed forces (in thousands)	Defense spending (in millions of dollars)
Ecuador	8.4	11.8	39	184
Egypt	45.8	32.2	447	2,679
El Salvador	4.8	3.7	28	150
Guatemala	7.8	8.8	19	209
Haiti	5.5	1.7	8	24
Honduras	4.1	2.7	14	55
Indonesia	165.8	93.4	280	2,049
Israel	4.0	21.4	180	6,229
Jordan	2.6	4.3	64	814
Kenya	18.6	6.5	18	138
Liberia	2.1	0.9	5	27
Malaysia	15.0	27.3	105	1,432
Mexico	74.7	157.6	131	872
Morocco	22.9	16.0	135	1,318
Oman	1.1	6.9	20	1,944
Pakistan	94.1	36.6	584	1,984
Panama	2.0	3.9	11	60
Paraguay	3.5	4.6	16	89
Philippines	54.3	41.6	157	771
Saudi Arabia	10.1	154.1	55	27,192
Senegal	6.3	2.7	18	60
Somalia	6.2	1.2	48	114
South Korea	41.4	80.7	602	4,717
Sudan	20.1	10.6	86	180
Thailand	50.7	39.4	250	1,539
Trinidad/Tobago	1.1	7.3	2	81
Tunisia	7.0	8.9	28	256
United Arab Emirates	1.2	23.7	49	1,867
Uruguay	n.a.	n.a.	n.a.	n.a.
Venezuela	16.8	69.5	56	920
Zaire	31.2	5.4	42	82
Total	979.7	$1,510.6	4,912	$ 71,708
China (People's Republic)	1,020.9	$ 401.0	4,100	$ 34,500

THE SOVIET ALLIANCE SYSTEM

Country	Population (in millions)	GNP (in billions of dollars)	Number in armed forces (in thousands)	Defense spending (in millions of dollars)
The Warsaw Pact				
Bulgaria	8.9	$52.7	177	$4,282
Czechoslovakia	15.4	120.6	214	7,157
East Germany	16.7	153.2	240	9,806
Hungary	10.7	73.2	105	3,134
Poland	36.6	212.9	430	12,282
Rumania	22.6	108.7	244	5,159
Soviet Union	272.5	1,843.4	4,400	258,000
Total	383.4	$2,564.7	5,810	$299,820

(*continued*)

Country	Population (in millions)	GNP (in billions of dollars)	Number in armed forces (in thousands)	Defense spending (in millions of dollars)
Other Soviet Allies				
Afghanistan	14.7	$4.0	75	$198
Algeria	20.7	48.9	130	1,334
Angola	7.5	6.7	54	1,558
Benin	3.8	0.8	7	20
Burundi	4.5	1.3	7	41
Cape Verde	0.3	0.1	4	2
Congo	1.7	2.1	11	79
Cuba	9.9	22.5	250	1,306
Equatorial Guinea	0.3	0.1	2	1
Ethiopia	31.3	4.8	199	385
Guinea	5.1	1.0	17	80
Iraq	14.5	25.2	500	11,900
Laos	3.6	0.3	46	50
Libya	3.5	24.1	68	4,223
Madagascar	9.4	2.9	29	61
Mali	7.4	1.1	11	30
Mongolia	1.8	1.2	38	150
Mozambique	13.0	4.8	32	175
Nicaragua	2.8	2.6	46	272
North Korea	19.2	21.6	784	3,600
PDRY	2.1	1.0	25	179
Sao Tome and Principe	0.1	0.3	0	n.a.
Seychelles	n.a.	n.a.	n.a.	n.a.
Syria	9.8	16.4	222	2,138
Tanzania	20.1	4.9	43	122
Vietnam	57.6	8.5	1,200	1,000
Zambia	6.3	4.0	16	n.a.
Total	271.0	$ 211.2	3,816	$ 28,904
India	730.6	$ 189.5	1,120	$ 6,546

n.a. = Data not available.
China and India are listed separately because their inclusion in either alliance network has an enormous impact on the total figures. Other countries are included here either because they have a formal treaty of alliance with one of the superpowers or because military advisers from one superpower are present on their territory. States with no treaty commitment, with no advisers, or with both Soviet and U.S. advisers were judged to be neutral and omitted. Data in this table are from ACDA, *World Military Expenditures and Arms Transfers 1985* (Washington, D.C., 1986).

Bibliography

The following abbreviations in the footnotes are spelled out in the bibliography: ACDA (U.S. Arms Control and Disarmament Agency), AID (U.S. Agency for International Development), CIA (U.S. Central Intelligence Agency), MECS (*Middle East Contemporary Survey*), MEJ (*Middle East Journal*), MER (*Middle East Record*).

"'Abd-al-Nasir's Secret Papers." Joint Publications Research Service. *Translations on Near East and North Africa*, no. 1865, Report 72223 (November 1978).

Abidi, Aqil H. S. *Jordan: A Political Study, 1948–1957*. New Delhi: Indian School of International Studies, 1965.

Abu-Jaber, Kamal S. *The Arab Ba'th Socialist Party: History, Ideology, and Organization*. Syracuse, N.Y.: Syracuse University Press, 1966.

Abu-Lughod, Ibrahim, ed. *The Arab-Israeli Confrontation of June 1967: An Arab Perspective*. Evanston, Ill.: Northwestern University Press, 1969.

Ajami, Fouad. *The Arab Predicament: Arab Political Thought and Practice since 1967*. Cambridge: Cambridge University Press, 1981.

——. "The End of Pan-Arabism," *Foreign Affairs*, 57, no. 2 (1978–1979).

——. "The Middle East: Important for the Wrong Reasons." *Journal of International Affairs*, 29, no. 1 (1979).

Albertini, Luigi. *The Origins of the War of 1914*. London: Oxford University Press, 1952.

Altfeld, Michael F. "The Decision to Ally: A Theory and Test." *Western Political Quarterly*, 37, no. 4 (1984).

Altfeld, Michael F., and Bruce Bueno de Mesquita. "Choosing Sides in Wars." *International Studies Quarterly*, 23, no. 1 (1979).

Anderson, Irvine. *Aramco, the United States, and Saudi Arabia: A Study of the Dynamics of Foreign Oil Policy, 1933–1950*. Princeton, N.J.: Princeton University Press, 1981.

Andreski, Stanislaw. *Military Organization and Society*. Berkeley: University of California Press, 1968.

Antonius, George. *The Arab Awakening: The Story of the Arab Movement*. New York: Putnam's, 1946.

Arab Ba'th Socialist Party. *Revolutionary Iraq, 1968–1973: The Political Report Adopted by the Eighth Regional Congress of the Arab Ba'th Socialist Party–Iraq*. Baghdad: Arab Ba'th Socialist Party, 1974.

Arab Political Documents 1963. Beirut: American University of Beirut, 1964.

Arab Political Documents 1965. Beirut: American University of Beirut, 1966.

Aronson, Shlomo. *Conflict and Bargaining in the Middle East: An Israeli Perspective*. Baltimore, Md.: Johns Hopkins University Press, 1978.

Aruri, Naseer H. *Jordan: A Study in Political Development (1921–1965)*. The Hague, Netherlands: Martinus Nijhoff, 1972.

Asparturian, Vernon V., ed. *Process and Power in Soviet Foreign Policy*. Boston: Little, Brown, 1971.

Bachrack, Stanley. *The Committee for One Million: "China Lobby" Politics*. New York: Columbia University Press, 1976.

Badeau, John S. *The American Approach to the Arab World*. New York: Harper & Row, 1968.

Baker, Raymond W. *Egypt's Uncertain Revolution under Nasser and Sadat*. Cambridge: Harvard University Press, 1978.

Barnet, Richard J. *Intervention and Revolution: The United States in the Third World*. New York: Meridian, 1968.

Bar-Siman-Tov, Ya'acov. *The Israeli-Egyptian War of Attrition, 1969–1970*. New York: Columbia University Press, 1980.

———. *Linkage Politics in the Middle East: Syria between Domestic and External Conflict, 1961–70*. Boulder, Colo.: Westview Press, 1983.

Bar-Ya'acov, N. *The Israel-Syrian Armistice: Problems of Implementation, 1949–1966*. Jerusalem: Magnes Press, 1967.

Bar-Zohar, Michael. *Ben-Gurion*. New York: Delacorte Press, 1977.

Batatu, Hanna. *The Old Social Classes and the Revolutionary Movements of Iraq: A Study of Iraq's Old Landed and Commercial Classes and of Its Communists, Ba'thists, and Free Officers*. Princeton, N.J.: Princeton University Press, 1978.

Bechtold, Peter K. "New Attempts at Arab Cooperation: The Federation of Arab Republics, 1971–?" *Middle East Journal*, 27, no. 2 (1973).

Beer, Francis A., ed. *Alliances: Latent War Communities in the Contemporary World*. New York: Holt, Rinehart and Winston, 1970.

Beling, Willard A., ed., *The Middle East: Quest for an American Policy*. Albany: State University of New York Press, 1973.

Ben-Dor, Gabriel, ed. *The Palestinians and the Middle East Conflict*. Ramat Gan, Israel: Turtledove Press, 1979.

Ben-Gurion, David. *Israel: A Personal History*. New York: Funk & Wagnalls, 1971.

Ben-Zvi, Abraham. *Alliance Politics and the Limits of Influence: The Case of the U.S. and Israel, 1975–1983*. Boulder, Colo.: Westview Press, 1984.

Berger, Earl. *The Covenant and the Sword*. London: Routledge & Kegan Paul, 1965.

Berry, Nicholas O. "The Management of Foreign Penetration." *Orbis*, 17, no. 3 (1973).

Bertram, Christoph, ed. *Prospects of Soviet Power in the 1980s*. Hamden, Conn.: Archon Books, 1980.

Bienen, Henry. "Soviet Political Relations with Africa." *International Security*, 6, no. 4 (1982).

Binder, Leonard. "The Middle East as a Subordinate Political System." *World Politics*, 10, no. 3 (1958).

———, ed. *Politics in Lebanon*. New York: Wiley, 1966.

Blalock, Hubert. *Basic Dilemmas in the Social Sciences*. Beverly Hills, Calif.: Sage Publications, 1984.

Blechman, Barry M. "Impact of Israel's Reprisals on the Behavior of Bordering Arab Nations Directed at Israel," *Journal of Conflict Resolution*, 16, no. 2 (1972).

Blechman, Barry M., and Stephen S. Kaplan. *Force without War: U.S. Armed Forces as a Political Instrument*. Washington, D.C.: Brookings Institution, 1978.

Bibliography

Blitzer, Wolf. *Between Washington and Jerusalem: A Reporter's Notebook*. New York: Oxford University Press, 1985.

Borkenau, Franz. *World Communism: A History of the Communist International*. Ann Arbor: University of Michigan Press, 1971.

Boulding, Kenneth A. *Conflict and Defense: A General Theory*. New York: Harper Torchbooks, 1962.

Bradlee, Ben, Jr. "Lobbying for Israel." *Arizona Republic*, 27 May 1984.

Brecher, Michael. *Decisions in Israel's Foreign Policy*. New Haven, Conn.: Yale University Press, 1975.

——. *The Foreign Policy System of Israel*. New Haven, Conn.: Yale University Press, 1972.

——. *Nehru: A Political Biography*. London: Oxford University Press, 1959.

Brecher, Michael, with Benjamin Geist. *Decisions in Crisis: Israel 1967, 1973*. Berkeley: University of California Press, 1981.

Brown, L. Carl. *International Politics and the Middle East*. Princeton, N.J.: Princeton University Press, 1984.

Brown, Seyom. *The Faces of Power: Constancy and Change in United States Foreign Policy from Truman to Johnson*. New York: Columbia University Press, 1968.

Bruun, Geoffrey. *Europe and the French Imperium: 1799–1814*. New York: Harper & Bros., 1938.

Brzezinski, Zbigniew. *Power and Principle: Memoirs of the National Security Adviser, 1977–1981*. New York: Farrar, Strauss, and Giroux, 1983.

——. *The Soviet Bloc: Unity and Conflict*. Cambridge: Harvard University Press, 1967.

Brzoska, Michael. "Arms Transfer Data Sources." *Journal of Conflict Resolution*, 26, no. 1 (1982).

Bueno de Mesquita, Bruce, and J. David Singer. "Alliance, Capabilities, and War." *Political Science Annual*, 4 (1972).

Bull, Hedley. *The Anarchical Society*. New York: Columbia University Press, 1977.

Burgess, Philip, and David Moore. "Inter-Nation Alliances: An Inventory and Appraisal of Propositions." *Political Science Annual*, 5 (1973).

Burns, William J. *Economic Aid and American Policy toward Egypt, 1955–1981*. Albany: State University of New York Press, 1985.

Buss, Robin. "Wary Partners: The Soviet Union and Arab Socialism." *Adelphi Paper No. 73*. London: International Institute for Strategic Studies, 1970.

Butow, Robert J. C. *Tojo and the Coming of the War*. Princeton, N.J.: Princeton University Press, 1960.

Campbell, Donald, and Julian Stanley. *Experimental and Quasi-Experimental Designs for Research*. Chicago: Rand McNally, 1963.

Campbell, John C. *Defense of the Middle East: Problems of American Policy*. New York: Praeger, 1960.

——. "The Middle East: A House of Containment Built on Shifting Sands." *Foreign Affairs*, 60, no. 3 (1981).

Caporaso, James A. "Dependence, Dependency, and Power in the Global System: A Structural and Behavioral Analysis," *International Organization*, 32, no. 1 (1978).

Carnegie Endowment for International Peace. *Challenges for U.S. National Security: Assessing the Balance: Defense Spending and Conventional Forces*. Washington, D.C.: Carnegie Endowment for International Peace, 1981.

Carter, Jimmy. *Keeping Faith: Memoirs of a President*. New York: Bantam Books, 1982.

Challener, Richard D. *The French Theory of the Nation in Arms*. New York: Columbia University Press, 1955.

Childers, Erskine B. *The Road to Suez*. London: MacGibbon and Kee, 1962.

Chubin, Shahram, and Sepehr Zabih. *The Foreign Relations of Iran*. Berkeley: University of California Press, 1974.

Churchill, Winston S. *The Second World War*, Vol. 1: *The Gathering Storm*. Boston: Houghton Mifflin, 1948.

———. *The Second World War*, Vol. 3: *The Grand Alliance*. Boston: Houghton Mifflin, 1950.

Clark, Asa, et al. *The Defense Reform Debate*. Baltimore, Md.: Johns Hopkins University Press, 1984.

Claude, Inis L. *Power and International Relations*. New York: Random House, 1962.

Cline, Ray S. *World Power Assessment 1977: A Calculus of Strategic Drift*. Washington, D.C.: Georgetown University Press, 1978.

Cohen, Eliot A. "The Long-Term Crisis in the Alliance." *Foreign Affairs*, 61, no. 2 (1982–1983).

Confino, Michael, and Shimon Shamir, eds. *The USSR and the Middle East*. New York: Wiley, 1973.

Congressional Quarterly. *The Middle East*. 5th ed. Washington, D.C.: Congressional Quarterly, 1981.

Cordesman, Anthony. "U.S. and Soviet Competition in Arms Exports and Military Assistance." *Armed Forces Journal International*, 118, no. 12 (1981).

Craig, Gordon A. *Germany: 1866–1945*. London: Oxford University Press, 1978.

Cremeans, Charles D. *The Arabs and the World: Nasser's Arab Nationalist Policy*. New York: Praeger, 1963.

Crosbie, Sylvia Kowitt. *A Tacit Alliance: France and Israel from Suez to the Six Day War*. Princeton, N.J.: Princeton University Press, 1974.

Curtiss, Richard H. *A Changing Image: American Perceptions of the Arab-Israeli Dispute*. Washington, D.C.: American Educational Trust, 1982.

Dallek, Robert. *Franklin D. Roosevelt and American Foreign Policy: 1932–1945*. London: Oxford University Press, 1979.

Dallin, David J. *Soviet Foreign Policy since Stalin*. New York: Lippincott, 1960.

Dann, Uriel. *Iraq under Qassem: A Political History, 1958–1963*. New York: Praeger/Pall Mall, 1969.

David, Steven R. "The Realignment of Third World Regimes from One Superpower to the Other: Ethiopia's Mengistu, Somalia's Siad, and Egypt's Sadat." Diss., Harvard University, 1980.

Dawisha, Adeed. *Egypt in the Arab World*. London: Macmillan, 1976.

———. "Saudi Arabia's Search for Security," *Adelphi Paper No. 158*. London: International Institute for Strategic Studies, 1979.

———. *Syria and the Lebanese Crisis*. London: Macmillan, 1981.

———. "Syria in Lebanon-Assad's Vietnam?" *Foreign Policy*, 33, (1978–1979).

———, ed. *Islam and Foreign Policy*. Cambridge: Cambridge University Press, 1983.

Dawisha, Adeed, and Karen Dawisha, eds. *The Soviet Union in the Middle East: Policies and Perspectives*. London: Holmes and Meier, 1982.

Dawisha, Karen. "The Roles of Ideology in the Decisionmaking of the Soviet Union." *International Relations*, 4, no. 2 (1972).

———. "Soviet Cultural Relations with Iraq, Syria, and Egypt, 1955–1970." *Soviet Studies*, 27, no. 3 (1975).

———. *Soviet Foreign Policy towards Egypt*. New York: St. Martin's Press, 1979.

Dayan, Moshe. *Breakthrough: A Personal Account of the Egypt-Israel Peace Negotiations*. New York: Knopf, 1981.

———. *Diary of the Sinai Campaign*. New York: Shocken Press, 1966.

Deese, David, and Joseph Nye, eds. *Energy and Security*. Cambridge, Mass.: Ballinger Publishing, 1981.

Bibliography

Dehio, Ludwig. *The Precarious Balance*. New York: Vintage, 1965.

Dekmejian, R. Hrair. *Egypt under Nasir: A Study in Political Leadership*. Albany: State University of New York Press, 1971.

Deutscher, Isaac. *Stalin: A Political Biography*. London: Pelican Books, 1966.

Devlin, John F. *The Ba'th Party: A History from its Origins to 1966*. Stanford, Calif.: Hoover Institution Press, 1968.

Diesing, Paul. *Patterns of Discovery in the Social Sciences*. Chicago: Aldine Atherton, 1971.

Dismukes, Bradford, and James M. McConnell, eds. *Soviet Naval Diplomacy*. New York: Pergamon, 1979.

Donaldson, Robert H., ed. *The Soviet Union in the Third World: Successes and Failures*. Boulder, Colo.: Westview Press, 1981.

Doyle, Michael. "Liberalism and World Politics." *American Political Science Review*, 80, no. 4 (1986).

Drucker. Peter. "A Changed World Economy." *Foreign Affairs*, 64, no. 4 (1986).

Duncan, George T., and Randolph Siverson. "Flexibility of Alliance Partner Choice in Multipolar Systems: Models and Tests." *International Studies Quarterly*, 26, no. 4 (1982).

Dupuy, Trevor N. *Elusive Victory: The Arab-Israeli Wars*. New York: Harper & Row, 1980.

Efrat, Moshe. "The Economics of Soviet Arms Transfers to the Third World—A Case Study: Egypt." *Soviet Studies*, 35, no. 4 (1983).

Eichenberg, Richard. "The Myth of Hollanditis." *International Security*, 8, no. 2 (1983).

Eisenhower, Dwight D. *The White House Years, 1956–61: Waging Peace*. Garden City, N.Y.: Doubleday, 1965.

Emerson, Steven. *The American House of Saud: The Secret Petrodollar Connection*. New York: Franklin Watts, 1985.

Eran, Oded, and Jerome E. Singer. "Soviet Policy towards the Arab World 1955–71." *Survey*, 17, no. 4 (1971).

Eveland, Wilbur Crane. *Ropes of Sand: America's Failure in the Middle East*. New York: Norton, 1980.

Fedder, Edwin. "The Concept of Alliance." *International Studies Quarterly*, 12, no. 1 (1968).

Feinberg, Richard E., and Kenneth A. Oye, "After the Fall: U.S. Policy toward Radical Regimes." *World Policy Journal*, 1, no. 1 (1983).

Feis, Herbert. *From Trust to Terror: The Onset of the Cold War, 1945–50*. New York: Norton, 1970.

Fest, Joachim. *Hitler*. New York: Vintage, 1974.

Feuchtwanger, E. J., and Peter Nailor, eds. *The Soviet Union and the Third World*. New York: St. Martin's Press, 1981.

Feuerwerger, M. C. *Congress and Israel*. Westport, Conn.: Greenwood Press, 1979.

Fidel, Kenneth, ed. *Militarism in Developing Countries*. New Brunswick, N.J.: Transaction Books, 1975.

Findley, Paul. *They Dare to Speak Out: People and Institutions Confront Israel's Lobby*. Westport, Conn.: Lawrence Hill, 1985.

Finer, Herbert. *Dulles over Suez: The Theory and Practice of His Diplomacy*. Chicago: Quadrangle Books, 1964.

Foreign Broadcast Information Service. "Daily Report for Middle East and North Africa," April 2, 1979.

Freedman, Robert O. *Soviet Policy in the Middle East since 1970*. New York: Praeger, 1975.
_____. *Soviet Policy in the Middle East since 1970*. Rev. ed. New York: Praeger, 1981.

Friedman, Julian R., Christopher Bladen, and Steven Rosen, eds. *Alliance in International Politics*. Boston: Allyn & Bacon, 1970.

Frye, R. N., ed. *The Near East and the Great Powers*. Cambridge: Harvard University Press, 1951.

Fuchs, Lawrence H., ed. *American Ethnic Politics*. New York: Harper Torchbooks, 1968.
Fukuyama, Francis. "A New Soviet Strategy?" *Commentary*, 68, no. 4 (1979).
――. "Soviet Threats to Intervene in the Middle East." *Research Note N–1577–FF*. Santa Monica, Calif.: RAND Corporation, 1980.
――. "The Soviet Union and Iraq." *Research Note 1924–AF*. Santa Monica, Calif.: RAND Corporation, 1980.
Gaddis, John Lewis. *Russia, the Soviet Union, and the United States: An Interpretive History*. New York: Wiley, 1968.
――. *Strategies of Containment*. New York: Oxford University Press, 1982.
Gaddis, John Lewis, and Thomas Etzold, eds. *Containment: Documents on American Policy and Strategy, 1945–1950*. New York: Columbia University Press, 1978.
Gazit, Mordechai. *President Kennedy's Policy toward the Arab States and Israel*. Tel Aviv: Shiloah Center for Middle Eastern and African Studies, 1983.
Geiss, Imanuel. *German Foreign Policy 1871–1914*. London: Routledge & Kegan Paul, 1977.
――. *July 1914*. New York: Norton, 1967.
George, Alexander L. "Case Studies and Theory Development." Paper presented to the 2d Annual Symposium on Information Processing, Carnegie-Mellon University, October 15–16, 1982.
George, Alexander L., and Richard Smoke. *Deterrence in American Foreign Policy: Theory and Practice*. New York: Columbia University Press, 1974.
George, Alexander L., David Hall, and William Simons. *The Limits of Coercive Diplomacy: Laos, Cuba, Vietnam*. Boston: Little, Brown, 1971.
George, Alexander L., ed. *Managing U.S.-Soviet Rivalry: Problems of Crisis Prevention*. Boulder, Colo.: Westview Press, 1982.
Gershoni, Israel. *The Emergence of Pan-Arabism in Egypt*. Tel Aviv: Shiloah Center for Middle Eastern and African Studies, 1981.
Glassman, Jon. *Arms for the Arabs: The Soviet Union and War in the Middle East*. Baltimore, Md.: Johns Hopkins University Press, 1975.
Golan, Galia. *Yom Kippur and After: The Soviet Union and the Middle East Crisis*. Cambridge: Cambridge University Press, 1977.
Golan, Matti. *The Secret Conversations of Henry Kissinger*. New York: Quadrangle Books, 1976.
Gooch, G. P., and Harold Temperley, eds. *British Documents on the Origins of the War, 1898–1914*. London: British Foreign Office, 1928.
Green, Stephen. *Taking Sides: America's Relations with a Militant Israel*. New York: Morrow, 1984.
Greenfield, Kent Roberts, ed. *Command Decisions*. New York: Harcourt, Brace, & World, 1959.
Grey, Sir Edward, Viscount of Fallodon, K.G. *Twenty-Five Years, 1892–1916*. New York: Frederick A. Stokes, 1925.
Griffiths, William. "Soviet Influence in the Middle East." *Survival*, 18, no. 1 (1976).
Grose, Peter. *Israel in the Mind of America*. New York: Knopf, 1983.
Gulick, Edward V. *Europe's Classical Balance of Power*. New York: Norton, 1955.
Haim, Sylvia, ed. *Arab Nationalism: An Anthology*. Berkeley: University of California Press, 1962.
Haley, P. Edward, and Lewis Snider, eds. *Lebanon in Crisis: Participants and Issues*. Syracuse, N.Y.: Syracuse University Press, 1979.
Halliday, Fred. *Arabia without Sultans*. New York: Vintage, 1975.
Halpern, A. M., ed. *Policies toward China: Views from Six Continents*. New York: McGraw-Hill, 1965.

Halpern, Manfred. *The Politics of Social Change in the Middle East and North Africa*. Princeton, N.J.: Princeton University Press, 1963.

Hammond, Paul Y., and Sidney S. Alexander, eds. *Political Dynamics in the Middle East*. New York: American Elsevier, 1972.

Handel, Michael. *The Diplomacy of Surprise: Hitler, Nixon, Sadat*. Cambridge, Mass.: Center for International Affairs, 1981.

_____. *Israel's Political-Military Doctrine*. Cambridge, Mass.: Center for International Affairs, 1973.

Harkabi, Yehoshofat. *Arab Attitudes to Israel*. Jerusalem: Keter Publishing, 1972.

Harkavy, Robert E. *Arms Trade and International Systems*. Cambridge, Mass.: Ballinger, 1975.

_____. *Great Power Competition for Overseas Bases: The Geopolitics of Access Diplomacy*. New York: Pergamon, 1982.

Haselkorn, Avigdor. *The Evolution of Soviet Security Strategy, 1965–1975*. New York: Crane Russak, 1978.

Hasou, Tawfiq Y. *The Struggle for the Arab World*. London: KPI Ltd., 1985.

Healy, Brian, and Arthur Stein. "The Balance of Power in International History: Theory and Reality." *Journal of Conflict Resolution*, 17, no. 1 (1973).

Heikal, Mohamed. *The Cairo Documents*. New York: Doubleday, 1971.

_____. "Egyptian Foreign Policy." *Foreign Affairs*, 56, no. 4 (1978).

_____. *The Road to Ramadan*. New York: Quadrangle Books, 1975.

_____. *The Sphinx and the Commissar*. New York: Harper & Row, 1976.

Helms, Christine Moss. *Iraq: Eastern Flank of the Arab World*. Washington, D.C.: Brookings Institution, 1984.

Heradstveit, Daniel. *Arab and Israeli Elite Perceptions*. Oslo: Universitetsforlaget, 1974.

_____. *The Arab-Israel Conflict: Psychological Obstacles to Peace*. Oslo: Universitetsforlaget, 1979.

Herzog, Chaim. *The Arab-Israeli Wars: War and Peace in the Middle East*. New York: Random House, 1982.

_____. *The War of Atonement*. Boston: Little, Brown, 1975.

Hinsley, F. H. *Power and the Pursuit of Peace: Theory and Practice in the History of Relations between States*. Cambridge: Cambridge University Press, 1963.

Hirschman, Albert O. *State Power and the Structure of International Trade*. Berkeley: University of California Press, 1945.

Hirst, David. *The Gun and the Olive Branch*. London: Futura Publications, 1978.

Hoffman, Erik P., and Frederic J. Fleron, Jr., eds. *The Conduct of Soviet Foreign Policy*. New York: Aldine, 1980.

Holden, David, and Richard Johns. *The House of Saud*. New York: Holt, Rinehart and Winston, 1981.

Holsti, K. J. *International Politics: A Framework for Analysis*. Englewood Cliffs, N.J.: Prentice-Hall, 1967.

Holsti, Ole, P. Terrence Hopmann, and John D. Sullivan. *Unity and Disintegration in International Alliances*. New York: Wiley, 1973.

Hoopes, Townsend. *The Devil and John Foster Dulles*. Boston: Little, Brown, 1971.

Hopmann, P. Terrence, Dina Zinnes, and J. David Singer, eds. "Cumulation in International Relations Research." *Monograph Series in World Affairs*. Graduate School of International Studies, University of Denver, vol. 18, bk. 3 (1981).

Hopwood, Derek. *Egypt: Politics and Society, 1945–1981*. London: George Allen & Unwin, 1982.

Horvath, W. J., and G. C. Foster. "Stochastic Models of War Alliances." *Journal of Conflict Resolution*, 7, no. 2 (1963).

Howard, Michael. *The Franco-Prussian War*. New York: Humanities Press, 1979.

Hudson, Michael. *Arab Politics: The Search for Legitimacy*. New Haven, Conn.: Yale University Press, 1977.

———. *The Precarious Republic: Political Modernization in Lebanon*. New York: Random House, 1968.

Hurewitz, J. C. *Middle East Politics: The Military Dimension*. New York: Praeger, 1969.

Hussein, King of Jordan. *My "War" with Israel*. As told to and with additional material by Vick Vance and Pierre Lauer. New York: Morrow, 1969.

———. *Uneasy Lies the Head*. New York: Bernard Geis, 1962.

Institute of International Education. *Open Doors: A Report on International Educational Exchange*. New York: various years.

International Monetary Fund. *International Financial Statistics*. Washington, D.C.: International Monetary Fund, 1981.

Isaacs, Stephen. *Jews and American Politics*. New York: Doubleday, 1974.

Ispahani, Mahnaz Z. "Alone Together: Regional Security Arrangements in Southern Africa and the Arabian Gulf." *International Security*, 8, no. 4 (1984).

Israeli, Raphael, ed. *The Public Diary of President Sadat*. Leiden, The Netherlands: E. J. Brill, 1978.

Jabber, Paul. *Not by War Alone*. Berkeley: University of California Press, 1981.

Jervis, Robert. "Cooperation under the Security Dilemma." *World Politics*, 30, no. 3 (1978).

———. "Hypotheses on Misperception." *World Politics*, 20, no. 3 (1968).

———. *Perception and Misperception in International Politics*. Princeton, N.J.: Princeton University Press, 1976.

Jervis, Robert, Richard Ned Lebow, and Janice Gross Stein, eds. *Psychology and Deterrence*. Baltimore, Md.: Johns Hopkins University Press, 1986.

Johnson, Lyndon B. *The Vantage Point: Perspectives of the Presidency 1963–1969*. New York: Popular Library, 1971.

Joshua, Wynfred, and Stephen Gibert. *Arms for the Third World*. Baltimore, Md.: Johns Hopkins University Press, 1969.

Kann, Robert A. "Alliances versus Ententes." *World Politics*, 28, no. 4 (1976).

Kaplan, Morton A. *System and Process in International Politics*. New York: Wiley, 1957.

Kaplan, Stephen S. *Diplomacy of Power: Soviet Armed Forces as a Political Instrument*. Washington, D.C.: Brookings Institution, 1981.

Karpat, Kamal H., ed. *Political and Social Thought in the Contemporary Middle East*. New York: Praeger, 1982.

Katz, Mark N. *Russia and Arabia: Soviet Foreign Policy toward the Arabian Peninsula*. Baltimore, Md.: Johns Hopkins University Press, 1986.

———. *The Third World in Soviet Military Thought*. Baltimore, Md.: Johns Hopkins University Press, 1982.

Kegley, Charles W., and Gregory A. Raymond. "Alliance Norms and War: A New Piece in an Old Puzzle." *International Studies Quarterly*, 26, no. 4 (1982).

Kekkonen, Urho. *A President's View*. London: Heinemann, 1982.

Kelly, J. B. *Arabia, the Gulf, and the West*. New York: Basic Books, 1980.

Kenen, I. L. *Israel's Defense Line: Her Friends and Foes in Washington*. Buffalo, N.Y.: Prometheus Press, 1981.

Kennan, George F. *The Decline of Bismarck's European Order*. Princeton, N.J.: Princeton University Press, 1978.

———. *Realities of American Foreign Policy*. New York: New American Library, 1951.

———. "The Sources of Soviet Conduct." *Foreign Affairs*, 25, no. 4 (1947).

Bibliography

Kennedy, Paul M. "The First World War and the International Power System." *International Security*, 9, no. 1 (1984).
——. *The Rise of the Anglo-German Antagonism, 1860–1914*. London: George Allen & Unwin, 1980.
——. *The Rise and Fall of British Naval Mastery*. London: Macmillan, 1983.
——. *Strategy and Diplomacy: Collected Essays*. London: George Allen & Unwin, 1983.
Keohane, Robert O. "The Big Influence of Small Allies." *Foreign Policy*, no. 2 (1971).
Kerr, Malcolm. *The Arab Cold War: Gamal 'Abdel Nasser and His Rivals*. London: Oxford University Press, 1971.
Khadduri, Majid. *Independent Iraq*. London: Oxford University Press, 1960.
——. *Political Trends in the Arab World*. Baltimore, Md.: Johns Hopkins University Press, 1970.
——. *Republican Iraq*. London: Oxford University Press, 1969.
——. *Socialist Iraq: A Study in Iraq's Politics since 1968*. Washington, D.C.: Middle East Institute, 1978.
Khairy, Majduddin Omar. *Jordan and the World System: Developments in the Middle East*. Frankfurt, Germany: Peter Bern, 1984.
Khalidi, Ahmed S. "The War of Attrition." *Journal of Palestine Studies*, 3, no. 1 (1973).
Khalidi, Rashid. "Soviet Middle East Policy in the Wake of Camp David." *Institute for Palestine Studies Papers, No. 3*. Beirut: Institute for Palestine Studies, 1979.
Khalidi, Walid. *Conflict and Violence in Lebanon*. Cambridge: Harvard Center for International Affairs, 1979.
——, ed. *International Documents on Palestine 1969*. Beirut: Institute for Palestine Studies, 1972.
Khouri, Fred J. *The Arab-Israeli Dilemma*. Syracuse, N.Y.: Syracuse University Press, 1976.
Khrushchev, Nikita S. *Khrushchev Remembers*. Edited by Strobe Talbott. Boston: Little, Brown, 1970.
Kissinger, Henry A. *American Foreign Policy*. New York: Norton, 1974.
——. *White House Years*. Boston: Little, Brown, 1979.
——. *Years of Upheaval*. Boston: Little, Brown, 1981.
Knorr, Klaus. "Is International Coercion Waning or Rising?" *International Security*, 1, no. 4 (1977).
——. *The Power of Nations*. New York: Basic Books, 1975.
——, ed. *Historical Dimensions of National Security Problems*. Lawrence: University Press of Kansas, 1976.
Koen, Ross Y. *The China Lobby in American Politics*. New York: Harper & Row, 1974.
Konigsberg, Karen B. "Red Star and Star of David: Soviet Relations with Israel." Senior thesis, Princeton University, 1986.
Korany, Bahgat, and Ali E. Hillal Dessouki, eds. *The Foreign Policies of Arab States*. Boulder, Colo.: Westview Press, 1984.
Krasner, Stephen D. *Defending the National Interest: Raw Materials Investments and U.S. Foreign Policy*. Princeton, N.J.: Princeton University Press, 1978.
——, ed. *International Regimes*. Ithaca: Cornell University Press, 1983.
Kuniholm, Bruce R. *The Origins of the Cold War in the Near East*. Princeton, N.J.: Princeton University Press, 1980.
Lacey, Robert. *The Kingdom*. New York: Harcourt Brace Jovanovich, 1981.
Lackner, Helen. *A House Built on Sand: A Political Economy of Saudi Arabia*. London: Ithaca Press, 1978.
Lambeth, Benjamin. "How to Think about Soviet Military Doctrine." *RAND Paper P–5939*. Santa Monica, Calif.: RAND Corporation, 1978.
Langer, William L. *The Diplomacy of Imperialism*. New York: Knopf, 1953.
——. *European Alliances and Alignments*. 2d ed. New York: Random House, 1950.

——. *Political and Social Upheaval: 1832–1852.* New York: Harper Torchbooks, 1969.

Laqueur, Walter Z. *The Middle East in Transition.* New York: Praeger, 1958.

——. *The Road to Jerusalem.* New York: Macmillan, 1968.

——. *The Soviet Union and the Middle East.* New York: Praeger, 1959.

——. *The Struggle for the Middle East.* New York: Macmillan, 1968.

Laqueur, Walter Z., ed. *The Israel-Arab Reader.* New York: Bantam Books, 1969.

Larson, Deborah Welch. "The Bandwagon Metaphor and American Foreign Policy." Paper delivered at the International Studies Association annual meeting, March 1986.

Lauren, Paul Gordon, ed. *Diplomacy: New Approaches in Theory, History, and Policy.* New York: Free Press, 1979.

Lebow, Richard Ned. "The Soviet Offensive in Europe: The Schlieffen Plan Revisited?" *International Security*, 9, no. 4 (1985).

Lenczowski, George. *The Middle East in World Affairs.* 4th ed. Ithaca: Cornell University Press, 1980.

——. *Soviet Advances in the Middle East.* Washington, D.C.: American Enterprise Institute, 1971.

Lerner, Daniel. *The Passing of Traditional Society: Modernizing the Middle East.* New York: Wiley, 1964.

Levite, Ariel, and Athanassios Platias. "Evaluating Small States' Dependence on Arms Imports: An Alternative Perspective." Ithaca: Cornell Peace Studies Program, 1983.

Levy, Jack S. "Alliance Formation and War Behavior: An Analysis of the Great Powers, 1495–1975." *Journal of Conflict Resolution*, 25, no. 4 (1981).

——. "The Offensive/Defensive Balance of Military Technology: A Theoretical and Historical Analysis." *International Studies Quarterly*, 28, no. 2 (1984).

——. "Theories of General War." Unpublished manuscript, 1984.

Lewis, Bernard. *The Middle East and the West.* New York: Harper Torchbooks, 1964.

Li, R. P. Y., and W. R. Thompson. "The Stochastic Process of Alliance Formation Behavior." *American Political Science Review*, 72, no. 4 (1978).

Lippmann, Walter. *The Cold War: A Study of U.S. Foreign Policy.* New York: Harper & Bros., 1947.

Liska, George. *Nations in Alliance: The Limits of Interdependence.* Baltimore, Md.: Johns Hopkins University Press, 1962.

Love, Kennett. *Suez: The Twice-Fought War.* New York: McGraw-Hill, 1969.

Lowe, C. J. *The Reluctant Imperialists.* New York: Macmillan, 1967.

Lowenthal, Richard. "Factors of Unity and Factors of Conflict." *The Annals*, 349, (1963).

——. *Model or Ally? The Communist Powers and the Developing Countries.* London: Oxford University Press, 1977.

——. *World Communism: The Disintegration of a Secular Faith.* New York: Oxford University Press, 1964.

Lundestad, Geir. *America, Scandinavia, and the Cold War: 1945–1949.* New York: Columbia University Press, 1980.

Luttwak, Edward N. *The Grand Strategy of the Roman Empire.* Baltimore, Md.: Johns Hopkins University Press, 1976.

Luttwak, Edward, and Daniel Horowitz. *The Israeli Army.* New York: Harper & Row, 1975.

McDonald, H. Brooke, and Richard Rosecrance. "Alliance and Structural Balance in the International System: A Reinterpretation." *Journal of Conflict Resolution*, 29, no. 1 (1985).

McDonald, Robert W. *The League of Arab States: A Study in the Dynamics of Regional Organization.* Princeton, N.J.: Princeton University Press, 1965.

MccGwire, Michael, and John McDonnell, eds. *Soviet Naval Influence.* New York: Praeger, 1977.

Mackinder, Halford. "The Geographical Pivot of History." *Geographical Journal*, 23, no. 4 (1904).

McLane, Charles. *Soviet-Middle East Relations*. London: Central Asia Research Centre, 1973.

McNaugher, Thomas L. *Arms and Oil*. Washington, D.C.: Brookings Institution, 1985.

McNeill, William H. *America, Britain, and Russia: Their Cooperation and Conflict, 1941–1946*. London: Oxford University Press, 1953.

Mangold, Peter. *Superpower Intervention in the Middle East*. New York: St. Martin's Press, 1978.

Mansfield, Peter. *The Middle East: A Political and Economic Survey*. 5th ed. London: Oxford University Press, 1980.

Mastanduno, Michael. "Strategies of Economic Containment." *World Politics*, 37, no. 4 (1985).

Mathias, Charles McC. "Ethnic Groups and Foreign Policy." *Foreign Affairs*, 59, no. 5 (1981).

Mattingly, Garrett. *Renaissance Diplomacy*. Boston: Houghton Mifflin, 1971.

Mearsheimer, John J. *Conventional Deterrence*. Ithaca: Cornell University Press, 1982.

Meo, Leila. *Lebanon: Improbable Nation*. Bloomington: Indiana University Press, 1965.

Meyer, Gail C. *Egypt and the United States: The Formative Years*. Cranbury, N.J.: Associated University Press, 1980.

Meyer, Stephen M. "Soviet Theatre Nuclear Forces, Part 1: Development of Doctrine and Objectives." *Adelphi Papers No. 187*. London: International Institute for Strategic Studies, 1984.

Middle East Contemporary Survey. London: Holmes and Meier, various years.

Middle East Record. Tel Aviv: Israel Universities Press, various years.

The Military Balance. London: International Institute for Strategic Studies, various years.

Miller, Aaron David. *Search for Security: Saudi Arabian Oil and American Foreign Policy, 1939–1949*. Chapel Hill: University of North Carolina Press, 1980.

Miller, Steven E. "Arms and Impotence." Paper delivered at the International Institute for Strategic Studies New Faces Conference in Bellagio, Italy, 1979.

Modelski, George. "The Study of Alliances: A Review." *Journal of Conflict Resolution*, 7, no. 4 (1963).

Monger, G. W. *The End of Isolation: British Foreign Policy, 1900–1907*. London: Thomas Nelson, 1963.

Morgenthau, Hans J. "A Political Theory of Foreign Aid." *American Political Science Review*, 56, no. 2 (1962).

——. *Politics among Nations*. 4th ed. New York: Knopf, 1967.

Mroz, John Edward. *Beyond Security: Private Perceptions among Arabs and Israelis*. New York: American International Peace Academy, 1980.

Neff, Donald. *Warriors at Suez*. New York: Linden Press, 1981.

Neumann, Robert G. "Assad and the Future of the Middle East." *Foreign Affairs*, 62, no. 2 (1983–1984).

Neustadt, Richard. *Alliance Politics*. New York: Columbia University Press, 1970.

Newman, David. "Security and Alliances: A Theoretical Study of Alliance Formation." Diss., University of Rochester, 1984.

Nicolson, Harold. *The Congress of Vienna*. New York: Harcourt, Brace, 1946.

——. *Diplomacy*. London: Oxford University Press, 1963.

Nutting, Anthony. *Nasser*. London: Constable, 1972.

Nye, Joseph S., ed. *The Making of America's Soviet Policy*. New Haven, Conn.: Yale University Press, 1984.

O'Ballance, Edgar. *The War in the Yemen*. London: Faber and Faber, 1971.

Olson, Mancur, and Richard Zeckhauser. "An Economic Theory of Alliances." *Review of Economics and Statistics*, 48, no. 3 (1966).

Osgood, Robert E., and Robert W. Tucker. *Force, Order, and Justice*. Baltimore, Md.: Johns Hopkins University Press, 1967.

[303]

Oye, Kenneth A., Robert J. Lieber, and Donald Rothchild, eds. *Eagle Defiant: United States Foreign Policy in the 1980s*. Boston: Little, Brown, 1983.

Pajak, Roger F. "Soviet Arms Relations with Syria and Iraq." *Strategic Review*, 4, no. 1 (1976).

Pennar, Jaan. *The USSR and the Arabs: The Ideological Dimension*. New York: Crane, Russak, 1973.

Penrose, Edith, and E. F. Penrose. *Iraq: International Relations and National Development*. Boulder, Colo.: Westview Press, 1978.

The Pentagon Papers: The Defense Department History of United States Decisionmaking in Vietnam. Senator Gravel edition. Boston: Beacon Press, 1971.

Peres, Shimon. *David's Sling*. New York: Random House, 1970.

Peterson, Horace C. *Propaganda for War: The British Campaign against American Neutrality, 1914–1918*. Norman: University of Oklahoma Press, 1939.

Peterson, J. E. "The Yemen Arab Republic and the Politics of Balance." *Asian Affairs*, 12, no. 3 (1981).

_____. *Yemen: The Search for a Modern State*. London: Croom Helm, 1980.

Peterson, Phillip A., and John G. Hines. "The Conventional Offensive in Soviet Theater Strategy." *Orbis*, 27, no. 3 (1983).

Petran, Tabitha. *Syria*. New York: Praeger, 1972.

Philips, Walter Alison. *The Confederation of Europe*. London: Longmans, Green, 1920.

Polk, William C. *The Arab World*. Cambridge: Harvard University Press, 1981.

Pollock, David. *The Politics of Pressure: American Arms and Israeli Policy since the Six Day War*. Westport, Conn.: Greenwood Press, 1982.

Porter, Bruce D. *The USSR and Third World Conflicts: Soviet Arms and Diplomacy in Local Wars, 1945–1980*. Cambridge: Cambridge University Press, 1984.

Posen, Barry R. "Measuring the European Conventional Balance: Coping with Complexity in Threat Assessment." *International Security*, 9, no. 3 (1984–1985).

_____. *The Sources of Military Doctrine: France, Britain, and Germany between the World Wars*. Ithaca: Cornell University Press, 1984.

Posen, Barry R., and Stephen W. Van Evera. "Reagan Administration Defense Policy: Departure from Containment." *International Security*, 8, no. 1 (1983).

Pridham, B. R., ed. *Contemporary Yemen: Politics and Historical Background*. New York: St. Martin's Press, 1984.

Quandt, William B. *Camp David: Peacemaking and Politics*. Washington, D.C.: Brookings Institution, 1986.

_____. *Decade of Decisions: American Policy toward the Arab-Israeli Conflict, 1967–1976*. Berkeley: University of California Press, 1977.

_____. *Saudi Arabia in the 1980s: Foreign Policy, Security, Oil*. Washington, D.C.: Brookings Institution, 1981.

_____. "Soviet Policy in the October 1973 War." *Research Report R–1864–ISA*. Santa Monica, Calif.: RAND Corporation, 1976.

Quandt, William B., Ann Mosely Lesch, and Fuad Jabber. *The Politics of Palestinian Nationalism*. Berkeley: University of California Press, 1972.

Qubain, Fahim I. *Crisis in Lebanon*. Washington, D.C.: Middle East Institute, 1961.

Quester, George. *Offense and Defense in the International System*. New York: Wiley, 1977.

Ra'anan, Uri. *The USSR Arms the Third World: Case Studies in Soviet Foreign Policy*. Cambridge, Mass.: MIT Press, 1969.

Rabin, Yitzhak. *The Rabin Memoirs*. Boston: Little, Brown, 1979.

Rabinovich, Itamar. *Syria under the Ba'th: The Army-Party Symbiosis*. New York: Halsted Press, 1974.

_____. *The War for Lebanon, 1970–1985*. Ithaca: Cornell University Press, 1985.

Rabinovich, Itamar, and Haim Shaked, eds. *From June to October.* New Brunswick, N.J.: Transaction Books, 1978.

Rahmy, Ali Abdel Rahman. *The Egyptian Policy in the Arab World: The Intervention in Yemen, 1962–1967 Case Study.* Washington, D.C.: University Press of America, 1983.

Randal, Jonathan. *Going All the Way: Christian Warlords, Israeli Adventurers, and the War in Lebanon.* New York: Vintage, 1984.

Record, Jeffrey. *Revising American Military Strategy: Tailoring Means to Ends.* Washington, D.C.: Pergamon-Brassey's, 1984.

Reich, Bernard. *Quest for Peace: United States–Israel Relations and the Arab-Israeli Conflict.* New Brunswick, N.J.: Transaction Books, 1977.

Report of the European Security Study. *Strengthening Conventional Deterrence in Europe: Proposals for the 1980s.* New York: St. Martin's Press, 1983.

Riker, William H. *The Theory of Political Coalitions.* New Haven, Conn.: Yale University Press, 1962.

Roi, Ya'acov. *Soviet Decisionmaking in Practice: The USSR and Israel, 1947–1954.* New Brunswick, N.J.: Transaction Books, 1980.

_____, ed. *From Encroachment to Involvement: A Documentary History of Soviet Foreign Policy in the Middle East, 1945–1973.* New Brunswick, N.J.: Transaction Books, 1974.

_____. *The Limits to Power: Soviet Policy in the Middle East.* London: Croom Helm, 1979.

Rokach, Livia. *Israel's Sacred Terror.* Belmont, Mass.: Association of Arab-American Graduates, 1980.

Rood, Robert, and Patrick McGowan. "Alliance Behavior in Balance of Power Systems." *American Political Science Review,* 79, no. 3 (1976).

Rosecrance, Richard, Alan Alexandroff, Brian Healy, and Arthur Stein. "Power, Balance of Power, and Status in Nineteenth Century International Relations." *Sage Professional Papers in International Studies.* Beverly Hills, Calif.: Sage Publications, 1974.

Rosen, Steven J. "The Strategic Value of Israel." *AIPAC Papers on U.S.-Israeli Relations.* Washington, D.C.: American-Israel Public Affairs Committee, 1982.

Rothenberg, Morris. "Recent Soviet Relations with Syria," *Middle East Review,* 10, no. 4 (1978).

Rothstein, Robert L. *Alliances and Small Powers.* New York: Columbia University Press, 1968.

Rubinstein, Alvin Z., ed. *The Foreign Policy of the Soviet Union.* New York: Random House, 1969.

_____. *Red Star on the Nile: The Soviet-Egyptian Influence Relationship since the June War.* Princeton, N.J.: Princeton University Press, 1977.

_____. *Soviet and Chinese Influence in the Third World.* New York: Praeger, 1975.

Russett, Bruce, and Donald R. Deluca. "Theatre Nuclear Forces: Public Opinion in Western Europe." *Political Science Quarterly,* 98, no. 2 (1983).

Rustow, Dankwart A. "Realignments in the Middle East." *Foreign Affairs,* 63, no. 3 (1984).

Sachar, Howard M. *Egypt and Israel.* New York: Richard Marek, 1981.

_____. *The Emergence of the Middle East: 1914–1924.* New York: Knopf, 1969.

_____. *Europe Leaves the Middle East: 1936–1954.* New York: Knopf, 1972.

_____. *A History of Israel: From the Rise of Zionism to Our Time.* New York: Knopf, 1979.

Sadat, Anwar el-. *In Search of Identity: An Autobiography.* New York: Harper & Row, 1977.

Safran, Nadav. "Arab Politics: Peace and War." *Orbis,* 18, no. 2 (1974).

_____. *From War to War: The Arab-Israeli Confrontation, 1948–1967.* New York: Pegasus, 1969.

_____. *Israel: The Embattled Ally.* Cambridge: Harvard University Press, 1981.

_____. *Saudi Arabia: The Ceaseless Quest for Security.* Cambridge: Harvard University Press, 1985.

——. *The United States and Israel*. Cambridge: Harvard University Press, 1963.

Said, Abdul Aziz, ed. *Ethnicity and U.S. Foreign Policy*. New York: Praeger, 1981.

Sayegh, Fayez. *Arab Unity*. New York: Devin-Adair, 1958.

Sayegh, Yusif A. *The Economies of the Arab World*. London: Croom Helm, 1978.

Schiff, Ze'ev. "Green Light, Lebanon." *Foreign Policy*, no. 50 (1983).

Schmidt, Dana Adams. *Yemen: The Unknown War*. London: The Bodley Head, 1968.

Schmitt, Bernadotte C. *The Coming of the War in 1914*. New York: Howard Fertig, 1968.

Schmitt, Bernadotte C., and Harold M. Vedeler. *The World in the Crucible: 1914–1918*. New York: Harper & Row, 1984.

Schroeder, Paul W. "Quantitative Studies in the Balance of Power: An Historian's Reaction." *Journal of Conflict Resolution*, 21, no. 1 (1977).

Schwartz, Morton. *The Failed Symbiosis: The USSR and Leftist Regimes in Less Developed Countries*. Santa Monica, Calif.: California Seminar on Arms Control and Foreign Policy, 1973.

Schwarzenberger, Georg. *Power Politics*. London: Jonathan Cape, 1941.

Scott, Andrew M. *The Revolution in Statecraft: Informal Penetration*. New York: Random House, 1965.

Seabury, Paul A., ed. *Balance of Power*. San Francisco: Chandler Publishing, 1965.

Seale, Patrick. *The Struggle for Syria: A Study of Arab Politics, 1945–1958*. London: Oxford University Press, 1965.

Sella, Amnon. *Soviet Political and Military Conduct in the Middle East*. New York: St. Martin's Press, 1981.

Shaked, Haim, and Itamar Rabinovich, eds. *The Middle East and the United States: Perceptions and Policies*. New Brunswick, N.J.: Transaction Books, 1980.

Shazly, Saad el-. *The Crossing of the Canal*. San Francisco: American Mideast Research, 1980.

Sheehan, Edward R. F. *The Arabs, Israelis and Kissinger*. Pleasantville, N.Y.: Reader's Digest Press, 1976.

Sheffer, Gabriel, ed. *Dynamics of a Conflict: A Reexamination of the Arab-Israeli Conflict*. Atlantic Highlands, N.J.: Humanities Press, 1975.

Sherwig, Robert. *Guineas and Gunpowder: British Foreign Aid in the Wars with France, 1793–1815*. Cambridge: Harvard University Press, 1969.

Shimshoni, Jonathan. "Conventional Deterrence: Lessons from the Middle East." Diss., Princeton University, 1985.

Shirabi, Hisham B. *Nationalism and Revolution in the Arab World*. New York: Van Nostrand, 1966.

Shlaim, Avi. "Conflicting Approaches to Israel's Relations with the Arabs: Ben-Gurion and Sharett, 1953–1956," *Middle East Journal*, 37, no. 2 (1983).

Shultz, George P. "New Realities and Ways of Thinking." *Foreign Affairs*, 63, no. 3 (1985).

Sinai, Anne, and Allen Pollock. *The Hashemite Kingdom of Jordan and the West Bank: A Handbook*. New York: American Academic Association for Peace in the Middle East, 1977.

——. *The Syrian Arab Republic: A Handbook*. New York: American Academic Association for Peace in the Middle East, 1976.

Singleton, Fred. "The Myth of Finlandisation." *International Affairs*, 47, no. 2 (1981).

Smith, Denis Mack. *Mussolini*. New York: Knopf, 1982.

Smoke, Richard. *War: Controlling Escalation*. Cambridge: Harvard University Press, 1977.

Smolansky, Oles M. *The Soviet Union and the Arab East under Khrushchev*. Lewisburg, Pa.: Bucknell University Press, 1974.

Snetsinger, John. *Truman, the Jewish Vote, and the Creation of Israel*. Stanford, Calif.: Hoover Institution Press, 1974.

Snyder, Glenn. "The Security Dilemma in Alliance Politics." *World Politics*, 36, no. 4 (1984).

Snyder, Glenn, and Paul Diesing. *Conflict among Nations: Bargaining, Decision, Making, and System Structure in International Crises.* Princeton, N.J.: Princeton University Press, 1977.

Snyder, Jack L. "Civil-Military Relations and the Cult of the Offensive." *International Security,* 9, no. 1 (1984).

Sontag, Raymond J. *European Diplomatic History, 1871–1932.* New York: Appleton-Century-Crofts, 1933.

Spiegel, Steven L. "Israel as a Strategic Asset." *Commentary,* 75, no. 6 (1983).

———. *The Other Arab-Israeli Conflict: Making America's Middle East Policy from Truman to Reagan.* Chicago: University of Chicago Press, 1985.

Springborg, Robert. "New Patterns of Agrarian Reform in the Middle East and North Africa." *Middle East Journal,* 31, no. 2 (1977).

Sprout, Harold, and Margaret Sprout. *Foundations of International Politics.* Princeton, N.J.: Van Nostrand, 1962.

Spykman, Nicholas. *America's Strategy in World Politics.* New York: Harcourt, Brace & World, 1942.

Starr, Harvey, and Benjamin Most. "The Substance and Study of Borders in International Relations Research." *International Studies Quarterly,* 20, no. 4 (1976).

Steinbruner, John, and Leon V. Sigal, eds. *Alliance Security: NATO and the No-First-Use Question.* Washington, D.C.: Brookings Institution, 1984.

Stephens, Robert. *Nasser: A Political Biography.* New York: Simon & Schuster, 1971.

Stern, Fritz. *Gold and Iron: Bismarck, Bleichroder, and the Building of the German Empire.* New York: Vintage, 1979.

Stinchcombe, Arthur L. *Constructing Social Theories.* New York: Harcourt, Brace & World, 1968.

Stock, Ernest. *Israel on the Road to Sinai.* Ithaca: Cornell University Press, 1967.

Stockholm International Peace Research Institute (SIPRI). *The Arms Trade with the Third World.* New York: Humanities Press, 1971.

Stookey, Robert W. *America and the Arab States: An Uneasy Encounter.* New York: Wiley, 1975.

———. *South Yemen: A Marxist Republic in Arabia.* Boulder, Colo.: Westview Press, 1982.

———. *Yemen: The Politics of the Yemen Arab Republic.* Boulder, Colo.: Westview Press, 1978.

Strategic Survey. London: International Institute for Strategic Studies, various years.

Sunday Times Insight Team. *Insight on the Middle East War.* London: Andre Deutsch, 1974.

Tansky, Leo. *U.S. and USSR Aid to Developing Countries: A Comparative Study of India, Turkey, and the UAR.* New York: Praeger, 1967.

Tanter, Raymond, and Janice Gross Stein. *Rational Decisionmaking: Israel's Security Choices, 1967.* Columbus: Ohio State University Press, 1980.

Tatu, Michel. *Power in the Kremlin.* New York: Viking Press, 1970.

Taylor, A. J. P. *The First World War.* New York: Perigee Books, 1980.

———. *The Struggle for Mastery in Europe: 1848–1918.* London: Oxford University Press, 1952.

Taylor, Alan R. *The Arab Balance of Power.* Syracuse, N.Y.: Syracuse University Press, 1982.

Taylor, Telford. *Munich: The Price of Peace.* New York: Vintage, 1980.

Thomas, Hugh. *Suez.* New York: Harper & Row, 1966.

Thompson, W. Scott. "The Communist International System." *Orbis,* 20, no. 4 (1977).

Tillman, Seth P. *The United States in the Middle East: Interests and Obstacles.* Bloomington: Indiana University Press, 1982.

Torrey, Gordon H. *Syrian Politics and the Military, 1945–1958.* Columbus: Ohio State University Press, 1964.

Touval, Saadia. *The Peace Brokers: Mediators in the Arab-Israeli Conflict, 1948–1979.* Princeton, N.J.: Princeton University Press, 1982.

Toynbee, Arnold, and Veronica Toynbee, eds. *Survey of International Affairs, 1939–46:*

Hitler's Europe. London: Oxford University Press for The Royal Institute for International Affairs, 1954.

Trice, Robert. "Congress and the Arab-Israeli Conflict: Support for Israel in the U.S. Senate, 1970–73." *Political Science Quarterly*, 92, no. 3 (1977).

Ulam, Adam. *Expansion and Coexistence: Soviet Foreign Policy, 1917–1973*. New York: Praeger, 1974.

U.S. Agency for International Development (AID). *U.S. Overseas Loans and Grants*. Washington, D.C.: Government Printing Office, various years.

U.S. Arms Control and Disarmament Agency (ACDA). *World Military Expenditures and Arms Transfers*. Washington, D.C.: Government Printing Office, various years.

U.S. Bureau of the Census. *Statistical Abstract of the United States 1977*. Washington, D.C.: Government Printing Office, 1976.

U.S. Central Intelligence Agency (CIA). *Communist Aid to Non-Communist Less Developed Countries, 1979 and 1954–1979*. Washington, D.C.: n.p., 1980.

———. *Handbook of Economic Statistics*. Washington, D.C.: n.p., various years.

U.S. Congress. House. Committee on Foreign Affairs. *The Soviet Union and the Third World: Watershed in Great Power Policy?* 97th Cong., 1st sess., 1977.

———. *The Soviet Union in the Third World, 1980–85: An Imperial Burden or Political Asset?* 99th Cong., 1st sess., 1985.

U.S. Congress. House. Committee on International Relations. *Military Sales to Saudi Arabia, 1975*. 94th Cong., 1st sess., 1976.

———. *Notes on Educational and Cultural Exchange between the United States and Countries of the Middle East*. 95th Cong., 1st sess., 1977.

———. *United States Arms Policies in the Persian Gulf and Red Sea Areas: Past, Present, and Future*. 95th Cong., 1st sess., 1976.

U.S. Congress. Joint Economic Committee. *The Political Economy of the Middle East: A Compendium of Papers*. 96th Cong., 2d sess., 1977.

———. *Soviet Economy in a New Perspective*. 94th Cong., 2d sess., 1976.

U.S. Congress. Senate. Committee on Appropriations. *U.S. Policy toward Anti-Communist Insurgencies*. 99th Cong., 1st sess., 1985.

U.S. Congress. Senate. Committee on Foreign Relations. *Hearings on Memoranda of Agreements between the Governments of Israel and the United States*. 94th Cong., 2d sess., 1975.

U.S. Department of Defense. *Foreign Military Sales and Foreign Assistance Facts*. Washington, D.C.: n.p., various years.

———. *The FY1987 Department of Defense Program for Research and Development*. Washington, D.C.: n.p., 1986.

———. *Soviet Military Power*. Washington, D.C.: n.p., various years.

———. "U.S. Military Strength Outside the U.S.: Fact Sheet." Washington, D.C.: n.p., quarterly, various years.

U.S. Department of State. "The Sandinista Military Buildup." Inter-American Series 119. Washington, D.C.: Government Printing Office, 1985.

U.S. Department of State. Bureau of Public Affairs. "Communist Influence in El Salvador." Washington, D.C.: n.p., 1981.

———. *Current Policy No. 264*. Washington, D.C.: n.p., March 19, 1981.

U.S. Departments of State and Defense. "The Soviet-Cuban Connection in Central America and the Caribbean." Washington, D.C.: Government Printing Office, 1985.

"U.S. Economic and Business Relations with the Middle East and North Africa." *Department of State Bulletin*, 14 June 1976.

U.S. Joint Chiefs of Staff. *U.S. Military Posture for FY1987*. Washington, D.C.: n.p., 1986.

Van Dam, Nikalaos. *The Struggle for Power in Syria: Sectarianism, Regionalism, and Tribalism in Politics, 1961–1978*. New York: St. Martin's Press, 1979.

Bibliography

Van Evera, Stephen W. "Causes of War." Diss., University of California, Berkeley, 1984.
Van Hollen, Christopher. "North Yemen: A Dangerous Pentagonal Game." *Washington Quarterly*, 5, no. 3 (1982).
Vatikiotis, P. J. *The Modern History of Egypt*. New York: Praeger, 1969.
———. *Nasser and His Generation*. New York: St. Martin's Press, 1978.
———. *Politics and the Military in Jordan: A Study of the Arab Legion, 1928–1957*. London: Frank Cass, 1967.
Viner, Jacob. *International Economics: Studies*. Glencoe, Ill.: Free Press, 1952.
Waltz, Kenneth N. "The Stability of a Bipolar World." *Daedalus*, 93, no. 3 (1964).
———. *Theory of International Politics*. Reading, Mass.: Addison-Wesley, 1979.
Ward, Michael Don. "Research Gaps in Alliance Dynamics." *Monograph Series in World Affairs*. Graduate School of International Studies, University of Denver, 19, no. 1 (1982).
Waterbury, John. *The Egypt of Nasser and Sadat: The Political Economy of Two Regimes*. Princeton, N.J.: Princeton University Press, 1983.
Webster, Charles K. *The Foreign Policy of Palmerston*. London: G. Bell and Sons, 1951.
Weinland, Robert G. "Land Support for Naval Forces: Egypt and the Soviet Escadra, 1962–1976." *Survival*, 20, no. 2 (1979).
Weinstein, Franklin B. "The Concept of a Commitment in International Relations." *Journal of Conflict Resolution*, 13, no. 1 (1969).
Wenner, Manfred. *Modern Yemen*. Baltimore, Md.: Johns Hopkins University Press, 1967.
Wheelock, Keith. *Nasser's New Egypt*. New York: Praeger, 1960.
Whetten, Lawrence. *The Canal War*. Cambridge: MIT Press, 1974.
White, Ralph K. "Misperception in the Arab-Israeli Conflict." *Journal of Social Issues*, 33, no. 1 (1977).
Wight, Martin, and Herbert Butterfield, eds. *Diplomatic Investigations*. London: George Allen & Unwin, 1966.
Williamson, James A. *Great Britain and the Commonwealth*. London: Adam and Charles Black, 1965.
Wilson, Evan. *Decision on Palestine: How the U.S. Came to Recognize Israel*. Stanford: Calif.: Hoover Institution Press, 1981.
Wohlstetter, Albert. "Illusions of Distance." *Foreign Affairs*, 46, no. 2 (1968).
Wolf, John. *The Emergence of the Great Powers*. New York: Harper Torchbooks, 1962.
Wolfers, Arnold, ed. *Alliance Policy in the Cold War*. Baltimore, Md.: Johns Hopkins University Press, 1959.
———. *Discord and Collaboration: Essays on International Politics*. Baltimore, Md.: Johns Hopkins University Press, 1962.
Wright, Claudia. "Libya and the West: Headlong into Confrontation?" *International Affairs*, 58, no. 1 (1981–1982).
Ya'ari, Ehud, and Ze'ev Schiff. *Israel's Lebanon War*. New York: Simon & Schuster, 1984.
Yodfat, Aryeh. *Arab Politics in the Soviet Mirror*. New Brunswick, N.J.: Transaction Books, 1973.
———. *The Soviet Union and the Arabian Peninsula: Soviet Policy towards the Persian Gulf and Arabia*. New York: St. Martin's Press, 1983.
Yost, Charles W. "The Arab-Israeli War: How It Began." *Foreign Affairs*, 46, no. 2 (1968).
Zagladin, V. V. *The World Communist Movement*. Moscow: Progress Publishers, 1973.
Zimmerman, William. *Soviet Perspectives on International Relations*. Princeton, N.J.: Princeton University Press, 1969.
Zinnes, Dina, and William Gillespie, eds. *Mathematical Models in International Relations*. New York: Praeger, 1976.

Index

Abdullah, King of Jordan, 55
Achille Lauro, hijacking of, 228n, 272n
Aden, British withdrawal from, 106
Afghanistan, Soviet invasion of, 3, 137, 140–41, 230, 279
Aflaq, Michel, quoted, 200
Aggregate Power, 22–24, 32, 147, 153–58, 161, 166, 171–72, 263–65, 276. *See also* Balance of threat theory
Aggressive intentions, 5, 87, 141, 144, 147–48, 176, 179–80; and Arab-Israeli conflict, 171–72; and balancing behavior, 25–26, 32, 167–71, 264–65; and foreign aid, 45; and regional powers, 170–71; and superpowers, 168–70, 278–79
Ahmed, Imam of Yemen, 56, 82; conflict with Great Britain, 60, 174, 197, 231, 248; relations with Egypt, 79; relations with Soviet Union, 60n, 231
Ajami, Fouad, quoted, 206
Algeria: as French colony, 63; joins Steadfastness Front, 136
'Ali, Rubay, 118, 142, 232n, 233
Alignment. *See* Alliance
Alliance: alternative approaches to study of, 6–11; definition of, 1n, 12, 14. *See also* Balancing behavior; Bandwagoning behavior; Foreign aid; Ideological solidarity; Penetration
Altfeld, Michael F., 9
Amer, Abdel Hakim, 72, 91n
American Israel Public Affairs Committee (AIPAC), 254–56, 258
Amitay, Morris, quoted, 258–59
Aqaba, Gulf of, 64
Arab Deterrent Force. *See* Riyadh Summit
Arabian Peninsula, 56, 106
Arab-Israeli conflict, 51–52, 86, 88, 95–96, 98, 143, 158, 165, 171, 202; impact of ideology on, 204–6; and inter-Arab relations, 61, 85–87, 103, 265–66; and peace process, 105, 114; Soviet policy toward, 106; U.S. policy toward, 52. *See also* Camp David Accords; October War; Six Day War; Suez Crisis; War of Attrition
Arab League, 59, 81n, 118n, 137, 205; intervention in Kuwait, 79, 171
Arab Legion, 60, 249n
Arab nationalism, 51–52, 66, 69–70, 80, 201–2. *See also* Arab-Israeli conflict; Arab solidarity; Ideological solidarity; Pan-Arabism
Arab socialism, 212n. *See also* Pan-Arabism
Arab Socialist Union, 90, 188
Arab solidarity, 51, 59; and Arab-Israeli conflict, 100–1, 111–13, 120–23, 166, 174, 204–6, 215, 236; as balancing behavior, 149; declining importance of, 131, 143, 270–71. *See also* Arab nationalism; Pan-Arabism
Arab Solidarity Agreement (1965), 87n
Arab Solidarity Pact (1955–56), 65–66, 68–69, 174, 207, 224, 243
Arab summits, 87n, 132, 136, 138. *See also* Cairo Summit; Khartoum Summit; Rabat Summit
Arab unity. *See* Pan-Arabism
Arafat, Yasser, 271n
Aref, Abdel Salam, 73–75, 83, 85, 92, 106, 190, 196; pan-Arab convictions of, 210; relations with Nasser, 73; relations with Soviet Union, 92
Arms transfers, 13n, 41. *See also* Foreign aid; Political leverage; Soviet Union; Tripartite Declaration; United States

Cornell Studies in Security Affairs

A series edited by

Robert Jervis
Robert J. Art
Stephen M. Walt